# The Rise of East Asia

The rise of East Asia has proceeded dramatically since the 1970s and the economic strength of Japan, South Korea and Taiwan is well established. By the 1980s industrialization was well under way in Thailand, Malaysia, Indonesia and China's coastal provinces. Now the governments of the Philippines, Vietnam and even India are attempting to follow the East Asian model, while the people of Australia and the US, and a growing number of other countries in the Americas and beyond, are being exhorted to meet the challenge of the rise of East Asia.

In the context of the rise of East Asia and the transition from the Cold War to the post-Cold War era in the Asia-Pacific, there are competing visions of both what is going on in the region today and of what the future holds. The first part of the book engages with the dominant narratives on the Pacific Century by looking at particular trends in specific nations and at particular areas of change within those nations. There is a thorough examination of the rise of East Asia and analysis of the significance of the emergence of the Asia-Pacific (and the Pacific Rim) as a new regional demarcation in the context of the wider trend towards globalization.

*The Rise of East Asia* is a challenging contribution to the debate concerning the rise of the region and its growing importance on a global scale. It will provide an invaluable overview of the most important issues for anyone interested in the implications of the Pacific Century.

**Mark T. Berger** is Lecturer in Asia Studies and Programme Chair of Development Studies in the School of Humanities at Murdoch University, Western Australia. **Douglas A. Borer** is Assistant Professor, Virginia Polytechnic Institute and State University.

# The Rise of East Asia

Critical Visions of the Pacific Century

Edited by Mark T. Berger and
Douglas A. Borer

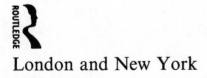

London and New York

First published 1997
by Routledge
11 New Fetter Lane, London EC4P 4EE

Simultaneously published in the USA and Canada
by Routledge
29 West 35th Street, New York, NY 10001

© 1997 Mark T. Berger and Douglas A. Borer, selection and editorial
matter; the contributors, individual chapters.

Typeset in Times by
BC Typesetting, Bristol
Printed and bound in Great Britain by
Hartnolls Ltd, Bodmin, Cornwall

*British Library Cataloguing in Publication Data*
A catalogue record for this book is available from the British Library

*Library of Congress Cataloguing in Publication Data*
The rise of East Asia: critical visions of the Pacific century/
   edited by Mark T. Berger and Douglas A. Borer.
      p.   cm.
   Includes bibliographical references and index.
   1. East Asia.  2. Asia, Southeastern.  I. Berger, Mark T., 1955–
. II. Borer, Douglas A., 1962–
DS504.5.R57   1996
950–dc20
                                                    96-43154
                                                    CIP

ISBN 0–415–161673 (Hbk)
ISBN 0–415–161681 (Pbk)

# Contents

# Figure and tables

**FIGURE**

**TABLES**

# Contributors

**Roger Bell** is Professor of History and Head of the School of History, University of New South Wales, Sydney, NSW, Australia. He is President of the Australian and New Zealand American Studies Association and has published widely on international relations, Australian history and the United States in the Pacific. His books include *Unequal Allies: Australian–American Relations and the Pacific War* (Melbourne University Press, 1977); *Last Among Equals: Hawaiian Statehood and American Politics* (University of Hawaii Press, 1984); *Implicated: the United States in Australia* (with Philip Bell) (Oxford University Press, 1993). He is editor of *Multicultural Societies: A Comparative Reader* (Sable, 1987); and senior editor of *Negotiating the Pacific Century: the United States, Australia and the New Asia* (Allen & Unwin, 1996).

**Mark T. Berger** is Lecturer in Asian Studies and Programme Chair of Development Studies in the School of Humanities at Murdoch University in Western Australia. He worked previously as a history/politics lecturer at the University of Western Sydney, the University of NSW and at the University of the South Pacific in Fiji. He has published articles in a number of international journals including *Bulletin of Concerned Asian Scholars, Positions: East Asia Cultures Critique* and *Third World Quarterly: Journal of Emerging Areas*. He is the author of *Under Northern Eyes: Latin American Studies and US Hegemony in the Americas 1898–1990* (Indiana University Press, 1995). His research interests include comparative history, comparative political economy, international relations and theories of development, with a geographical focus on the Asia-Pacific and the Americas. He is currently working on a book on the relationship between the international development debate and the changing twentieth-century global political economy with particular emphasis on the Asia-Pacific.

**Douglas A. Borer** is Assistant Professor of Political Science at Virginia Polytechnic Institute and State University in Blacksburg, Virginia, USA. Previously he worked as a lecturer in international politics at the University of Western Australia in Perth, and the University of the South Pacific in Fiji. He has published book chapters, articles and reviews in international journals including *Comparative Strategy*, *War & Society*, and *The Journal of Pacific Studies*. His research interests include comparative foreign policy, international relations theory, Soviet/Russian politics, and the political economy of the Asia-Pacific.

**Martin F. Farrell** is Professor of Politics and Government, and Director of Global Studies, Ripon College, Ripon. Wisconsin, USA. He taught previously at the University of Chicago, the College of William and Mary, Hampton University and the University of Wisconsin – Eau Claire. He has contributed articles and chapters to several international journals and reference works, including *The Journal of Pacific Studies* and *The World Encyclopedia of Political Systems and Parties*. His research interests include comparative politics and the philosophy of the social sciences.

**Shigeko N. Fukai** is Professor of International Politics in the Law Faculty of Okayama University, Okayama, Japan. Previously she served as Japan Program Director at the Center for International Commerce and Associate Professor in the Department of Political Science at Auburn University in the United States, as a visiting scholar in the Faculty of Law, Tokyo University, and as senior researcher in the Center for International Affairs, Harvard University. She has published articles in a number of journals, including *Asian Survey, World Politics, Current History, PS: Political Science and Politics, Journal of Japanese Studies* and *Chuo Koron* ('Japanese Monthly'). She has also contributed chapters to a number of books, including Gail Lee Bernstein and Haruhiro Fukui, eds, *Japan and the World: Essays in Japanese History and Politics in Honour of Ishida Takeshi* (Macmillan, 1988) and T. David Mason and M. Turay, eds, *Japan, NAFTA and Europe: Trilateral Cooperation or Confrontation?* (Macmillan Press, 1994). Her research interests include international political economy and comparative politics, with a focus on land problems, policy making and electoral and party politics in Japan.

**Haruhiro Fukui** is Professor of International Politics in the Institute of Policy and Planning Sciences at the University of Tsukuba, Tsukuba, Japan. From 1968 to 1994, he taught in the department of political science at the University of California, Santa Barbara. During that period, he also held visiting professorships at the University of Hawaii, the University of Sydney, and El Colegio de Mexico and a visiting fellowship at All Souls College, Oxford. He has authored or co-authored a number of books and articles on Japanese politics and foreign policy, including *Party in Power: The Japanese Liberal-Democrats and Policy Making* (Australian National University Press and University of California Press, 1970), *The Textile Wrangle: Conflict in Japanese–American Relations, 1969–71* (Cornell University Press, 1979), *Japan and the New Ocean Regime* (Westview Press,

1984), and *Japan and the World: Essays in Japanese History and Politics in Honour of Ishida Takeshi* (Macmillan, 1988). His current research interests include informal politics in Asia, Japanese–American relations, and regime formation in the Asia and Pacific region.

**Gerard Greenfield** writes on workers and trade union issues in the Asian region. He has lived and travelled extensively in Vietnam and is currently based in Hong Kong.

**Kwan S. Kim** is Professor of Economics and Faculty Fellow of the Kellogg Institute for International Studies at the University of Notre Dame, USA. He is an international development economist, occasionally serving as an economic consultant for governments and for international agencies. His career includes: four years as a Rockefeller Foundation scholar in East Africa; two years as a senior economist with the United States Agency for International Development. More recently he spent a year as a visiting professor at Hitotsubashi Institute of Economic Research in Tokyo, and has spent short periods as an economic researcher at the Economic Research Center, Monterrey, Mexico; the Hudson Institute; UNIDO; and the National Financiera in Mexico. He has published nine books and over fifty professional journal articles in the areas of economic development, international economics, and quantitative methods. His latest books include: *The State, Markets and Development* (Edward Elgar, 1994), *The Acquisition, Adaptation and Development of Technologies: Japan's Experience* (Macmillan, 1994), *Trade and Industrialization* (The Netherlands Institute for International Management, 1994), and *Economic and Corporate Restructuring* (Lansa Publishing, 1996).

**Timothy W. Luke** is Professor of Political Science, Department of Political Science, Virginia Polytechnic Institute and State University, Blacksburg, Virginia, USA. He was the Fulbright Professor on the Politics of Information Society at the Victoria University in Wellington, New Zealand, in 1995. His articles appear in many international journals, including *Alternatives, Environment and Planning, International Studies Quarterly, Political Geography, Telos* and *Theory, Culture and Society*. Currently he is working in the areas of contemporary social theory, the politics of information society, and environmental politics. He is the author of *Screens of Power: Ideology, Domination and Resistance in Informational Society* (University of Illinois Press, 1989); and *Social Theory and Modernity: Critique, Dissent and Revolution* (Sage, 1990). His latest book is *Ecocritique: Contesting the Politics of Nature, Economy and Culture* (University of Minnesota Press, 1997).

**Steve Majstorovic** is Assistant Professor in the Department of Political Science and in the Graduate Center for Social and Public Policy at

Duquesne University in Pittsburgh, Pennsylvania, USA. He has published articles in numerous journals including *World Affairs*, *Political Research Quarterly* and *Nationalism and Ethnic Politics*. He is a former Fellow at the Hoover Institution at Stanford University and his research interests include Western and Eastern European politics, Russian politics, ethnic and minority politics cross-nationally, ethnic conflict and conflict resolution, and international political economy. He is currently at work on a book that examines the ethnocultural barriers to democratic transition in Eastern Europe.

**Yao Souchou** is a Lecturer in the Department of Anthropology at the University of Sydney, NSW, Australia. His research and teaching focuses on the anthropology of the overseas Chinese and cultural studies of modern China. Previously he was a Fellow at the Institute of Southeast Asian Studies in Singapore. He has carried out fieldwork in Hong Kong and more recently in Sarawak, East Malaysia. His publications include articles in *SOJOURN (Journal of Social Issues in Southeast Asia)*, *Journal of Asian Communications*, *Journal of the South Seas Society* and *Journal of Cultural Critique*. He is currently working on a project on Confucian capitalism.

# Editors' preface and acknowledgements

The idea for this book began when both editors were based at the University of the South Pacific in Fiji. While in Fiji Doug Borer served as editor of a special issue of the *Journal of Pacific Studies* (vol. 17, nos 1–2, 1993) on the Pacific in the New World Disorder. The success of that project encouraged Doug Borer, with the collaboration of Mark Berger, to embark on a more substantial book. As the edited volume evolved, and the editors moved on to other institutions, the project shifted focus in various ways. While some of the original contributors to the 1993 issue of *Journal of Pacific Studies* remained involved, almost all the contributors to this volume are new and the subject matter is much more East Asian in its focus. Whatever strengths and insights this book has are undoubtedly due to the many people who have influenced the editors during the book's gestation. To this end we want to thank our colleagues in the School of Social and Economic Development at the University of the South Pacific, Suva Fiji, the School of Humanities at Murdoch University, Perth Western Australia, the Department of Political Science at the University of Western Australia, Perth Western Australia and the Department of Political Science, Virginia Polytechnic Institute and State University, Blacksburg Virginia, as well as many other colleagues and friends who are part of an increasingly transnationalized academic community. The perseverance of the contributors and their tolerance of the sometimes heavy-handed intervention of the editors should also be acknowledged. Thanks also to Penelope Claringbull, who worked as research assistant on this project, the funding for which was provided by the School of Humanities at Murdoch University. We also want to thank Victoria Smith, Asian Studies Editor at Routledge, for her commitment and support for this project. The smooth transition from manuscript to book was facilitated by Diane Stafford (Senior Desk Editor), Rosamund Howe (Copy Editor), James Whiting (Senior Editorial Assistant) and Mark Kavanagh (Editorial Assistant) at Routledge and we thank them for their work. Most importantly we would like to thank our partners, Catherine Waldby and Jodi Stiles, for their support and encouragement.

Mark T. Berger and Douglas A. Borer
December 1996

# Introduction: The rise of East Asia: Critical visions of the Pacific Century

*Mark T. Berger and Douglas A. Borer*

## INTRODUCTION: CRITICAL VISIONS OF THE PACIFIC CENTURY

The coming of the Pacific Century has been proclaimed ever more frequently since the mid-1980s.[1] The rapid economic growth of East Asia (particularly Japan, South Korea, Taiwan, Hong Kong and Singapore) was already setting the region apart from the rest of the world by the 1970s.[2] By the 1980s the trend was seen to have spread southward to Thailand, Malaysia and Indonesia, while China's coastal provinces had also become integral to the regional economic boom. Now the governments of the Philippines, Vietnam and even India are attempting to follow East Asia, while the people of Australia and the USA, and a growing number of other countries in the Americas and beyond, are being exhorted to meet the challenge of the rise of East Asia. From one influential point of view, a growing number of countries in East Asia have 'gone from being dominoes to dynamos'. This was the expression used by US President Bill Clinton in a speech he gave at the November 1993 Asia Pacific Economic Cooperation forum (APEC) meeting in Seattle. First set up in 1989, APEC reflects the effort to manage the transition from the Cold War to the post-Cold War era. It is also an organizational manifestation of post-Cold War attempts to shift the focus of international relations from geopolitics to geo-economics, and it is seen in some circles as a possible new force for global liberalization.[3]

In the context of the transition from the Cold War to the post-Cold War era in the Asia-Pacific, APEC is emerging as a key institutional nexus of liberal Anglo-American visions of the Pacific Century. At the same time, there are competing narratives on the region's future among the members of APEC. The differences within APEC reflect the differing elite visions of the rise of East Asia which dominate the debate about what is going on in the Asia-Pacific today. Despite challenges inside and outside APEC, brought on by the dramatic industrial success of East Asia and the end of the Cold War, Anglo-American narratives on the coming of the Pacific Century remain the most influential within and beyond the region. This is the main point of departure for this book. The various contributors all focus on particular countries and/or issues in an effort to engage critically with those elite visions which see the rapid economic growth of Northeast and Southeast Asia and the passing of the Cold War as heralding the dawn of a Pacific Century, the hallmark of which will be the dissemination and consolidation of economic prosperity and political stability throughout the region.

Most of the chapters in Part I, Asia-Pacific nations, engage with the dominant discourses on the Pacific Century by looking at politico-economic, social and cultural trends in specific 'nations' and/or at particular locations of change within those 'nations'. The range of contributions in Part I also reflects the important changes brought on by the rise of East Asia and the end of the Cold War, insofar as traditional Cold War analytical divisions have less salience than they did in the past. Thus, in addition to chapters on China, Japan, South Korea, Vietnam, Indonesia and Malaysia, Part I includes contributions on Russia and Australia, two countries which do not normally fall inside the boundaries of Asian Studies as it was constituted during the Cold War. While two of the chapters in Part II, Asia-Pacific patterns, examine the debate over the causes of the rise of East Asia from different angles, one of these, along with a third contribution, also addresses the significance of the emergence of the Asia-Pacific (and the Pacific Rim) as a 'new' regional demarcation in the context of the wider trend towards globalization.

In order to provide both the background for, and some preliminary discussion of, the various chapters that follow, this Introduction begins with a historical political economy of the Cold War in East Asia. This is followed by an attempt briefly to characterize the post-Cold War era in the Asia-Pacific, before turning to a more detailed examination of the rise of APEC. In an effort to contextualize APEC and the wider efforts to manage the transition to the post-Cold War era, the dominant Anglo-American discourses on the coming of the Pacific Century will then be considered. While Anglo-American liberalism is still hegemonic in international relations, powerful conservative approaches are reflected in the continued force of cultural/racial discourses in North America (and Australia) which see the rise of the 'East' as a threat to the 'West'; and these too are briefly charted. With the industrialization of East Asia and the end of the Cold War, Anglo-American liberalism has also been increasingly challenged, and the more conservative 'Yellow Peril' approaches have been fuelled, by powerful East Asian-based cultural/racial narratives. The enhanced strength of East Asian-centred discourses which challenge Anglo-American hegemony are discussed in some of the contributions in Part II. The growing power of East Asian narratives, embedded in the dynamic politico-economic and social forces of Northeast and Southeast Asia, demonstrates that the rise of East Asia, combined with the end of the Cold War, represents a world-historical turning point the significance of which should not be underestimated.

## EAST ASIA RISING: THE POLITICAL ECONOMY OF THE COLD WAR IN THE ASIA-PACIFIC

The Cold War provided the overall context for the industrial rise of East Asia after 1945. Stretching from the end of World War II until the collapse of the state-socialist regimes in Eastern Europe in 1989, and the subsequent disintegration of the Soviet Union in 1991, the Cold War can now be seen as a relatively discrete era in twentieth-century history. For most of that period international power relations were dramatically shaped by the imperatives and imaginings that attended the rivalry between the USA and the Soviet Union. While some commentators point to the success of US efforts to contain the Soviet Union and characterize the Cold War as a 'long peace', such a characterization betrays an Atlantic-centred perspective.[4] Northeast and Southeast Asia represented a particularly important and far less peaceful arena of the Cold War, as did the eastern Pacific Rim (Latin America), particularly Central America. The major Cold War fault line which ran through Northeast and Southeast Asia was the site of at least four full-scale wars (the Chinese Civil War 1945–1949, the Korean Civil War 1950–1953, and the complex colonial and civil wars in Vietnam, Cambodia and Laos known as the First Indochina War 1946–1954 and the Second Indochina War 1965–1975). These conflicts, along with innumerable smaller confrontations and incidents, all had local and regional dynamics, but were bent to the wheel of superpower geo-politics in various ways.

While military conflict in Northeast and Southeast Asia appears to have subsided, in contrast to an earlier era and in contrast to many other parts of the world, the popular post-Cold War notion that international relations can now focus on geo-economics, rather than the geo-politics of the Cold War, betrays both an excessively optimistic conception of what the future holds and a very selective reading of the history of the Cold War. The apparent centrality of politico-military strategy to the Cold War and the end of the US–Soviet military confrontation following the dramatic events of 1989–1991 has obscured the way in which politics and economics were inseparable during the Cold War, and the way in which post-Cold War economics continue to be embedded in wider politico-military questions. The Cold War was a long-standing politico-military effort to contain the USSR in the interests of the USA and its allies, at the same time as the projection of US power was also directed at ensuring the continued existence of a relatively open capitalist world economy which benefited US-based corporations and transnational capital generally. These interconnected objectives ensured that right up until the dramatic end of the Cold War, the USA played a key role in the wider dynamics of the global political economy. And, following the events of 1989–1991, the USA continued to possess considerable influence over the world's two other main industrial powers: Germany and Japan. US leverage over Germany and Japan stemmed from the very beginning of the Cold War. While Europe, particularly a partitioned Germany, was the main axis of the early Cold War, events in Northeast Asia by the late 1940s were serving to give the Cold War its increasingly global character. At the end of 1949 the Communist Party came to power in China, followed by the outbreak of war on the Korean peninsula. Although US policy in Japan had already begun to shift by 1947 towards the rebuilding of Japan as a buffer to Soviet power in the region, it was not until the Korean War (1950–1953) that the US defence industry, and the governmental institutions and bureaucratic structures of US Cold War hegemony, began to develop into distinct instruments of global power.[5]

Against the backdrop of the rise of communist China and the Korean War, the USA accelerated its support for the economic reconstruction and stabilization of Japan (as well as South Korea and Taiwan), while Washington's assistance to the beleaguered French effort to hold on to their colonial empire in Indochina increasingly became the focal point of a wider commitment to containing communism in Southeast Asia.[6] By late 1953 President Eisenhower was particularly concerned about the economic and political impact of a French collapse on Japan, which was seen by then as the linchpin of US efforts to contain China and the Soviet Union in East Asia. Despite US aid, the French were brought to their knees at Dien Bien Phu in May 1954. The country was 'temporarily' divided between the Viet Minh-controlled North and what became a US client regime in the South. While North Vietnam gravitated into the communist bloc, the Southeast Asian Treaty Organization (SEATO), comprised of the USA, France, Great Britain, Australia, New Zealand, Thailand, Pakistan and the Philippines, was set up, and its zone of defence was defined as including Cambodia, Laos and South Vietnam. With the Cold War well established, the USA increasingly sought to shape events in Vietnam and Southeast Asia. While the communist 'contagion' was prevented from spreading beyond the former French empire in Indochina, the sustained effort to project US power in the region over the next twenty years could not avert the eventual collapse of the Washington-backed Saigon regime in April 1975. In broad terms, the US defeat in Vietnam flowed from Washington's failure to lay down a politico-economic framework which could provide the basis for a military victory. In the post-1945 era the USA had increasingly sought to achieve impossible goals, failing in spectacular fashion in the jungles of Southeast Asia by the early 1970s.[7]

The war was already being seen as a 'failure' by the late 1960s, but the USA did not pull out of Vietnam completely until the fall of Saigon in April 1975. Vietnam epitomized the way in which the US mission to 'modernize' the world along liberal capitalist lines was increasingly challenged outright by social revolution and nationalism in Asia, Latin America, the Middle East and Africa, and in North America by those concerned with the limits of US power.[8] While the USA was the hegemonic military and economic power in Northeast and Southeast Asia for at least twenty years following the end of World War II, by 1968 the foreign policy consensus in North America, based on Truman's version of global containment, was breaking down and the country was at the centre of a wider hegemonic crisis. In 1969, Richard Nixon entered the White House promising that his administration would find an 'honorable solution' to the war in Southeast Asia. However, the approach to foreign policy articulated by the Nixon administration was a relatively conservative reaction to Washington's problems of empire and the incoming administration made a *realpolitik* reassessment of the United States' means, not its goals. The Nixon Doctrine began as a relatively spontaneous assertion about a new US role in Asia. Nixon emphasized that the USA would seek to avoid direct intervention to contain revolution and increasingly move to assist its allies with military and economic aid. The Nixon Doctrine was explicitly aimed at avoiding another Vietnam; however, it did little to alter a deeply rooted Cold War outlook, nor did it serve to curtail covert interventions.[9] At the beginning of the 1970s, Nixon and his foreign affairs adviser Kissinger perceived no need for a large number of allies. From their perspective, regimes and/or revolutions around the world were incapable of threatening US interests, unless they were backed by a major power, as had happened in Vietnam.[10]

Nixon and Kissinger's relatively traditional balance-of-power outlook guided US overtures to China, and in 1972 the two governments embarked on a series of diplomatic exchanges that by 1979 resulted in the establishment of ambassadorial-level relations. The successful rapprochement between China and the USA flowed primarily from their joint concern about the 'Soviet threat'.[11] This shift in US–Chinese relations was related not only to changes in the US regional and global position, but also to the vicissitudes of post-1949 Chinese history. Close relations between China and the USSR, and the initial Chinese commitment to a technocratic Soviet-style industrial development model in the 1950s, had given way by the 1960s to the Sino-Soviet split and a more rural-oriented communism based on mass mobilization. This ideological rift culminated in the Cultural Revolution which stretched from 1966 until Mao's death in 1976. By the late 1970s, as the US–China rapprochement moved ahead, the Cultural Revolution was increasingly being seen as the ten 'lost years'. The passing of Mao from the Chinese political stage and the growing awareness of the economic shortcomings associated with the Cultural Revolution paved the way for the rise of Deng Xiaoping and the Central Committee decision of December 1978 to shift the country's overall economic policy in a market-oriented direction, staking the legitimacy of the Chinese Communist Party (CCP) on the ability of a more liberal economic policy to raise the standard of living of the population. In the late 1970s the Chinese state began to wind back the central planning system in favour of market mechanisms. This was accompanied by a dramatic opening to foreign capital and technology and foreign consumer goods, as well as the accessing of external export markets.[12] It is worth noting that in China, at least eight years prior to the rise of Gorbachev in the Soviet Union, the process of economic *perestroika* (restructuring) was well under way, but political *glasnost* (openness) was minimal and was eventually snuffed out in Tiananmen Square in 1989.

By the 1980s communist China, while remaining a totalitarian political regime, was clearly becoming a capitalist economic power and was increasingly perceived as another East Asian success story. By the early 1990s China was being represented as a 'new superpower'.[13] The shift in Sino-US relations and China's (re)turn to capitalism signalled an important change in the political economy of the Cold War in the region. At one level it marked an implicit acknowledgement of the relative 'success' of capitalism generally, and the post-war capitalist dynamism of South Korea, Taiwan and Japan more particularly. At the same time, 'actually existing socialism' in China and elsewhere had sought from the outset to 'mimic the economic achievements of capitalism', setting goals which capitalism was 'obviously much better equipped than socialism to achieve'.[14] From this perspective, the (re)turn to capitalism was a logical expression of the pursuit of those goals and it also served to regain some legitimacy for the CCP which continues to exercise centralized state control over China's increasingly capitalist trajectory. As Martin Farrell points out in Chapter 2 of this book, the Chinese leadership confronts 'daunting obstacles' in its efforts to sustain the kinds of economic growth rates the country has experienced since the beginning of the 1980s. Farrell examines these various trends, concluding that even if China maintains its current economic growth rate for the next ten or twenty years, the CCP's efforts to retain its monopoly of political power and guide the country to superpower status will be increasingly challenged from various quarters. Regardless of the outcome, he concludes that the centre will hold and a dynamic capitalist China will play a key role in regional and international politics as the Pacific Century approaches.

The earlier capitalist success of Japan, South Korea and Taiwan, which were the closest and most obvious challengers to state socialism in North Korea, China and Vietnam, flowed in part from US Cold War efforts to contain China. A growing number of writers now emphasize the central role of the USA in the economic rebirth of Japan and in the industrialization of South Korea and Taiwan, and the subsequent importance of Japanese corporations and the Japanese state in the region.[15] Because Northeast Asia was a major arena of the Cold War, Japan, South Korea and Taiwan received sustained US economic and military aid, and capital. Their key positions in the Cold War also resulted in the implementation of land reforms, under US auspices, which contributed to economic growth and industrialization. Despite the reforms carried out in Japan between 1945 and 1950, it took purchases worth billions of dollars during the Korean War to kick off real economic growth. By the 1950s Japanese-based corporations had clearly begun to (re-)emerge as a key element in the wider US-centred Cold War political economy of Northeast Asia. At the same time, in the 1950s, 75 per cent of Taiwan's infrastructure investment came from US aid, while US economic aid to South Korea from 1945 to 1973 was US$5.5 billion. This was more than all the US economic aid to Africa and half the figure for all of Latin America over the same period. In the 1950s more than 80 per cent of South Korean imports were financed by US economic assistance, and US military aid to South Korea between 1945 and 1979 was US$7 billion. In a wider sense US Cold War imperatives in the form of the Vietnam War in the 1960s also provided an important economic stimulus in South Korea and Taiwan. This was reflected in the dramatic increase in US purchases of agricultural and industrial commodities, not to mention US spending on 'rest and recreation' in Taiwan, and US contracts to Taiwanese firms for work in Vietnam, while South Korean firms such as Hyundai and Daewoo gained major war-related construction contracts.[16]

In the late 1950s and 1960s, manufacturers based in Japan, South Korean and Taiwan also gained privileged access to the North American market. South Korea, Taiwan, Singapore and Hong Kong all entered the world export markets in the 1960s when a consumer boom was under way, when transnational corporations (TNCs) were looking for places to set up and expand production, and when the USA remained intent on facilitating 'successful' capitalist models in a part of the world where communism was seen to be a particularly serious threat. The USA also tolerated Taiwan and South Korea's protected markets and their governments' tight controls on foreign investment – even as the International Monetary Fund (IMF) and the World Bank were increasingly exhorting the rest of the world to end their restrictions on imports and foreign capital. In the Cold War era South Korea's foreign investment code was one of the most restrictive in the world. This, and South Korea's protected domestic markets, provided a secure base from which its subsidized conglomerates (*chaebôl*) were able to pursue their entry into foreign markets. At the same time, Japanese companies avoided the rising cost of labour in Japan by relocating operations to their former colonies in the 1960s and 1970s. By the 1970s Japanese trading companies controlled 50–70 per cent of the international trade of South Korea and Taiwan. When Taiwanese and South Korean industrialization began to take off in the 1970s, Japanese corporations provided a substantial portion of the machinery and the other components needed, and they were also an important source of technology licences.

Against the backdrop of the overall importance of Cold War political economy to East Asia's industrial trajectory, one of the things that is increasingly emphasized by those trying to explain post-1945 industrial success in South Korea and Taiwan (and in Northeast and Southeast Asia generally) is the role of a 'strong' interventionist state. A growing interest in identifying, and/or building, 'strong states' (usually defined as states which have a high degree of coercive capability and relative independence or 'autonomy' from certain classes or sectors of society, and are capable of intervening to restructure society or direct the market) has underpinned debates about economic and political change for a number of years. By the end of the 1980s the statist and wider institutionalist approaches to capitalist development in East Asia had gained some influence within wider international economic policy debates.[17] In Part II, Asia-Pacific patterns, Chapter 11 by Mark Berger and Chapter 9 by Yao Souchou offer cultural critiques of the capitalist developmental state and/or various emerging conceptions of 'Asian' capitalism. At this point it should simply be emphasized that the 'state' in late-industrializing South Korea and Taiwan or elsewhere has a particular history which flows from the character of the wider social formation. Furthermore, even if the state appears to have a degree of independence or relative autonomy this should not be seen as conferring on it a status separate from society. States are at once products of and embedded in wider social formations and those states that appear to have relative autonomy reflect a particular historical conjuncture, at once local, regional and world-historical. The state is not so much autonomous from society; rather, the particular social formation in which it is embedded has produced a 'strong' state as a result of a particular history.

From this perspective the relative autonomy of the state in South Korea and Taiwan flowed directly out of the colonial period. These states were strengthened by the way in which their continued survival was central to US geo-strategic concerns after World War II and by the support they received as a consequence of US policy. Apart from the highly centralized authoritarian states which were a legacy of the colonial period (and in Taiwan's case a result of the Guomindang's history on the mainland) the power of Cold War authoritarian states was grounded in the relative weakness of their capitalist elites, who were dependent on, or created by, the 'state'. Autonomous state power was also enhanced by the undercutting or the elimination of powerful landowners after 1945. The role of the state in industrialization in East Asia and the importance of the history of Japanese colonialism in the region are readily apparent in the way in which the South Korean state financed industrialization in the 1970s. Park Chung Hee (1961–1979), who had been an officer in the Japanese Kwantung Army during the Pacific War, was one of many post-war South Korean leaders who clearly remembered and was influenced by the Japanese colonial industrial pattern, most importantly the state's close links with the *zaibatsu* (pre-1945 Japanese conglomerates).[18] From the 1960s to the 1980s the authoritarian state in South Korea operated closely with the country's burgeoning conglomerates: the *chaebôl*. The centrality and predominance of the South Korean state and the complexity of its relationship to the *chaebôl* in the context of the country's overall development trajectory are drawn out by Kwan Kim in Chapter 3. He argues that a 'striking and persistent feature' of South Korea during industrialization has been the 'preservation' of the authority of the state and this has flowed from South Korea's historical legacy, particularly Japanese colonial rule and the geo-politics of the Cold War. Kwan Kim also emphasizes the way in which the rapid economic growth of the 1960s and 1970s paved the way for the relative decline of the authoritarian capitalist developmental state in South Korea in the late 1980s.

In the 1980s, the complex East Asian matrix of Cold War developmentalism, which came into being after World War II, and provided the context for the economic resurgence of Japan and the dramatic rise of South Korea and Taiwan in particular, underwent a shift as Washington increasingly began to question the financial and trading practices which it had overlooked in an earlier era when geo-political considerations loomed larger. At the same time, domestic pressures for political and economic liberalization worked to undermine the state-centred authoritarian approach to capitalist development which characterized South Korea and Taiwan and ushered in an elite-negotiated transition to democracy.[19] Liberalization and the waning of the tight linkage between government and business in South Korea (which exploded in 1996 in the form of a major scandal involving the discovery of a secret US$650 million 'slush fund' controlled by former President Roh Tae Woo which had been built up by contributions from virtually all the major corporations in South Korea) have meant many of the *chaebôl* setting up operations elsewhere in Northeast Asia, as well as in Southeast Asia and beyond. The 1980s also saw an increase in the shifting of operations by Japan and Taiwan-based companies offshore, as a result of rising wages and increased production costs. The industrial rise of a growing number of countries in Southeast Asia and of coastal China was fuelled in part by the dramatic influx of capital from Northeast Asia. Since the second half of the 1980s there have been significant increases in Northeast Asian investment flows into Southeast Asia linked to the wider trend towards globalization, a process which is perceived to have accelerated with the end of the Cold War.

## FROM GEO-POLITICS TO GEO-ECONOMICS? THE POLITICAL ECONOMY OF THE POST-COLD WAR ASIA-PACIFIC

While the dramatic scaling back of the US–Russian conflict had important implications for other parts of the world, many of the boundaries and configurations of power of the Cold War in East Asia persist in a less attenuated form than elsewhere. The sharp reversal in late 1989 of the politico-military imperatives and distinct social and economic spheres which had divided Western Europe from Eastern Europe for over forty years was not paralleled by a similar trend in East Asia (the Tiananmen uprising in 1989 went the way of the Prague Spring in 1968 rather than following the successful rebellions which toppled the Soviet proconsular regimes in Eastern Europe in late 1989–1990). The Chinese Communist Party remains at the helm of an ostensibly 'socialist state' and the post-1949 division between mainland China and the Chinese nationalist government in Taiwan remains in place. At the same time, since the late 1980s the Taiwanese economy has become increasingly integrated with mainland China's coastal provinces as trade, capital and technology flows put new strains on political boundaries. Because there are still no direct lines of trade, travel and communication, people, goods, capital and information pass through third countries. Following the lifting in 1987 of the ban on family visits (as long as they took place through a third country) 4 million people, out of a population of 22 million in Taiwan, had visited China by 1992, often for business. There is an increasingly large quantity of investment capital flowing from Taiwan to China which seeks to shift land-intensive and labour-intensive production to the mainland where both are in large supply, and trade flows are as marked as capital flows. An important facet of the dramatic growth in trade between Hong Kong (which officially returns to Chinese rule in July 1997) and China, and the dramatic emergence of the Pearl River Delta as the fifth Dragon, can be attributed to the activity of Taiwanese traders and investors operating through Hong Kong.[20] Some optimistic observers see these trends leading to a gradual but inexorable 'rapprochement' between Beijing and Taipei.[21] At the same time, as Taiwanese politics are liberalized and democratized, there is continued concern that moves towards political 'independence', and the renunciation of the 'two governments one China policy', could spark an invasion and a forced reunification attempt by Beijing. A 1994 novel which predicted a Chinese invasion of Taiwan quickly became a best seller in the erstwhile Chinese province.[22] However, Chinese efforts to influence the March 1996 presidential elections in Taiwan by carrying out large and dramatic war games close to the island did not lead to either a military invasion or the election result preferred in Beijing.

Further to the south, Vietnam, which was reunified in 1975, continues to be governed by the Communist Party, and, as in China, the governing elite has presided over a major shift towards the market beginning in the late 1970s.[23] Vietnam's reintegration with the capitalist world economy was accelerated by the promulgation of *doi moi* (renovation programme) in 1986, the loss of its Soviet patron in 1991, and by the normalization of US–Vietnamese relations in early 1994. In July 1995 Vietnam was formally inducted into the Association of South-East Asian Nations (ASEAN) as its seventh member. Chapter 5 on Vietnam by Gerard Greenfield focuses on the implications of the country's dramatic transition to capitalism for its workers and peasants, with particular attention to coal miners in Quang Ninh, in the country's northeast. He examines the new nationalist discourses which are emerging in the context of the Vietnamese elite's dramatic appropriation of public sector assets and its establishment of lucrative new connections with transnational capital. He emphasizes that despite the elite narratives that seek to mobilize the Vietnamese population around the continued leadership of the Communist Party, the transition to capitalism in Vietnam has been characterized by profound dislocation and fragmentation. Quang Ninh is just one of many sites of localized resistance where the national elite and their vision of Vietnam's position in the Pacific Century are being subverted and challenged.

Even the diplomatically isolated and autarkic North Korean regime, following the death of Kim Il Sung, has begun to make cautious attempts to make more links with the international political economy and join the Pacific Century. Under his son, Kim Jong Il, North Korea has reached a *modus vivendi* with the USA and with South Korea regarding nuclear weapons, while a number of South Korean companies, with the support of the South Korean state, are beginning to move into North Korea.[24] At the same time considerable uncertainty remains regarding the future of the Korean peninsula. North and South Korean soldiers are still lined up along the 38th parallel and the USA remains forward-deployed in support of its South Korean ally. North and South Korea's prospects remain tied up with the uncertainty surrounding the continued division of the peninsula, a direct legacy of the Cold War.[25]

Meanwhile, the Japanese government has only just begun to question the constraints on it established by the Cold War system. This was clear from its deliberations during the Gulf War. Even though almost 65 per cent of Japan's oil supplies come from the Middle East, the government had to reverse an initial decision to dispatch a small number of 'non-combatants' to the Gulf. Its significant financial support (at least US$13 billion) for the US-led military machine also generated heated domestic debate. More recently, the debate over the continued presence of almost 50,000 US military personnel in Japan, which was sparked by the rape in October 1995 of a young girl in Okinawa where most of the US troops are based, has again highlighted the wider question of Japan's politico-military position in post-Cold War Asia.[26] At the same time, many Chinese and Koreans continue to regard Japan with considerable suspicion and animosity, as demonstrations about compensation for 'comfort women' and the Nanjing Massacre make clear.[27] Also, the Communist parties that remain in power in China and North Korea are products, in part, of the earlier struggle against Japan, while many Japanese citizens remain deeply committed to pacifism and the pacifist movement which flowed from Japan's own experience of the war. Although Japan is generally seen as a rising power in the Asia Pacific and beyond, US hegemony in the Asia-Pacific has not necessarily come to an end with the passing of the Cold War.[28] For example, as Haruhiro Fukui and Shigeko N. Fukai suggest in Chapter 1, concerns in Japan about the country's position in post-Cold War Asia have been partially subsumed by the relative uncertainty and instability of domestic politics and the apparent waning of the 'economic miracle'. Ironically Japanese politics since the 1970s has been characterized by a growing policy 'convergence' between virtually all the main interest groups and political parties in Japan, at the same time as 'political instability' has increased as a result of the 'heightened volatility' of the Japanese electorate. At the same time, contrary to many commentators, Fukui and Fukai argue that the Japanese development model is 'dying', if not already 'dead'. Furthermore, they take the view that Japan's previous economic success was directly linked to the 'political stability' of the Cold War era, concluding that the celebrated Japanese developmental state, which presided over the post-1945 economic miracle, has, like the Cold War itself, passed into history.

With regard to the overall shape of the emerging post-Cold War era in the Asia-Pacific, Tim Luke argues, in Chapter 10 that the emerging 'flows' of the post-industrial economy will alter traditional notions of nation-states, sovereignty and identity in the Asia-Pacific and beyond. Meanwhile, Mark Berger argues in Chapter 11 on the East Asian Miracle and post-Cold War capitalism that the region continues to be shaped by a transitional type of Anglo-American liberalism which remains grounded in the politico-military power of the United States of America. However, it is also pointed out that even at its height US power was not a homogenizing force, and with the rise of East Asia and the passing of the Cold War this new phase of global capitalism is shaping up to be an even less stable arrangement than that which characterized US-centred Cold War capitalism. Berger emphasizes that if there is a 'key nexus of power' in the post-Cold War Asia-Pacific, it is not the USA but the USA–Japan relationship, which has emerged as an increasingly complex 'web of economic rivalry and interdependence' linked to Japan's continued reliance on the USA for military support. And even if the end of the Cold War does not represent as immediate a shift in US hegemony in the Asia-Pacific as first it appeared, it has served to accelerate a number of trends that flowed out of the end of the 'golden age' of capitalism in the early 1970s.[29] First, in the Asia-Pacific, even before the end of the Cold War, it was abundantly clear that although Japan was not a rising military power, the Japanese government and Japan-based corporations had emerged as key actors. While 'national' trade measurements indicate that both Japanese and US trade has declined relative to most of the other countries in the region, the US figure has dropped much further than the Japanese one. More significantly, the role of Japanese-based foreign investors has now clearly surpassed US-based foreign investors in the region.[30] By the mid-1990s, 75 per cent of the economic activity in East Asia was centred on Japan and that figure is not expected to drop below 70 per cent before the end of the century.[31] Furthermore, Japan clearly surpasses the USA as the primary distributor of foreign aid in the Pacific, especially in Northeast and Southeast Asia, and in the world.[32] Second, the economic growth of a growing number of Northeast and Southeast Asian states has meant that, in economic terms, the Asia-Pacific is more integrated and complex than it was twenty years ago. Third, the military role of the USA in the Pacific has been cut back. While Ronald Reagan's rejuvenation of the Cold War in the early 1980s led to increased US and Soviet naval and military deployment in the Pacific, by 1990 a growing number of states in the region no longer perceived the Soviet Union as a serious military threat. This perception undermined the relevance of US military power even before the USSR disappeared from the scene in December 1991.[33]

At the same time, the Asia-Pacific is one region of the globe which has witnessed steady increases in military spending on the part of a number of states in the post-Cold War years.[34] Furthermore, despite the perceived shift towards geo-economics, the interdependence of economics and politics as expressed in disputes over the control of valuable natural resources continues, the best-known example being the dispute over the Spratly Islands in the South China Sea, where sovereignty claims have been made by the governments of China, the Philippines, Taiwan, Malaysia, Vietnam and Indonesia. At the same time, questions about North Korea's nuclear programme and the transfer of missile technology and China's acquisition of power-projection weapons systems are receiving greater attention. While a growing and technologically advanced Japanese military potential means that some states remain interested in the projection of US military power in the Asia-Pacific, they appear to want the USA to fulfil a balance-of-power function, rather than occupy a singularly hegemonic position. At the same time, the growth of East Asia more generally remains linked to both the Japanese and the North American economy in a myriad ways. East Asian economic growth has built on and strengthened ongoing connections with the USA and Japan, but the growing significance of East Asia (North and South) means that it has the economic potential to rival the power of the North American economy. With the overall political-economic equation becoming increasingly complex, negotiations have become more frequent and more intense, while the results have tended to be incremental and/or disappointing to all sides.[35] This is apparent in US–Japan and US–China trade disputes in the first half of the 1990s, and represents the context for the emergence of APEC and the trend towards Pacific economic cooperation.

## PACIFIC ECONOMIC COOPERATION? THE END OF THE COLD WAR AND THE RISE OF APEC

The Asia-Pacific Economic Cooperation forum did not emerge until 1989, even though on more than one occasion since at least the 1960s the idea of some form of regional governmental association had been proposed.[36]

For example, in major speeches in 1961, and again in 1965, Lyndon Johnson, in his capacity as Vice-President and then as President of the USA, called for the establishment of a security and development organization comprised of the 'free nations' of the region. However, this initiative was apparently viewed with some suspicion in the Asia-Pacific itself, insofar as it was seen as an attempt by the USA to withdraw rather than project military power. Meanwhile, the Asian Development Bank was set up in 1966, primarily under Japanese auspices, and two subregional security initiatives were also undertaken. SEATO was set up in 1954 and the Asian and Pacific Council (ASPAC) also came into being; however, neither organization lasted beyond the 1970s and no regional intergovernmental economic institution was established, although one significant subregional economic intergovernmental organization did take shape in the form of ASEAN, comprising Thailand, Malaysia, Singapore, Indonesia, Brunei and the Philippines.[37]

In 1967 the Japanese government put forward an official proposal for a 'Pacific free trade area' as a reaction to the emergence of the European Economic Community (EEC). It did not gain widespread government support, but it did ease the way for the Pacific Basin Economic Council (PBEC) founded in April 1967 and made up of nationally based business organizations. At the beginning of 1968 a regional organization for economists, the Pacific Trade and Development Conference (PAFTAD), had its first meeting in Tokyo. In the 1970s, no direct governmental initiatives took hold, although Japan, with Australian support, floated the idea of a pan-Pacific government organization on more than one occasion. This led, in late 1980, to the formation of the Pacific Economic Cooperation Conference (PECC), which had its first meeting in Canberra and included representatives from the USA, Japan, Canada, Australia, New Zealand, South Korea, Malaysia, Thailand, Indonesia, Singapore and the Philippines. During the 1980s the governments of China, Taiwan, Brunei and the South Pacific Forum (a regional organization which includes all the governments of Oceania) began sending delegates to the PECC. Hong Kong and then Mexico, Chile and Peru had joined by 1991–1992, while a number of other Latin American countries, along with the USSR (Russia after 1991), held observer status. While the PECC brought together academics, business and government officials a key characteristic of its operation is the 'unofficial' role played by governments. Although the PECC produces a host of reports and recommendations they are not binding in any fashion.[38] The rise of the PECC paralleled a growing Pacific awareness in the United States in the 1970s and 1980s. In the early 1980s the former US ambassador to Japan, Michael Mansfield, emphasized that trade across the Pacific was now more important to the USA than trade across the Atlantic.[39] In 1984 Ronald Reagan noted publicly that 'the Pacific is where the future of the world lies'.[40] The US crisis of hegemony in the 1970s provided the context in which the concept of the 'Pacific Rim' and the 'Pacific Community' emerged; however, the US-centred discourse on the Pacific Rim and a Pacific Community faded somewhat with the initial decline of the Soviet 'threat', the economic recession, and the growing US–Japan trade friction of the late 1980s and early 1990s.[41] Although the end of the Cold War may have altered the security and alliance framework and demarcated the end of a US-centred 'imagined community' in the Pacific, the early 1990s have been characterized by the emergence of new visions of the Pacific which build on, but depart from, the proto-Pacific Community of the Cold War era.

Since the late 1980s elites in the Asia-Pacific have become concerned that the post-Cold War international economy is shifting towards economic blocs centred on Western Europe and North America. While both European economic integration and the North American Free Trade Agreement (NAFTA) have been represented by their proponents as liberalizing rather than protectionist initiatives there is considerable scepticism about this in Northeast and Southeast Asia. It was against this background that Australian Prime Minister Bob Hawke managed to bring about the founding meeting of APEC in Canberra at the end of 1989.[42] APEC represented a major element in a wider turn to Asia on the part of the Australian government and Australian-based corporations, which was already apparent in the 1970s but was given new impetus with the end of the Cold War. Chapter 8 by Roger Bell charts the Australian government's attempt to keep up with the dramatic changes in the Asia-Pacific. He explores some of the implications of the Australian effort at integration with Asia. As Bell makes clear, economic realities provided a powerful incentive for the Australian government and Australian-based companies to attempt increasingly to integrate with Asia; however, social forces in Australia continue to stand in some contrast to the politically and socio-culturally diverse, and geographically large, region which is poorly captured by the term 'Asia'. As the government in Canberra attempts to pursue 'national interests' in the Asia-Pacific and around the world, which are driven less by historic ties to Britain and the USA, there are related and growing efforts in Australia, argues Bell, to define the nation in new and more 'distinctive' ways. The Australian government's leading role in APEC is a manifestation of this trend insofar as Australian approaches to the organization, and to various key actors in it such as Japan and Indonesia, clearly reflect the changes to Australia's relationship with the USA brought on by the end of the Cold War and the decline of Soviet military power in the region.

Even though the Soviet Union no longer exists, Chapter 4 by Douglas Borer makes a case for the continued significance of Russia as a major player in the region. He emphasizes that, in the context of continued economic growth in the Asia-Pacific, Russia's position in the Pacific Century, initially as a supplier of weapons, oil, gas and various other raw materials and then subsequently as a site for investment and trade, will not be insignificant. The Russian government hopes to join APEC at some stage and, as Borer argues, although an increasingly authoritarian post-Soviet state may be unfavourably received in North America and Western Europe, such a trend may be seen as 'necessary' by governments in Asia, given that authoritarianism is often presumed to have underpinned the dynamic economic development of Taiwan, South Korea, Singapore and China, and more recently Indonesia (and to a lesser extent Thailand and Malaysia).

In the context of the wider theme of a changing post-Cold War world, Chapter 7 by Mark Berger, on Indonesia, questions the viability of Soeharto's authoritarian rule in that country. His contribution traces the history of the New Order state and emphasizes the way in which decades of uneven capitalist development have seen the nation of Indonesia become a Java-centred empire grounded as much in its Dutch colonial legacy as in the promise of the Indonesian nationalist struggle which brought about independence from Holland in the 1940s. At the same time, Berger emphasizes that this Java-centred empire is being challenged by the emergence of new social forces (a process which involves the reconfiguration of ethnic and social identities all across Indonesia) that are linked to major shifts in the global political economy associated with the rise of East Asia and the end of the Cold War.

Meanwhile, Chapter 6 by Steve Majstorovic, on Malaysia, focuses on the continued, if not increased, 'salience' of ethnicity after the Cold War, taking a historical approach to the rise of an 'ethnic state' in Malaysia. Directly linked to Malaysia's explicitly multiethnic history has been the growing effort on the part of the Malaysian elite to seek to generate national unity via a constant emphasis on Asian unity *vis-à-vis* the West. The ostensible need to put the community ahead of the individual, and a fixed cultural/racial conception of 'Asia', are key aspects of the East Asian vision articulated by Malaysian Prime Minister Mahathir Mohamad.[43] While the Malaysian government is a member of APEC, Mahathir has repeatedly sought to create an East Asian Economic Group (EAEG) which would include all the main East Asian countries but would explicitly exclude non-'Asian' countries such as New Zealand, Canada, the US and Australia, not to mention Chile and Mexico, all currently members of APEC.

Both the rise of APEC and the challenge to APEC in the form of Mahathir's aspirations for an East Asian economic bloc clearly reflect the growing strength of the idea that the twenty-first century will see the global centre of economic gravity shift to the Pacific Rim. The optimistic rhetoric which attended APEC's emergence carried through to its first major meeting in Seattle in late 1993 hosted by a recently elected Bill Clinton.[44] On the eve of a second major meeting in Bogor, Indonesia, in November 1994, President Clinton reiterated his 'vision of a new Asia-Pacific community with no artificial dividing line down the middle of the

Pacific'.[45] On the final day of the Bogor meeting the leaders from the eighteen member countries agreed in principle to the virtual elimination of tariff barriers and obstacles to capital flows within the APEC region by the year 2020.[46] From the point of view of sympathetic observers at least, the annual meeting in Osaka, Japan, in November 1995 resulted in further progress (the Philippines hosted the November 1996 meeting and it will be in Vancouver, Canada, in November 1997). The Japan meeting produced an 'Action Agenda' which eschewed binding trade agreements in favour of what Fidel Ramos (President of the Philippines) called the 'Asian way'. This amounts to verbal assurances by all member governments that they will make every effort to meet the economic liberalization goals of APEC. However, this result also points to the real limitations of the organization, as no enforcement mechanisms were formulated and no legally binding commitments were made.[47] The so-called developing countries in APEC fear that US and Japan-based corporations might squeeze out their own infant industries if protectionist measures are removed too soon, Japan continues to promote special treatment for its agricultural sector, and the USA has not offered to cut tariffs ahead of schedule as APEC countries are expected to do.[48] The emergence and survival of APEC can be seen as indicative of the wider regional transition to a weakened form of transnational economic liberalism which is still grounded in US politico-military power. The global political economy is shifting from a Cold War era in which the USA continued to occupy a hegemonic position to a post-Cold War era in which the US role is far more fluid. While the 1970s were a major turning point, the end of the US–Soviet conflict and the resurgence of global economic competition have accelerated the reconfiguration of state and social power in the Asia-Pacific and beyond.[49] In this context APEC represents an effort on the part of regional and transnational elites to manage the post-Cold War political economy and APEC is, potentially, the key institutional nexus of the Pacific Century.

## MANAGING THE PACIFIC CENTURY: EAST ASIAN DYNAMISM AND ANGLO-AMERICAN LIBERALISM

Linked to the emergence of APEC and the end of the Cold War are the major Anglo-American narratives on the Pacific Century. The continued power of Anglo-American liberalism is grounded in the historical dominance of the British empire of the nineteenth and early twentieth centuries and the US global hegemony of the twentieth century. Since the nineteenth century, liberalism has reinforced and informed British and then US hegemony world-wide. Despite the relative decline of the USA and the end of the Cold War, the English language provides the main means of communication for transnational capitalist elites and Anglo-American conceptions of political and economic activity remain central to the day-to-day functioning of the international political economy.[50] One of the best-known exponents of a particularly triumphant strand of Anglo-American liberalism is Francis Fukuyama, a RAND consultant and former US State Department employee. At the end of the 1980s he articulated a liberal utopian vision of the Pacific Century and suggested that the end of the Cold War might be the 'end of history'. In a now famous article he characterized the waning of the conflict between Washington and Moscow as the 'end point of mankind's ideological evolution and the universalisation of Western liberal democracy as the final form of human government'. He emphasized that the liberal 'victory' was still unfinished, and it had occurred mainly 'in the realm of ideas or consciousness'. The process was 'as yet incomplete in the real or material world'. However, with regard to East Asia he saw liberalization as well advanced. In Japan, where 'the essential elements of economic and political liberalism' had been 'successfully grafted onto uniquely Japanese traditions and institutions', he was confident that liberalism's 'survival in the long run' was assured. In the case of South Korea he argued that 'political liberalism' had been trailing 'economic liberalism, more slowly than many had hoped but with seeming inevitability' and that South Korea 'could not possibly be isolated from the larger democratic trends' which were sweeping the globe.[51] Then, in 1992, Fukuyama argued that East Asia's 'postwar economic miracle' makes clear that 'capitalism is a path toward economic development that is potentially available to all countries'. More specifically, he argued that 'the established industrial powers' have not been 'capable of blocking the development of a latecomer, provided that country plays by the rules of economic liberalism'. From his point of the view the 'newly industrialized economies' (NIEs) of Asia 'have proven that economic liberalism allows late modernizers to catch up with and even overtake' established industrial powers.[52]

Fukuyama's emphasis on the superiority and universality of Anglo-American liberalism points to the power of the assumption that the demise of state socialism was a victory for the type of capitalism that predominated in Britain and North America in the 1980s.[53] Fukuyama's writings capture the spirit of the late 1980s and early 1990s, and reflect the dominant Anglo-American narrative which continues to find in the East Asian 'Miracle' confirmation of the superiority of the modes of political and economic organization associated with an idealized North America and Great Britain. At the same time, he has also allowed that an East Asian-style capitalist development model led by Japan may embody a major challenge to, rather than a recapitulation of, the Anglo-American model.[54] However, other voices of economic liberalism continue to find in the rise of the 'East' a replication of the rise of the 'West'. According to the former Prime Minister of Britain, Margaret Thatcher, 'such success as Asia now enjoys is the result of unremitting hard work, an unquenchable spirit of enterprise, and sound economic policies'.[55] In an article in

*The Economist*, on the occasion of the fiftieth anniversary of the IMF and the World Bank, Jeffrey Sachs, a Harvard University economics professor who has acted as an adviser to the Polish and Russian governments as well as governments in Latin America and elsewhere in Eastern Europe, mapped out what he saw as the progress made by the IMF and the World Bank and its future direction. He asserted that 'the world' was 'closer than ever before to the global, co-operative, free-market arrangements championed 50 years ago by the visionaries who met at Bretton Woods, New Hampshire'. For the first time in history, said Sachs, 'the world had the opportunity to adopt an international system built on law, in which the weak and strong are treated equally, and where all have a chance to benefit from an open market-based, global economy'.[56]

In contrast to the rampant triumphalism of some variants of post-Cold War Anglo-American liberalism, an equally powerful and related narrative which rests on a more managerial, less overtly *laissez-faire* conception of the global political economy has continued to shape national, regional and international approaches to the Pacific Century. This liberal managerial discourse complements, and flows out of, the liberal internationalist tendency in US policy and the emergence of trilateralism which attended the relative decline of US hegemony in the 1970s. In the context of the wider shift in the 1970s towards greater influence on the part of Asian, Latin American and African governments at the United Nations, and in related organizations such as the International Labour Organization (ILO), the United Nations Conference on Trade and Development (UNCTAD) and the United Nations Development Program (UNDP), along with the call for a New International Economic Order (NIEO), liberal managerialism substituted a Cold War view of international relations for a North–South emphasis. Liberal managerialism advocated accommodation, mild reform and selective intervention, rather than confrontation with Asian, Latin American and African revolutions and regimes, seeking a limited amount of reform in order to maintain long-term stability. A major nexus of liberal managerialism was the Trilateral Commission which was founded in 1973 by prominent North American, European and Japanese academics, politicians and corporate heads. One of the co-founders and first directors of the Trilateral Commission, Zbigniew Brzezinski (in keeping with George F. Kennan's original economic prescriptions for US containment doctrine), emphasized that the Trilateral Commission's overall approach to international relations rested on the assumption that US relations with Japan and Western Europe represented the 'strategic hard core for both global stability and progress'.[57] The major goal of the Trilateral Commission was to develop a cohesive, and semi-permanent, alliance which embraced the world's major capitalist-industrial democracies, to better promote stability and protect their interests. The Trilateral Commission was devoted to the maintenance and strengthening of the liberal international economic order.[58]

By the 1970s the dominant liberal discourses increasingly emphasized the profound socio-economic forces at work in Asia and around the world and the dangers involved in US failure to recognize them. The emphasis was on managing the international political and economic order and responding to challenges by means of reform, negotiation and diplomacy. This approach reflected the liberal concern to discard the discredited anti-communist modernizing mission in favour of an approach which recognized the limits of US power, and the increased economic and political influence of many governments in Asia and elsewhere. At the same time this discourse reflected the continued survival of the assumption that the interests of the people and governments of Asia and the interests of the USA and the other major industrial states could be harmonized, and that greater understanding on both sides could lead to less conflict and greater prosperity for all concerned. The influence of liberal managerialism on US policy during the Nixon years remained marginal; however, policies followed by the Carter administration in its first two years meshed with a growing emphasis on managing the international political economy. However, the Carter administration eventually shifted back to a conventional Cold War policy, when the July 1979 revolution in Nicaragua was followed by the Soviet invasion of Afghanistan at the end of that year.

The conservative revival in North America and Western Europe (most notably in Britain) looked with considerable approval on the values and institutions which they believed were at the core of 'Western' civilization. From their perspective the 'West' was in the midst of a crisis of leadership. They were convinced that the continued existence of democracy and liberty in North America and Western Europe required the vigorous projection and expansion of US power around the globe. They pointed to the need for a new anti-communist crusade, and unrelentingly emphasized that a Moscow-inspired communist threat was the cause of unrest around the world. From Ronald Reagan's point of view, which was as black-and-white as his early movies, US ideals were under siege world-wide from 'Soviet Russia' and 'left-wing totalitarianism'.[59] However, the conservative attempt to return to a golden age, in which the USA stood as a beacon of liberty against an international communist movement centred in Moscow, had foundered by the end of Reagan's first term. Throughout the 1980s US foreign policy continued to be framed in the context of powerful conservative political discourses grounded in socio-economic forces in North America; however, the influence of the new Cold Warriors declined dramatically in the second half of the Reagan years. This decline in influence flowed from questions regarding the legitimacy of Reagan's huge defence build-up and the impact of massive deficit spending on the ability of the US economy to sustain a global military role, issues which were underscored in Paul Kennedy's highly regarded popular work, *The Rise and Fall of the Great Powers*.[60]

By the mid-1980s liberal managerialism had undergone a resurgence in the face of the still powerful but increasingly compromised conservatism which had brought Reagan to power. Between 1985 and 1988 a managerial approach, emphasized by the liberal critics of Reagan's foreign policy, was partially reincorporated into US foreign policy. The shift away from conservative revivalism was highlighted by James Baker's emergence as Treasury Secretary in 1985. In this position, Baker, who went on to be Secretary of State under Bush, was far less opposed than his predecessor to government intervention in the economy, looked favourably on international economic and financial cooperation, and began to pursue a series of initiatives to secure agreements with the Japanese government and the world's other major economic and financial powers, resulting in the 1985 Plaza Agreement and the Louvre Accord of 1987. These agreements were aimed at mitigating the negative effects of Reaganomics on the international market, international debt repayment and the decline in world investment. The Baker initiatives flowed from a perceived need for greater cooperation between the major capitalist powers in the management of the international economic order. When Baker emerged as Bush's Secretary of State in 1989 his appointment was well received in the Democratic Congress. And the trend towards a new consensus accelerated once Bush entered the White House intent on a more multilateral and managerial approach to foreign policy and international economic relations.[61] In the context of the end of the Cold War, a resurgent liberal managerialism has shaped the dominant discourses on international affairs and was connected to the restoration of a managerial and internationalist approach guiding the practice of US foreign policy and international affairs more generally.[62] And with all the criticism of US policy under Clinton, the liberal managerial trajectory which was reasserted in the Bush era has continued with ups and downs, as evidenced by a US emphasis on working with a now far more prominent United Nations, the ratification of NAFTA and GATT (as well as turning the General Agreement on Trade and Tariffs into the World Trade Organization (WTO)) and US support for APEC.[63]

In institutional terms APEC clearly reflects the continued force of liberal managerialism. Unlike its more triumphalist manifestations, liberal managerialism is characterized by greater concern about the many problems involved in the transition to the Pacific Century. For example, in his book *Rethinking the Pacific*, Gerald Segal lamented that, despite the 'growing sophistication' of politics in the Pacific, there is little evidence that the foreign policies being pursued by the governments of the Asia-Pacific are 'dominated by a Pacific-consciousness' at least in contrast to the Atlantic. In his view the element which is most clearly missing from an alleged 'Pacific community' is any 'sense of shared cultures and ideologies'. In the face of what he regarded as an excess of 'speculation' about the coming of the Pacific Century, he argued that in contrast to 'the coherence of the North Atlantic community, the Pacific will not fulfil its supposed promise'.

He anticipated that the two major 'trading states' of the USA and Japan would persist as the dominant economic powers in the Pacific, noting that both have important trade and investment linkages with Western Europe. Writing just as the Cold War was coming to an end, he also saw the Pacific as being the preserve of four major military powers: the USA, the USSR, Japan and China. However, he was optimistic that the overall security situation in the Pacific would improve. He perceived a trend towards the blurring of distinctions between socialism and capitalism, arguing that the 'success' of 'state capitalism' in Japan (not to mention countries such as South Korea and Taiwan) 'offers a bridge of sorts between the two ideals of "East" and "West"'. At the same time, he envisioned a Pacific region which would remain characterized by cultural and ideological fragmentation and anticipated that the 'alliances' which develop will continue to extend well outside the region. Ultimately, for Segal, 'thinking Pacific' did not mean 'thinking only in regional terms' and the future 'success' of states in the Pacific will flow more from 'their ability to play the global game' than their position in the region.[64]

The liberal managerial perspective is also reflected in the well-known work of history by Mark Borthwick, entitled *Pacific Century*. This book, which is a key text in the liberal discourse on the Pacific Century, emphasizes that a transition is under way from the US-centred Pacific Century to a new Pacific Century. Borthwick, who is US director of the PECC (discussed on p. 14), argues that it should come as no surprise that North Americans are expressing misgivings and ambivalence about this transition. However, in his view the USA has 'achieved a long-cherished national goal': that is, that the Pacific region is now 'a group of stable, economically vibrant and generally friendly (albeit competitive)' nation-states. At the same time some kind of 'confrontation' could emerge out of the rivalry between the capitalist giants of the USA and Japan, and governments in the Pacific are 'concerned' because their economic well-being is heavily dependent on the successful management of US–Japanese relations. According to Borthwick the end of the Cold War has encouraged Pacific states to rethink what being part of a region actually involves and to look at the way in which 'ongoing adjustments in the structures of interdependent economies can be made more smoothly'. He emphasizes that this process of rethinking and economic management is taking place in the context of two historically grounded visions of cooperation in the Asia-Pacific. One vision is based on the rise of Japan and the Japan-sponsored 'co-prosperity' sphere of the 1930s and the other on the post-1945 US drive to contain communism, both of which had calamitous results in the form of the Pacific War (Japan) and the Vietnam War (the United States). In Borthwick's view, both 'visions' have passed and, with the end of the Cold War, Japan now 'aspires to the leadership of a Pacific economic renaissance' in alliance with the USA which continues to work to 'bind the region to its global political and economic foreign policy'. Borthwick argues that 'collisions of interests and cultures between Asia and the West have subsided in intensity but not disappeared' and that the 'resolution' of a variety of concerns is being pursued at a time of 'significantly lowered political and military tensions' in the region.[65]

Borthwick's book clearly reflects a liberal managerial perspective on the Pacific Century which is part of the wider post-Cold War liberal discourses on international relations. While this perspective emphasizes the growing economic interdependence of the Asia-Pacific, drawing attention to what has become known as globalization, it is assumed that current economic trends in the region are going to deliver prosperity to an ever growing number of people. This view makes limited or no reference to the social inequities which are characteristic of interdependence and globalization even in the economically booming Asia-Pacific. Liberal managerialism also tends to assume that in the post-Cold War era the elites of the region can give preference to geo-economics, as the threat of military confrontation subsides; however, as we have seen, Northeast and Southeast Asian economic growth has been accompanied by dramatic increases in arms spending, while industrialization itself has generated new or reconfigured rivalries, and the end of the Cold War has altered the politico-military balance. Although it is profoundly misleading to view the rise of East Asia as a recapitulation of the rise of the 'West', it is still worth remembering that an important dynamic of the historic rise of capitalist Western Europe was interstate conflict and warfare (as has been the case in East Asia for much of this century). While liberal managerialism is not necessarily overtly utopian, it does subscribe in varying degrees to the idea that the rise of East Asia and the end of the Cold War have produced increased opportunities for the dissemination and consolidation of economic prosperity and political stability throughout the region as the global centre of economic gravity shifts to, or at least tilts in the direction of, the Pacific.

In the context of the rise of East Asia and the end of the Cold War, some conservatives in North America, Western Europe and Australia are far more doubtful about the promise of the Pacific Century. They perceive a growing threat to the 'West', flowing particularly from the resurgence of Japan and/or China in East Asia (Islam in the Middle East is also seen as a major threat). By the second half of the 1980s the rise of Japan in particular, and the rise of East Asia more generally, resulted in the appearance in North America and Australia of an increasingly strident concern about Asian immigration and about the growing presence of Japanese companies and the 'unfair' trading practices of Japanese and East Asian corporations.[66] In 1985 a *New York Times*–CBS poll found that 8 per cent of the US citizens it interviewed represented their view of Japan as 'generally unfriendly'. By July 1989 the figure was 19 per cent and by February 1990 it had risen to 25 per cent.[67] This perception of 'general unfriendliness' was symbolized in North America by the furore in the US media surrounding the purchase of the Rockefeller Center in New York by Japanese capital, not to mention the 1989 purchase of Columbia Pictures by Sony and the controlling interest in MCA acquired by Matsushita in 1990.[68] Approaches which represent East Asia as a 'threat' often continue to rest on an explicitly racial understanding of Japan, and of East Asia more generally. This view was reflected in Michael Crichton's novel *Rising Sun* which became a major movie. Interestingly Crichton's book came complete with a bibliography and an afterword in which the author warned that: '[s]ooner or later, the United States must come to grips with the fact that Japan has become the leading industrial nation in the world.' He argued that 'the Japanese have invented a new kind of trade – adversarial trade, trade like war, trade intended to wipe out the competition – which America has failed to understand for several decades. In his view it was time 'for the United States to wake up, to see Japan clearly, and to act realistically' because '[t]he Japanese are not our saviours' but 'our competitors' and 'we should not forget it'.[69] The novel and the movie reinforced the image of US–Japan relations as primarily a racial war which the USA was losing. At the same time, Japanese corporate investment in the USA has remained smaller than the investment flow from corporations based in Western Europe. Furthermore, by the mid-1990s a number of the Japanese investments had proved to be unprofitable, while the anticipated 'control' of the film industry by the Japanese did not materialize, and in some cases Japanese companies have now divested themselves of their stake in the film industry.[70]

While a preoccupation with the Japanese, or East Asian, 'threat' to North America lost some of its strength as a result of the recession in Japan in the early 1990s (and the apparent economic recovery in North America), culturally/racially deterministic discourses on the rise of the 'East', centred in North America, Western Europe and Australia, have certainly not disappeared. A recent and widely debated effort by Samuel Huntington to view post-Cold War international relations as a 'clash of civilizations' reflects the continued influence of culturally (if not racially) deterministic discourses on East Asia specifically, and on international politics more generally.[71] Huntington is also a prominent critic of writers such as Fukuyama. In the late 1980s Huntington reiterated that major 'obstacles to the expansion of democracy exist in many societies'. From his perspective many of these were cultural. What he saw as the 'third wave' of democratization (from the mid-1970s to the end of the 1980s) would not necessarily 'last forever' and it could be succeeded 'by a new surge of authoritarianism', although he did not 'preclude a fourth wave of democratization developing some time in the twenty-first century'.[72]

The cultural determinism which underpins Huntington's earlier writings gained more significance with the end of the Cold War. In his 1993 *Foreign Affairs* article he argued that 'the fundamental source of conflict' in the future would be 'cultural'. In his view, while '[n]ation-states' will continue to be the key 'actors' in the international arena it is '[t]he clash of civilizations' which 'will dominate global politics'. He postulated seven or eight primary 'civilizations', the interaction of which would shape the future. These were Confucian, Western, Japanese, Hindu, Islamic, Slavic-Orthodox, Latin American and 'possibly African civilization'. He emphasized that civilizational 'differences' were 'basic', far more basic than 'ideologies'. He also argued that interaction between 'peoples of different civilizations' reinforces 'civilization-consciousness' which in turn invigorates animosities and differences 'stretching or thought to stretch back deep into history'. In his view civilizations were also gaining strength because social change and economic modernization were undermining loyalty to 'nation-states' and detaching people from more localized identification. Also, increasing 'civilization-consciousness' was being strengthened by the way the 'West', at the height of its 'power', increasingly 'confronts non-Wests' with the aspiration, 'the will and the resources to shape the world in non-Western ways'. He argues that cultural characteristics are less open to compromise than economic and political issues. For example, he argues that Japan confronts serious obstacles to any effort to set up an economic entity in East Asia comparable to NAFTA because the 'convergence' of Canadian, Mexican and US 'cultures' is not possible in the Japanese case. From his perspective, 'Japan is a society and civilization unique to itself' and, regardless of the strength of investment and trading linkages it forms with the rest of East Asia, the 'cultural differences' between Japan and the rest of the region represent a serious obstacle and may well 'preclude' the economic integration of the region to the degree that is occurring in North America and Europe. At the same time, in his view, cultural similarities were hastening the steady increase in economic relations between Singapore, Hong Kong, Taiwan, mainland China and the overseas Chinese throughout the region. As a result the main 'East Asian economic bloc' could well coalesce around China rather than Japan.[73] Huntington cites Murray Weidenbaum who has argued that:

> [d]espite the current Japanese dominance of the region, the Chinese-based economy of Asia is rapidly emerging as a new epicenter for industry, commerce and finance. This strategic area contains substantial amounts of technology and manufacturing capability (Taiwan), outstanding entrepreneurial, marketing and services acumen (Hong Kong), a finance communications network (Singapore), a tremendous pool of financial capital (all three), and very large endowments of land, resources and labor (mainland China). . . . From Guangzhou to Singapore, from Kuala Lumpur to Manila, this influential network – often based on extensions of the traditional clans – has been described as the backbone of the East Asian economy.[74]

Huntington and Weidenbaum's analysis of a 'Greater China' reflects a deterministic approach to culture which treats China and the Chinese diaspora as a fixed and monolithic entity, while downplaying or overlook-ing the innumerable lines of tension and fracture within mainland China and between the mainland and the Chinese inhabitants elsewhere in the region, not to mention the fissures and complicated loyalties within the wider Chinese diaspora.

Huntington's approach also rests heavily on a sharp distinction between the 'West' and the non-West. In his view the main axis of international politics is increasingly converging on the conflict between the 'West' and the rest of the world, and on the reaction of 'non-Western civilizations to Western power and values'. He points with concern to a 'Confucian-Islamic connection' which has risen to challenge the power, interests and values of the 'West': in particular the build-up of military power in China is at the centre of the 'development of counter-West military capabilities'. He argues that major confrontations in the near future are going to pit the 'West' against several 'Islamic-Confucian states', a formulation which appears to encapsulate neatly the fear in North America and Western Europe of the diffuse threats embodied by militant Islam and the rising 'developmental states' of East Asia, especially China. Huntington empha-sizes that he is not in favour of 'conflicts between civilizations', and in the near future it is in the West's 'interest' to encourage more unity and co-operation 'within its own civilization', especially in North America and Western Europe. He urges the US and Western European governments to reach out to Latin America and Eastern Europe because their 'cultures are close to those of the West'. He also highlights the need to sustain good relations with Tokyo and Moscow. He advises the 'West' to try and contain the growing military power of Islamic and Confucian states at the same time as ensuring continued Western 'military superiority' in South-west Asia and East Asia.[75]

Ultimately, like Huntington's earlier work, his now famous vision of a coming 'clash of civilizations' can still be located within a wider liberal managerial discourse. At the same time, it represents a clear instance of ahistorical and culturally deterministic analysis which continues to rely on a homogeneous conception of the 'West' while reducing Asia to its main cultural and/or religio-philosophical traditions. While triumphalist liberal narratives, as already noted, rest on the assumption that Northeast and Southeast Asia are travelling down the same historical road as North America and Western Europe, the wider liberal managerial discourses to which they are linked appear to allow for a somewhat more multilinear conception of social and political change. However, as in the case of Huntington's work, this can be manifested as cultural/racial determinism and remains committed, at least implicitly, to assumptions about the super-iority of North American and Western European institutions and values. Ultimately, liberal managerial discourses, despite their differences, still work to complement national and international institutions and arrange-ments that originate in, and often remain centred on, North America and

Western Europe. At the same time, as will be reviewed in Chapter 11 by Mark Berger in Part II, Asia-Pacific patterns, the industrial success of East Asia and the end of the Cold War have provided the context in which culturally/racially determined North American and West European narratives are paralleled by increasingly powerful East Asian discourses, centred on the industrializing states of Northeast and Southeast Asia, which represent the rise of East Asia as a function of 'Asian' cultural/racial superiority. In addition to these new or reconfigured anti-Western (or anti-US) initiatives in East Asia, Douglas Borer in Chapter 4 discusses the new Russian state's emerging 'Eurasian' doctrine, which seeks to revitalize and make relevant Russia's place in the post-Cold War era. Eurasianism stresses Russia's unique historical role as both a European and an Asian power, and it attempts to bridge the new West–East divide.

## CONCLUSION: THE RISE OF EAST ASIA

The dominant narratives on the rise of East Asia and the coming of the Pacific Century have repeatedly emphasized the miraculous economic success of a growing number of countries in the region over the course of the Cold War and into the post-Cold War era. The dramatic industrialization of various nations in East Asia is also increasingly represented as a trend which is carrying the Asia-Pacific towards a new era of prosperity and even democratic stability. This image, with variations and qualifications, has been generated in part by a large number of commentators whose writing complements the wider efforts of regional elites to manage the post-Cold War political economy of the Asia-Pacific and beyond. Despite our attempt to position ourselves in opposition to the dominant managerial narratives on the Pacific Century, some of the contributions to this book, and maybe the book as a whole, can still be located within the liberal managerial discourse on the Pacific Century. At the same time, the chapters which follow all attempt to take a critical approach to the coming of the Pacific Century by looking at many of the main nations in the region and at a number of key debates and patterns which can be discerned with the rise of East Asia and the end of the Cold War. What these chapters have in common is a commitment to critical engagement with the dominant narratives on the rise of East Asia and a concern that the most influential visions of the coming of the Pacific Century are deployed by elites in an effort to maintain or expand their power and interests. While a shared critical engagement with the elite visions of the processes which are sweeping the Asia-Pacific at the end of the twentieth century gives the chapters in this book an overall unity, the authors come to their chosen topics from a range of disciplinary backgrounds and occupy differing politico-intellectual positions.

Martin Farrell's chapter on China, Douglas Borer's chapter on Russia and Steve Majstorovic's on Malaysia reflect the authors' background in the disciplines of political science and international relations as they have developed in North America. At the same time, these authors have all been influenced directly or indirectly by the important shift in the social sciences in North America in the 1980s towards 'bringing the state back in'.[76] They have all tried to a greater or lesser degree to foreground the particular history of the 'state' as a key to understanding the wider 'national' trajectories of China, Russia and Malaysia. In his chapter on South Korea, Kwan Kim, an economist by training, also focuses on the history of the state as an important element in South Korea's overall path to its current position as an industrialized 'nation'. The approach taken in Roger Bell's chapter on Australia points to the author's background in the disciplines of history and international relations and he foregrounds the importance of Australia's relations with a series of 'great powers' as crucial to the country's political history and to the current search for national identity in the antipodes. Haruhiro Fukui and Shigeko N. Fukai's chapter on Japan bears clear traces of the influence of marxism, and is testimony to the relatively important, albeit declining, place a particularly Japanese marxist intellectual tradition has occupied within popular and academic discourses on political, economic and social change in Japan.[77] From a somewhat different angle, Gerard Greenfield's contribution on Vietnam, and Mark Berger's chapters on Indonesia and on the East Asian Miracle, flow from the marxist tradition at the same time as they also reflect the fruitful engagement between marxism and various trends in post-structuralism which has been taking place over the past decade or more. Timothy Luke's chapter is also best viewed as yet another strand of the emerging synthesis between marxism and post-structuralism, while Yao Souchou's chapter is clearly informed by a framework drawn directly from post-structuralism. Despite their different politico-intellectual positions it should be reiterated that the various contributors all seek to engage critically with the dominant narratives on the rise of East Asia and the coming of the Pacific Century. It should also be reiterated that even as we attempt to challenge the dominant narratives, some chapters (if not the book as a whole) are readily assimilated to elite efforts to manage the Pacific Century in a direction commensurate with the interests and concerns of powerful minorities rather than in a direction beneficial to the majority of the inhabitants of the Asia-Pacific.

## NOTES

1 Staffan Burenstam Linder, *The Pacific Century: Economic and Political Conse-quences of Asian-Pacific Dynamism* (Stanford, Calif.: Stanford University Press; 1986); David Aikman, *Pacific Rim: Area of Change, Area of Opportunity* (Boston, Mass.: Little Brown, 1986); Brian Kelly and Mark London, *The Four Little Dragons: Inside Korea, Taiwan, Hong Kong and Singapore at the Dawn of the Pacific Century* (New York: Simon & Schuster, 1989); Robert Elegant, *Pacific Destiny: Inside Asia Today* (London: Headline, 1991; first published

1990); Simon Winchester, *Pacific Rising: The Emergence of a New World Culture* (New York: Prentice Hall, 1991); William McCord, *The Dawn of the Pacific Century: Implications for Three Worlds of Development* (New Brunswick: Transaction Publishers, 1991); Frank Gibney, *The Pacific Century: America and Asia in a Changing World* (New York: Macmillan, 1992); Mark Borthwick (with contributions by selected scholars), *Pacific Century: The Emergence of Modern Pacific Asia* (Boulder, Colo.: Westview Press, 1992); James C. Abegglen, *Sea Change: Pacific Asia as the New World Industrial Center* (New York: Free Press, 1994); John Naisbitt, *Megatrends Asia: The Eight Asian Megatrends That Are Changing the World* (London: Nicholas Brealy, 1995); Jim Rohwer, *Asia Rising: How America Will Prosper as Asia's Economies Boom* (New York: Simon & Schuster, 1995).

2 The area encompassed by the term 'East Asia' fluctuates. Sometimes East Asia is used to mean Northeast Asia, while at other times it is seen to include both Northeast and Southeast Asia. The term is used in this book to refer to both Northeast and Southeast Asia.

3 C. Fred Bergsten, 'APEC and the World Economy: A Force for Worldwide Liberalisation' *Foreign Affairs* vol. 73, no. 3, May/June 1994.

4 John Lewis Gaddis, *The Long Peace: Inquiries into the History of the Cold War* (New York: Oxford University Press, 1987), This criticism is made in Bruce Cumings, 'The Wicked Witch of the West is Dead. Long Live the Wicked Witch of the East' in Michael J. Hogan, ed., *The End of the Cold War: Its Meaning and Implications* (Cambridge: Cambridge University Press, 1992), p. 87.

5 Bruce Cumings, 'Japan in the World-System' in Andrew Gordon, ed., *Post-War Japan as History* (Berkeley: University of California Press, 1993), pp. 45–51.

6 Andrew J. Rotter, *The Path to Vietnam: Origins of the American Commitment to Southeast Asia* (Ithaca, NY: Cornell University Press, 1987); Lloyd C. Gardner, *Approaching Vietnam: From World War II Through Dienbienphu 1941–1954* (New York: W. W. Norton, 1988).

7 Gabriel Kolko, *Anatomy of A War: Vietnam, the United States and the Modern Historical Experience* (New York: New Press, second expanded edition, 1994; first published, 1985), p. 545.

8 Charles Gati, 'Another Grand Debate?: The Limitationist Critique of American Foreign Policy' *World Politics* vol. 21, no. 1, 1968.

9 Robert S. Litwak, *Détente and the Nixon Doctrine: American Foreign Policy and the Pursuit of Stability 1969–1976* (Cambridge: Cambridge University Press, 1986; first published 1984), pp. 193–194.

10 Enrico Augelli and Craig Murphy, *America's Quest for Supremacy and the Third World: A Gramscian Analysis* (London: Pinter, 1988), p. 144.

11 Thomas G. Paterson, *Meeting the Communist Threat: Truman to Reagan* (New York: Oxford University Press, 1988), p. 75.

12 Stephen White, John Gardner, George Schöpflin and Tony Saich, *Communist and Postcommunist Political Systems: An Introduction* (London: Macmillan, 1990), pp. 247–260.

13 William H. Overholt, *The Rise of China: How Economic Reform is Creating a New Superpower* (New York: W. W. Norton, 1994).

14 Arif Dirlik, *After the Revolution: Waking to Global Capitalism* (London: Wesleyan University Press, 1994), p. 44.

15 Bruce Cumings, 'The Origins and Development of the Northeast Asian Political Economy: Industrial Sectors, Product Cycles and Political Consequences' *International Organization* vol. 38, no. 1, 1984; reprinted in Frederic C. Deyo, *The Political Economy of the New Asian Industrialism* (Ithaca, NY: Cornell University Press, 1987).

16  Richard Stubbs, 'The Political Economy of the Asia-Pacific Region' in Richard Stubbs and Geoffrey R. D. Underhill, eds, *Political Economy and the Changing Global Order* (London: Macmillan, 1994), pp. 366–371.

17  Gary Hawes and Hong Liu, 'Explaining the Dynamics of the Southeast Asian Political Economy: State, Society, and the Search for Economic Growth' *World Politics* vol. 45, no. 4, 1993, pp. 630–633.

18  Jung-En Woo, *Race to the Swift: State and Finance in Korean Industrialization* (New York: Columbia University Press, 1991), pp. 20–21, 40.

19  James Cotton and Kim Hyung-a van Leest, 'The New Rich and the New Middle Class in South Korea: The Rise and Fall of the "Golf Republic"' in Richard Robison and David S. G. Goodman, eds, *The New Rich in Asia: Mobile Phones, McDonalds and Middle-Class Revolution* (London: Routledge, 1996).

20  David S. G. Goodman and Feng Chongyi, 'Guangdong: Greater Hong Kong and the New Regionalist Future' in David S. G. Goodman and Gerald Segal, eds, *China Deconstructs: Politics, Trade and Regionalism* (London: Routledge, 1994); Yun-Wing Sun, Pak-Wai Liu, Yue-Chim Richard Wong and Pui-King Lau, *The Fifth Dragon: The Emergence of the Pearl River Delta* (Singapore: Addison Wesley, 1995).

21  Abegglen, *Sea Change*, pp. 116–120.

22  Julian Baum, 'Fear of Falling: Prophet of Chinese Invasion Makes Many Nervous' *Far Eastern Economic Review* 13 October 1994, p. 24; Nayan Chanda, 'Fear of the Dragon' *Far Eastern Economic Review* 13 April 1995, p. 26.

23  Gerard Greenfield, 'The Development of Capitalism in Vietnam' *The Socialist Register: 1994* (London: Merlin Press, 1994).

24  Shim Jae Hoon, 'Bridging the Divide: South Korea's Daewoo Makes Headway in North Korea' *Far Eastern Economic Review* 14 September 1995, p. 63.

25  Ian Buruma, 'Will the Wall Come Tumbling Down' *The New York Review of Books* 3 November 1994, pp. 24–31.

26  Andrew Higgins, 'US Military on Trial in Okinawa' *The Guardian Weekly* 7 January 1996, p. 7.

27  Charles Smith, 'War and Remembrance' *Far Eastern Economic Review* 25 August 1994, pp. 22–24.

28  Bruce Cumings, 'The Political Economy of the Pacific Rim' in Ravi Arvind Palat, ed., *Pacific-Asia and the Future of the World-System* (Westport, Conn.: Greenwood Press, 1993).

29  Andrew Glyn, Alan Hughes, Alain Lipietz and Ajit Singh, 'The Rise and Fall of the Golden Age' in Stephen A. Marglin and Juliet B. Schor, eds, *The Golden Age of Capitalism: Interpreting the Postwar Experience* (New York: Oxford University Press, 1990).

30  Donald Crone, 'Does Hegemony Matter?: The Reorganization of the Pacific Political Economy' *World Politics* vol. 45, no. 4, 1993, pp. 507–508.

31  Abegglen, *Sea Change*, pp. 2–4, 18.

32  Dennis Yasutomo, *The Manner of Giving: Strategic Aid and Japanese Foreign Policy* (New York: D. C. Heath, 1986).

33  Crone, 'Does Hegemony Matter?', pp. 508–512.

34  Steven Ratuva and Douglas Borer, 'The Myth of Post-Cold War Disarmament: Post-Soviet Disorder and Rearmament in the Asia-Pacific Region' *The Journal of Pacific Studies* vol. 17, 1993, pp. 107–131; 'Asian Security: East Asia Wobbles' *The Economist* 23 December 1995–5 January 1996, p. 27.

35  Stubbs, 'The Political Economy of the Asia-Pacific Region', pp. 373–374.

36 Hadi Soesastro, 'Pacific Economic Cooperation: The History of an Idea' in Ross Garnaut and Peter Drysdale, eds, *Asia Pacific Regionalism: Readings in International Economic Relations* (Sydney: Harper Collins, 1994).

37 Crone, 'Does Hegemony Matter?', pp. 512–513.

38 ibid., pp. 513–515.

39 Michael Mansfield, 'Prospects for a Pacific Community' in Paul F. Hooper, ed., *Building a Pacific Community: The Addresses and Papers of the Pacific Community Lecture Series* (Honolulu: University of Hawaii Press/East-West Center, 1982), p. 86; cited and discussed in Rob Wilson and Arif Dirlik, 'Asia/Pacific as Space of Cultural Production' *boundary 2* vol. 21, no. 1, 1994, p. 2.

40 Ronald Reagan quoted in Winchester, *Pacific Rising*, p. 24; cited and discussed in Wilson and Dirlik, 'Asia/Pacific as Space of Cultural Production', p. 3.

41 Christopher L. Connery, 'Pacific Rim Discourse: The US Global Imaginary in the Cold War Years' *boundary 2* vol. 21, no. 1, 1994, pp. 31–32, 54–56.

42 While the Australian government has tended to be seen as the originator of APEC there is now evidence that the Japanese Ministry for International Trade and Industry (MITI) was an early advocate of an Asia-Pacific trade organization and encouraged the Australian government to take the initiative because it was felt that the idea would be better received in the region if it came from Australia rather than Japan. See Richard McGregor, 'How the Japanese Gave Us APEC' *The Australian* 4 January 1996, pp. 1–2; also see Yoichi Funabashi, *Asia Pacific Fusion* (Washington, DC: Institute for International Economics, 1996).

43 Khoo Boo Teik, *Paradoxes of Mahathirism: An Intellectual Biography of Mahathir Mohamad* (Kuala Lumpur: Oxford University Press, 1995).

44 James Walsh, 'Toward the Pacific Age' *Time International* 22 November 1993, pp. 22–27.

45 Cited in Michael Gordon, 'APEC's Great Leap Forward?' *The Weekend Australian* 12–13 November 1994, p. 21.

46 'A Dream of Free Trade' *The Economist* 19–25 November 1994, pp. 29–30. The member states of APEC in 1989 were Australia, Brunei, Canada, Indonesia, Japan, Malaysia, New Zealand, the Philippines, Singapore, South Korea, Thailand and the United States. China, Hong Kong and Taiwan joined in 1991. Mexico and Papua New Guinea joined in 1993 and Chile joined in 1994. As of 1996 the Russian government was preparing to apply.

47 Frank Ching, 'APEC Moving Along "Asian Way"' *Far Eastern Economic Review* 7 December 1995, p. 48.

48 Sandra Sugawara, 'Lingering Trade Disputes Cloud Asia-Pacific Summit' *Washington Post* 12 November 1995, p. A24.

49 Stephen R. Gill, 'Neo-Liberalism and the Shift Towards a US-Centred Transnational Hegemony' in Henk Overbeek, ed., *Restructuring Hegemony in the Global Political Economy: The Rise of Transnational Neo-Liberalism in the 1980s* (London: Routledge, 1993), pp. 246–247, 280.

50 Leslie Sklair, *Sociology of the Global System* (London: Harvester, 1991), p. 26.

51 Francis Fukuyama, 'The End of History?' *The National Interest* vol. 16, no. 8, 1989, pp. 3–4, 15.

52 Francis Fukuyama, *The End of History and the Last Man* (London: Hamish Hamilton, 1992), pp. 101–107.

53 William Keegan, *The Spectre of Capitalism: The Future of the World Economy After the Fall of Communism* (London: Vintage, 1993; first published 1992), p. 4.

54 Fukuyama, *The End of History and the Last Man*, p. 243; Francis Fukuyama, 'Capitalism and Democracy: The Missing Link' *Journal of Democracy* vol. 3, no. 3, 19, pp. 108–110. But, even in his latest book, Fukuyama argues that

'civil society' in the 'West' rests on a greater degree of 'social trust' than 'civil society' in many East Asian societies (Japan is emphasized as 'high trust', while China is 'low trust') which continues to be based mainly on family networks. He takes the view that 'high trust' societies have more long-term capacity for the generation of economic growth. See Francis Fukuyama, *Trust: The Social Virtues and the Creation of Prosperity* (New York: Free Press, 1995).

55 Margaret Thatcher, 'The Triumph of Trade' *Far Eastern Economic Review* 2 September 1993, p. 23.

56 Jeffrey Sachs, 'Beyond Bretton Woods: A New Blueprint' *The Economist* 1–7 October 1994, pp. 23–29. For a thorough critique of Sachs's ideas and his role in the transition to capitalism in Eastern Europe see Peter Gowan, 'Analysing Shock Therapy: Neo-Liberal Theory and Practice for Eastern Europe' *New Left Review* no. 213, 1995.

57 Zbigniew Brzezinski, *Power and Principle: Memoirs of the National Security Advisor 1977–1981* (London: Weidenfeld & Nicolson, 1983), pp. 5–6, 49, 288–289.

58 Stephen Gill, *American Hegemony and the Trilateral Commission* (Cambridge: Cambridge University Press, 1990), p. 1.

59 Robert Dallek, *Ronald Reagan: The Politics of Symbolism* (Cambridge, Mass.: Harvard University Press, 1984), cited in Charles W. Kegley, Jr. and Eugene R. Wittkopf, *American Foreign Policy: Pattern and Process* (New York: St Martin's Press, third edition 1987), p. 575.

60 Paul Kennedy, T*he Rise and Fall of the Great Powers: Economic Change and Military Conflict from 1500–2000* (New York: Random House, 1987).

61 Gill, *American Hegemony and the Trilateral Commission*, pp. 108, 119–121.

62 For example, see The Commission on Global Governance, *Our Global Neighbourhood: The Report of the Commission on Global Governance* (New York: Oxford University Press, 1995).

63 Martin Walker, 'Clinton Hits Global Path to Re-election' *The Guardian Weekly* 3 December 1995, p. 6.

64 Gerald Segal, *Rethinking the Pacific* (Oxford: Oxford University Press, 1991; first published 1990), pp. 1–2, 367–368, 385–386, 390–391.

65 Borthwick, *Pacific Century*, pp. 1–3, 543–545. Another good example of the liberal managerial approach is Steve Chan, *East Asian Dynamism: Growth Order and Security in the Pacific Region* (Boulder, Colo.: Westview Press, second edition, 1993; first published 1990), pp. 131–137. He draws explicitly on R. O. Keohane and J. S. Nye, *Power and Interdependence: World Politics in Transition* (Boston, Mass.: Little Brown, 1977), For other books which exemplify post-Cold War liberal managerialism and internationalism see James Chace, *The Consequences of the Peace: The New Internationalism and American Foreign Policy* (New York: Oxford University Press/Twentieth Century Fund, 1992); Tony Smith, *America's Mission: The United States and the Worldwide Struggle for Democracy in the Twentieth Century* (Princeton, NJ: Princeton University Press/Twentieth Century Fund, 1994).

66 For example, see Clyde Prestowitz, *Trading Places: How We Are Giving Our Future to Japan and How to Reclaim It* (New York: Basic Books, expanded edition 1989; first published, 1988); George Friedman and Meredith Lebard, *The Coming War With Japan* (New York: St Martin's Press, 1991).

67 Connery, 'Pacific Rim Discourse', p. 46.

68 Giovanni Arrighi, *The Long Twentieth Century: Money, Power, and the Origins of Our Times* (London: Verso, 1994), pp. 17–18.

69 Michael Crichton, *Rising Sun* (London: Arrow, 1992), pp. 401–402.

70 In April 1995 Matsushita sold 80% of its shares in MCA to Seagram. See Nigel Holloway, 'Star Struck' *Far Eastern Economic Review* 11 January 1996, p. 64.
71 Samuel P. Huntington, 'The Clash of Civilizations?' *Foreign Affairs* vol. 72, no. 3, 1993. The succeeding issue of *Foreign Affairs* had a range of responses, as did *Asian Studies Review* vol. 18, no. 1, 1994. Also see Samuel P. Huntington, *The Clash of Civilizations and the Remaking of World Order* (New York: Simon and Schuster, 1996).
72 Samuel P. Huntington, 'Democracy's Third Wave' *Journal of Democracy* vol. 2, no. 2, 1991, p. 33; cited and discussed in Georg Sørensen, *Democracy and Democratization: Processes and Prospects in a Changing World* (Boulder, Colo.: Westview Press, 1993), p. 120. See also Samuel P. Huntington, *The Third Wave: Democratization in the Late Twentieth Century* (Norman: University of Okalahoma Press, 1991), For an approach to 'democracy' similar to Huntington's see Larry Diamond, 'The Globalization of Democracy' in Robert O. Slater, Barry M. Schutz and Steven R. Dorr, eds, *Global Transformation and the Third World* (Boulder, Colo.: Lynne Rienner, 1993); Larry Diamond, 'The Global Imperative: Building a Democratic World Order' *Current History* vol. 93, no. 579, 1994.
73 Huntington, 'The Clash of Civilizations?', pp. 22–28.
74 Murray Weidenbaum and Samuel Hughes, *Greater China: The Next Economic Superpower?* (St Louis, Mo.: Washington University Center for the Study of American Business, Contemporary Issues Series 57, February 1993), pp. 2–3; cited in Huntington, 'The Clash of Civilizations?', p. 28. Also see Murray Weidenbaum, *The Bamboo Network: How Expatriate Chinese Entrepreneurs Are Creating A New Economic Superpower in Asia* (New York: Martin Kessler Books, 1996).
75 Huntington, 'The Clash of Civilizations?', pp. 41, 45–49.
76 Theda Skocpol, 'Bringing the State Back In: Strategies of Analysis in Current Research' in Peter B. Evans, Dietrich Rueschemeyer and Theda Skocpol, eds, *Bringing the State Back In* (New York: Cambridge University Press, 1985).
77 Tessa Morris-Suzuki, 'Introduction: Japanese Economic Growth, Images and Ideologies' in Tessa Morris-Suzuki and Takuro Seiyama, eds, *Japanese Capitalism Since 1945: Critical Perspectives* (New York: M. E. Sharpe, 1989), pp. 14–21; Germaine A. Hoston, *Marxism and the Crisis of Development in Prewar Japan* (Princeton, NJ: Princeton University Press, 1986).

# Part I
# Asia-Pacific nations

# 1 The end of the miracle: Japanese politics in the post-Cold War era

*Haruhiro Fukui and Shigeko N. Fukai**

## INTRODUCTION: JAPANESE POLITICS IN THE POST-COLD WAR ERA

For three and a half decades, from the mid-1950s to the late 1980s, Japan enjoyed a double blessing: phenomenal economic growth and equally phenomenal political stability. To many observers, the two blessings were in fact causally connected: the economic miracle was, to an important extent, both a cause and a consequence of the political stability.[1] The political stability was in turn due substantially to permanent rule by a single party, the Liberal Democratic Party (LDP), which ensured continuity and consistency in economic policy making and implementation. In other words, a domestic regime of hegemonic rule provided the Japanese for three and a half decades with generous amounts of key public goods such as political stability, personal safety and, above all, prosperity.

This felicitous combination attracted the attention and interest of not only scholars and journalists but also governments, especially in Asia. By the mid-1980s, it had spawned a whole new literature on the 'developmental state' and the 'new capitalism'. In his influential and pioneering 1982 study of the modern Japanese political economy, Chalmers Johnson elaborated a model of a state that nurtures a highly capable elite bureaucracy and guides and directs the national economy vigorously but judiciously – by market-conforming means.[2] In an article published two years later, Bruce Cumings named the model Bureaucratic-Authoritarian Industrializing Regime, or BAIR, and traced the route of its migration from pre-war imperialist Japan to its colonies, Taiwan and Korea.[3]

A BAIR is, by definition, a politically closed regime in the sense that participation in decision making on important political and economic issues is open only to members of the dominant group or groups.[4] The fact of being closed, however, enables the regime to adapt rapidly and flexibly to changing domestic or international economic circumstances. It thus helps the regime to govern the market in such a way as to achieve its developmental goals by, as Wade suggests, effectively controlling and manipulating the ownership of farm land, the financial system, exchange and interest rates, prices, the import and export trade, and the acquisition and development of new technologies.[5] Japan has been the model developmental state, or 'Asian-style democracy', as some euphemistically call it, not only for Taiwan and Korea but increasingly also for a number of other Asian nations.[6] Prime Minister Mahathir Mohamad of Malaysia 'looks east' as intently and enthusiastically as the late President Park Chung Hee of South Korea.

However, Japan's vaunted image and reputation as a strong and quintessential developmental state, spearheading a 'new' form of capitalism, was sullied by the early 1990s.[7] Not only was its economy mired in a protracted recession, triggered by the burst of a speculative bubble at home and compounded by the soaring value of the yen abroad, but political stability guaranteed by continuous rule by an invincible conservative party was no longer the reliable marker of its politics. Intractable economic trouble began in early 1990 with a sudden collapse of stock prices. Political trouble had begun several months earlier, when the LDP suffered the worst electoral defeat in its history and, for the first time, lost the majority in the upper house, or House of Councillors, of the Japanese Parliament, or the Diet. Far more damaging to the stability of Japanese politics and government, as well as to the LDP's position and role in them, were the results of the 1993 lower house election. For the first time, the LDP lost its majority in the House of Representatives, which is the larger and more powerful of the two chambers. This led to an end of the LDP's thirty-eight-year-long rule and the formation of the first of a series of unstable coalition governments.[8] All these events that took place in a rapid sequence in the early 1990s were unexpected and surprising. The most unexpected and surprising, however, was the party make-up of the coalition governments formed in the wake of the 1993 general election, particularly the third such government formed in the spring of 1995.

In the discussion that follows, we try to demonstrate that the dramatic developments in Japanese politics in the last few years of the 1980s and the first few years of the 1990s had deeper and more complex roots than casual observers realized. We point out that, in addition to a long and seemingly endless series of political scandals, an important change in Japanese economic and political culture triggered by the oil crisis of the early 1970s paved the way for the fall of the LDP's hegemonic rule in the early 1990s. We document how that crisis led to a change in the attitude and behaviour, first, of the leadership of organized labour, and then of the leadership of organized business, and to the formation of a 'neocorporatist' regime of tripartite cooptation and cooperation among the LDP government, big business and the main unions. The emergence of the neo-corporatist regime in turn paved the way for cooperation and coalition, first between the LDP and centrist parties and, eventually, between the LDP and the Socialists as well.

Paradoxically, however, Japanese politics became increasingly unstable even as the rapprochement between big business and the main unions and between the LDP and the major opposition parties progressed. This was due mainly to increases in the number of floating voters not attached to any particular party and of abstainers. These increases in turn reflected the growing disillusion and alienation among the Japanese electorate that resulted from the series of political scandals. They also resulted, however, from the apparent convergence among the parties on major policy issues, which, as we argue in the Conclusion, made elections irrelevant to the serious concerns of most voters.

## PROXIMATE CAUSES OF THE 'GREAT REVERSALS'[9]

The LDP suffered a disastrous defeat in the July 1993 lower house general election and, as a result, lost its legendary status as Japan's permanent ruling party. The SDPJ suffered even greater losses, but these were not as surprising to most observers because it had been in opposition since 1955 when the two parties were founded. The LDP won 223 of the 511 lower house seats in the 1993 general election, compared to the 275 it had won in the previous general election of 1990, while the SDPJ won 70, compared to 136 in 1990. None of the three smaller parties which had been in existence since the 1960s – the DSP, the CGP, and the Japan Communist Party (JCP) – made significant gains or suffered significant losses.[10] On the other hand, the three new parties founded by defectors from the LDP no more than fifteen months before the general election – the JNP, the JRP, and the NPH – won, respectively, 35, 55 and 13, or a total of 103 seats. Simple arithmetic thus suggests that the bulk of the LDP's and SDPJ's losses of, respectively, 52 and 66 seats went to the new parties. The same conclusion seems compelling when we look at the parties' gains and losses in terms of actual numbers of votes. The LDP won about 7.3 million fewer votes than in 1990 and the SDPJ won about 6.3 million fewer than in 1990. The two parties thus lost about 13.6 million votes between them. On the other hand, the three new parties together collected just about 13 million votes. The commonsense conclusion that the new parties took both their votes and their seats from the LDP and SDPJ is in fact corroborated by survey data as well.[11]

Why did the LDP and SDPJ lose and the three new parties win so spectacularly? The answer seems simple: nearly one-third of the voters who had voted for LDP candidates and nearly two-thirds of those who had voted for SDPJ candidates in the 1990 elections were so unhappy with each party in 1993 that they defected to the new parties. Why were they so unhappy? They were unhappy and angry about the series of political scandals that had made one newspaper headline after another over a span of several years. A deeper search for the underlying causes of the voter disaffection suggests, however, a far more complex and ambiguous psychological state in contemporary Japanese society. For example, the unhappiness and alienation of many voters was not about any specific policy issue, such as the liberalization of agricultural imports, a proposed tax increase, greater contributions to international aid, that had been debated by some candidates.[12] Nor were the disaffected voters particularly interested in a candidate's party affiliation or legislative track record. Incumbency was not as significant an asset for candidates in the 1993 election as in previous elections.[13] Widespread malaise generated by the exposure of pervasive political corruption and compounded by a prolonged recession thus appears to have led to the rejection of the political status quo in general and of both the ruling and the major opposition parties in particular.

This state of public sentiment explains, at least partly, the results of the 1995 upper house election as well: a key partner in the ruling coalition, the SDPJ, suffered another devastating defeat, while the newly formed major opposition party, the New Frontier Party (Shinshinto), made substantial gains, especially where proportional representation applied.[14] Judging by the record low voter turnout (44.5 per cent, compared with the previous low of 50.7 per cent in 1992), however, it seems sensible to regard the new party's advance as a sign of voters' rejection of the ruling coalition, rather than as a sign of their positive approval of the opposition. As Charles Maier suggests, similar trends can be seen in North America and Europe but in Japan the feeling of anticlimax following the collapse of the Soviet Union and international communism was a far less important factor than disillusion caused by domestic problems, such as the series of political scandals and the protracted recession.[15]

Incidentally, the year 1995 was memorable for the Japanese for several other events that singly and collectively undermined their self-image as a people living in a uniquely peaceful and safe society. They had long been used to, and proud of, this self-image, and willing to tolerate the bureaucratic red tape and government regulations that went with it. In early 1995, however, a disastrous earthquake hit Kobe, a major city and hub of maritime transportation in western Japan, claiming well over 5000 lives and exposing the Japanese government's inability to cope effectively with a national crisis, as well as revealing the shoddy construction of public highways and port facilities. This was followed by a lethal sarin gas attack on Tokyo's subway system and the shooting in broad daylight of the top official of the National Police Agency. Both events, which were blamed on a fanatical new religious group called Aum Shinrikyo (Supreme Truth), further shook the Japanese sense of personal security and confidence in their own society and government. So did media reports of the proliferation of guns and gang violence. These events were seen by many as symptomatic of widespread social malaise and frustration, and as evidence of the potential for even greater violence.[16] Nor did Japan appear to be an isolated case but part of an increasingly unstable and tormented world in the last decade of the twentieth century.[17]

How and why the post-1993 coalition governments took the form they did are considerably more complex and difficult questions than how and why the LDP and the SDPJ lost the 1993 general election to the new parties. For example, an *Asahi shinbun* telephone poll conducted in the wake of the election found the majority of the respondents (56 per cent) to be anticipating the formation of a coalition between the LDP and one other party or more, while only a third of the respondents (33 per cent) expected a coalition government without the LDP to be formed.[18] What followed, however, was the formation of a coalition government led by the JNP leader, Morihiro Hosokawa,which not only did not include the LDP as a coalition partner but was openly anti-LDP. Given the results of the general election reviewed above, however, this development was not particularly surprising. In fact, the news of the event was received with little surprise by the media. The nation's press reported the event under remarkably bland titles such as 'Prime Minister Hosokawa has arrived'.[19]

Proximate causes provide similarly plausible explanations for the subsequent comings and goings of the post-1993 governments. The Hosokawa government lasted for only nine months before it resigned in April 1994. The timing of Hosokawa's decision to resign and his announcement of that decision were precipitous and caught many observers by surprise, but the decision itself was perfectly understandable. He had been accused of borrowing a large sum of money (¥100 million) from a scandal-tainted parcel carrier company, Sagawa Kyubin, under suspicious circumstances, and of involvement in dubious stock transactions in his father-in-law's name.[20] His resignation thus had little to do with any policy issue. Hosokawa had claimed and won premiership ostensibly to stamp out political corruption and 'money politics', but now found himself accused of the same kind of practices. A scion of an old aristocratic family to whom politics was probably no more than an honourable service to society, if not a diversion, he called it a day when the job became much too serious, personal and unpleasant.[21]

Hosokawa was succeeded by Tsutomu Hata, the leader of the largest coalition partner, the JRP. However, on the day he was elected by the Diet, the creation of a new coalition which excluded the SDPJ was reported by the media. The SDPJ, which had not even been informed of, much less consulted about, the planned coalition, felt itself to be the victim of a plot by its conservative partners to punish it for its left-wing beliefs, and quickly defected from the existing government coalition.[22] Such a plot may have existed, but the timing of its disclosure by the media was clearly not what its members wanted. The SDPJ's defection made Hata's new cabinet a minority government at its birth, and the subsequent failure of the coalition leaders' frantic efforts to lure the party back into the government doomed it to a predictably short life.

The Hata government thus lasted for only two months and was replaced in June 1994 by the third coalition cabinet since the great electoral reversal of less than a year before. This new coalition government, led by Tomiichi Murayama, was also the oddest of the three. To many observers' consternation and disbelief, the June 1994 government brought together, under a Socialist Prime Minister, the long-time arch-enemies, the LDP and SDPJ, along with the NPH, this being a group of centrist politicians who had defected from the LDP on the eve of the 1993 general election, then joined the Hosokawa coalition, but, defected from the Hata coalition at the same time as the SDPJ. This was patently, and unabashedly, a marriage of convenience. But a marriage of convenience has its own rationale, in this case including a shared enmity towards the JRP's *de facto* leader, Ichiro Ozawa, who had masterminded the defection of forty-four LDP Diet members from the party in June 1993, paving the way for the great electoral reversal of the following month, and who was believed also to have masterminded the sometimes unintended sequence of events leading to the defection of the SDPJ in April 1994.[23] Ozawa's reformist statements earned him many admirers among both his political peers and the general public, but his Machiavellian political style brought him many enemies and critics. His alliance with CGP Secretary-General Yuichi Ichikawa was known as the Ichi-Ichi Line (from the first syllable of Ozawa's first name and the second syllable of Ichikawa's last name). The LDP–SDPJ–NPH coalition that came to power in June 1994 was an avowed anti-Ichi-Ichi Line alliance.

Another, and more important, reason for the strange union was no doubt the desire of both parties to come to power and claim, or reclaim in the case of the LDP, the obvious electoral and patronage advantages of a ruling party. The LDP in particular was faced with the threat of an unstoppable stream of defections while it remained out of power, stuck with the unenviable reputation of a thoroughly corrupt party, irresponsible beyond redemption. The SDPJ, on the other hand, was only used to opposition, and was inexperienced in and unprepared for a governing role. Sharing the power and responsibility of government with a party that had been in power for nearly forty years was obviously prudent and consequently welcome to the SDPJ leadership (interestingly, Murayama was eventually succeeded as Prime Minister at the end of 1995 by Ryutaro Hashimoto, the new leader of the LDP).

Notwithstanding the pragmatic considerations mentioned above, as well as the pervasive antipathy towards the Ichi-Ichi Line among the Liberal Democrats and the Socialists alike, the marriage of convenience had a number of vocal opponents in both parties. Within the LDP, Toshiki Kaifu and Yasuhiro Nakasone, a former LDP chairman and Prime Minister, led the opposition to what they believed was an unholy alliance, while within the SDPJ, moderate and conservative groups, including the group known as the Democrats, and the majority of party office-holders opposed the alliance in the beginning. On the other hand, the LDP's mainstream group led by party President Yohei Kono and the SDPJ's leftist groups led by Chairman Tomiichi Murayama supported the marriage of convenience.[24] Kono's ideological affinity and long-standing personal relationship with many SDPJ leaders no doubt contributed to his willingness to forge a conservative–progressive alliance. One of the most liberal and dovish LDP politicians, Kono had long known and worked with SDPJ leaders, such as the former SDPJ chairwoman and current lower house speaker, Takako Doi, who was a fellow member of a non-partisan group of dovish Diet members called the Diet Members' League for International Cooperation and Disarmament.[25]

The advocates of the LDP–SDPJ coalition eventually prevailed over their opponents and sceptics, and in a closely contested vote in the lower house to elect a new Prime Minister, Murayama, by 261 votes to 214, beat Kaifu, who had by then left the LDP in protest against the unholy alliance. Most of the opponents of the coalition within the SDPJ had changed their minds by this time and voted for Murayama as leader of the strangest and most unlikely coalition that the nation had ever seen. The party's main patron, the 8 million-member Rengo (Japanese Trade Union Confederation), was also initially opposed to the coalition, but eventually acquiesced.[26] As an SDPJ leader remarked at the time, the Murayama coalition government thus brought into being was largely a result of a pure and simple power game devoid of ideological or policy identity.[27] As such, it was, like any other marriage of convenience, an inherently unstable arrangement which faced the threat of a rupture and disintegration from the very beginning.

## LONGER-TERM CAUSES OF THE GREAT REVERSALS

The foregoing review of the 1993 lower house general election and the subsequent changes of government provides a succinct and basically accurate account of the most dramatic developments in the history of post-war Japanese politics. It is, however, a good journalistic account at best and captures only the superficial ongoing events in a limited short-term perspective. It does not take account of the longer-term patterns and trends that lay behind those events. In this sense, it is a very incomplete account that needs to be complemented, though not replaced, by one based on a longer-term perspective.

Political corruption, for example, was nothing new, having been a virtual constant in Japan since the beginning of party politics and parliamentary government there in the late nineteenth century. During the last two decades alone, proved or alleged charges of involvement in pecuniary crimes had been made against a former Prime Minister in the mid-1970s (the Lockheed scandal), against another former Prime Minister and a former Defence Agency director-general in the late 1970s (the Douglas–Grumman scandal), against a Prime Minister, a Finance Minister and a former Prime Minister in the late 1980s (the Recruit-Cosmos scandal), and against a lesser cabinet member and two other LDP Diet members in the early 1990s (the Kyowa scandal).[28] What angered the voters in 1993 was thus not just a few scandals that immediately preceded the general election but a long and widely publicized record of greed and venality left by a succession of the nation's political leaders.

Another important long-term trend that contributed to the electoral reversal of 1993 was a significant increase during the previous two decades in the volatility of voting behaviour among the Japanese electorate. This was due importantly to an increase in the number of floating voters from less than 10 per cent of the total electorate in the late 1960s to more than 30 per cent by the 1980s.[29] A year before the 1993 general election, more than a quarter of Japanese voters told *Asahi shinbun* pollsters that they did not support any particular party, while nearly 15 per cent refused to say whether they did or not (see Table 1.1). Moreover, even among those voters who continued to support and identify with a particular party, the degree of commitment weakened. As a result, about one-quarter of LDP supporters voted for candidates of other parties in 1993 and about 22 per cent of those who had voted for LDP candidates in 1990 voted for new party candidates in 1993.[30]

Some, if not all, of those who defected from the LDP in the 1993 lower house election, and in the elections of either house in the late 1980s and early 1990s, may have been motivated largely by economic dissatisfaction. This is suggested by the results of opinion polls that found that the percentage of respondents who identified themselves as members of the 'middle of the middle' group in society increased in the 1960s and the 1970s, reaching more than 90 per cent by 1973, but decreased in the 1980s and early 1990s, while those who identified themselves as members of the 'lower-middle' group increased.[31] The main marker of the widening status difference was the quantity of material or financial assets owned by members of each group.

Japanese wages steadily rose between the early post-war years and the late 1980s, but the value of real estate and stocks rose even faster. This

*Table 1.1* Findings of opinion polls conducted by *Asahi shinbun* on the two types of floating voters (percentages)

|                   | 1983 | 1986 | 1989 | 1990 | 1992 |
|-------------------|------|------|------|------|------|
| Support no party  | 17.6 | 18.1 | 24.5 | 18.7 | 26.4 |
| No answer         | 15.7 | 21.5 | 16.5 | 13.5 | 13.8 |
| Total             | 33.3 | 39.6 | 41.0 | 32.2 | 40.2 |

*Source:* Yasuharu Okino, *Gendai nihon no seiji: Seido to senkyo katei* (Tokyo: Ashi shobo, 1995), p. 154, Table 8-3; p. 232, Table 9-12.

led to widening gaps in both wealth and status between those who owned substantial material and/or financial assets and those who did not. Land and stock prices in large cities soared particularly during the late 1980s as a speculation-driven 'bubble economy' rapidly expanded, making it virtually impossible for the average worker to buy even a small piece of property in any of the nation's major cities. This bred a sense of inequity, despite a generally egalitarian pattern of income distribution that prevailed in the society.[32] The widespread dissatisfaction thus generated added significantly to the social 'impetus' behind the 'great reversals'.[33]

The SDPJ's problems with voters were neither new nor surprising. The party had been fighting, unsuccessfully, a long-term decline in its electoral strength, due mainly to a steady erosion of class consciousness and loyalty among Japanese workers. The erosion in turn resulted principally from structural changes in the Japanese economy, such as an expansion of the service sector and a corresponding increase in the number of temporary and part-time employees, an increase in the proportion of middle management personnel and a decrease in that of blue-collar workers in the manufacturing sector.[34]

The spread of what may be called a 'middling class' identity among Japanese workers during the high-growth period also contributed to the decline of unionism. In a 1992 Office of the Prime Minister survey, 90 per cent of respondents considered themselves to be members of the middling class.[35] As one Japanese sociologist argues, their identity may have been based largely on an illusion created by the steadily rising standard of living during the high-growth period.[36] It was, however, also based on a pattern of income distribution during that period which was one of the most egalitarian in the world.[37]

In any event, and as we will discuss in greater detail below, structural changes in the national economy, and the concomitant value changes, substantially attenuated ideological fervour on both sides of management–labour relations and turned most Japanese employees, and therefore most Japanese voters, into ideological middle-of-the-roaders.[38] These changes worked against both the LDP and the SDPJ, and in favour of the new parties, in the 1993 general election and probably also in the 1995 upper house election.[39] Supporters of the new parties tended to be more centrist than those of either the LDP or the SDPJ.[40]

The emergence of the middle-of-the-road Hosokawa and Hata coalition governments in the wake of the 1993 general election was thus logical and to be expected. However, the logic behind the formation of the Murayama coalition government that succeeded the short-lived Hata government in June 1994 is far more elusive and harder to explain. After all, the LDP was a party dominated by business and agricultural interests, while the SDPJ was one dominated by labour unions. We may, however, seek a deeper explanation in the sea changes that have occurred in Japanese economic and political culture since the mid-1970s or so.

The standard Japanese form of labour union, known as the company union, is inherently micro-corporatist and management–labour cooperation was an important aspect of it in the 1960s, if not earlier, in some industries, such as coal mining and steel, if not in all.[41] Corporatism at the macro-level, however, did not become an integral part of the basic outlook and strategy of the Japanese labour movement until the mid-1970s.

Faced, for the first time since the 1950s, with a realistic threat of massive lay-offs in the wake of the first oil crisis, the leadership of the Japanese labour movement was split between a radical wing, represented by the federation of public sector unions, Sohyo (General Council of Japanese Trade Unions), and a moderate wing, represented by the federation of private sector unions, Domei (Japanese Confederation of Labour). The moderates soon prevailed over the radicals and led the entire movement away from the customary confrontational posture to both management and the LDP government and towards reconciliation and compromise.[42]

After 1975, the union demands in the nationally coordinated annual wage negotiations known as the 'spring (labour) offensive' were kept at such modest levels that a former Sohyo leader declared in his book published in 1975 that the 'spring offensive' was dead.[43] In the 1975 wage negotiations, the coordinating committee of the employer organizations recommended an annual increase of 15 per cent on average, while Sohyo and Domei demanded, respectively, 30 per cent or more and 27 per cent or more. In the end, the acceptance of the employer group's increase by the federations of unions in the steel and shipbuilding industries led to acceptance of even lower rates of increase, averaging about 13 per cent, by most unions around the nation.[44] In the 1976 negotiations, the employer group's even lower offer of 13 per cent was immediately accepted not only by unions in the steel and shipbuilding industries but also by those in the electrical and automobile industries, thus rendering the negotiations, not to mention the 'offensive', no more than formalities in four of the nation's major industries.[45]

More important in the long run than the change in labour's attitude towards wage negotiations was the change in its attitude towards and role in the formulation of broad government policies. At a union leader's initiative, an existing management–labour consultative group, called Sanrokon (Tripartite Roundtable Conference on Industrial and Labour Issues), invited government representatives to participate in its sessions in early 1975; thereafter the Prime Minister, Deputy Prime Minister and EPA director-general became regular participants. By early 1976, labour leaders from Sohyo, Domei and other major labour organizations began frequently, and increasingly regularly, to submit policy recommendations to the government and consult with relevant government agencies on such issues as employment, consumer prices and social security. A new forum set up by those labour organizations later that same year, named the Labour Council for Policy Promotion, began to take up a vastly expanded range of policy issues, including pension programmes, public health, land ownership and prices, housing, resources and energy, women's status, administrative reform and industrial policy, in consultation not only with government agencies but also with all major political parties.[46]

In the late 1980s and early 1990s, labour representatives from the Labour Council for Policy Promotion and its successors, as well as Sohyo and Domei and their successor Rengo, actively participated in a number of official advisory groups. Particularly noteworthy in this regard was their involvement in the cabinet-appointed groups on political reform which had considerable impacts on the debates in the government and the media on a variety of policy issues ranging from land price inflation to local autonomy to the deregulation of the economy.[47] Participation in these advisory groups brought the labour leaders in frequent and direct contact, in collegial rather than adversarial settings, not only with government and party officials but also with leaders of the major employer organizations.[48]

Not surprisingly, employers and their organizations welcomed and reciprocated the wholesale change in union leaders' attitudes and actions. For example, labour leaders' restraint in wage negotiations in the wake of the 1973 oil crisis led many employers, especially in the steel industry, to refrain from raising the prices of their products to help combat rising inflationary pressure. More importantly, most corporations refrained from laying off their regular employees during the period of stagflation that followed the initial inflationary phase of the crisis. They resorted instead to other expedients to cut costs, such as redeploying regular employees, often to subsidiaries, laying off temporary and part-time employees, and reducing overtime and new recruitment.[49] Unions responded by refraining from strikes and industrial action. At the same time, they began to participate actively in regional and local development projects alongside employer groups throughout the nation. This, too, contributed to management–labour accommodation.[50] Both the number of union-initiated work stoppages and the amount of damage done by them declined sharply after the mid-1970s (see Table 1.2).

*Table 1.2* Union-initiated work stoppages in Japan, 1975–1990

|                  | *1975*    | *1980*    | *1985*  | *1990*  |
|------------------|-----------|-----------|---------|---------|
| Work stoppages   | 3,391     | 1,133     | 627     | 284     |
| Workers involved | 2,732,000 | 563,000   | 123,000 | 84,000  |
| Man-days lost    | 8,016,000 | 1,001,000 | 264,000 | 145,000 |

*Sources:* International Labour Office, *Year Book of Labour Statistics* (Geneva: International Labour Office, annual); Solomon B. Levine, 'Labor' in *Kodansha Encyclopedia of Japan* vol. 4 (Tokyo: Kodansha, 1983), p. 349, Table 1.

The management–labour accommodation not only reinforced the quasi-communal character of many Japanese companies but also gave rise to a neo-corporatist regime in which organized labour became an influential player.[51] By the early 1990s, the leading employer organization with special interest in management–labour relations, Nikkeiren (Japan Federation of Employer Associations), was co-sponsoring with Rengo the establishment of a joint enterprise called Working People's Rental Housing Association, a joint study of consumer price gaps between Japan and other industrial nations, and a joint proposal to the government on a ¥5 trillion tax cut. The LDP government was likewise receptive to the reformed, and de-radicalized, labour movement. The first union representative to be sent to a Japanese embassy abroad was dispatched to Bangkok as a labour attaché in 1986. In 1992, another union representative was assigned to the Japanese embassy in Washington, DC.[52]

'Corporatism without labour' may have been an appropriate label for the Japanese political economy before the 1973 oil crisis.[53] Labour was largely absent and excluded from both the formal and the informal arenas of decision making on important domestic and foreign policy issues which were dominated by the conservatives, that is the LDP, from the mid-1950s. The exclusion of labour resulted from the combination of the conservatives' refusal to let labour representatives participate in decision-making processes and labour leaders' refusal to seek participation in a period of intense East–West conflict internationally, and equally intense LDP–opposition antagonism domestically. This corporatism proved remarkably stable and, in a period when rapid economic growth was almost the sole concern of the Japanese state, was remarkably effective in helping to achieve that end. It was, in other words, a key condition of the Japanese model of a developmental state.

The neo-corporatist regime that emerged in the wake of the first oil crisis, on the other hand, was one very much 'with labour' within its fold. Not only were the conservatives now willing to accept labour representatives as legitimate participants in decision making on wide-ranging policy issues but leaders of the labour organizations were equally willing to participate in such processes. As suggested already, the sudden change of attitude on both sides was no doubt due, in large measure, to an acute sense of vulnerability and profound concern about the fragility of the trade-dependent Japanese economy, triggered by the oil crisis. It was as if the nation reverted psychologically to the early post-war years when it fought the ever present spectre of hunger and starvation, and looked to the future with dread. But the change was also due to a thaw in the Cold War, both internationally and at home, in the post-Vietnam War period. For many Japanese in key social positions, such as leaders of the major political parties, employer organizations and labour federations, the end of the Cold War thus began nearly two decades before the fall of Soviet communism. To them, the outcome of the Vietnam War signalled the end

*Table 1.3* Lower house elections

|  | 1960 | 1963 | 1967 | 1969 | 1972 | 1976 |
|---|---|---|---|---|---|---|
| LDP seats | 296 | 283 | 277 | 288 | 271 | 249 |
| Total seats | 467 | 467 | 486 | 486 | 491 | 511 |

*Source: Asahi shinbun*, various dates.

of American hegemony in the region, and the end of American hegemony foreshadowed the end of the Cold War long before the collapse of the Soviet empire.

The management–labour accommodation and the emergence of a neo-corporatist regime had inevitable and profound repercussions in Japanese party and parliamentary politics. The change here was accelerated by the steady decline of the LDP's popularity at the polls in the 1960s and the first half of the 1970s until the party lost its predominant position in the Diet (see Table 1.3). The situation of 'parity' in the parliamentary strengths of the ruling LDP and the opposition forced the government to seek compromise and accommodation with the non-communist opposition, rather than try to dictate unilateral decisions to the opposition. The LDP government made overtures to the non-communist opposition, and the opposition responded to them, mainly through informal negotiations in the House Management Committee of each chamber and in frequent meetings of the chairs of the major parties' Diet Policy Committees. Reliance on such informal behind-the-scenes channels for bargaining and deal-making gave rise to a dualistic, and duplicitous, style of parliamentary politics. For public relations purposes and media consumption, the LDP continued to maintain a tough, uncompromising posture, often railroading controversial bills through the Diet, while the opposition continued to stage vociferous protests on the Diet floor against the LDP's 'undemocratic' conduct. For purposes of real legislative business and policy making, however, the two sides struck bargains and abided by them.[54]

By the early 1980s, all opposition parties except the JCP had thus joined the neo-corporatist regime erected in the wake of the 1973 oil crisis as a consortium of the LDP, the government bureaucracy, and both big business and the main labour organizations. By then, the opposition parties, including the SDPJ (then called Japan Socialist Party, or JSP), had begun to co-sponsor candidates in local elections and it soon became common-place for the LDP to participate in such candidate-sharing arrangements. By the late 1980s the centrist DSP and CGP began to cooperate actively with the LDP in the legislative arena, as, for example, in passing a contro-versial 1988 bill to introduce a new sales tax and an even more controver-sial 1992 bill to authorize Japanese participation in United Nations-sponsored peace-keeping operations.

The centrist parties also began to explore the possibilities of 'power sharing', and the formation of a coalition government with the LDP. Serious efforts to bring about an LDP–centrist coalition government were made from time to time throughout the 1980s.[55] All such efforts failed, except for the nominal participation of a minor group of defectors from the LDP, the New Liberal Club (NLC), in the Nakasone government following the 1983 general election. The failure was due almost entirely to the LDP's still preponderant power relative to any of the centrist parties, or even all of them combined, and refusal to make any substantive concession, such as an offer of an important cabinet post, to its would-be partners. For a viable coalition government to materialize, the ruling party had to be further, and substantially, weakened through, for example, a disastrous electoral defeat or a split. Such events did not happen until the early 1990s.

An LDP–SDPJ coalition was unthinkable in the 1980s, not only because the LDP was too strong but also because the SDPJ was still 'unreformed' and remained committed, at least theoretically, to its role as a 'mass class party' with the mission to transform Japan's capitalist order by peaceful means, socialize the key industries, and introduce a planned economy.[56] The party also renounced both the Japanese Self-Defence Forces and the US–Japan Mutual Security Treaty as unconstitutional, characterized the development and use of nuclear energy for power generation as unacceptably hazardous, and viewed South Korea as both a product of and a contributing factor to the Cold War. It was not until the mid-1980s that the party redefined itself as a 'people's party', renounced its commitment to socialist revolution, and implicitly accepted the capitalist economy in its revised party manifesto.[57] Thereafter, the party temporized over its patently outdated and untenable positions on the Self-Defence Forces, the US–Japan Mutual Security Treaty, South Korea, nuclear energy and so on, but refused to renounce them officially until after the fall of the LDP government in the wake of the 1993 general election.[58]

In short, in the 1970s and 1980s, an LDP–centrist coalition failed to materialize due to the great power gap between the potential partners, while an LDP–SDPJ coalition was impractical because of both a power gap and ideological and policy incompatibilities. Meanwhile, however, cooperative, and in some cases even collusive, relationships were being forged between the LDP and the centrist parties within the Diet, among all parties, including the LDP and SDPJ but not the JCP, in local elections, and between the LDP's main patron and benefactor groups, such as the big business organizations, and the SDPJ's main labour federations. From a longer-term perspective, then, it appears to have been only a matter of time before an LDP–centrist, an SDPJ–centrist, or even an LDP–SDPJ coalition government was born. Such coalitions would become not only feasible but also necessary if the LDP lost its predominant legislative position as a result of a disastrous defeat in a Diet election or large-scale defections by its Diet members. Both happened in 1993, spawning a succession of coalition governments.

A non-LDP coalition government was increasingly acceptable, or decreasingly unacceptable, to Japan's big business in the post-oil crisis period. This was partly because the extravagance of the LDP's election campaigns had become ever more burdensome to the big businesses which paid the bulk of the party's bills. Big businessmen had therefore become vocal and influential advocates of political reform, especially a reform of the multi-seat election system, which they blamed for the rampant 'money politics'. Their unhappiness with the LDP had also to do with the party's continuing protection of agricultural and small-business interests. The policy had become a central issue in disputes with Japan's major trading partners, especially the United States, threatening to provoke US retaliation in the form of import restrictions against Japanese manufactured exports.[59] In the early 1990s, Japan's big business was thus not as loyal and reliable a supporter of the LDP as it used to be in the 1960s, although it was still firmly committed to political conservatism.

The reception the Hosokawa government met in August 1993 illustrated the readiness of the neo-corporatist state that had evolved since the mid-1970s to accept a non-LDP coalition government. The new government was warmly, if not enthusiastically, received not only by the nation's largest labour federation, Rengo, but also by all its largest employer organizations.[60] Moreover, the new government's policy agenda virtually replicated the set of policy recommendations prepared by a quintessential neo-corporatist public advisory group, the Political Reform Promotion Council, led by a prominent businessman acting as chairperson, a triumvirate comprising a labour leader, an academic and a former journalist serving as the board of directors, and staffed by dozens of other eminent businessmen, labour leaders, scholars and journalists. As we have noted, this government did not last long, nor did its immediate successor. Their very short life-span had little to do with their policy or ideological positions, however, but was almost exclusively due to the Prime Minister's personal problems and, more importantly, the dictates of inter-party power games. The LDP–SDPJ coalition government that followed was as susceptible as its predecessors to the same kind of problems and proved to be short-lived.

The post-1993 phase of Japanese politics thus appears to be one of tremendous volatility in which the parties come together and then separate in a rapid and unpredictable succession in a political environment virtually devoid of serious conflicts of opinion or even debates on policy issues. It is as if, in a vulgar version of the end of history, non-partisan national consensus had formed on all important policy issues in the post-Cold War era and politics had become a game of musical chairs revolving around the distribution and redistribution of executive and legislative offices inside government and of pork barrel outside. Reality, however, is seldom what it appears to be. What has ended is conventional partisan politics and not politics as fights over the allocation of values which now go on, and even grow more intense, across and in disregard of party lines.

## THE FUTURE OF JAPANESE POLITICS

Like the future of anything else, the future of Japanese politics, even its near future, is very difficult to predict. What appears reasonably certain and predictable at this point, however, is that the volatility both of the voting behaviour of the Japanese electorate and of the patterns of alignment and realignment among the Japanese parties will remain high. There are several broad reasons for this. One relates to the as yet unknown effects of a change, or reform as its promoters prefer to call it, in the method of electing lower house members. Japan has thus given up the nearly unique election system known as SNTV (single non-transferable vote), first introduced in the 1920s, under which several members were elected from each district by voters who cast only one non-transferable ballot. The most important features of the new method approved by the Diet in 1994 include the following: first, the total number of lower house seats is 500, or eleven fewer than under the old system; second, 300 of the 500 seats will be filled by members elected from as many newly created single-seat districts by the standard 'first-past-the-post' method; and, third, the remaining 200 seats will be filled by members elected from eleven newly created electoral regions ('blocs') by the so-called d'Hondt version of proportional representation.

The alleged purpose of the change was to purge Japanese politics in general and Diet elections in particular of the pervasive and highly corrosive influence of money which gave Japanese politics and, especially, the LDP government such a bad name. The standard argument used to justify the change ran as follows: the SNTV system forces a major party intent on winning the majority or a large plurality of seats in the house to run more than one candidate in many, if not all, districts; those candidates of the same party compete therefore for votes not on policy issues, on which there is, as a rule, broad agreement among them, but on a variety of constituency service activities, which tend to cost the candidates a great deal of money; the SNTV system thus breeds 'money politics' and political corruption.

However, whether the new formula, which mixes a single-seat plurality district system with a party-list proportional representation system, will actually bring an end to 'money politics' and restore public trust and respect for the key institutions of democratic government remains to be seen. The record of past electoral reforms in Japan shows that their outcomes have been consistently perverse; they were invariably at odds with their promoters' intent.[61] It should not be surprising, then, if the latest system based on the German model proved ineffectual in combating 'money politics' and corruption and if, as a result, voters' frustration and, therefore, volatility rose rather than fell.[62] The presence of a large number – at least one-third of the entire electorate – of floating voters is also a factor that is likely to contribute to the volatility. Another reason for predicting a high level of volatility in Japanese politics is the presence of a number of highly divisive policy issues, the appearance of national consensus on all important policy issues notwithstanding. Two such issues are particularly potent: revision of the post-war constitution and Japan's international role.

Dormant since the late 1950s, the constitutional issue has regained some saliency both among politicians and in the media. An important landmark in the current debate on the issue was the publication of a draft revised constitution by the nation's largest newspaper, *Yomiuri shinbun*, in November 1994.[63] The draft revised Article IX of the present constitution, the so-called 'peace clause', in such a way as unambiguously to permit the nation to develop and maintain armed forces for self-defence. The conservative newspaper's editors may have taken the initiative in the belief that the Japanese public was increasingly receptive to a reconsideration, and possible revision, of the constitution drafted by the Americans and imposed on a Japan under military occupation. However, they may have jumped the gun.

Public opinion on the constitutional issue remains not only sharply divided but also highly unstable. For example, a poll taken by another national daily, *Mainichi shinbun*, in April 1993 found 44 per cent of the respondents for and 25 per cent against revision, but another poll taken by the same newspaper in December 1994 found only 28 per cent for and 27 per cent against revision.[64] The number of 'don't know' answers, as high as 29 per cent and 41 per cent in the two polls respectively, suggests the great difficulty many people have in making up their minds one way or the other. Opinion among Diet members seems more convergent, but against, rather than for, revision. A June 1994 *Asahi shinbun* poll, based on direct interviews with Diet members, found 38 for and 109 against revision among LDP members, none for and 72 against among SDPJ members, and 14 for and 99 against among members of the other parties.[65] If it was put to a vote, the issue would no doubt prove to be extremely divisive and could tear up the façade of national consensus that has been carefully nurtured during the last two decades.

Japan's international role is a similarly sensitive, difficult and divisive issue among the Japanese public. For example, an overwhelming majority approves Japan's bid for a permanent seat in the United Nations Security Council, but only if Japan is not to be asked to contribute to any military action. An *Asahi shinbun* poll taken in autumn 1994 found 70 per cent for and 16 per cent against Japan's bid for a permanent Security Council seat free of military obligations, but 29 per cent for and 57 per cent against such a bid at the price of accepting military obligations.[66] Moreover, opinion on the issue is divided in at least as complex a way among Diet members, including LDP members.

A third broad factor that is likely to contribute to volatility in Japanese politics is the dramatic changes the Japanese economy is undergoing in the post-Cold War period. In the late 1980s and early 1990s, the sharp appreciation of the yen has forced Japan's leading manufacturing firms to relocate their factories abroad, and their subcontractors and parts suppliers to follow in their wake. The exodus threatens to deprive Japan of many of its 'best and brightest' firms and thus to 'hollow out' its domestic economy that was once the foundation of a model developmental state.[67] According to one survey, all Japan's major consumer electronics makers have already shifted their production of audio equipment abroad, mostly to other Asian nations. This recalls the hollowing out of manufacturing industries in the United States in the last three decades. The Japanese case, however, may be more serious. Whereas the USA has lost some of its key industries to offshore production, such as consumer electronics and machine tools, it has retained others, such as computer software and aerospace industries. In Japan's case, by contrast, virtually all its leading industries have moved out.[68] Whereas in the USA the hollowing out of some key industrial sectors has in a way helped to strengthen others, in Japan the process has been far more extensive and potentially more damaging to its long-term employment prospects and productivity gains.[69]

The arrival of migratory Japanese industries has contributed to economic development in the host nations, especially in East Asia. It has also helped to turn many industries in the region into strong competitors with Japan's own industries. The global process of rapid cross-national and cross-regional migration of capital and technology, called delocalization by some and globalization by others, is particularly visible in the region.[70] Developing countries that appeared condemned indefinitely to peripheral status and reliance on labour-intensive low-technology industries barely a decade ago, such as Malaysia, Thailand and Indonesia, now frown upon such industries and hurry to move up the rungs of the technological ladder. Meanwhile, US manufacturers are making an impressive comeback in some sectors, such as automobiles and microchips.[71] The appearance of these new competitors and reappearance of the old ones keep the diminishing number of home-based Japanese industries under growing pressure to cut production costs while innovating and improving product quality in order to stay alive.

Moreover, Japan's heavily regulated economy, especially its service sector, tends to inhibit, rather than encourage, the growth of new businesses and creation of new jobs in cutting-edge knowledge-intensive industries. The Japanese economy is thus under growing pressure for drastic deregulation for its revitalization and survival in the intensely competitive post-Cold War world markets.[72] Meanwhile, many of the traditional business practices, such as the use of cross-sectoral inter-corporate cartels, known as *keiretsu*, and exclusive manufacturer–subcontractor ties to suppress competition, are crumbling as Japanese firms move their production facilities abroad and increasingly obtain both raw materials and parts from local suppliers.[73]

These changes in the character of the Japanese economy under the relentless pressure of multinationalization and globalization undermine some of the basic conditions of the successful developmental state that Japan once was. For example, unemployment has become a real and serious threat again for the first time since the oil crisis two decades ago. Should the threat materialize, it would further destabilize the Japanese political situation, which has already lost the stability based on the LDP's one-party dominance.

There is a host of other complex and divisive domestic and foreign policy issues, including, for example, an overhaul of the entire tax system to finance the rising costs of social welfare programmes in the rapidly 'greying' society, the interminable and worsening trade disputes, especially with the United States, response to China's ongoing and North Korea's potential nuclear weapons programmes, and so on. Any of these and other policy issues could bring down future governments one after another. As we have already suggested, meaningful partisanship may no longer exist in post-1993 Japanese politics, but political conflicts not only continue but have grown increasingly undisciplined and out of control. A high level of volatility and instability thus appears to be a very likely attribute of Japanese politics in the remainder of this century and the first decade of the next.

## CONCLUSION: THE END OF THE MIRACLE

Somewhat ironically, the increasing convergence of opinion on important policy issues among the major political parties and among the major interest groups in Japan during the last two decades has been accompanied by increasing political instability. A plausible explanation for this seeming paradox might sound somewhat circular: the political instability is a result of the heightened volatility of Japanese voting decisions; the heightened volatility among voters is due, at least partly, to the increasing convergence of opinion on important policy issues among the parties, which makes politics in general and elections in particular uninteresting, even boring, for the average voter. Add to this an endless series of political scandals amidst a seemingly endless recession, and we are likely to have growing ranks of disillusioned and increasingly cynical voters. Such voters not only destabilize politics by suddenly and unpredictably switching their support from one candidate to another and from one party to another, but even endanger the election system on which the modern democratic government depends, by simply refusing to vote.

The Japanese model of a developmental state or new capitalism, then, is probably dead or dying. Japan was not a model simply because it was developmentalist or new capitalist; many other nations and, certainly, most 'developing' nations are developmentalist or new capitalist in the sense that they mix some rules of a market economy with some of a planned economy under the direction or guidance of an aggressively interventionist state. However, only a few of them have ever been cited as a model of the developmental state or of new capitalism in action, as Japan and some of its East Asian neighbours have been. This is because Japan and the few others have been, or once were, successful in achieving rapid economic development and maintaining political stability at the same time. In fact, the two achievements were causally related: political stability made rapid economic growth possible. Chalmers Johnson's Japan was not just a developmental state but a successful one, thanks to the strong and effective leadership of its highly educated and competent bureaucrats. And so was T. J. Pempel's Japan as an exemplary case of 'creative conservatism'. We have tried to show that their Japan now belongs to history.

## NOTES

* All Japanese personal names in this chapter are written with the given name first, rather than surname (family name) first which is Japanese practice.

1 See, for example, Chalmers Johnson, *MITI and the Japanese Miracle: The Growth of Industrial Policy, 1925–1975* (Stanford, Calif.: Stanford University Press, 1982); and T. J. Pempel, *Policy and Politics in Japan: Creative Conservatism* (Philadelphia, Pa.: Temple University Press, 1982).
2 Johnson, *MITI*, pp. 315–320.
3 Bruce Cumings, 'The Origins and Development of the Northeast Asian Political Economy: Industrial Sectors, Product Cycles, and Political Consequences' *International Organization* vol. 38, no. 1, 1984, pp. 1–40.
4 Frederic C. Deyo, 'Coalitions, Institutions, and Linkage Sequencing – Toward a Strategic Capacity Model of East Asian Development' in Frederic C. Deyo, ed., *The Political Economy of the New Asian Industrialism* (Ithaca, NY: Cornell University Press, 1987), p. 230.
5 Robert Wade, *Governing the Market: Economic Theory and the Role of Government in East Asian Industrialization* (Princeton, NJ: Princeton University Press, 1990), pp. 24–28.
6 Clark D. Neher, 'Asian Style Democracy' *Asian Survey* vol. 34, no. 11, 1994, pp. 949–961.
7 For a discussion of Japan as a representative strong state, see Stephen D. Krasner, 'US Commercial and Monetary Policy: Unravelling the Paradox of External Strength and Internal Weakness' in Peter J. Katzenstein, ed., *Between Power and Plenty: Foreign Economic Policies of Advanced Industrial States* (Madison: University of Wisconsin Press, 1978), pp. 60–61. For a now classic treatise on 'new capitalism', see Peter L. Berger, *The Capitalist Revolution: Fifty Propositions about Prosperity, Equality and Liberty* (New York: Basic Books, 1986). For our own general statement on specifically 'Japanese-style'

capitalism, see Haruhiro Fukui, 'The Japanese State and Economic Development: A Profile of a Nationalist-Paternalist State' in Richard Appelbaum and Jeffrey Henderson, eds, *States and Development in the Asian Pacific Rim* (Newbury Park, Calif.: Sage Publications, 1992), pp. 199–225.

8 Following the July 1993 general election, the Social Democratic Party of Japan (SDPJ), Democratic Socialist Party (DSP), Clean Government Party (CGP), Social Democratic League (SDL), Japan Renewal Party (JRP), Japan New Party (JNP), New Party Harbinger (NPH) and a minor group called Democratic Reform League formed a coalition government led by the JNP leader, Morihiro Hosokawa. Both the Hosokawa government and its immediate successor, led by the JRP leader, Tsutomu Hata, were very short-lived and, by the summer of 1994, had been succeeded by a third coalition government led by the SDPJ leader, Tomiichi Murayama.

9 The term 'great reversal' is borrowed from the title of a book by reporters of a local newspaper: Kanagawa shinbun hodobu, *Seikai daigyakuten: Tsuiso Murayama seiken tanjo made no 83-nichi kan* ('The great political reversals: a record of developments during the 83 days before the birth of the Murayama government') (Yokohama: Kanashin shuppan, 1995).

10 The DSP, CGP and JCP won, respectively, 15 (14 in 1990), 51 (45 in 1990) and 15 (16 in 1990). The SDL, which had split from the SDPJ in the late 1970s, won 4 (4 in 1990). Thirty independents (21 in 1990) also won. See *Asahi shinbun* 19 July 1993, p. 1.

11 See *Asahi shinbun* 19 July 1993, evening edition, p. 4; and Ikuo Kabashima, 'Shinto no tojo to jiminto itto-yui taisei no hokai' ('The emergence of the new parties and the collapse of the one-party rule by the LDP') *Leviathan* 15, Fall 1994, pp. 9–12.

12 Kabashima, 'Shinto no tojo to jiminto itto-yui taisei no hokai', p. 15.

13 Ichiro Miyake, 'Shinto no shutsugen to kohosha hyoka moderu' ('The emergence of the new parties and a model of candidate assessments') *Leviathan* 15, Fall 1994, pp. 39, 44, 50–51.

14 The Japanese upper house, known as the House of Councillors, has 250 seats, of which 100 are held by members elected by a party-list proportional representation (PR) method from a single nationwide district, while 150 are held by members elected by a single non-transferable vote (SNTV) method from 47 prefecture-wide districts. In each triennial election, half of the members, 125 people, are elected for a fixed six-year term, 50 by PR and 75 by SNTV.

15 Charles S. Maier, 'Democracy and Its Discontents' *Foreign Affairs* vol. 73, no. 4, 1994, p. 48.

16 See, for example, 'Wakamono ni shintou suru "shumatsu shudan": bukimi nano wa Aum dake dewa nai' ('"End of the world" groups gaining a wide following among youth: Aum is not the only scary one') *Sentaku* May 1995, pp. 122–125; Inada Nada, 'Aru seishinka no mita shinshinshukyo' ('The new new religions as seen from a psychiatrist's perspective') *Sekai* June 1995, pp. 129–134; Kiyoshi Kasai, 'Fuyuu suru mokujirokuteki ishiki' ('Roaming revelatory consciousness') *Sekai* June 1995, pp. 135–139; and Tamotsu Aoki, 'Kaihatsu to shumatsuron: posuto baruru nihon no futatsu no kyoku' ('Development and the end of the world: the two poles in post-bubble Japan') *Chuokoron* May 1995, pp. 30–35.

17 Stephen J. Del Rosso, Jr., 'The Insecure State: What Future for the State?' *Daedalus* Spring 1995, p. 175. See also Robert D. Kaplan, 'The Coming Anarchy' *The Atlantic Monthly* February 1994, pp. 44–76.

18 Yasuharu Okino, *Gendai nihon no seiji: Seido to senkyo katei* ('Politics in contemporary Japan: the system and electoral processes') (Tokyo: Ashi shobo, 1995), pp. 157–158.

19 *Asahi shinbun* 7 August 1993, p. 1.
20 See, *inter alia, Asahi shinbun* 13 March 1994, p. 2, 19 March 1994, p. 2, 31 March 1994, pp. 34–35, 1 April 1994, p. 34.
21 Hosokawa is a member of one of Japan's most illustrious aristocratic families which traces its roots to an early fourteenth-century clan of warlords which was well represented among the most powerful *daimyo* during the Tokugawa period (1600–1868), Morihiro Hosokawa served as an LDP member of the upper house from 1971 to 1983 and as governor of Kumamoto Prefecture from 1983 to 1993, when he was elected to the lower house as leader of the Japan New Party.
22 For a blow-by-blow account of this development, see Kanagawa shinbun hodobu, *Seikai daigyakuten*, pp. 96–101.
23 ibid., pp. 212–214.
24 ibid., pp. 216–217, 221–222, 230–232.
25 ibid., p. 232.
26 ibid., pp. 207–210.
27 See the comments by an SDPJ Election Committee member, Ken'ichiro Sato, cited in ibid., p. 250.
28 For a list of the major political scandals in post-war Japan, see *Joho chishiki IMIDAS 1995* ('IMIDAS: a yearbook of information and knowledge') (Tokyo: Shueisha, 1995), pp. 366–367.
29 See Michio Muramatsu, Mitsuharu Ito and Yutaka Tsujinaka, *Nihon no seiji* ('Politics in Japan') (Tokyo: Yuhikaku, 1992), p. 126, Figure 7-2; and Joji Watanuki, 'Shussei kohoto' to nihon yukensha' ('The birth cohort and the Japanese electorate') *Leviathan* 15, Fall 1994, p. 58.
30 Kabashima, 'Shinto no tojo', pp. 18-19, Figure 6.
31 Nihon hoso kyokai, ed., *A Bilingual Guide to the Japanese Economy* (Tokyo: Kodansha International, 1995), p. 232.
32 See Economic Planning Agency, *Economic White Paper 1989–90* (Tokyo: Okurasho insatsukyoku, 1990), pp. 187–208.
33 Kabashima, 'Shinto no tojo', p. 29.
34 See Muramatsu, Ito and Tsujinaka, *Nihon no seiji*, p. 129.
35 ibid., p. 130.
36 See Takatoshi Imada, *Shakai kaiso to seiji* ('Social stratification and politics'), vol. 7 (Tokyo: Tokyo daigaku shuppankai, 1989), in Takashi Inoguchi, ed., *Gendai seijigaku sosho* ('Contemporary political science textbook series').
37 Martin Bronfenbrenner and Yasukichi Yasuba, 'Economic Welfare', in Kozo Yamamura and Yasukichi Yasuba, eds, *The Political Economy of Japan. Vol. 1 Domestic Transformation* (Stanford, Calif.: Stanford University Press), 1987, p. 111.
38 The Economic Planning Agency (EPA) of the Japanese government reported in December 1994 that Japan had achieved the world's highest nominal per capita GNP in that year. According to a World Bank study published at about the same time, however, Japan's per capita GNP, measured by purchasing power parity, ranked seventh in the world. See *Nikkei Weekly* 13 February 1995, p. 2.
39 The spread of 'middle-class consciousness' may have turned voters' attention and interest away from public issues and towards matters that directly concerned their private lives. This in turn may have bred political complacency and apathy towards political parties. See Juichi Aiba, Tadashi Iyasu, and Shoji Takashima, *Nihon seiji wo yomu: sono soshiki to fudo* ('Readings on Japanese politics: the organization and clime') (Tokyo: Yuhikaku, 1987), pp. 234–238.
40 Kabashima, 'Shinto no tojo', p. 12, Figure 4.

41 Ikuo Kume, 'A Tale of Twin Industries: Labor Accommodation in the Private Sector' in Gary D. Allinson and Yasunori Sone, eds, *Political Dynamics in Contemporary Japan* (Ithaca, NY: Cornell University Press, 1993), pp. 158–180. On the susceptibility of the company union to micro-level corporatism, see Yutaka Tsujinaka, 'Rengo and Its Osmotic Networks' in Allinson and Sone, *Political Dynamics*, p. 207. See also Ronald Dore, 'Japan: A Nation Made for Corporatism?' in C. Crouch and R. Dore, eds, *Corporatism and Accountability* (Oxford: Clarendon Press, 1990), pp. 45–62.

42 See Lonny E. Carlile, 'Party Politics and the Japanese Labor Movement: Rengo's "New Political Force"' *Asian Survey* vol. 34, no. 7, 1994, pp. 610–611.

43 Kaoru Ota, *Shunto no shuen* ('The demise of the spring offensive') (Tokyo: Chuo keizaisha, 1975).

44 Nobuhiro Hiwatari, 'Explaining the Transformation of the Postwar Party System in Japan', paper presented at the 47th annual meeting of the Association for Asian Studies, Washington, DC, 6–9 April 1995, p. 3; Naoto Oumi, 'Gendai nihon no makuro koporatizumu: Chingin kettei to seisaku sanka' ('Macro-corporatism in contemporary Japan: wage determination and participation in policy making'), in Takeshi Inagami *et al.*, *Neo-koporatizumu no kokusai hikaku* ('International comparison of neo-corporatism') (Tokyo: Nihon rodo kenkyu kiko, 1992), pp. 280–281.

45 Oumi, 'Gendai nihon no makuro koporatizumu', pp. 281–282.

46 ibid., pp. 283–284, 287–289.

47 ibid., pp. 289, 294–298; Tsujinaka, 'Rengo and Its Osmotic Networks', pp. 209–210; Carlile, 'Party Politics and the Japanese Labor Movement', p. 617.

48 Carlile, 'Party Politics and the Japanese Labor Movement', p. 617; Oumi, 'Gendai nihon no makuro koporatizumu', pp. 327–329; Toru Shinoda, 'Ima mata koporatizumu no jidai nano ka: mezo koporatizumu to sono nihonteki tenkai' ('Is this another era of corporatism? Mezo-corporatism and its Japanese-style manifestation') in Inagami *et al.*, *Neo-koporatizumu no kokusai hikaku*, p. 363.

49 Hiwatari, 'Explaining the Transformation of the Postwar Party System', p. 3. See also Takaaki Ogata, 'Koyo Seisaku to Genjitsu' ('Employment policy and the reality') in Kikuo Ando *et al.*, eds, *Nihon-teki Keiei no Tenki* ('A turning point in the Japanese-style management practices') (Tokyo: Yuhikaku, 1980), pp. 227–239; and Shinoda, 'Ima mata koporatizumu no jidai nano ka', p. 361.

50 Shinoda, 'Ima mata koporatizumu no jidai nano ka', p. 367.

51 This is not to argue that labour's influence had become, or has since become, equal to that of organized business either in Japanese politics in general or in public advisory councils more specifically. See Frank Schwartz, 'Of Fairy Cloaks and Familiar Talks: The Politics of Consultation' in Allinson and Sone, *Political Dynamics in Contemporary Japan*, pp. 217–241; and various chapters of Inagami *et al.*, *Neo-koporatizumu no kokusai hikaku*, especially D. Hugh Whittaker, 'Atarashii seiji keizai moderu no tansaku: "shuren no shuen" no owari ka' ('An exploration for a new political-economic model: is the "end of convergence" over?'), pp. 484–485. See also Minoru Nakano, *Gendai nihon no seisaku katei* ('Policy process in contemporary Japan') (Tokyo: Tokyo daigaku shuppankai, 1992), pp. 5–6, 120.

52 Oumi, 'Gendai nihon no makuro koporatizumu', pp. 327, 329.

53 T. J. Pempel and Keiichi Tsunekawa, 'Corporatism without Labor? The Japanese Anomaly' in Philippe C. Schmitter and Gerhard Lehmbruch, eds, *Trends toward Corporatist Intermediation* (Beverly Hills, Calif.: Sage, 1979), pp. 231–270.

54 Nakano, *Gendai nihon no seisaku katei*, pp. 113, 115.

55 Hiwatari, 'Explaining the Transformation of the Postwar Party System', pp. 20–23.
56 Okino, *Gendai nihon no seiji*, pp. 101–102.
57 Hiwatari, 'Explaining the Transformation of the Postwar Party System', p. 10.
58 See *Asahi shinbun* 3 December 1993, p. 7, 4 September 1994, p. 1.
59 J. Mark Ramseyer and Frances McCall Rosenbluth, *Japan's Political Marketplace* (Cambridge, Mass.: Harvard University Press, 1993), pp. 194–195.
60 Tsujinaka, 'Hikaku koporatizumu no kisoteki suryo bunseki: Kankoku to amerika, nihon no hikaku rieki shudan bunseki' ('A basic quantitative analysis of comparative data on corporatism: a comparative analysis of interest groups in South Korea, the United States and Japan') in Inagami *et al.*, *Neo-koporatizumu no kokusai hikaku*, p. 426.
61 Haruhiro Fukui, 'Electoral Laws and the Japanese Party System' in Gail Lee Bernstein and Haruhiro Fukui, eds, *Japan and the World: Essays in Japanese History and Politics in Honour of Ishida Takeshi* (London: Macmillan Press, 1988), pp. 119–143.
62 For a broad and perceptive prognosis of the potential effects of the electoral reform see Raymond V. Christensen, 'Electoral Reform in Japan: How It Was Enacted and Changes It May Bring' *Asian Survey* vol. 34, no. 7, 1994, pp. 602–605.
63 See *Yomiuri shinbun* 3 November 1994, pp. 1–3.
64 *Mainichi shinbun* 29 December 1994, p. 1.
65 *Asahi shinbun* 14 June 1994, p. 1. For examples of divergent views on the constitutional and related issues among conservatives, see Kiichi Miyazawa, *Shin goken sengen* (Tokyo: Asahi shinbunsha, 1995), pp. 85–129; Ichiro Ozawa, *Nihon kaizo keikaku* (Tokyo: Kodansha, 1993), pp. 122–126.
66 *Asahi shinbun* 22 September 1994, p. 1.
67 Henny Sender, 'Nippon's Choice' *Far Eastern Economic Review* 8 June 1995, p. 38.
68 ibid.
69 Young-Kwan Yoon, 'The Political Economy of Transition: Japanese Foreign Direct Investments in the 1980s' *World Politics* vol. 43, no. 1, 1990, pp. 1–27.
70 Klaus Schwab and Clause Smadga, 'Power and Policy: The New Economic World Order' *Harvard Business Review* November–December 1994, p. 41.
71 Toru Hirose, 'Hollowing Out: Can New Growth Replace Japan's Pruned Industries?' *Nikkei Weekly* 16 January 1995, p. 1.
72 See, for example, Richard Koo, 'Closed Markets Hurting the Domestic Economy' *Nikkei Weekly* 20 February 1995, p. 7; and 'Advisory Panel to Urge Greater Deregulation' *Nikkei Weekly* 17 July 1995, p. 2.
73 Masato Ishizawa, 'Subcontractors Hurt by Imports, Shift of Production Abroad' *Nikkei Weekly* 17 July 1995, p. 3.

# 2 Global power or East Asian tinderbox? China in the post-Deng, post-Cold War era

*Martin F. Farrell*

## INTRODUCTION: CHINA IN THE POST-DENG, POST-COLD WAR ERA

Faced with the task of assessing China's likely role in the closing years of this century and on into the next millennium, one is reminded of Winston Churchill's famous reference to the Soviet Union as 'a riddle wrapped in a mystery inside an enigma'. Yet, at least in retrospect, the Stalinist system seems relatively easy to understand.[1] The Communist Party controlled virtually every aspect of society, and Stalin controlled the Party. Party domination was exercised over almost every facet of political, economic and cultural life. Ethnic minorities, while given broad *de jure* powers to run their own affairs and even secede from the Union, were in fact tightly controlled by the central Party apparatus through a combination of tactics ranging from cooptation to severe repression. Revolutionary rhetoric and some erratic decisions notwithstanding, foreign policy was generally guided by traditional notions of power politics serving the perceived national interest.

Granted that these simple descriptions gloss over important subtleties in the Soviet system, it still seems clear that the Chinese situation today is far more complex and uncertain than that of the USSR in all but its last days of existence. While the Chinese Communist Party (CCP) still enjoys a formal monopoly of power, signs of its dwindling control are everywhere. With its legitimacy seriously and perhaps irretrievably undermined by the Tiananmen Square massacre of 1989, followed by growing charges of corruption, the Party seems more and more a parasitic organism living at the expense of the rest of society; yet no alternative organization or structure seems available to replace it. Under the slogan 'Socialism with Chinese characteristics' (or now, more oxymoronically, 'Market Leninism'), non-state enterprises and market-based exchanges have been permitted to expand to the extent that they now account for over half of all economic activity and are still growing. One result has been growth rates since 1980 rivalling or exceeding those of the 'Little Dragons' of East Asia. Yet historical evidence and legitimation theory both show that rapid economic growth may bring increased social strain and political instability rather than enhanced support for the political system whose policies facilitated or at least allowed the growth. As for ethnic conflicts, China's 94 per cent Han population might at first glance seem to provide a much more stable foundation than that enjoyed by the former Soviet Union, with over 400 identifiable ethnic minorities and with the majority Russians comprising just over 50 per cent of the national population. Once again, however, the Chinese reality is considerably more complex than it appears on the surface, with some observers baldly predicting an imminent break-up of the country along ethnolinguistic, religious and/or regional lines. Given all these complexities, unique features, gigantic scale, weight of history and current 'crazy quilt' combination of institutions in China, no prudent person would attempt to make ironclad predictions about its national role and performance in even the near term. Yet its size and importance, both actual and potential, require at least a provisional assessment of the role China may play as its mantle of leadership passes to a new generation in an international arena itself just beginning to take shape in a new era.

## CHINA'S SUPERPOWER POTENTIAL

There seems little doubt that if China can maintain its unity and continue its economic growth rates of the past fifteen years, its power and influence will expand greatly, first regionally and then in the world arena, perhaps permitting it to become a global superpower as early as 2015 or 2020. Even bracketing for the moment the two huge assumptions underlying this projection, it still may seem incredible to those who know that China's per capita GNP, even after a decade and a half of impressive growth, is still listed at a mere $370 per year by the World Bank. How could a nation so apparently mired in poverty be projected to become a superpower so rapidly, no matter how large its population and territory? In fact, however, the unreliability of what have served, until very recently, as conventional economic measurements, such as GNP per capita, is becoming increasingly apparent. After all, these measures would have us believe that after achieving an annual average real growth of 7.5 per cent over fifteen years and an average 1.5 per cent annual population increase over the same period, China is worse off today than in 1976. The reason for this absurd conclusion is, of course, that these measures have been based on *international* rather than *local* purchasing power. This means that the decline in the official value of the yuan from 1.7 per US dollar in 1978 to 5.5 today would, by these conventional measures, have wiped out all the real economic growth of this period and more.[2]

It is for this reason that the World Bank and independent economists have recently sought more realistic ways of measuring incomes and living standards. In particular, the Purchasing Power of Currencies (PPC) has been advanced as a superior measure. It is defined as 'the number of units of a country's currency required to buy the same amounts of goods and services in the domestic market as one dollar would buy in the United States'.[3] By this measure, China's 1991 GDP per capita has been estimated at somewhere between $1000 and $2040, a range which seems to correspond more accurately to first-hand observations on the ground in China.[4] Adopting the upper estimate yields a total GDP for China today of over $2 trillion, or about 36 per cent of that of the US. Moreover, if both countries' recent growth rates remain roughly the same, China's GDP would exceed that of the US by 2010 and would be 80 per cent of that of all the Organization of Economic Cooperation and Development (OECD) countries *combined* by 2020.[5] If these measures are indeed more realistic, and if China can sustain its recent economic growth rates while keeping its population growth reasonably in check, the prediction of its emergence as a superpower in the relatively near future seems not so far-fetched. Even if one assumes, quite reasonably, some slowing in China's recent rates of economic growth, this only delays by a decade or two China's assumption of true superpower status in the world arena.

## THREATS TO CHINA'S UNITY

Obviously, however, this assessment rests on several critical assumptions, both technical and substantive. By far the most important of these, and therefore the one which will be the primary focus of this chapter, is simply whether the entity China will even *exist* as a unified nation by the year 2010 or 2020. The notion that China's continued existence cannot simply be taken for granted is supported by a number of considerations. First, the dissolution of central authority and the division of China into a number of smaller, often feuding, entities has been a recurring feature of Chinese history. By one count, China has been so divided for a total of about 452 years since it was first unified by the Qin emperor in 221 BC, or for 20 per cent of its history since then. Moreover, even putative central control of such outlying areas as Tibet, Xinjiang, Mongolia and Manchuria was achieved only relatively recently, in the Qing dynasty, about 200 years ago. At that, major portions of these areas were not brought under *de facto* modern control until 1949 or even later.

In addition to these historical considerations, some specialists have recently cast doubt on the depth and breadth of nationalist sentiment in today's China. This line of thought is based on a serious revision of earlier analyses which made Chinese nationalism the keystone of Maoist ideology and the linchpin of the communist regime's legitimacy.[6] To be sure, the claim that its identification with and ability to tap into the deep wellspring of Chinese nationalism was the *primary* reason for the success of the CCP has always been controversial and has stimulated one of the biggest debates among Sinologists over the past thirty years.[7] Reasonable people can, and certainly have, differed over the relative weight assigned to nationalism, the communists' social and economic programmes, the incompetence of the Guomindang, international assistance and other factors associated with the communist victory. To this author, it seems futile to attempt to assign absolutely precise weights to the various aspects of this undeniably complex phenomenon. That nationalism was a *major*, if not necessarily *primary*, factor in the success of the CCP has been accepted by virtually every serious student of recent Chinese history and politics.

Now, however, revisionist historians are beginning to contend that the rise of Chinese nationalism around the May Fourth Movement and the success of the CCP in eventually capturing its mantle in the struggle against Japanese imperialism and the Guomindang is simply a myth created almost out of whole cloth by Mao, an ambitious and resourceful 'totalizing cosmocrat'.[8] In the words of Edward Friedman, 'What appeared as permanent national truth was merely passing national mythos. . . . The anti-imperialist nationalism embodied in Maoism that once won Chinese hearts has been discarded.'[9]

On this view, the Marxist–Leninist–Maoist project of constructing an anti-bourgeois, anti-imperialist identity is so fatally flawed at its core that any nation which has relied upon it for any length of time is bound to fly apart once its 'cover' is blown. Hence, China is likely to follow the path of the former Soviet Union, Czechoslovakia or even Yugoslavia. In response to the argument that China is different from these cases because it is much more ethnically homogeneous, with 94 per cent of the population classified as Han Chinese, revisionists identify a host of resurgent primary identifications that are not simply 'ethnic' but cultural, regional, linguistic and/or religious in nature. Friedman cites examples of such identities, including

> the Muslim, Buddhist, Maoist, Christian or non-Confucian; the Cantonese, Fukienese or Wu speaking; the Yueh, Chu or Ba ancestry in Jiangsu, Hunan, and Sichuan; the Manchu, Mongol, Turkic, Tibetans and Hakka. The prior national chauvinism that celebrated the Han people is reexperienced as a fraud. No Chinese asserts intrinsically 'I am a Han.' None![10]

While this last observation will strike many observers as extreme or simply wrong, the historical record shows, as noted above, that the possible break-up of China must be taken seriously.[11] For one thing, it is becoming increasingly clear that all the variants of modern nationalism must be understood in terms of what, or who, they were *against* as much as what they were *for*. So, for example, modern British nationalism, which encompassed the Scots and Welsh as well as the English, coalesced in the face of the perceived threat mounted by the French in the seventeenth and eighteenth centuries. Similarly, Yugoslav nationalism can be understood as developing in opposition to the Nazi occupiers and being maintained out of a fear of the Soviet Union. Once that threat was removed, and in the absence of any other credible threat to replace it, Yugoslav nationalism quickly disintegrated, with disastrous results. In the case of China, nationalism originally focused on opposition to the Western imperialist powers, followed by Japan, the United States and the Soviet Union. Following the normalization of relations with the United States, the end of the Cold War, the dismemberment of the Soviet Union, and with no other major threat to China currently on the horizon, this line of thinking suggests that Chinese nationalism may be growing thinner every day.

It is, of course, exceedingly difficult, if not impossible, to gauge precisely how much of this thinning has actually occurred. However, virtually all observers agree that a breakdown in central authority or the emergence of any sort of power vacuum at the centre could precipitate such fragmentation. Indeed, in the view of many, it was just such a paralysis of the centre which allowed events in early 1989 to 'get out of hand' with such disastrous effects. Here we must also consider the role of a strong, charismatic leader in the Chinese past and present. In traditional China, as Pingti Ho has pointed out, elaborate steps were taken to strengthen the prestige and charisma of the emperors, even to the point of near or actual deification.[12] The extreme fragmentation and mass chaos experienced in the early Republican period, similar to what some argue may soon happen again, may be seen as stemming, at least in part, from the overthrow of this emperor cult and the absence of a readily available modern equivalent. The later glorification of Chiang Kaishek, the near deification of Mao and the continued reliance upon and recently intensified glorification of Deng Xiaoping, even well into the tenth decade of his life and long after he has relinquished all official posts, can all be read as continuations of this historical/cultural imperative. In Ho's arresting words, it is a 'stark historical fact that for more than two thousand years the Chinese nation has never experienced any system of state and government which is not easily identifiable by a single charismatic leader, whether the emperor or his modern counterpart'.[13]

Of course, it is possible that Deng could live to be over 100 or, like Moses, even 120. He can continue to serve as the symbolic leader the Chinese seem to need probably as long as he lives since much, if not most, of the prestige he lost due to his initial indecisiveness and subsequent endorsement of brutal repression in 1989 has been restored through the success of the economic reform process he has continued to champion. But the probabilities are great that he will die soon. Granted that the Chinese, both historically and in the current regime, have been masters at creating 'charisma' out of even relatively unpromising material, it is extremely difficult to conceive of a Li Peng, Zhu Rongji or Jiang Zemin (Deng's designated successor) assuming such a role. Zhao Ziyang might have sufficient residual popularity and prestige to assume this role and, while his current status remains ambiguous, it is not inconceivable that a

Party desperate to survive might return him to power if he is the only one deemed capable of playing this essential leadership role. After all, the rehabilitation of a formerly disgraced leader would scarcely be a novel event in the history of Chinese communism. By early 1995, the regime's leaders were attempting to assert that the succession question was a non-issue: Jiang Zemin had been installed as both President and Party Chair, governing in tandem with a collective leadership team. However, by mid-1996 observers had detected one leadership stumble and hesitation after another in matters both foreign and domestic over the previous eighteen months.[14] All things considered, it seems that a major power struggle still looms on China's horizon. Hence, a crucial test of the regime's ability to survive and, with it, of the unity of the nation, will come no later than the occasion of Deng's death.

At this point, we must consider a second historical continuity discussed by Ho in his seminal 1968 article, namely, the 'persistent historical fact . . . that the Chinese state has always derived its ultimate power from the army, and this has largely predetermined its authoritarian character'.[15] Especially considering the crucial role of military force in bringing the Communist Party to power in 1949 and in re-establishing central control in 1968–1969 and again in 1989, it is clear that whether or not it has an heir-apparent ready at the time of Deng's death, the Party will rely pre-eminently on the People's Liberation Army (PLA) both to preserve its monopoly position of power and to prevent breakaways by ethnic minorities or regions. But here, too, crucial questions arise which are extremely difficult to answer in advance. Will the Party still be able, in such a crisis, to continue to 'command the gun'? Equally important, will the Chinese military, whether loyal to the Party and its new leadership or acting on its own behalf, even be capable of containing the centrifugal forces which will be unleashed?

Neither the experience of 1989, nor developments within the PLA since then, nor the current state of PLA–Party relations support definite affirmative answers to these key questions. The divisions in the Party in the face of the Tiananmen demonstrations were mirrored in the military, which showed a great deal of hesitancy, confusion and internal conflict before overwhelming force could finally be brought to bear. In the initial aftermath of Tiananmen, several steps were taken to strengthen the PLA's loyalty to the Party and its role in preserving the unity of the country, but with far from certain results. It is difficult to credit as even marginally effective the granting of medals to selected soldiers, the revival of the preposterous campaign to 'Learn from Lei Feng', temporarily intensified Marxism study sessions, or expanded research and publication on the PLA's glorious past, especially when army action had produced ambiguous if not counterproductive results.[16] Potentially more significant was the waxing power of the 'Yang Family Village', i.e. Yang Shangkun, Yang Baibing and assorted relatives and supporters. However, by the end of the Fourteenth Party Congress in October 1992, Yang Shangkun had been retired from all his positions, including that of Vice-Chair of the powerful Central Military Commission (CMC), and Yang Baibing had been removed from both the CMC and the Party Secretariat, although he was placed, in a face-saving move, on the Politburo.[17] Since then Yang Baibing has also relinquished his military posts, and with the retirement of Defence Minister General Qin Jiwei, there is now only one serving military officer, General Liu Huaqing, a close colleague of Deng, on the Politburo and its Standing Committee, the PLA's smallest representation ever and especially noteworthy since only a few years ago half or more of these elite posts were held by men in uniform.[18] The 'second foot' in this process fell in January 1993, with the complete reshuffling of the entire chain of command, including the dismissal of at least 300 of the nation's estimated 500 to 600 generals, a shake-up unprecedented in PRC history.[19] One telling move was the transfer of Zhang Gong, the spokesman for martial law forces in 1989 who became the Political Commissar of Beijing, to the more peripheral Chengdu military region. In all, these moves would seem to have radically reduced the likelihood of an attempted military takeover or, less dramatically, of the replacement of Deng's chosen successor, Jiang Zemin, by the Yang Family following Deng's death. With Jiang retaining his position as Chair of the CMC (while simultaneously serving as CCP Chair and President of the People's Republic, giving him the greatest concentration of authority in one man's hands in the history of the People's Republic of China), and with such strong Deng supporters as Liu at the top of the military command, it is obviously Deng's hope that both the unity and the loyalty of the PLA to the Party will be solidified.

A number of recent analyses of the Chinese military and the attitudes of its current leaders indicate that this hope may not be in vain. For example, Ellis Joffe argues that nationalism remains, and has indeed recently been strengthened, as the paramount value of China's military leaders.[20] The demise of Mao Zedong's and Lin Biao's messianic revolutionism and the obsolescence of the paradigm centred on a global struggle to the death between capitalism and socialism, both serve to strengthen nationalism and China's drive to superpower status as core values. The commitment to defend China's territorial integrity and to project its power, at first regionally and then, perhaps, globally, is fully congruent with the major efforts under way since 1989 to professionalize and modernize China's forces. Joffe argues that:

> Although the Soviet threat has disappeared and the United States is reducing its forces, China will probably try to step up this pace for several reasons: its nationalistic foreign policy aims; the rise of the United States to the position of sole superpower; the urgency created by the need to fill a power void in the Pacific; the availability of more funds and advanced arms; and the desire of the new leadership to gain the full support of the military. As modernization progresses, military

professionalism will be even more firmly in command. And the stronger it becomes, the less likelihood there will be of the military supporting or initiating moves towards regionalism.[21]

Hence, the CCP leadership has apparently calculated that professionalization will enhance rather than weaken trends supporting central control within the military and that, in any case, if breakaway movements need to be contained, a slimmed down, depoliticized and professionalized force will be able to do the job as well or better than one subjected to large volumes of political indoctrination, the policy instituted immediately following the 1989 crackdown. It is also known that in May 1992 new directives regarding protest and crowd control were circulated internally in the PLA, calling for the application of force in carefully controlled stages from warnings to tear gas, with actual use of lethal ammunition as the final stage.[22] Had such a plan been in place in 1989, along with the requisite training and equipment, it is entirely possible that the worst aspects of the Tiananmen disaster could have been averted.

## CENTRIPETAL FORCES IN CHINA

In addition to the forces supporting nationalism and centralized authority within the Chinese military, there are other features of the current landscape indicating that China's unity may not be as precarious as the revisionist scholars have alleged. First of all, the fate of the former Leninist states following the 'revolutions' of 1989 and the dissolution of the Soviet Union in 1991 has not been comforting for those favouring either the break-up or the rapid democratization of China. East and Central European hopes for a smooth transition to pluralist-democratic politics and thriving market economies have been dashed by the realities of economic collapse, resurgent tribalism and tenacious authoritarianism. Given this recent experience, Richard Baum has cautioned, 'Increasingly, the only viable alternative to the scylla of communism and the charybdis of chaos appears to be not pluralist democracy, but some form of post-Leninist neo-authoritarianism.'[23] This last, of course, resembles closely the 'New Authoritarianism' advocated by Zhao Ziyang and his supporters since the mid-1980s as well as the actual situation in virtually every other East Asian state, including the 'Little Dragons' of South Korea, Taiwan, Singapore and Hong Kong and others such as Indonesia, Malaysia and Thailand. Advocates of this position argue that concepts such as individual rights, civil liberties, freedom of the press, human rights and the like are Western in their origins and can be applied in the Asian context gradually, selectively and only in the wake of significant economic progress. It is not only Deng and his Leninist cohorts who fear the effects of 'bourgeois liberalization' and 'spiritual pollution'. As a Singaporean official, Kishore

Mahbubani, has recently argued, 'In the face of growing evidence of social, economic and occasionally moral deterioration of the fabric of many Western societies, it would be increasingly difficult for a Westerner to convince Asians that the West has found universally valid prescriptions for social order and justice.' The recent experience of the former Leninist states in Europe would seem to reinforce these doubts. Mahbubani goes on to argue that 'Economic development is the only force that can liberate the Third World. . . . If the West wants to bury forever Mao's totalitarian arrangements, it should support Deng's reforms to the hilt, even if he occasionally has to act firmly to retain political control.'[24]

Of course, such arguments can be dismissed as the self-serving rationalizations of elites out to protect their power and privileges at all costs. But the fact remains that all the developing nations of East Asia, without exception, have seen their days of repression and even massacres as bad or worse than Tiananmen. But it is equally true that several of these nations by now have also witnessed economic growth which has spread economic resources more widely in society, leading, in turn, in at least some cases such as South Korea and Taiwan, to modest but discernible steps towards lessened repression and greater democracy.

There is also strong evidence that such a vision is shared by the overwhelming majority of Chinese. Horrifying as the repression of 1989 and its follow-up undoubtedly were, by now, on the account of numerous observers, most Chinese are 'really uninterested in what has happened to the Tiananmen dissidents – or in any other dissidents – who were jailed. . . . [M]ost Chinese seem too busy pursuing new ideas, promotions, second jobs and economic ventures to bother worrying about human rights issues'.[25] Given these Asian traditions and current Chinese attitudes, Deng's strategy of avoiding explicit political reform while continuing to push economic reform and rapid growth may well present a successful formula for stability and gradual democratization in China. Moreover, there is abundant evidence that at least some aspects of the political liberalization and democratization which are anticipated in the wake of economic growth are beginning to occur in China, as they already have in some other nations of East Asia. For example, in the areas of cultural and personal, as distinct from political, freedoms, Suzanne Ogden reports that 'the level of tolerance, openness, experimentation, and freedom is high. . . . [M]any Chinese say that since the inception of communist rule in 1949 they have never "felt" as free as they do now – even compared to the heady period directly preceding the Tiananmen crackdown in 1989.' She continues:

> The CCP is now willing to tolerate a vibrant street scene – one where the formerly standard blue Mao jacket, white shirt and baggy trousers have given way to spandex and body-hugging dresses, high heels, and makeup; permed hair, leather jackets and boots, blue jeans and designer

labels. Almost anything goes: from sidewalk noodle shops to snake oil salesmen, from stereos blasting Western rock music with strobe lights to nostalgic paeans to Mao Zedong in songs written in the Cultural Revolution, sidewalk bands, shaves and acupuncturists.[26]

Similarly, Elizabeth Perry points to the 'proliferation of pricey restaurants, coffee shops and *karaoke* bars'. While all of this may be dismissed by some as simply the regime's attempt to coopt political dissent through rampant materialism, she adds that 'such places of entertainment also provide an arena for the once tightly controlled citizenry to complain about the state's abdication of responsibilities, to forge a "civil society" as it were'.[27]

Moreover, the growth in personal incomes which has accompanied the dramatic reduction of the state-run portion of the economy puts rapidly increasing resources in the hands of individuals and local governments which can be used to make demands on the state in a variety of ways and at a variety of levels. This process is already under way in China and is most evident in those areas which have experienced the greatest economic growth. Local elections and other pseudo-democratic mechanisms of party control are subtly but perceptibly being transformed into more genuine instruments of popular control and government accountability. As Ogden has observed,

> The sense of empowerment at the local level, even if rooted in economic and not (originally) political power, is not only creating substantial numbers of people who will insist that a government be accountable to them, it is also training people in leadership skills, in conflict resolution and in the give and take of compromise. In short, local leaders who will make their own decisions, take responsibility for them and learn about governing, rather than merely implementing changes dictated at the center, are bound to emerge from this process. They will provide a critical element for democratization in China.[28]

## NEW FAULT LINES IN THE PEOPLE'S REPUBLIC

Now, this scenario of a formerly totalitarian society in which the engine of rapid economic growth gradually creates the basis for a democratic civil society and a liberal political culture may be entirely too rosy. While there are many arguments which stress that China's success in economic reform to date augurs well for its avoidance of an East European or Soviet-style break-up,[29] it is well known that rapid economic growth can have destabilizing effects, as well. One classic formulation of this idea is traced to Tocqueville's analysis of the French Revolution of 1789 as stemming not from immiseration but from a relative improvement in living standards which was suddenly threatened by a 'feudal reaction' as the nobles sought to recapture lost privileges. More recently, James Davies has argued that

[t]he background for political instability is economic and social progress. A populace in a static socio-economic condition [as in Maoist China] is very unlikely to listen to the trumpet or siren call to rebellion. . . . Progress in other words is most of the time a necessary but insufficient cause for violent political change.[30]

In the case of contemporary China, scholars such as Friedman and Helen F. Siu believe that it is the southern coast of China, centred on the metropolis of Guangzhou (Canton), which is the most likely to break away, in part precisely because it has led the way to China's growing prosperity. On this analysis, the southerners, not really Han,[31] totally reject the Maoist myth of the 'liberation' and see themselves as having been conquered by northern guerrillas who 'had been ruling the South in state-imposed collectives of virtual serf (or slave) labour since 1949'.[32] On this view, the south's true liberation came when the xenophobic, isolationist know-nothings returned to the north and local people resumed control (around 1980) to reopen China to the outside world and to a new activist dynamic of trade, commerce and enterprise. The reform policies of Deng emanating from Beijing are given no credit in this economic success story; it was all done by skirting the obstacles posed by the parasitic bureaucrats of the north. Nor has economic success brought contentment. Those who have enjoyed the fruits of this success, including successful entrepreneurs and Party cadres, show blatant disrespect for national aspirations; those who have not obtained a share of the new resources have become cynical and have fallen adrift in a sea of gambling, drug addiction and violent crime.[33]

Is south China today a tinderbox, awaiting only a spark or the first sign of irresolution from the centre to jettison all attachments to the ersatz 'nation' of China and join a new orbit with Hong Kong and, perhaps, Taiwan? Theory as well as empirical evidence indicates that while this scenario is not entirely implausible, some key elements are not yet in place. It is true that recent work in the area of nationality formation acknowledges that it need not be based on any sort of primordial ethno-linguistic or ethno-religious identity.[34] Rather, it is a socially and, above all, politically constructed phenomenon which can be made, if not out of whole cloth, from what may initially appear to be rather skimpy material and which can be brought together with astonishing rapidity. In the case of south China, however, the crucial *political* elements are still missing. For example, Paul Brass has argued that one necessary ingredient in creating such a movement is the emergence of a counter-elite which explicitly challenges the established national elite as part of a conscious effort to create an alternative political consciousness and national identity.[35] All kinds of 'objective' conditions apparently conducive to revolt or secession may be present, but unless they are capitalized upon by an emerging counter-elite, they can go virtually unnoticed, or at least unacted upon, indefinitely. By the same token, even slight differences in condition can be seized upon by enterprising elites as the material to construct a nationalist or secessionist movement. Interestingly, these need not involve the absolute or even relative deprivation of the target group; their greater prosperity can actually become the *casus separationis*, as, for example, among the Sikhs of the Punjab or the partisans of the Lombardy League in Italy. But what is missing in the case of south China, at least to date, is a new myth or narrative to substitute for the discredited Maoist one and the counter-elites who must create and disseminate it. Of course, one thing the current regime can be counted upon to do is to come down hard on anyone who steps forward to play just such a role. But suppression can actually serve to create the leadership and self-consciousness which such a movement needs, as in the cases of Nelson Mandela in South Africa and Lech Walesa in Poland. These are the main considerations, then, which have led many Sinologists to conclude that conditions are ripe for the breakaway of south China.

In this regard, two specific events can be visualized which could, given the needed enterprising leadership, serve as triggering mechanisms for such a movement. One would be a reversal or even significant retrenchment in the economic reform programme, especially as it has been pursued since 1989. Here the analysis of Tocqueville presented above would appear to be pertinent, despite the obvious differences between France in 1789 and south China today. Such a reversal can, of course, never be ruled out, especially given the need periodically to slow the engine of growth to prevent overheating, the emergence of bottlenecks, inflation, speculative pressures and the like. However, Deng's much-heralded trip to Guangdong in January 1992, in which he held up the region as a model for the rest of the country, shows that Beijing understands the need not only to avoid any hint of such a reversal but also to reinforce the initiatives of the past fifteen years and, especially, to renew the reform impulse following the brief retrenchment after 4 June 1989.

The second shock capable of igniting an effective separatist movement in south China could arise from difficulties in the process of transferring the sovereignty of Hong Kong from Britain to China in 1997. This process is sufficiently sensitive and complex to require detailed study in its own right. For now it will have to suffice to point out that Beijing has a tremendous economic and national stake in preventing just such a shock. The use of force alone in an attempt to hold Hong Kong and a south China which wanted to join it in separating from China would have devastating economic, political and diplomatic repercussions. This is not to say that blunders cannot or will not be made or that uncontrollable forces cannot arise from unanticipated sources. As in all these considerations, one factor can affect the others in ways that intensify the effects. So, for example, a Beijing regime left without a strong leader and wracked by internal divisions might be more likely to make missteps in this hypersensitive area, just as it would lack the will or resolve to act decisively and effectively in a crisis. All one can do at this point is reiterate the statement above, namely that any sensible national leadership must understand the importance of handling the transition process in a way which avoids sparking separatist sentiments in this increasingly volatile area.

Nor is south China the only area which could pose a threat to the continued unity of the Chinese nation. Another obvious possibility involves the minority areas on China's periphery, which will be discussed on pp. 74–77. Yet another threat to China's unity which has been brought to the fore recently is that of peasant revolt. Once again, such an event is scarcely unheard of in China's history, but its recurrence now would represent a crowning irony since the communist regime came to power in 1949 on the crest of what has been touted as the greatest peasant rebellion in world history. This irony would be deepened by the fact that the rural areas in general were the first to benefit from Deng's reform policies in the post-1978 period. The *de facto* privatization of land, vast expansion of free markets, establishment of 'specialized households' and cooperative village and township enterprises along with greater peasant mobility led to rapid increases in prosperity and living standards for most, though not all, living in the countryside. However, this growing rural prosperity sparked-resentment and protests in China's cities. By 1986, recognizing the imminent dangers of urban unrest, the regime shifted attention and resources increasingly to the coastal areas and urban centres. Soon rural living standards began to slip further behind those areas newly favoured with economic incentives and privileges. The result is a classic case of the 'revolution of rising expectations'. Having tasted the possibilities of a better life but now able, through the more extensive and freer channels of communication and transportation, to watch at least their relative standing slip behind that of the urbanites, the peasants are growing increasingly restive. Specific grievances include a contraction of land available for cultivation due to local development projects (including some illegally initiated by local officials for their own benefit), erosion, contamination and salinization; rapacious officials who attempt to extort 'taxes' on everything from old radios to bicycles and then imprison those who are unwilling or unable to pay; the issuance of IOUs instead of cash for state-required staple crops, money orders and the like; rapidly rising prices for agricultural inputs and daily necessities; and the rampant corruption of Party cadres who demand payment for dozens of services which are supposed to be provided free. Internal government documents reported in Hong Kong refer to over 200 rural protests in the year following July 1992, the bulk occurring in interior provinces.[36]

Yet here, too, the trend is not clearly in the direction of revolution, separation or even decentralization. Nicholas D. Kristof, who recently concluded five years of reporting from China, concurs that the peasants have plenty to be furious about. Yet he quotes one villager as follows on the mood of his compatriots: 'Overall life has gotten much better. My family eats meat maybe four or five times a week now. Ten years ago, we never had meat. Now the peasants can go into the cities and earn 18 yuan (about $3.15) a day doing odd jobs. Of course the peasants are content.'[37] Of course, it is difficult to know how much analytical weight can be made to hang on such statements. One way of attempting to gauge these sentiments, public opinion surveys, are only in their infancy in China and to date none has dealt directly with such sensitive issues.[38] What can be said with certainty, however, is that with three-quarters of China's 1.2 billion people still living in the countryside, it is crucial for the regime to avoid allowing these areas to fall any further behind south China and the eastern coastal areas. But as with so many other matters discussed here, this advice is much easier to give than to follow. Here too is a massive challenge, to the current regime or to any successor regime attempting to maintain a unified country.

Nor are China's cities immune from disorders resulting from dynamic economic change. Despite the explosive growth of private, cooperative, township and foreign enterprises, China's state-owned factories still employ, at least nominally, around 150 million industrial workers. Most of these state-owned enterprises are ripe for drastic downsizing or elimination, but given the recent creation of what has been termed 'a reserve army of migrant rural workers', there are insufficient employment opportunities in the private sector to absorb those who would lose their 'iron rice bowl' positions in the state-run enterprises.[39] The result has been a dramatic upsurge in labour disputes, as state-sector workers and managers fight to maintain their positions even as inflation regularly outstrips their meagre salary gains. While to date the authorities have been able to contain these disputes, any one of a number of possible adverse turns in China's economic situation could result in labour protests and strikes on a massive scale. Although urban disorders might seem to be more easily contained or repressed than those occurring in the far-flung hinterlands, they too could easily spread, especially in a context of leadership uncertainty and hesitation such as that displayed in early 1989.

The final challenge to China's unity to be discussed here is perhaps the most obvious, yet is no less serious for its evident nature, namely that of unrest among those of China's ethnic minorities which are concentrated in the western, northwestern and northern peripheries of the Chinese empire. This question has commanded rapidly growing attention in the aftermath of the break-up of the Soviet Union and the tragic turn of events in the former Yugoslavia. The provinces of Tibet, Xinjiang and Inner Mongolia are remote, sparsely populated and peripheral to the historical development of China. However, they will play a crucial part in determining China's role and the extent of its influence in the coming decades. Together they comprise over 40 per cent of China's total land mass, and while much of their area may be vacant or nearly so, their location is critical. Indeed, retention of all its 'peripheral' areas is geopolitically essential to China's expanding influence, first as a regional power and eventually as a global power or superpower, quite apart from their significance economically or with regard to their resources. For example, south China is crucial as a link to both the maritime and continental facets of Southeast Asia. Similarly, Tibet gives China a presence on the South Asian land mass and encompasses the two major border conflicts China has with its main rival in this area, India. Xinjiang, with its borders on Afghanistan, Tajikistan, Kyrgyzstan and Kazakhstan, links China to the strategically vital Middle East. Inner Mongolia connects China to the steppes of Central Asia, Outer Mongolia (still claimed by China) and its giant neighbour to the north, the Russian Republic. Manchuria, in turn, provides the bridge to China's status as a player in Northeast Asia *vis-à-vis* Russia, Japan and the Korean peninsula. Moreover, these areas simultaneously serve, as they have historically, as security shields or buffers for China proper, or 'Inner' China, against hostile neighbours. Lillian Craig Harris's statement that '[n]o Chinese leadership could voluntarily relinquish China's sovereignty over Xinjiang and expect to remain in power'[40] can probably be generalized to all these border regions. Among them, Manchuria will probably be the easiest to retain, for historical and demographic reasons, and Tibet the most difficult, with the others arrayed somewhere in between. Tibet's quest for autonomy or independence is by far the most advanced among these regions, especially with respect to leadership, with the Dalai Lama almost universally recognized among Tibetans and, as a Nobel Peace laureate, greatly respected internationally as well. Although Tibet, unlike other border regions, is not known to harbour significant oil, coal or other strategic resources, its important geo-strategic location, the fate of the 6 million Han who have moved to Tibet in recent decades and the need to 'set an example' for other minority areas all mean that the current Chinese leadership, and probably any likely future Chinese leadership, will use all the means at their command to keep effective control over Tibet. At the same time, Chinese interests in Tibet need not be interpreted in a way which would rule out all hope of compromise. The Dalai Lama's avowed pacifism has not prevented the occurrence of violent clashes, but it may actually make continued Chinese control somewhat easier. When asked how the Dalai Lama believed Tibet can win its freedom without resort to violence, one of his supporters is reported to have replied, 'He believes it's not possible. Only if China falls apart again, as it did when the Manchus were overthrown in 1911.'[41] Once again, the crucial role of unity and the maintenance of central control to China's future is displayed.

The situation in Xinjiang is somewhat different. With its direct ties to the Muslim world and the Middle East, its geo-strategic significance is greater than Tibet's. With respect to resources, too, Xinjiang is much more significant, having already been tapped as China's next major source of oil, vitally needed to replace the rapidly shrinking reserves of the eastern provinces, and also thought to possess significant stores of natural gas, iron ore and arable land. Major clashes between Muslim separatists and the Chinese People's Armed Police had begun even before the ill-fated Soviet coup attempt of 1991 led to the independence of the neighbouring Muslim-dominated states. Since then, the emergence of these independent states has further heightened tensions, leading Chinese officials to speak of the need to 'form a steel wall to safeguard socialism and the unification of the motherland' and to back these words up with increased troop movements, stiffer prison sentences for 'troublemakers' of any kind and a purge of religious leaders on the government payroll.[42] Favourable factors from the Chinese viewpoint include the lack of recognized leaders anywhere approaching the status of the Dalai Lama in Tibet, the absence of a single dominant nationality in the region (Xinjiang's Muslims are divided into no fewer than ten ethnically, historically and linguistically distinct groups) and the help of other governments who also have much to fear from either pan-Turkic or pan-Islamic movements. As in Tibet, but with more success, the Chinese are attempting to use economic development as a means of defusing separatist sentiment. Measures have included the signing of economic cooperation pacts with the new Central Asian states, upgraded transportation links with these states and with eastern China, tourism promotion and the like. As a result, exports from Xinjiang were said to have increased 55 per cent in the first half of 1992.[43] In all, while the situation here is not as volatile as in Tibet, the potential for a conflagration remains high, especially with the disintegration of central authority in Tajikistan and the violent clashes taking place in the nearby Ferghana Valley. As one pessimistic Chinese analyst summed it up, 'Either way we lose. If the Central Asian states fall apart, chaos spreads to China. If they manage to survive, Chinese minorities say, "Look, it works there. Why can't we, too, have a state of our own?"'[44]

The situation in Mongolia differs from that of both Tibet and Xinjiang, but offers its own reasons for concern. First of all, Mongols in Inner Mongolia outnumber their counterparts in Outer Mongolia by about 50 per cent (3.4 million compared to 2.3 million). Both groups, however, are dwarfed by the over 15 million Han settlers who have migrated to Inner Mongolia over the past forty years at the urging of the Chinese government.[45] Han settlements have also served to water down minority populations in Tibet and Xinjiang, but not nearly to this extent. Any idea that Inner Mongolia might join Outer Mongolia in a unified nation is given pause by the need either to expel or somehow drag along 15 million Chinese. Nor does Outer Mongolia serve as a powerful magnet for Mongols now living in China. To the contrary, living standards are on average higher for those in China and recent trends are widening the gap. Indeed, the main fear in Ulan Bator is that the ongoing experiment with pluralistic politics and market economics will fail and that a weakened or crumbling independent Mongolia will not be able to resist absorption into China's orbit of influence. Heightening this fear is the indifference of the rest of the world, with the exception of China, to the newly independent (*de facto* as well as *de jure*) Mongolian Republic. Chinese economic dominance over independent Mongolia is already being felt. At the same time, residents of the two Mongolias seem to have serious reservations about unification. Inner Mongolians tend to see their northern brethren as uncivilised bumpkins while the latter view the Inner Mongolians as 'Sinicized half-breeds'.[46] Still, such events as the Dalai Lama's deliriously received 1991 visit to Ulan Bator and Outer Mongolia's emerging role as a platform for dissidents from China are major irritants to Beijing. In a situation of weakened authority at the centre coupled with breakaway efforts in other regions, even the presently secure position of Inner Mongolia could deteriorate and add yet another threat to the unity of China.

One final threat to the unity and national integrity of China remains to be examined: while of a different nature from those examined to this point, it is all the more ominous because it serves to compound all the others, namely corruption. That the levels of corruption have skyrocketed apace with economic growth is acknowledged by everyone. Most observers agree that the 1989 demonstrations which mushroomed into the Tiananmen disaster were initially sparked more by disgust at corruption than by a thoroughgoing commitment to principles of Western-style liberal democracy.[47] While the former image of the Chinese Communist Party cadres as incorruptible, self-sacrificing patriots is now known to have been grossly exaggerated, the levels of official corruption today are startling to all but the most jaundiced eyes. The Party's monopoly on power is compounded by the lack or weakness of auditing and other forms of supervisory mechanisms to produce a truly mind-boggling variety and level of official freebooting. From illegally charging peasants a 0.5 per cent 'commission' on entitlement payments to the fraudulent sale of a dilapidated merchant ship for a profit of 1 million yuan, the creativity and *chutzpah* of Chinese officials seem to know no bounds.[48] While prosecutions and convictions for official misdeeds have doubled and tripled in recent years, no one denies that they are merely scratching the surface. Indeed, in a survey conducted by the Chinese Academy of Social Sciences in the late 1980s almost two-thirds of the officials questioned *admitted* to involvement in corrupt practices.[49] To be sure, some of these illegal exchanges are made attractive or even unavoidable by the dual pricing structure still applied to some goods and by particular shortages and bottlenecks resulting from China's recent rapid growth within an inadequate transportation, communication and energy-producing infrastructure. Indeed, some may even be functional, at least towards the goal of economic growth and efficiency, though the evidence indicates that the vast majority are not.[50] More generally, however, these astonishing levels of corruption appear to be a byproduct of the tacit deal the Party and its leaders have made with the Chinese people: 'Don't question our right to rule, and we'll permit you to make as much money as you can as quickly as you can; we won't even look too closely at how you do it.'[51]

At this point, however, the question arises of just how much corruption can go on for how long before it begins to rot away the last vestiges of support for, or acquiescence in, the communist system. While of course it is difficult or perhaps even impossible to give a precise, quantified answer to such a question, it is almost universally acknowledged that endemic corruption was one of the major factors contributing to the defeat of the Guomindang in 1949.[52] Of course, the CCP today faces no enemy as well organized, well armed and highly motivated as it itself posed against the Guomindang then, nor does it show the slightest intention of permitting one to emerge. Nevertheless, when a retired senior official and Party member admits that 'Corruption is much worse now than it ever was under the Nationalists',[53] one must wonder whether this system, with its irrelevant and even oxymoronic ideology and its severely frayed legitimacy now hanging from the single thread of 'delivering the goods', has not entered the stage of terminal decay.

## CONCLUSION: GLOBAL POWER OR EAST ASIAN TINDERBOX?

In all, then, China's potential for leadership in the new era in world politics is great, but it faces daunting obstacles in attempting to reach that potential. First, simply continuing the economic growth rates of the past fifteen years will not be easy. The sort of conversion from an almost totally state-dominated economy to a dynamic, predominantly free-market economy which China is now attempting has never been done before. Hence, the Chinese must make it up as they go along. Critically necessary measures yet to be taken include currency reform and the establishment of sound banking and financial institutions, including auditing and supervisory mechanisms, commercial and civil legal systems, institutions of fiscal and monetary policy and many more such institutions which are required in even the freest of free market systems. However, the clear lesson of this study is that *even if* all these problems are solved and China continues its recent rates of economic growth for another generation, it still faces huge threats to the stability and unity which are prerequisites for the realization of its superpower potential. First, there is the question of leadership and the successor(s) to Deng Xiaoping, which threatens the unity of the Party and its continuing viability as the guiding political force of the country. Then there is the matter of the unity and loyalty of the armed forces, including their ability and will to contain disorders which may arise from a multitude of sources. We have also examined the substance and meaning of Chinese nationalism today and found it badly frayed, understandably enough in peripheral areas but also in such economically vital and dynamic areas as south China. We have also seen that the peasantry, long considered the backbone of the Chinese revolution, is becoming increasingly alienated from the Party and even from its generally popular reform programmes. Finally, we have seen how the acid of corruption is eating away the last vestiges of the regime's legitimacy and effectiveness. Simply to review these challenges should be enough to make the leaders of most other countries count their blessings; very few face the range and complexity of hazards facing China today. Given China's tremendous potential, however, the rewards for meeting these challenges will also be very great. No one can pretend to know with certainty how all these contingencies will be resolved; what is certain is that the contours of world politics in the twenty-first century will be significantly shaped by their outcome.

## NOTES

1 In fairness, it must be noted that Churchill's remark, made in a radio broadcast of 1 October 1939, specifically referred to the future *actions* of the Soviet Union, not to its system *per se*.

2 Jim Rohwer, 'When China Awakes' *The Economist* 28 November 1992, p. A6.

3 The World Bank, *World Development Report 1993: Investing in Health* (New York: Oxford University Press, 1993), p. 320.

4 ibid., p. 288.

5 Lawrence Summers of the World Bank, cited by Rohwer, 'When China Awakes', p. 3.

6 For the earlier view, see, for example, Chalmers A. Johnson, *Peasant Nationalism and Communist Power: The Emergence of Revolutionary China, 1937–1945* (Stanford, Calif.: Stanford University Press, 1962).

7 This debate is ably summarized by Shum Kui-Kwong in *The Chinese Communists' Road to Power: The Anti-Japanese National United Front, 1935–45* (New York: Oxford University Press, 1988), pp. 1–16.

8 David E. Apter, 'Yan'an and the Narrative Reconstruction of Reality' *Daedalus* vol. 122, no. 2, 1993, p. 210.

9 Edward Friedman, 'A Failed Chinese Modernity' *Daedalus* vol. 122, no. 2, 1993, p. 2.

10 ibid., pp. 3–4.

11 Benedict Anderson, 'The New World Disorder' *New Left Review* no. 193, May–June 1992, pp. 3–13.

12 Pingti Ho, 'Salient Aspects of China's Heritage' in Pingti Ho and Tang Tsou, eds, *China's Heritage and the Communist Political System* (Chicago: The University of Chicago Press, 1968), p. 16.

13 Ho, *China's Heritage* 1968, pp. 17–18.

14 Lincoln Kaye, 'Disorder Under Heaven' *Far Eastern Economic Review* 9 June 1994, pp. 22–23. See Patrick E. Tyler, 'Is China Stumbling? Some See Mishandling of Ties With U.S., Raising Questions About Deng's Successor' *The New York Times* 5 February 1995, pp. A1–A6.

15 Ho, *China's Heritage*, p. 16.

16 June Teufel Dreyer, *China's Political System: Modernization and Tradition* (New York: Paragon House, 1993), pp. 260–261. Lei Feng was a young PLA recruit who died on duty in 1962 after being struck by a truck filled with telegraph poles. Lin Piao concocted the first 'Learn from Lei Feng' campaign the

following year in an attempt to instil in other recruits such virtues as unquestioning loyalty, self-sacrifice and devotion to duty. Such campaigns have been repeated on several occasions during times of ideological stress or uncertainty.

17 Tai Ming Cheung, 'Back to the Front: Deng Seeks to Depoliticize the PLA' *Far Eastern Economic Review* 29 October 1992, p. 15.

18 ibid.

19 Sheryl Wu Dunn, 'Beijing Shuffles Military to Avert Power Struggle' *The New York Times* 27 January 1993, p. A8.

20 Ellis Joffe, 'Regionalism in China: The Role of the PLA' *The Pacific Review* vol. 7, no. 1, 1994, pp. 24–32.

21 ibid., p. 25. Peter Kien-hong Yu comes to much the same conclusion, based mainly on the argument that China's political, economic and military regions have been purposely made overlapping and incongruent so as to discourage the growth of what he terms 'regional military separatism'. See his 'Regional Military Separatism After Deng Xiaoping?' *Journal of Northeast Asian Studies* vol. 11, no. 1, Spring 1992, p. 10.

22 Elizabeth J. Perry, 'China in 1992: An Experiment in Neo-Authoritarianism' *Asian Survey* vol. 23, no. 1, 1993, p. 18.

23 Richard Baum, 'The China Syndrome: Prospects for Democracy in the Middle Kingdom' *Harvard International Review* vol. 15, no. 2, Winter 1992, pp. 32–33.

24 Kishore Mahbubani, 'Live and Let Live: Allow Asians to Choose their Own Course' *Far Eastern Economic Review* 17 June 1993, p. 26.

25 Suzanne Ogden, 'The Changing Content of China's Democratic Socialist Institutions' *In Depth* Winter 1993, p. 241.

26 ibid., p. 239.

27 Perry, 'China in 1992', p. 17.

28 Ogden, 'The Changing Content', p. 239.

29 See, for example, Richard Baum, 'The China Syndrome', p. 33.

30 The theories of Tocqueville and Davies, among many others, are discussed in Chalmers Johnson, *Revolutionary Change* (Boston, Mass.: Little, Brown & Company, 1966), pp. 62–63 and *passim*.

31 Siu points to classified surveys from the 1950s which showed that those southerners who claimed to be Han were 'largely the upwardly-mobile part of an indigenous population who became Han as they actively acquired the cultural symbols of the larger polity'. Or, we might say, they were Han 'wannabes'. Helen F. Siu, 'Cultural Identity and the Politics of Difference in South China' *Daedalus* vol. 122, no. 2, 1993, p. 22.

32 Edward Friedman, 'A Failed Chinese Modernity', p. 10.

33 Siu, 'Cultural Identity', p. 21.

34 E. J. Hobsbawm, *Nations and Nationalism Since 1780: Programme, Myth, Reality* (Cambridge: Cambridge University Press, 1992, rev. edn), pp. 63–67 and *passim*.

35 Paul R. Brass, *Ethnicity and Nationalism: Theory and Comparison* (New Delhi: Sage Publications, 1991), p. 25.

36 Carl Goldstein *et al.*, 'Get Off Our Backs' *Far Eastern Economic Review* 15 July 1993, pp. 68–69.

37 Nicholas D. Kristof, 'Riddle of China: Repression as Standard of Living Soars' *The New York Times* 7 September 1993, pp. A1, A10.

38 See, for example, Andrew J. Nathan and Tianjin Shi, 'Cultural Requisites for Democracy in China: Findings from a Survey' *Daedalus* vol. 122, no. 2, 1993, pp. 95–124.

39 Lincoln Kaye, 'Labour Pains: Worker Unrest Could Challenge the Party's Legitimacy' *Far Eastern Economic Review* 16 June 1994, p. 32.

40 Lillian Craig Harris, 'Xinjiang, Central Asia and the Implications for China's Policy in the Islamic World' *China Quarterly* no. 133, March 1993, p. 116.
41 Alex Shoumatoff, 'The Silent Killing of Tibet' *Vanity Fair* May 1991, p. 37.
42 Lincoln Kaye, 'China Feels the Chill' *Far Eastern Economic Review* 9 January 1992, p. 14.
43 Craig Harris, 'Xinjiang, Central Asia and the Implications for China's Policy in the Islamic World', p. 124.
44 Quoted in ibid., p. 125.
45 Lincoln Kaye, 'Faltering Steppes' *Far Eastern Economic Review* 9 April 1992, p. 16.
46 Christopher Atwood *et al.*, 'The Han Hordes' *Far Eastern Economic Review* 9 April 1992, p. 18.
47 See, for example, Lee Feigon, *China Rising: The Meaning of Tiananmen* (Chicago, Ill.: Ivan R. Dee, 1990), p. 246.
48 For abundant examples and a thorough analysis, see Jean-Louis Rocca, 'Corruption and its Shadow: An Anthropological View of Corruption in China' *China Quarterly* no. 130, June 1992, pp. 402–417.
49 Ellen Salem, 'Fighting Sticky Fingers' *Far Eastern Economic Review* 16 June 1988, p. 22.
50 Rocca, 'Corruption and its Shadow', p. 414, quotes A. J. Heidenheimer as saying, 'The official who squeezes a bribe out of a poor peasant and diverts the money to investment is . . . seen as a potential benefactor to economic growth', but not if 'the bribe-giver is an investment-prone well-to-do peasant and the bribe taker a big spender in night clubs'.
51 On the nature of this 'deal' and its politico-cultural ramifications see Perry Link, 'China's "Core" Problem' *Daedalus* vol. 122, no. 2, 1993, pp. 189–206.
52 See, for example, Suzanne Pepper, 'The KMT-CCP Conflict, 1945–1949' in Lloyd E. Eastman *et al.*, *The Nationalist Era in China, 1927–1949* (Cambridge: Cambridge University Press, 1991), p. 306.
53 Quoted in Nicholas D. Kristof, 'China Sees "Market-Leninism" as Way to Future' *The New York Times* 6 September 1993, p. A5.

# 3 From neo-mercantilism to globalism: the changing role of the state and South Korea's economic prowess*

*Kwan S. Kim*

## INTRODUCTION: THE CHANGING ROLE OF THE STATE AND SOUTH KOREA'S ECONOMIC PROWESS

South Korea's 'rags-to-riches' development, cited as a 'man-made' miracle, is miraculous in the sense that in a single generation the country achieved the kind of structural transformation (from a subsistence agrarian economy to a modern industrial power) that today's industrialized countries took almost a century to achieve. Well into the 1960s South Korea's economy continued to centre on subsistence agriculture. The infrastructural base built during Japanese colonial rule was mostly destroyed during the Korean War of 1950–1953. Its per capita income of $87 in 1962 was lower than that of Haiti, Ethiopia and Yemen and about 40 per cent below India's. The population growth of nearly 3 per cent a year in an already densely populated country meant that it had to depend on foreign aid for sheer survival. If ever there was an economic basket case, South Korea in the 1950s was it. Capitalism during the 1950s had done little for South Korea.

Today, the country, with some 42 million people and a per capita income which was more than US$8000 dollars in 1995, is the world's eleventh largest trading nation, and is on the threshold of joining the ranks of the industrialized democracies. Politically, the year 1992 saw the inauguration of a civilian government after three decades of authoritarian military rule. The transition to democracy has now culminated in the recent implementation of local autonomy.[1] Externally, South Korea has been assuming an increasingly active role in global affairs by exporting technology, investing abroad and donating foreign aid to countries in Asia, Africa and Latin America. The current civilian government has initiated a globalization campaign, heralding South Korea's active participation in the GATT–WTO system and the Pacific Community.

Behind this transition from a subsistence to a modern economy has been the evolution in the complex and subtle ways the economy is managed. Indeed, the South Korean experience, especially in the early stage of industrialization, demonstrates the evolving and yet coherent role of the state in economic development. As in other newly industrialized countries in East Asia, such as Taiwan and Singapore, capitalist development in South Korea has been achieved under a strong state whose direction and intervention in resource allocation, rather than through market processes, contributed to the development of areas of the economy perceived to have longer-run potential. The South Korean experience suggests that a well-managed state-led economy can function better than an economy based on market forces, particularly in the early stage when a country is trying to catch up with the industrialized world. South Korea's tightly controlled economic devolution from state-guided capitalism to managed globalism has defied the conventional economic doctrine emphasizing the efficiency of unbridled capitalism.

In the literature, views on the role of the East Asian states have ranged from that of a minimalist state to that of an interventionist state.[2] The interventionists see the state as coercing the private sector to achieve the kinds of economic restructuring perceived to facilitate rapid growth of the economy. The other side of the spectrum in the controversy is the minimalist view, according to which the South Korean state intervened essentially to correct market failures. Many economists with a neoclassical bent attribute East Asia's success to an efficient state action in compliance with market principles.[3] Market forces are seen essentially as providing the self-regulating mechanism for efficient resource allocation and therefore rapid economic growth: the extreme position among the neoclassical scholars holds that state involvement is merely a structural necessity useful to create an environment suitable for capitalist development.

In the context of the above debate, the present study takes the case of South Korea and assesses the intermingling roles of state and market during periods of both authoritarian rule (1961–1987) and political liberalization (1988–1994). While the first period witnessed persistent and comprehensive state intervention, during the second period state activism was much weaker, being limited to a number of industrial sectors. It will be argued that the South Korean state, certainly during the initial period of rapid economic growth, played a critical role in the making of industrialization, prevailing in every sector of the economy. The glaring feature of state actions in South Korean development is that market rationality has been compromised by the paramount goal of industrialization even as the economy matures into a fully capitalist stage.

This chapter analyses the historical process and the social structure that gave birth to both an authoritarian and a democratic state in South Korea. The intention here is not to develop a theory of the state, but to draw attention to the particular features of the developmental state in East Asia. The next section presents an overview of industrial development in South Korea from a historical perspective, looking closely at the choice of development strategies and their consequences over the different phases of industrialization. The third section surveys the origin and scope of state authority, assessing the role of the state in the process of industrialization. A specific question addressed is how the state in post-liberation South Korea has been able to maintain its dominance over civil society. Finally, as South Korea enters a new era of globalization and internal political and economic stability, it faces new opportunities and new constraints associated with globalization. The concluding section explores the prospects for South Korea in the coming Pacific Century.

## INDUSTRIALIZATION IN HISTORICAL PERSPECTIVE: STRATEGIES AND CONSEQUENCES

The transition from a feudal agrarian economy to a modern industrial state in Korea began under Japanese colonial rule which lasted from the early twentieth century until 1945. Japan was a late-comer in the global struggle for colonies. Its ultimate interest in Korea and Manchuria was to integrate them closely to the metropolis and to use the conquered territories as a basis to supply human and physical resources in resisting the West. Japan's ultimate intention to make Korea a permanent part of the metropolis subsequently prompted heavy investments in administrative infrastructure, railroads, ports, communications and other physical facilities. The colony was used as the location for industry by drawing on the indigenous labour and raw materials. To facilitate the process of industrialization, the colonial administration exercised a strict control over the economy, relying on a tripartite apparatus made up of the business conglomerates or *zaibatsu*, the central bank and the administrative bureaucracy. The colonial state stepped in to fill the role of an absent or incipient entrepreneurial class in the colony. Japan's efforts to assimilate the colony were made easier by the fact that Koreans and Japanese are ethnically and culturally similar.

The colonial state, despite its harsh rule, contributed to the building of basic physical infrastructure, laying down the foundations for the partial industrialization of the Korean peninsula. In terms of value added, for instance, the share of manufacturing rose from 2 per cent in the early 1910s to around 13 to 15 per cent of GNP by 1940, while the share of primary activities declined from about two-thirds of GNP to about a half.[4] More significantly, it provided a model of a highly articulated, disciplined bureaucracy, later to be adopted by South Koreans for state-guided development. The Japanese suppressed the indigenous bourgeoisie, and introduced Japanese business conglomerates, the *zaibatsu*. In the post-war period South Korean conglomerates, called *chaebôl*, emerged as a close replica of the *zaibatsu* system. The corporate system is organized around a familial and ethical structure emphasizing filial piety. As for the other aspects of the colonial legacy, Bruce Cumings aptly summarizes them as follows:

The strong colonial state, the multiplicity of bureaucracies, the policy of administrative guidance of the economy, the use of the state to found new industries, and the repression of labour unions and dissidents that always went with it provided a surreptitious model for both Koreas after World War II. Japan showed them an early version of the 'bureau-cratic–authoritarian' path to industrialization, and it was a lesson that seemed well learned by the 1970s.[5]

Liberation from Japan in 1945 left the Korean economy, which had been closely integrated with the Japanese economy, crippled. The subsequent separation of the North from the South in the peninsula further disabled the economy: while heavy industries, electrical power resources and mineral deposits were mostly located in the northern part of the country, industries in the South consisted mainly of manufactures of agricultural and light consumer goods. The fragile, industrial infrastructure left in the South was soon destroyed during the Korean War (1950–1953), this time almost entirely. The South had to industrialize out of the ruins left in the wake of the war. For analytical purposes the post-Korean War era can be divided into three phases of development: the period of inward orientation (1953–1960), outward orientation (1961–1979), and liberalization and balanced growth (1980–1994).

The years between 1953 and 1960 mark the era of reconstruction under import substitution. An important goal of government policy in this period was to develop non-durable consumer and intermediate goods behind a protective wall of tariffs and quotas. The domestic currency was maintained persistently at an overvalued rate, which resulted in debilitating the export potential of the economy. As a result, exports remained negligible throughout the period, amounting to, on average, less than 1 per cent of GNP. Imports, on the other hand, which were mostly financed by American grants-in-aid, accounted for more than 10 per cent of GNP. Any kind of systematic, longer-run commitment by the state to sustained development was conspicuously absent. The South Korean economy in the 1950s possessed all the characteristics of an extremely poor Third World nation. In 1953, its per capita GNP was about $130 in 1970 prices. About half of its GNP was generated by the agricultural sector where nearly two-thirds of the total working population was located. The manufacturing sector contributed to a mere 6 per cent of GNP. The average annual growth rate of the economy during the period was 4 per cent.

The military coup in 1961 was a turning point in South Korean development. It marked the beginning of the era during which the state pursued systematic, aggressive, outward-oriented policies to achieve rapid economic growth. Initially, the government decided to start with an intensified effort to push import substitution. However, the inflow of US aid, which peaked in 1957, started its irreversible decline in the late 1950s. The government had no recourse but to rely on foreign borrowing and export promotion, along with fiscal and interest rate reforms to mobilize domestic savings.[6] Besides, by the early 1960s, internal markets for most import-substitutable products were already saturated. The shift towards exports was a timely, necessary and logical move. During the period of outward orientation, persistent state intervention in major economic activities became the rule rather than the exception. Three aspects of state actions are worth pointing out. The first is the practice of targeting the 'strategic' sectors and firms for special support; the second relates to a neo-mercantilist trade policy of maximizing exports while minimizing imports; and the third concerns the policy dilemma concerning an overall balance between industry and agriculture.

The South Korean government slipped into the practice later known as 'industrial targeting'. In the attempt to nurture infant industries, the South Korean planners selected for government support a set of 'strategic' industries over a series of five-year development plans.[7] With the notable exception of the first five-year plan (1962–1966) during which developmental priority was assigned to infrastructure development, the dynamic sequencing of industrial sectors over subsequent five-year plans was to reflect the country's prospective patterns of comparative advantage. State support of strategic industries started with labour-intensive sectors, moving on to capital- and skill-intensive sectors in subsequent plans. The industries targeted for support ranged from sophisticated electronics to heavy and chemical sectors, iron and steel, shipbuilding and automobiles. Rather than channelling funds and adopting projects on an *ad hoc* base, the government made systematic efforts to adapt to the technological changes occurring in the industry world-wide, to reflect scale economies and inter-industrial linkages, and to direct the economy along the desired path as perceived by policy makers.[8]

As for trade policy, South Korea's outward-oriented policy was in effect an eclectic one. While emphasizing exports, protection for import substitution of selected domestic industries – especially of intermediate and capital goods – was accorded no less importance. The government decided to give balanced attention to promoting development of capital and intermediate industries to strengthen vertically integrated production structures. This would lessen the economy's dependence on imports. The government's longer-term strategy was aimed at establishing a viable industrial structure adaptable to the shifting comparative advantage patterns in international markets. In the case of South Korea import substitution and export promotion proceeded together.

The final aspect of government strategy worth mentioning concerns the development of the agricultural sector. South Korean agriculture, despite its importance, has on the whole been subordinated to the goal of industrialization. President Park's technocrats were more concerned with the pace of industrialization, although South Korea had a substantial food deficit in this period. Park's strategy was to mobilize resources for activities that accelerated the pace of industrialization. For example, in order to assure lower industrial wages through cheap imported food, the government denied to agriculture any protection from foreign competition, allowing virtually duty-free imports of food grains. The resulting deterioration in the rural sector's terms of trade ensured continual inflows of rural labour to urban factories. Throughout the 1960s, the rural population, relative to urban workers, remained impoverished. By the early 1970s, political instability in the countryside began to pose a threat to the Park regime. The political leadership saw the promotion of farming interests as a viable route to retaining political power.[9] To put the brakes on the rapid deterioration in the rural economy, the Park government initiated, along with provisions of extension services through the rural-oriented New Village Movement (*Saemaul*), a massive rice procurement programme at prices several times the world market price. The farm support programme during the first half of the 1970s resulted in government deficits and, at the same time, substantial increases in rural income, making it possible for the rural population to have improved health, high levels of educational attainment, and access to basic services. Industrial success eventually facilitated agricultural development through the reallocation of an industrial surplus back to agriculture. The policies which sought to force growth with equity by supporting declining agriculture turned out to be economically costly. From the early 1970s on, the government found itself committed to heavy subsidies for fertilizer and for the difference between the price it paid to farmers for rice and barley and the lower price at which it sold them to consumers. The financial costs of supporting agriculture added to the economic costs to the nation of protecting agriculture against competing imports. The labour-intensive small farm sector became a hindrance.

The results of these state actions were predictable. South Korea achieved a significant level of import substitution behind heavy protective tariffs in such products as cement, fertilizer, refined petroleum, textile yarn and fabrics, which in due course emerged as a new generation of exportable goods. Also, export promotional policies gathered momentum over time. Taking advantage of the favourable trade environment in the 1960s and privileged access to US offshore procurements during the Vietnam War, the government resorted to an all-out effort for exports. Exports rose dramatically: over the period 1962–1979, South Korea's real exports grew at the average annual rate of 33.7 per cent. The growth performance was also spectacular: the average growth rate in real GNP during the 1965-79 period was 9.7 per cent; real per capita income showed an eighteen-fold increase to $1481 in 1980 from $87 in 1962. Rapid economic growth brought with it a drastic transformation in South Korea's industrial structure: the primary sector, which accounted for 40 per cent of total economic activity in 1962–1964, declined to 18.3 per cent by 1980 while manufacturing and mining rose from 18.1 per cent to 30 per cent (see Table 3.1).

*Table 3.1* Annual growth rates in real GNP

| Regime | Period | % |
| --- | --- | --- |
| | 1965–1969 average | 10.0 |
| Park | 1970–1974 average | 9.1 |
| | 1975–1979 average | 10.1 |
| Transition | 1980 | −5.2 |
| Chun | 1981–1986 average | 7.3 |
| Roh | 1987–1992 average | 8.3 |
| Kim | 1993–1994 estimate | 5.6 |

*Sources:* Economic Planning Board and the Bank of Korea.

Towards the late 1970s, the distribution of income deteriorated as the government drastically reduced farm subsidies and continued with anti-labour policies while sheltering the interests of industrial capitalists. Pro-*chaebôl* policies, in particular, led to the widening of intra-industry income gaps. Moreover, as fiscal policies focused on industrial infrastructure development and ignored social sectors, the incidence of poverty became more acute in urban areas and among economically disadvantaged groups such as the elderly, disabled and female-headed households. Regional disparities also emerged as a result of the regional proclivities of economic policy makers. It is worth noting that despite the sector-specific distribution inequities in South Korean development, the country is still considered to be reasonably egalitarian by international standards. Two factors, both cultural and historical, have contributed to this: (1) the universal spread of education; and (2) relatively even asset ownership in rural areas.[10] Successful land reforms prior to industrialization eliminated land tenancy, and although the average farm size has been insufficient to provide satisfactory income relative to the urban counterpart, with the aid of the state they have enabled peasants to escape impoverishment. The high literacy rate in South Korea is attributed to the wide dissemination of education among the populace. Reflecting culturally rooted enthusiasm for education, primary education was nearly universal already at the time of the state initiative for industrialization. The state did not have to spend a particularly large share of the budget for education in comparison to other developing countries. By the late 1970s, however, it had become clear that the state's implementation machinery was working too effectively. The bureaucracy's excessive zeal to surpass targets and excessive interference in market functions gradually generated serious distortions and imbalances in the economy. Private companies blindly followed the government's lead without paying much attention to the underlying economic distortions and rent-seeking activities; too many production units were crowded into too few strategic sectors, resulting in too much capacity too fast. Wage suppression and pro-business policies also aggravated income distribution. Although South Korea's rapid growth was achieved under a fairly equitable income distribution by international standards, the distribution began to worsen from the mid-1970s.

Coming to the late 1970s, a series of economic setbacks took place, including a crop failure and the impacts of the second oil shock and the subsequent global recession. They provoked a decline in real GNP in 1980 for the first time since 1953 and high inflation. The economic crisis was compounded by a series of political crises, epitomized by the 1980 Kwangju uprising against Chun Doo Hwan's military regime. After brutally repressing the uprising and consolidating the authoritarian political state, Chun set to the tasks of economic stabilization and reforms. The stabilization programmes which were imposed included aggregate demand control through restrictive monetary policy, the elimination of subsidies, the reduction of government expenditure, and the realignment of exchange rates on a floating basis.

The basic component of Chun's reforms was economic restructuring aimed at longer-term balanced growth and the liberalization of the economy. Excessive aspects of the command structure were to be gradually discarded in favour of greater initiatives from the private sector. The business sector was urged to pay more heed to market signals and profits. A gradual and cautiously scheduled import liberalization programme was introduced in recognition of the importance of market forces in an already complex and highly sophisticated economy. New initiatives, in addition, included denationalization of the banking system, elimination of cartel arrangements and price fixing, and allocation of policy loans to restore a proper balance between small- and large-scale firms. With the help of timely Japanese loans and aid, the state initiated comprehensive programmes for sectoral reorganization; for instance, to avoid the waste from excessive competition, the Chun government adopted the principle of one *chaebôl* for each industrial sector. Chun's structural adjustment policies abetted the performance of the economy, while bringing down inflation. Partly helped by the recovery of the world market, beginning in 1983, the South Korean economy was on its way to expansion, registering an average GNP growth rate of 7.3 per cent during the 1981–1986 period.

The departure in 1987 of President Chun was followed by a wave of labour and student unrest. The subsequent years of rapid democratization under President Roh saw a general weakening of the overall performance of the economy. Wage increases began to outstrip productivity gains by wide margins, fuelling inflation and sharply eroding South Korea's export competitiveness. As inflation accelerated with imports rising rapidly under ongoing trade liberalization, the nation's trade balance which reached a surplus of $14 billion in 1988 worsened in the last two years of Roh's administration. South Korea was going through a critical period of transition from authoritarian rule to political liberalization, and at the same time from excessive statism to economic liberalization.

The transition to democracy created a new context in which economic policy makers had to work. Externally, Roh's government was committed to internationalizing the economy by opening domestic markets to foreign trade and investment. The state's role in industrial development was limited to assisting in the development of technology and human capital. Internally, a wider participation in political decisions forced the state to pay close attention to social welfare and equity. The policy makers faced the challenge of striking a proper balance between growth and equity. Accordingly, priorities in government spending were given to the basic needs of the working poor, public assistance programmes, and low-income housing subsidies for those who were particularly disadvantaged.[11] The increased participation of civil society began to have a salutary impact on the provision of social services, while the prospects of high growth policies were held in check. The annual growth rate, in fact, slowed down considerably from a 13 per cent high in 1986–1987 to 7 to 9 per cent by 1989–1990. On the other hand, the redistribution policies began to exert cumulatively equalizing effects on the distribution of income in South Korea.

Turning to the civilian administration, President Kim's policies have essentially aimed at establishing sound economic fundamentals in the economy, relying less on the 'hands on' approach of the previous regimes. Critical reform measures have included the rationalization of the financial system, the reduction of corruption and tax evasion, and the internationalization of the economy via the improvement of the investment environment. Some intervention, none the less, is still seen as necessary. There will be the continuing need for the government to monitor and supervise the process of fiscal and financial reforms. And the state, in collaboration with the private sector, also needs to prepare and implement strategies for industrial development. Kim's reform policies led to the initial slowing down of the economy, with the GDP growth rate around 5 per cent in 1993, a figure somewhat higher than anticipated. The reform measures, however, appear to have quickly injected new dynamism in the economy as export-oriented manufacturing activities, partly helped by the high value of the yen, began to show signs of regaining momentum after a period of deep stagnation since the 1980s.

## THE CHARACTER AND ROLE OF THE STATE IN CAPITALIST DEVELOPMENT

South Korea's success in rapid industrialization is, to a large extent, attributable to a strong state regime capable of energetically executing plans and strategies. The questions that need to be answered are: Where has the primacy of the state derived from? What has been the extent of state control? How autonomous has the South Korean state been in relation to various groups of civil society? And how has the state elicited compliance from the private sector? The rise of a modern bureaucratic state in South Korea can be traced to Japanese colonial rule. Upon colonizing the country, the colonial state promptly swept away the traditional feudalistic order, replacing it by a centralized bureaucratic state apparatus. The modernization of the colony was to be facilitated by sweeping changes from above. The consolidation of a new political order was followed by the introduction of new capitalist social relations in industry in which a tripartite alliance of the colonial state's bureaucracy, central banking and *zaibatsu* conglomerates dominated, while in pre-capitalist agriculture the state introduced landlord–tenant relations designed to produce surplus grain for export from Korea. The colonial mode of production influenced the indigenous class structure. While tenancy in agriculture pauperized indigenous farmers, turning them into urban proletarians in industries dominated by Japanese capital, there also emerged a new class of indigenous capitalists, mainly in trade and small-scale industry, and a significant number of indigenous landlords. The emerging propertied class tended to rely on the colonial state apparatus in sharing surpluses, as a way to retain its wealth and privilege. In the case of agriculture, the rural society continued to retain the feudalistic land-tenure system serving the interests of the colonial state, which turned into a factor contributing to the peasant uprisings immediately after Korea's liberation from Japan.

In post-liberation Korea, the anti-communist stance of the US Military Government in the South was a decisive factor in the making of the South Korean state. From the beginning, the leftist political parties were precluded from participation in the emerging government in the South. The American security interest in South Korea during the rapidly evolving Cold War years prompted the build-up of a strong, anti-communist state apparatus. The occupation regime's immediate task was to suppress the unwieldy labour movements mobilized by the leftist coalition, and for this, the Japanese-built administrative system was quickly resurrected, with a national police backed up by a revived form of the colonial police. The ensuing land reforms initiated by the Military Government redistributed land to the tiller and outlawed tenancy, which led to the virtual elimination of the landowning class as a contending political force. A few remaining, indigenous industrial capitalists in the wake of Japanese withdrawal from Korea constituted a disorganized, weakened economic force. The conservative coalition led by Syngman Rhee, which succeeded the US Military Government in 1948, could act autonomously, free from the interference and demands of elite groups.

The tragic experience of the Korean War (1950–1953) and the continued threat of renewed war by North Korea reinforced the authoritarian rule of Syngman Rhee with a strong backing of the military forces. While the post-liberation state in the South formally professed to resemble a Western democracy with free elections and civil liberty, the state's coercive apparatus was used to suppress civil rights and political oppositions in the name of national security. The state, in particular, enforced anti-labour policy as organized labour was seen as a left-leaning disruptive social force.[12] Clearly, the state apparatus in independent South Korea, inheriting the colonial military-administrative organization, was in a position to subordinate all the contending political and social forces. No particular interest groups or forces could dare to challenge state authority. The South Korean state was in a position to appropriate directly a large part of economic surplus, deploying it in bureaucratically directed activities.

In the wake of the termination of the Korean War a number of family-based industrial conglomerates, the *chaebôl*, began to emerge as the core of the new economic elite. As a result of extensive damages inflicted by the war, the South Korean economy had to depend heavily on imported consumer goods, which were financed mostly by US aid. The Rhee regime's plan was to develop domestic manufactures and gradually replace consumer goods imports. As the import substitution-based industrialization plan relied heavily on foreign aid, this left the door open for the possibilities of windfall gains that could be had through privileged access to foreign exchange and import licences. The corruption of the Rhee regime led to the rise of new economic elites who exploited every opportunity of expediting accumulation in sheltered domestic enterprises. Because of the close relationship between the state and private capital, the benefits of state policies accrued largely to the emerging *chaebôl*.

The emergence of new capitalists did not detract from the state's autonomy. Under the Rhee regime, private capital was created and supported to serve as an instrument of the state, while often working closely with state functionaries in the sharing of the spoils of rent-seeking activities. What prompted the demise of these particular capitalist social relations in the 1950s was the indignation of the populace directed against the rent-seekers under commercial capitalism, and the inability of commercial capital to provide for the needs of the people. Despite some advances made in import substitution, developments in the 1950s fell far short of paving the way towards a self-sustaining economy. The South Korean economy, under an inefficient and corrupt administrative infrastructure, remained stagnant and dependent, with import dependence rising in many manufacturing sectors and, most significantly, in agriculture.

The economic and moral crisis engendered by the inept and corrupt regime of Syngman Rhee made it easier for Park Chung Hee's military faction to legitimize its military coup in 1961 by invoking national security and economic survival. After coming to power, Park's immediate task was to institutionalize an authoritarian and interventionist rule in carrying out a kind of economic revolution from above. The military coup was organized by a previously isolated section of the state apparatus with no linkages to particular social groups. The coup came under the revolutionary mandate to eliminate the rent-seeking activities and to restore national security and economic prosperity. There were no countervailing forces to check the huge military institution. The military regime was soon able to institutionalize authoritarian rule. Learning from Japanese experience in the Meiji Restoration (*Ishin*), Park saw sweeping changes from above as the only way to facilitate the modernization of South Korea. Under the pretext of national 'revitalization' (*yshin*), the constitution was amended to consolidate the dominance of the executive under one-party rule. After amassing sweeping presidential powers, the Park regime set itself the task of designing and implementing strategies for accumulating industrial capital. Park saw rapid industrialization as the way to modernize the nation. A system of meritocratic bureaucracy backed by military muscle was ushered in to implement policies to develop modern manufacturing industry. The political system envisioned as ideal to carry out such a strategy was one wherein the policy makers, backed up by a coalition of competent bureaucrats, business people and the military, were able to make decisions with a minimum of interference.[13] The elimination of leftist forces, which continued throughout the 1950s, freed the government from the need to pursue populist policies, making it easier for the state to circumscribe debates on policy alternatives. The period of the Park regime witnessed the rebirth of a kind of Japanese colonial rule based on military control, decisive economic planning and the all-out mobilization of resources for industrial development.[14]

The state's strategy for accumulation of industrial capital has had far-reaching consequences upon class structure in South Korean society. One particular class viewed by the state as a potential threat to the success of economic growth was industrial labour. The export success during the early period of rapid growth required the mobilization of cheap and disciplined labour. The military regime played a critical role in shaping the labour movement and labour processes. Historically, South Korea's trade unions were created or controlled by the state to support the anti-communist struggle against a left-wing labour movement. Workers were long denied the right to organize unions that might foster class consciousness. Industrial unions were typically organized at the enterprise level so that collective bargaining had to be carried out at this level. This internal company unionism precluded the possibility of unions forming a united front on common economic and social interests, and thereby diminished their influence on national policies. The politics of labour demobilization continued throughout the 1970s. When the average real wage rate rose in response to tightened labour market conditions in the early 1970s, South Korea was threatened with a deterioration in the competitive edge of labour-intensive exports. The government quickly enacted a series of measures to restrain wage increases by curtailing the power of trade unions.[15] As a result, real wages fell in relation to improvements in labour productivity between 1967 and 1978 (see Figure 3.1). The slower growth in relative wages reflected labour's declining share in output.[16] Labour's

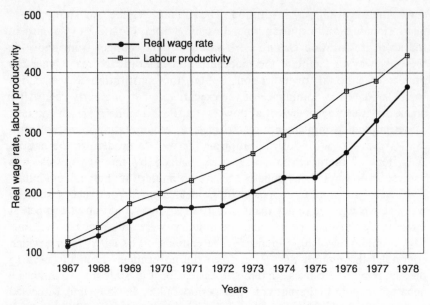

*Figure 3.1* Real wages and labour productivity in manufacturing

*Sources:* For wage series, Bureau of Labor; and for productivity series, Center of Productivity.
*Note:* After 1977 real wages gained some ground over productivity increases. These gains reflect the impact of structural adjustment in labour markets, which was instituted in response to increasingly militant labour movements.

share in manufacturing value added declined from 36.6 per cent in 1958 to 23 per cent by 1975.

While repressing labour movements, the state reorganized the capitalist class. At the time of the advent of the military regime, the old bourgeoisie, discredited by the downfall of Rhee, was on the verge of extinction. When Park decided to pursue a capitalist strategy for industrialization, he needed to enlist business support. The previous industrialists were given the opportunity to collaborate with the state while creating new business interests. The business sector was not, however, allowed to become autonomous in relation to the state. The nurturing of big businesses was seen as an imperative for the development of heavy industry in South Korea. Economic logic favoured large-scale production, as a minimum scale in plant size would be required for efficiency in production in such sectors as automobiles, steel, and shipbuilding. The *chaebôl* would have to compete in international markets with the large-scale, foreign multinationals. The size of the firm was also an important factor to consider in joint ventures with foreign partners, since there would be the risk that these could dominate and control the domestic counterparts.[17]

As a result, the breadth and speed in the rise of the *chaebôl* have been unprecedented in South Korea's history of enterprise. There were some fifty major conglomerates with each unit composed of half a dozen to

*Table 3.2* Growth of conglomerates (the *chaebôl*)

| Number of conglomerates | Annual growth rates (1973–1978) | As percentage of GDP | |
|---|---|---|---|
| | | 1973 | 1978 |
| 5 | 35.7 | 8.8 | 18.4 |
| 10 | 30.0 | 13.9 | 23.4 |
| 20 | 27.5 | 21.8 | 33.2 |
| 46 | 21.4 | 31.8 | 43.0 |
| GDP total | 17.2 | 100.0 | 100.0 |

*Source:* Korean Development Institute.

fifty member firms that were horizontally and vertically integrated in the industrial structure.[18] Between 1973 and 1978 the annual rate of growth in value added contributed by the ten largest conglomerates was as high as 30 per cent. In terms of the share of their contribution to GDP, they accounted for 14 per cent in 1973, rising to 23.4 per cent by 1978. The top forty-six firms, taken together, accounted for 31.8 per cent of GDP in 1973, which rose to 43 per cent over the same period (see Table 3.2). These measures clearly show the extent of progress in industrial concentration during the military regime.

To elicit compliance from private capital, the state resorted to a strictly enforced 'carrot and stick' system. Incentives were offered to those who complied with the directions of the state. The most important instrument was the allocation of bank credit and of access to foreign capital. Businesses in South Korea critically depended on bank credits, as over two-thirds of the cash flow of manufacturing firms came from borrowing from financial institutions controlled by the state. The debt–equity ratio in the private sector typically ranged from four to six, and the industrial capitalists were put in a weak bargaining position *vis-à-vis* the state. In the public sector, which included state-run enterprises, heavy pressure was exerted on the bureaucrats, frequently by imposing output targets, to execute their jobs well. The forms of intervention ranged from a 'friendly' telephone call from the President's office to the allocation of bank loans. One influential administrative institution is the tax authority. It has sanctioned non-compliant enterprises by inspecting their returns more strictly. The state also controlled prices to subsidize export- and targeted-sector activities through reductions in imported input prices or through increases in monopolistic prices for profits. The 'carrot and stick' system worked well for South Korea; industrial capitalists soon realized that compliance with government directions would be the only way to survive and prosper. In sum, the South Korean state during the export-led phase was free from the constraints of civil society, and could direct the economy so as to pursue the national goals perceived and formulated by technocratic bureaucrats. State involvement turned out to be most extensive and substantial during the export-led phase in South Korean development.

The decade of the 1980s began with political and economic crises. The assassination of President Park in 1979 was followed by a brief move towards civilian constitutionalism, ending with the Kwangju riot. At Kwangju the military suppressed an incipient pro-democracy rebellion with considerable force, causing hundreds of casualties. As already discussed (p. 89), economically Korea was severely affected by the global economic downturn during the late 1970s and early 1980s. For the first time since 1961, the economy was plunged into stagnation precipitated by the social unrest and a crop failure in 1980. Under the new President, General Chun Doo Hwan, state intervention revolved around the two major themes of macroeconomic stabilization and balanced growth, in the context of piecemeal economic liberalization. As far as the basic character of the state was concerned, it was still close to the bureaucratic authoritarian state, described by O'Donnell (see Note 13). The control of the state continued to remain comprehensive, technocratic and repressive. The goals of the state were to be attained at all costs. When the market system worked in the desired way, it was to be left alone; when it did not, state intervention directed it in the desired way. Thus, despite the economic mandate for liberalization and decentralization, the subordinate relations of business to the state remained unchanged under the Chun regime. Ignoring the alarming trends in industrial concentration, the Chun government continued to work with big businesses as large firms with economies of scale could be counted on to complete crucial projects for national development more successfully.[19] Funds flowed more readily into larger companies since they were generally in a better position to outbid smaller firms in government-financed projects.

The impressive economic growth combined with low inflation rates during the Chun regime was attained at the expense of workers and farmers. To maintain export competitiveness, the state repressed the labour movement, outlawing strikes and unions, and reduced farm subsidies while attempting to liberalize agricultural imports. Chun's government initially evinced greater interest in promoting balanced growth with equity. In reality, the reforms for equitable development had been incremental. There were no drastic structural reforms to the political economy. At the same time, Chun's structural adjustment policies relied on the effective working of the state bureaucracy. The capacity of the state to formulate and execute strategies under the Chun regime was not very different from that under the Park regime. The state continued to influence class formation. While some differences existed in the choice of economic strategy between the two regimes, the character and structure of the state remained essentially the same. At the same time, the deepening of industrialization in South Korea gradually weakened the state's strength and autonomy in relation to various groups of the political economy. As the economy grew in size and complexity, state intervention became more costly. As the number of labourers increased and the *chaebôl* became more powerful, they both became increasingly vocal about the negative aspects of the centralized role of the state. The labourers and even the acquiescent farmers became increasingly outspoken in their demands for a larger share of the benefits from economic growth.

The year 1987, when Chun stepped down from the presidency, was a turning point in South Korea. A crisis of state authority had erupted in February 1985 when the opposition parties gained strength in parliamentary elections. However, the ensuing presidential election saw the emergence of Roh Tae Woo, a former military general and ally of Chun Doo Hwan, as President of the Sixth Republic. Roh organized a coalition with two of the opposition parties, creating the Democratic Liberal Party, and attempted to initiate broad reformist policies of political and economic liberalization. Roh sought political legitimacy for his regime by winning the crucial support of the middle class. Like the previous regimes, his economic policies focused on maintaining sustained economic growth to appease the middle class. For continuous success in the export drive, he was forced to resort to measures, when necessary, to contain the potentially explosive forces for 'democratization from below'. Grass-roots labour movements were specifically targeted for containment. His reformist measures proved to be unpopular; they were greeted by growing dissension within his own party and were sharply criticized by the largest remaining opposition party, led by Kim Dae Jung. John Lie explains the dilemmas of Roh's reformist policies as follows:

> He is intimately tied to the authoritarian past, being himself a general and Chun's close associate. Most critically, his range of actions is constrained: he cannot simultaneously satisfy his crucial support bases. On the one hand, his reliance on the military and allied authoritarian institutions prevents him from undertaking serious reforms. Yet unlike Park and Chun, he cannot easily wield brute force; his crucial middle class support proscribes overtly authoritarian measures, an outright suppression of the labour or dissident movement would risk a revolutionary confrontation. Moreover, the perennial source of legitimacy, economic growth, became unstable. The *chaebôl* that Park and Chun nurtured have become independent power bases in their own right, resistant to government control.[20]

The political reforms under Roh led to a reduction of state autonomy, as the state became more prone to pressures from such influential interest groups as labour, peasants and the *chaebôl*. The Roh era continued to be characterized by a strong but certainly not omnipotent state: under Roh there was simply a transition from a 'hard' to a 'soft' developmental state.

The turning point in South Korean democracy arrived in 1992 with the incumbency of Kim Yong Sam, who was elected as the first civilian President after three decades of authoritarianism. The civilian regime quickly undertook economic reforms in three areas, which began to reshape the South Korean economy. First, there was an urgent task of fuller liberalization of the economy. Concerned about the poor economic performance in 1992, the new regime decided to expedite the restructuring of the economy as a focal point of revitalization.[21] By the 1990s, the statism of the previous regimes was seen not only as being in conflict with political democracy, but also as stifling South Korea's highly complex and sophisticated economy. Economic liberalization under Kim entailed the restructuring of the industrial sector. Also, many of the effective tools of state intervention in the past (such as loans policy, quantitative targeting and industrial licensing) were gradually eliminated. Second, the emergence of pluralistic forces in the South Korean polity made it a political imperative to create more equitable economic opportunities for all citizens. Political liberalization has brought with it a change in political environment where the state is open to, and tolerant of, divergent groups' needs and demands.[22] The new regime responded more readily, in particular, to increased demands from the popular sector by increasing the provision of national welfare services and by adopting policies for a more equitable distribution of resources.[23] The challenges facing the new democracy are to meet the pluralistic demands for economic support and social services more effectively and efficiently when the state's political capacity to do so is diminished. Finally, the new regime continues to face growing external pressures to participate more fully in the global economy. As a successful exporter, South Korea will benefit from intra-regional trade within a Pacific free trade area and from pursuing the multilateral free trade agreement under the new WTO. Accordingly, President Kim's policy emphasizes the continued internationalization of the economy, via the deregulation of foreign investment and the liberalization of financial markets, pursuing the country's fuller globalization through active participation in economic cooperation in the Asia-Pacific.

There is at the same time a serious concern whether the country will ultimately succeed in the structural transformation of the economy needed to sustain export competitiveness. South Korea's international competitiveness has dulled in the early 1990s and the country has already reached its maximum point of growth as a labour-intensive exporter. The export sector, hitherto seen as the main engine of growth, faced mounting difficulties – internal and external in origin. Externally, the protectionist mood in developed countries and growing competition from Asia's emerging economies, such as China and Indonesia, have eroded South Korea's international market share in labour-intensive exports. Internally, the surges in labour costs, often exceeding growth in productivity have undermined South Korean price competitiveness in international markets.[24] South

Korea's technology and productivity are not yet at a level to make its exports competitive, in high value-added, technology-intensive products, with Japan, the United States and Western Europe. The South Korean economy also suffers from a macro imbalance between manufacturing and service activities.

While the relative autonomy of South Korea's civilian state has diminished with the emergence of a pluralistic civil society, strong state actions continue to be seen as indispensable for sustained industrialization and for the prevention of structural distortions in the economy, growing income inequality or deepening foreign dependence.[25] In this respect, the civilian regime managed to retain state capacity for effective policy implementation. A sophisticated state apparatus that facilitates such implementation, which has been reorganized for increased efficiency and effectiveness, is kept in place. The new constitution endows the single-term President with virtually unlimited executive authority while the legislature's powers are severely curtailed. The constitutionally empowered executive authority, coupled with a deep-seated, traditional culture that respects social hierarchy and authority, will enable the democratically elected government of South Korea to continue to intervene in the economy when this is deemed to be in the nation's best interests. Kim's regime has thus assumed from the beginning a relatively confined (regulatory rather than developmental) but decisive role in the country's economic development. It has succeeded in reprioritizing industrial policies in the sectors of the economy where an abrupt transition of power to the market is seen to be harmful. For instance, the government adopted various measures to induce a quantum jump in the high-tech field by stimulating research and development investment. Loans and other discreet forms of subsidies continue to be provided to a limited number of industrial sectors.[26] The state in South Korea will thus continue to play a substantial role in the country's development as long as developmental policies and services provided by the state are not opposed by the dominant economic classes.

## STATE AUTHORITY, CAPITALIST DEVELOPMENT AND EAST ASIAN CULTURE

Given the complexity of the developmental process in South Korea, it is impossible to quantify the consequences of state intervention. Nor would it be possible to appraise the counterfactual case, had South Korea followed a non-interventionist strategy. Thus, the most one can conclude from the available data is that rapid economic growth in South Korea has taken place under a strong interventionist state dedicated to economic development. The particular contribution of state intervention is more discernible, however, when the judgement involves the efficacy of implementation. A major characteristic of bureaucratic organization under Park was the centralization of economic policy formulation and implementation by the Economic Planning Board. The Board, staffed by well-trained, competent technocrats and headed by a Deputy Prime Minister who was directly accountable to the President, had the ultimate power to plan and execute economic policies. Centralism was viewed as necessary to facilitate speed and flexibility in decision making and implementation. If the effectiveness of state intervention is judged on the basis of how closely the targeted goals have been achieved, the South Korean case can be seen as a success. The South Korean planners in the earlier period were known to have a tendency to set output targets in over-ambitious, quantitative terms. Despite this practice, actual performance exceeded planned targets by substantial margins in all the plan periods from 1962 to 1986, except during the fourth plan period (1977–1981) when the economy encountered unusually adverse external and internal shocks.

The preceding discussion has related the primacy of the South Korean state to historical factors. We have argued that the state authority in South Korea has not been derived from linkages to a particular civilian base of support. The state has, on the contrary, determined the formation of class structure, creating alliances with particular classes as it sees necessary. The emergence in South Korea of a 'hard state' – one that is strongly committed to economic development and capable of implementing it – cannot, however, be viewed as a simple historical accident. The question remains: Why has statism, despite its many potential pitfalls, worked in East Asia? In accounting for the legitimacy of state authority, one must go beyond the historical process in the development of state capitalism in East Asia. The primacy of the state, in conjunction with a tenuous development of any competing social and political classes, has been embedded in the culture and tradition of East Asia during the entire phase of modernization.

In East Asian societies, the centuries-old teachings of Confucius have long served as the norms of social morality, influencing personal, familial and institutional relationships, and the system of governance. In South Korea, perhaps the most Confucian country in East Asia, Confucianism is a long-lived tradition, providing the overall terms of reference for social morality and order. Some of the main behavioural norms in South Korean society which reflect the Confucian influence include reverence for education and social harmony, respect for authority, ancestor worship, and emphasis on the importance of personal relationships and the family. A particularly important aspect of the Confucian ideology is reverence for a patrimonial social and political order with a strong emphasis on the family, the state and the ruler as the institutions of primary loyalty. At the political level, this has been used by the ruler as a useful ideological construct for legitimizing the status quo, or for strengthening the system of governance. From a historical perspective, ever since the adoption and promotion of Confucianism as the only court-sanctioned ideology during the five-century reign of the Yi Dynasty (1392–1910), it has put down deep roots in Korean society. The Japanese also continued to promote Confucianism during the colonial era.[27] The post-colonial authoritarian military regimes similarly recognized the value of Confucianism in supporting their perceived interests and officially promoted Confucian values. The ideology which inculcates the virtue of authority emanating from a vertical social order was seen as useful in legitimizing state intervention.

South Korea's Confucian cultural heritage facilitated the operation of the country's hierarchical bureaucracy. First of all, there is a cultural undercurrent which sanctions hierarchical organizational structures in society. The traditional value system inculcated by Confucianism underscores status and hierarchy in social relations. Second, in Confucianism the highest prestige is attached to scholar-bureaucrats. This has induced some of the most talented people to work for the government, which in turn ensured the relative quality of the South Korean bureaucracy. Traditionally in Korea, meritocratic examinations have been used to recruit the best minds into the state bureaucracy. As the military regimes gained autonomy from civil society, a meritocratic recruitment system targeting elite universities was used to build a bureaucracy with the competence to manage the process of industrial transformation.

Under the Confucian system, the business community is subservient to the rulers of the state; and the non-elite classes respect the guidance of the ruling elites. Thus, the concept of a horizontal social order is at odds with Confucian ethics which value 'the wisdom and moral ethics of the supreme ruler and ruling elite'.[28] This has made rule by a strong state easier and more acceptable to many people in East Asia. In the case of South Korea, the linguistic and cultural homogeneity in a territorially compact nation further facilitated the formation of a centralized polity. At the same time, because Confucianism has served historically as an ideological construct deployed by the ruler in response to changing needs, the concept of morality in its ideology has been fluid and evolving. None the less, South Koreans, by and large, have continued to retain the core values of Confucianism in their daily lives and the influence of the Confucian cultural context on South Korea's bureaucracy and system of governance remains evident.

## CONCLUSION: FROM NEO-MERCANTILISM TO GLOBALISM

The striking and persistent feature of the history of South Korea's industrial development has been the preservation of state authority *vis-à-vis* particular class interests. The legitimacy of state primacy in South Korea is embedded in its culture and historical legacy. The historical process which accorded the state a large degree of autonomy, free from the constraints of civil society, was critical to South Korea's industrial success. State autonomy, particularly in South Korea's earlier phases of industrialization, combined well with a competent technocratic and private-entrepreneurial infrastructure to pursue the national objective of industrial development.[29] From a historical perspective, the post-1945 South Korean model reflected a hard state capitalism. Perceiving the building of a modern industrial economy as the supreme national interest, the state, organized in the fashion of a corporate unit, intervened whenever this seemed to be in the national interest. The state pursued an essentially pragmatic and nationalist approach to industrial development, accommodating to market forces only when they worked. Thus, the market did not serve as an organizing principle of the economy. It was used as an instrument to facilitate the national goal towards industrial capital accumulation. Also, the private sector played an important role only because the state was willing to reward entrepreneurial risk. As Kim Jae Ik, a top economic adviser to President Chun, noted, 'Ultimately, it was the government that ignited high growth and put South Korea on the fast track.'[30] The *raison d'être* of statism has none the less been re-evaluated and redefined by the South Korean state as economic development evolves. The earlier policies that yielded rapid growth during the 1960s and 1970s sowed the seeds for the developmental state's decline. As the complexity and the size of the economy grows, an overextended state must be replaced by a more open and decentralized economic structure. At the same time, however, the political liberalization set in motion since the mid-1980s has brought with it the need to redefine the state's role; for instance, the new democracy in South Korea must provide a social safety net, both to safeguard the basic welfare of the working poor and the sustainability of the political and economic reform process itself.

On the external front, South Korea can no longer depend on the neo-mercantilist policies of the past, which protected the domestic market from imports while promoting exports via strategic intervention. The offensive forms of industrial policy have already shown their own limitations and internal contradictions; as domestic industries become sophisticated and internationally competitive, the intervention and market protection reach the point of diminishing returns, often resulting in liabilities rather than in benefits. Furthermore, past practice will not be acceptable as a strategy for viable globalization in the context of the new GATT-WTO system and strategic offensives by trade partners such as the United States. It is imperative that South Korea continues to pursue an open and market-conforming strategy for domestic adjustment in the context of globalization. The main challenge for the South Korean state, which is deeply ingrained in statist tradition, is thus to articulate an alternative restructuring strategy – one that will conform to the GATT rules of a multilateral, open trading system and at the same time will safeguard the international competitiveness of South Korean exports. While the South Korean economy, as it is fully integrated to global markets, needs less of the state, it will probably need more of the state in other contexts. The sustainability of the domestic economy and its capacity for integration with the global and regional economies will hinge on the success and the speed with which the proper roles of the state and markets are articulated. The situation, however, is complicated by the fact that the democratic process of policy formulation and implementation is taking place against the backdrop of a culture and tradition which have not been as conducive to political modernization as they have been to economic modernization.

## NOTES

* An earlier version of this article was presented at a Korean Economic Association seminar in Seoul. The author is indebted to Mark Berger for valuable comments and suggestions.

1 A free election was held in 1995 in which the candidates from the opposition parties won two-thirds of the seats they contested.
2 See, for instance, L. P. Jones and I. L. Sakong, *Government, Business, and Entrepreneurship in Economic Development: The Korean Case* (Cambridge, Mass.: Council on East Asian Studies, Harvard University Press, 1980), A. H. Amsden, *Asia's Next Giant: South Korea and Late Industrialization* (Oxford: Oxford University Press, 1989).
3 See for instance, B. Balassa, ed., *Development Strategies in Semi-industrial Economies* (Baltimore, Md.: Johns Hopkins University Press, 1982); C. R. Frank, Jr., K. S. Kim and L. Westphal, *Foreign Trade Regimes and Economic Development: South Korea* (New York: Columbia University Press, 1975); L. E. Westphal, 'Industrial Policy in an Export-Propelled Economy: Lessons from South Korea's Experience' *Journal of Economic Perspectives* vol. 4, no. 3, 1990, pp. 41–59.
4 See Kwan S. Kim, 'An Analysis of Economic Changes in Korea under Japanese Colonial Rule' in A. Nahm, ed., *Korea under Japanese Colonial Rule: Studies of the Policy and Techniques of Japanese Colonialism* (Kalamazoo: Western Michigan University Press, 1973), pp. 99–112.
5 Bruce Cumings, *The Two Koreas: On the Road to Reunification?* (New York: Foreign Policy Association, 1991), pp. 20–21.
6 The interest rates on time and savings deposits and loans (except export credits) almost doubled in 1965. As a result, the share of time and savings deposits in the rapidly expanding total loan funds of the banks increased from less than 20 per cent before 1965 to nearly half in 1971.
7 Enterprises in targeted industries were provided with subsidized loans, tax breaks and tariff exemptions. In the 1970s, for example, six target industries were selected in the context of developing the heavy and chemical sectors. By 1986, subsidies given to targeted enterprises were substantially reduced in amount, and were given a time limit of three years.
8 In passing, it must be noted that the practice of sector targeting, beginning in the fifth five-year plan during the 1980s, has been gradually phased out as the economy becomes increasingly sophisticated and complicated to manage. Except for the high-tech sector which continues to receive government support, measures that can benefit all indiscriminately are now being implemented.
9 General Park was concerned with the possibility of losing rural votes in the 1971 presidential election.
10 The Korean data for income distribution for the 1960s and 1970s are limited in sample size and exclude the extreme lower- and upper-income classes. This

makes the determination of the precise patterns of distribution difficult. Nevertheless, the available studies tend to indicate a slight deterioration in income distribution, with the exception of the mid-1970s when the overall distribution slightly improved, the income share of the lowest 40 per cent continued to decrease from 19.3% in 1965 to 15.5% in 1978. On the other hand, the share of the top 20 per cent rose from 41.8% to 45.3% over the same period with the overall Gini coefficient changing from 0.28 to 0.38. Poverty incidence (the percentage of the population considered as poor) was calculated at 7 per cent in 1988. See United Nations Development Programme, *Human Development Report 1991* (New York: Oxford University Press, 1991).

11  Government expenditure amounted to about 0.5% of GNP in 1990. In the 1960s it was a trivial amount.

12  Open leftist and lower-class movements virtually disappeared by the mid-1950s. See Bruce Cumings, 'The Origins and Development of the Northeast Asian Political Economy: Industrial Sectors, Product Cycles, and Political Consequences' *International Organization* vol. 38, no. 1, 1984, p. 41.

13  The Korean state has often been compared to the bureaucratic authoritarian state described in G. A. O'Donnell, *Modernization and Bureaucratic-Authoritarianism in South American Politics* (Berkeley: University of California Institute for International Studies, 1973).

14  See G. Henderson, 'Constitutional Changes from the First to the Sixth Republics: 1948–1987' in I. J. Kim and Y. W. Kihl, eds, *Political Changes in South Korea* ( New York: Paragon House, 1988), pp. 22–43.

15  An example of this was the 1971 Special Emergency Law enacted under the umbrella of a series of national security provisions: in a situation of emergency threatening national security, the settlement of labour disputes would automatically fall under the jurisdiction of the government-controlled labour tribunals. Open walk-outs would then be illegal and other forms of restrictions would be imposed on collective bargaining.

16  Note that the rate of change in labour's share of GDP reflects the difference between the rates of change in real wages and productivity.

17  Another important benefit from supporting big business was the political funds the President could count on from it.

18  The largest four conglomerates are Hyundai, Dae Woo, Samsung and Gumsung, which together recently accounted for close to 10 per cent of total exports. Furthermore, ten Korean conglomerates were listed in 1995 among the top 500 corporations in the world, excluding the United States, in *Fortune* vol. 132 (7 August 1995), p. F37.

19  In terms of output, the largest group of firms employing more than 500 people grew at an annual rate of 27.6% between 1967 and 1979 compared to 11.1% for the smallest units employing fewer than nine people. In Korea any establishments employing fewer than 500 people are considered as small or medium units.

20  John Lie, 'Democratization and Its Discontents: Origins of the Present Crisis in South Korea' *Monthly Review* vol. 42, no. 9, 1991, p.48.

21  The performance of the South Korean economy in 1992 was respectable but less than that planned by the government. The growth rate for the year was 4.8%, a big drop from the 8.4% recorded in 1991, although the trade deficit shrank to US$4.3 billion compared to $8.7 billion in 1991.

22  The *chaebôl* and labour are the two most influential interest groups. Both have demanded significant changes in economic policies, with their demands often diametrically opposed.

23  By 1990 social and welfare services accounted for close to 40% of the government budget, up from 25% in 1976. Under the Kim regime, specific policy

measures were expanded to include: the expansion of employment and educational opportunities, the development of small-scale firms, increased health care and the improvement of living conditions for low-income classes, the introduction of a national pension system, and the extension of national medical insurance.

24 In 1992 wages rose by 17.4%, which far exceeded the government's target of a 5% increase. The legendary Korean work ethic is also questionable as evidence shows that workers increasingly avoid so-called '3-D' (dirty, difficult and dangerous) jobs.

25 Foreign direct investment is still heavily screened and regulated by the government to protect indigenous industry. For example, the Korean government has a habit of intervening in the stock market to prevent violent price swings, and foreign investment is subject to the ceiling of 15% of a domestic company's shares as of May 1995.

26 One of the reasons that high-tech industries in South Korea expanded rapidly in the mid-1990s is aggressive research and development in the corporate sector with strong support and funding from the government. For instance, in September 1994 the Korean government pledged disbursement of $63 million over the next four years to accelerate localization of semiconductor facilities, also backing the advancement of application-specific integrated circuits.

27 N. Jacobs, *The Korean Road to Modernization and Development* (Urbana: University of Illinois Press, 1985), p. 242.

28 Richard Luedde-Neurath, 'State Intervention and Export-Oriented Development in South Korea' in Gordon White, ed., *Development States in East Asia* (New York: St Martin's Press, 1988), p. 98.

29 The argument made here is not to refute the critical role of private capital. On the contrary, without the effective collaboration of the high-quality entrepreneurial elite, Park's growth-oriented policy would not have succeeded.

30 *The Wall Street Journal* 3 May 1982.

# 4 The new Eurasian state: Russia, the forgotten Pacific player

*Douglas A. Borer*

## INTRODUCTION: RUSSIA, THE FORGOTTEN PACIFIC PLAYER

As of the middle of 1996, international focus on Russia remains centred on events emanating from the political theatre of Boris Yeltsin's troubled presidency, on the resurgence of communists in the December 1995 parliamentary elections, and on the volatile northern Caucasus (most notably Chechnya). Occasionally, when nuclear waste is dumped in the Sea of Japan, or when President Yeltsin rejects Japanese earthquake aid as a guileful 'political ploy' in the decades-long dispute over the future sovereignty of the northern Kurile Islands, Russia is momentarily remembered in the West as being a state on the Pacific Rim. In general, Russia is the only historically important great power in the Pacific that is not perceived as an integral actor in the euphoric visions of the Pacific Century. As the hapless successor to the now-discredited Soviet regime, Russia is viewed as being shackled by its marxist inheritance. Its greatest challenge is to transform a centralised economic system whose fundamental market characteristics and processes are the antithesis of those factors giving rise to the East Asian 'success story'. However, it is argued here that Russia's authoritarian political culture, and its attempts at economic restructuring, are similar to those of today's successful East Asian states. Authoritarianism, combined with capitalist economic reform directed by the state, are the two pillars upon which East Asian states have achieved economic prosperity. If East Asia is seen as a role model for successful economic modernization, these factors are likely to be promoted as crucial to Russia's own success in the Pacific Century.

This chapter attempts to forecast Russia's probable role in the coming era. To do so, a brief narrative of Russia's historic role in the Pacific region, Russia's evolution from dictatorial to democratic rule, and the politics of Boris Yeltsin are charted. Underpinning this narrative is an analysis of the crucial political structures which currently maintain Russia as a unified state, and the contrasting socio-cultural forces which threaten to destroy it. Of particular importance is a review of three key elements in contemporary Russian political culture: first, the enduring use of military force as a means of imposing state legitimacy; second, the complex mixture of democratic and autocratic tactics employed by Boris Yeltsin in the creation of the present Russian state – with special focus on the development of Russian federalism and centre–periphery relations; and third, a look at the possible ramifications of 'Eurasianism' as the emerging post-Cold War ideological consensus among Russian political elites.

A clearer understanding of Russia's probable role in the Pacific Century is important. Due to the greater security threats posed by neighbouring states in the West, the Pacific region has always been of secondary concern to leaders in Moscow. With the end of the Cold War, these traditional security concerns have been replaced by cooperation. Thus, as Russia attempts to rejoin the international economic community, its eastern regions will inevitably gain greater status in Moscow, as the centre of the global political economy shifts to the Pacific Basin. At present, Russia's war-making capabilities in Asia, though in decline, remain backed by substantial nuclear and conventional force capabilities. In the post-Soviet era, Russia is generally perceived as a low-risk security threat *vis-à-vis* its traditional opponents. However, today's relatively cordial relations remain tenuously grounded in the West's lasting support for and faith in the political virtues of President Boris Yeltsin. With Yeltsin in charge, Russia is seen in the West as relatively stable and non-threatening. However, serious ongoing questions regarding his health, and his hospitalization for heart trouble in both 1995 and 1996, remind us that Yeltsin will not endure for ever. What of Russia in the post-Yeltsin era? Will Russia go the way of Yugoslavia bereft of the strong unifying hand of Tito? Rising ethnic tensions and civil war in the post-Soviet states and the ongoing bloody civil war in Chechnya raise significant fears of ethnic conflict spreading throughout the former Soviet Union. An understanding of Russia's role in the coming Pacific Century can only be projected from a solid grasp of Russia's internal processes, structures and recent political dynamic.

## THE PAST: THE GEO-POLITICS OF PACIFIC EXPANSION AND CONTRACTION

Russia's eastern territories make up 60 per cent of the Russian Federation.[1] Thus Russia is both a European and an Asia-Pacific state. As noted by regional specialist Gerald Segal, Russia has been an important actor in the Pacific region for over three centuries, and it was the first European power to see its future as tied to both the West and the East:

Although Russia was by no means the first European power to reach the Pacific, it was the only one to come by land and was one of the few that attempted to build bridges of trade and politics across its waters. Russia may not have been a genuine East Asian power in the sense that its population was always weighted towards Europe, but it was certainly a genuine Pacific power in the sense that *it was one of the first to think Pacific*.[2]

Today's Russia originated in the crucible of violent struggle against an Asian power – Genghis Khan's, whose Golden Horde conquered the Slavic peoples in the mid-thirteenth century. Two hundred and fifty years later, forces originating from Moscow defeated the western outposts of the Mongol empire and began Russia's own counter-conquest of the east. Military victories were followed by colonization as the czars' subjects moved to fill the void left by the crumbling Mongol empire. Explorers established czarist rule on the Pacific in the mid-seventeenth century, with the first port settlement being established at Okhotsk in 1647. When this eastward expansion turned south, Russia entered into conflict with the Chinese in the Amur River basin.[3] In a historic precursor to the modern Soviet 'imperial overstretch', made famous in Paul Kennedy's landmark 1986 work, *The Rise and Fall of the Great Powers*, this early military advance against the Chinese was economically unsustainable.[4] Following military setbacks and faced with probable defeat, circumstances dictated that Russia sign the Treaty of Nerchinsk in 1689. China was recognized as sovereign over the Amur River basin, the existing Russian fortifications were destroyed, and Russian subjects retreated from the region. An early critical analysis of Russian policy in the region was provided in 1914 by historian F. A. Goulder:

> at no time was there a clear and far reaching policy; the officers at Moscow followed blindly whatever opening her lawless bands made instead of directing their actions. Not a single one of her leaders on the Amur showed high class statesmanship or capacity other than brute force. Not one of them could see farther into the future than the immediate acquisition of a pack of fur. Force which succeeded in Siberia was not in itself sufficient on the Amur.[5]

A north–south territorial status quo with the Chinese had been reached which would remain intact for the next 170 years; however, Russia's eastward expansion continued across the waters of the Pacific Ocean. During the reign of Peter the Great (1682–1725), Kamchatka was annexed and the historic quest for a Russian warm-water port was begun in the north Pacific. Under Elizabeth I (1741–1762) and Catherine the Great (1762–1796) Russian Pacific advances were galvanized by European great-power competition, especially by the growing British presence in China and by the Spanish in North America. By 1784, Russia had established settlements in Alaska. In 1804, Russia sent an expedition to Polynesia and Russian ships landed in Hawaii in 1809. In 1808, expeditions were sent to Oregon and California, and in 1812 Fort Russ (later corrupted to Fort Ross) was established near today's San Francisco.[6] However, Russia had again over-extended itself. These far-flung Pacific settlements showed that Moscow's desire to project power globally was far greater than its economic/logistic capability to sustain it. Furthermore, the czars' main interests remained focused on political events in the West, most notably Russia's primary role as the gendarme of the *ancien-régime* in post-revolutionary, post-Napoleonic Europe. Russian traders faced fierce competition from both British and American interests on the American West Coast. A shortage of naval power and financial capital following the Crimean War, and the evolution of more profitable investment, trade and territorial expansion opportunities in China, provided the impetus for Russia's slow withdrawal from its remote outposts across the Pacific Ocean. In 1867, Russia's only attempt at establishing overseas colonies ended with the sale of Alaska to the United States.[7]

In the mid 1840s, Russia had begun shifting its focus from North America to China, and its military forces began infringing on Chinese territory in the Amur basin. Russia, like the rest of Europe's major imperial powers, was bent on exploiting internal Chinese weakness and extracting maximum benefits from Beijing. Russia's involvement in the 'carving of China' was formalized by the Aigun Treaty (1858) and the Beijing Treaty (1860) in which China ceded the territory now consisting of portions of the Amur Oblast, the Khaborovsk Region and the Maritime Region administrative divisions of the Russian Federation. Russia also pursued an aggressive 'railroad diplomacy' in which treaty provisions regarding the Russian-built Chinese Eastern Railway were utilized to give Moscow *de facto* administrative control over much of Manchuria.[8]

Russia's great-power status in the Pacific was severely challenged by competition with Japan over Manchuria, resulting in military defeat in the Russo–Japanese War (1904–1905). Russia's defeat marked the beginning of Japan's rise in modern great-power politics. Under the terms of the 1905 Treaty of Portsmouth, Russia gave up Liodong and Port Arthur and control over the southern railways in China and southern Sakhalin.[9] During the Bolshevik revolution and subsequent Russian Civil War (1918–1922), Japan was the only allied interventionist power openly intent on expanding its territory at the expense of Russia's internal instability.[10] Only under intense international pressure from the United States and looming conflict with Trotsky's Red Army did Japan grudgingly withdraw its troops from Soviet territory. These actions firmly entrenched a negative view of Tokyo in the minds of the new Bolshevik leadership, helping to magnify further a xenophobic perception that security was only maintained by autarky backed by force of arms. In the 1990s, Russia's relative intransigence over the Kurile Islands, seized from Japan at the end of World War II, must be seen as a product of a long historical record of conflict and territorial conquest among the states of the North Pacific region.

During the Soviet period, efforts were made to develop the Pacific region further. From the time of the Civil War, Moscow's primary concerns in the east were military and strategic. Generally speaking, following Japanese and American occupation from 1918 to 1920, the Soviets were haunted by the thought of having to fight simultaneously in both Europe and Asia. Thus, Soviet efforts to develop infrastructure and industry, and to exploit the vast resources in the East, were driven primarily by security concerns. During World War II, the Soviets were careful to maintain a non-conflictual stance towards Japan. At the end of the war in Europe, Stalin agreed to declare war, but only after it was clear that Japanese military forces could no longer directly threaten Soviet territory, and that Soviet power could be extended in the Northern Pacific by aiding in Japan's final demise. During the Cold War, North Asia was an important theatre of operations against America's allies; however, the Soviet state was never under direct military threat until the early 1960s. The Sino-Soviet split further inspired the militarization of Soviet Asia, but domestic industrial and infrastructure developments remained hindered by the vast distances, inclement weather and sparse labour pool that had also plagued the czars.

## BEYOND *KTO KOVO*: FROM LENIN TO THE END OF HISTORY

Despite egalitarian rhetoric, the Bolsheviks exhibited many traits common to their czarist predecessors. One of the most enduring was the crucial role played by military force and police violence to maintain the power of the ruling elite, to defend the state from outside aggression, and to ensure Moscow's sovereignty over territories conquered by the czars. Soviet policies, both external and internal, were based on Lenin's stark zero-sum world view of the nature of politics. According to Sovietologist Walter Clemens:

> Lenin taught that the fundamental quest of politics is 'Kto kovo' – [meaning] Who, whom? Which side will destroy the other? Armed with this view, he and his successors built a system that could seize and hold power but not one that interacts optimally with other states and systems or even with its own subjects.[11]

The use of military force and the application of coercive state power was the primary foundation of the new regime. Force enabled the Bolsheviks originally to seize power at the Second All-Russian Congress of Soviets in October 1917, and heavily armed Red Guards later disbanded the Constituent Assembly, following the Bolsheviks poor showing in the November 1917 free election. Clearly, Lenin's *kto kovo* (who will conquer whom) ethic applied to dealings not only with the czarist regime, but also with other revolutionary parties that might challenge the Bolsheviks' dictatorial power. An almost pure expression of Lenin's *kto kovo* thinking reached its peak during Stalin's reign of terror, when all challengers (real, potential and imagined) within the ranks of the Party, the army or the populace were systematically exiled, imprisoned or shot. However, even following Stalin's death in 1953, domestic political order remained dependent on the use of coercive force to repress dissenting elements in Soviet society (albeit in a less totalitarian form than during Stalin's regime). In Soviet foreign policy, the *kto kovo* ethic became fused with crucial ideological policy statements such as the Brezhnev Doctrine.[12]

It would be a terrible mistake, then, to underemphasize the pervasive importance of coercive state violence in both Russian and Soviet political history. Coercive force had maintained the czars in absolute power for over six hundred years; aggressive military force had created the Russian empire and allowed it to expand across Central Asia and the Pacific. Defeat at the hands of a stronger military power (Germany) had helped to unleash a civil upheaval that witnessed the triumph of the faction which most ruthlessly organized and used coercive force – the Bolsheviks. The Red Army under Trotsky ensured the survival of the Soviet state by defeating the White Armies during the Civil War. Massive state violence was effectively utilized by Stalin to industrialize the country rapidly and forcibly. Military force had proved to be the only effective tool for protecting the state from outside threats during World War II; and force had been effective in expanding and maintaining the Soviet sphere of influence during both World War II and the Cold War – as witnessed by the military occupation of the Baltic states and Eastern Europe, and by the direct Soviet invasions of Hungary in 1956, Czechoslovakia in 1968, and Afghanistan in 1979.

The crucial importance of repressive means of control for the survival of the Soviet regime is perhaps best illustrated by the fact that the collapse of the Soviet empire in Eastern Europe and the destruction of the Soviet state itself were direct results of Gorbachev's policy reforms, which fundamentally rejected Lenin's *kto kovo* ethic. The end of the Soviet empire would not have occurred in 1989–1991 without the rejection of the use of force as enshrined within Gorbachev's *glasnost* (openness) and *perestroika* (restructuring) policies. In 1989, the Brezhnev Doctrine, the ideological linchpin justifying military occupation throughout the Soviet sphere, was unmistakably revoked when Soviet soldiers completed their withdrawal from Afghanistan and when Solidarity candidates in Poland were allowed to run for office and remain victorious in parliamentary elections. These events initiated a domino effect that rapidly swept through the Eastern bloc and culminated in the destruction of the USSR in December 1991. Once Gorbachev broke the ideological constructs of the 'Socialist Commonwealth' and renounced the use of force to maintain Communist Party dictatorship, there was nothing to hold the old regime together. The end of force resulted in the end of empire and the end of union.[13]

According to Francis Fukuyama, Gorbachev's recognition of the failures of the 'Leninist Experiment', his reform policies of *perestroika* and *glasnost*, and the final breakdown of the 'Socialist Commonwealth' were indicators of the 'end point of mankind's ideological evolution and the universaliz-ation of Western liberal democracy as the final form of human govern-ment'. Fukuyama emphasised that the liberal 'victory' was still unfinished globally, and that victory had occurred mainly 'in the realm of ideas or consciousness'. He believed that the process was 'as yet incomplete in the real or material world'.[14] However, in commenting on communism and the USSR itself, Fukuyama would write:

> In retrospect, Walt Rostow's much-maligned characterization of com-munism as a 'disease of the transition [to mature development]' seems quite accurate: however monstrous in other ways, communism was a per-fectly adequate *economic* system for making the leap from an agrarian to an urban-industrial society, but it proved itself unable to meet the requirements of post-industrial modernity, and therefore had to be tran-scended or abolished.[15]

At first glance, in the period from 1990 to 1993, Fukuyama's vision of the 'end of history' seemed to be confirmed in Russia by multiple events. The free election of President Boris Yeltsin appeared to be proof that commun-ism was being actively 'transcended' and 'abolished' and was being replaced by democracy. Proof was also manifest in Yeltsin's successful battle against the neo-Stalinist coup and his leadership role in dissolving the USSR in 1991, in his implementation of capitalist-inspired and World Bank-guided economic reforms in 1992, and even in his October 1993 use of military force to purge the 'disease' of communism lingering in the Russian Parliament. However, questions remain regarding the viability, vitality and long-term prospects for both capitalism and democracy co-existing peacefully in post-Soviet Russia.

## YELTSIN'S AUTHORITARIAN DEMOCRACY

Since the beginning of 1992, Russia's future as a unified state has rested primarily in the complicated and controversial actions of its first and only democratically elected President, Boris Yeltsin. Yeltsin is a political sur-vivor, characterized by his ability to achieve goals through both democratic and autocratic means. The political quagmire that gave rise to Yeltsin's political dominance began with the election of the Russian Federation's Supreme Soviet in March 1990. This relatively free and open election was the second during Gorbachev's reform period in which non-communist parties could put forward candidates, and both communists and non-communists (representing a range of ideas) were elected. In addition, the post of President of the Russian Federation was created as the result of a popular referendum. Of crucial importance, however, was the fact that the referendum failed not only to define the powers of the office clearly, but also to differentiate clearly between the powers of the President and those of the Russian Parliament. In June 1991, still under the Soviet regime, Yeltsin became the first and only freely elected President in Russian history. Thus, at the birth of the first post-Soviet Russian state, the institutional structures of power were an incongruous mixture of old and new. The Parliament (the Russian Republic's Supreme Soviet) had its legal base in the now defunct 1978 Soviet constitution; however, its members had been freely elected – and the presidency had been created *extra-constitutionally* as a result of a democratic referendum, but with Yeltsin having achieved a broad mandate as Russia's most popular freely elected leader.[16]

Initially, because of his popular heroics in facing down the plotters, Yeltsin had the support of a majority of parliamentarians from across the political spectrum, and he quickly acted to increase his power. Soon after the coup, he requested and was granted from Parliament the temporary right to pursue economic reform through decree. In addition, power was granted to Yeltsin by Parliament to appoint and dismiss heads of the regional administration, thus giving him direct leverage within Russia's regional governments, with the stated intent of appointing leaders who would rapidly implement his economic reform policies.[17]

However, disagreement over economic 'shock therapy' proposals quickly ended the post-Soviet honeymoon between Yeltsin and a growing body of critics.[18] By 1993, the battle between Yeltsin and his parliamentary opponents had become so acrimonious that the Russian economy and government had largely ceased to function. Yeltsin, having been granted temporary power by the Parliament to rule the economy, later refused to acknowledge Parliament's sovereignty. As a result, the decisive issue in the struggle for power essentially boiled down to the final drafting of and voting on a new constitution for the Russian Federation. All sides in the conflict agreed that a new document was necessary to break the political deadlock over economic policy; however, the design of the new government was a highly contentious issue, with Yeltsin promoting a stronger executive, and various factions in the Parliament supporting a stronger legislature. Both sides became increasingly less willing to compromise as time went on.[19]

On 21 September 1993 Yeltsin acted unilaterally and ordered Parliament to be dissolved. When the Russian Constitutional Court declared that Yeltsin had violated the Soviet-era constitution, and when Parliament members refused to concede to presidential authority, a tense two-week stand-off ensued, during which Parliament impeached the President and set up a dual government at the Russian White House. Heavily armed opponents of Yeltsin seized the Ostankino television station, killing a number of unarmed people in the process. This act gave Yeltsin a convenient pretext for eliminating his political enemies. After receiving statements of support from various parts of the government, some regional leaders, the central bank and most importantly, the armed forces and Interior Ministry, Yeltsin forcibly terminated the stand-off by blasting the White House with tank fire on 4 October. Lenin's *kto kovo* ethic had returned to Russian politics after its brief hiatus during Gorbachev's final years in power.[20]

In December 1993 elections were held for the new State Duma, and the President's version of the new constitution was adopted by a majority of voters.[21] Despite his ability to dictate the structures of state power as stipulated in the new constitution, Yeltsin could not control the electorate. For instance, in the Pacific region three governors (who had been removed by Yeltsin because of their support for his opponent, Vice-President Rutskoi), Yevgeny Nazdratenko (Governor of the Maritime Region), Viktor Ishaev (Governor of the Khabarovsk Region) and Mikhail Nikolaev (Governor of the Sakha Republic) were elected to the new upper house of the State Duma (designated as the Federation Council). Likewise, many of Yeltsin's strongest supporters in the old Parliament, mainly those representing the more radical free-market and liberal-democratic beliefs, were not re-elected to the new Duma. Clearly Yeltsin had achieved a paradoxical victory: the new constitution that increased his own power was approved by the voters; however, the new Parliament was dominated by freely elected delegates who had successfully campaigned on various anti-Yeltsin, anti-Gaidar, anti-reform themes. In the President's favour, no single party or coalition was strong enough to dictate legislation entirely, and Yeltsin can veto any legislation, but the anti-Yeltsin forces definitely held the balance of power and dominated the legislative agenda.[22] The economic problems that gave rise to Yeltsin's new opponents in 1993 had not abated by April 1995 when the Russian Labour Ministry reported that from 30 to 40 per cent of Russians earned less than the minimum subsistence level and that the number of Russians below the poverty line was steadily increasing.[23]

In keeping with his pattern of making and abandoning politically expedient alliances, Yeltsin dropped the unpopular Gaidar as Prime Minister and distanced himself from his now emasculated democratic allies in the new Parliament. However, the growing separation of a more authoritarian Yeltsin from the democratic reformers was mutually reinforcing following his decison to use massive military force to impose central control in the breakaway Republic of Chechnya. As a result of the indiscriminate violence and large numbers of civilian casualties and refugees, many of Yeltsin's long-time supporters in the Parliament, namely the liberal Democratic Russia and Russia's Choice factions, denounced the attack and stated that they would not support Yeltsin in the 1996 presidential election.[24] Politically, the Chechen civil war has had a much greater impact in Moscow than any one could have expected, and the greatest political 'loser' has been President Yeltsin. Among the general public the war has been very unpopular, and the military intervention had the exact opposite of the planned effect on Yeltsin's popularity – which plummeted. However, within the government, the hard-liners who promoted resolving the crisis by crushing the Chechens militarily, gained significant new influence with the President, while moderates and liberals were marginalized.[25]

As the election approached Yeltsin reached out for financial support from the business and industrial elite who had benefited most from his reforms. Although campaigning laws limited spending to US$10 million/candidate, no enforcement mechanisms were in place and most observers agree that Yeltsin spent at least US$100 million in the re-election effort.[26] The President utilized to his great advantage the significant state bureaucratic controls over the Russian media to blanket Russia with pro-Yeltsin campaign messages and to hinder the media access of his opponents. Yeltsin also signed a widely publicized cease fire with the Chechen leadership whose ground forces had been decimated by heavy military assaults and who were politically fractured following the death of their charismatic leader Dzhokhar Dudaev at the hands of a well aimed Russian artillery barrage. One of his most effective campaign tactics was to use the decree powers of the 1993 constitution – in effect Yeltsin turned the Federal Treasury into a personal campaign slush fund, making literally billions of dollars in government pledges to local constituencies during his nationwide campaign.[27]

Only hours after results of the first round of the election had been tabulated, indicating the President had won a narrow plurality of 35 per cent of the vote and that he would face the Communist candidate Zyuganov in the second round, came one of Yeltsin's most important end-game tactical manoeuvers. The Kremlin announced that ex-general Alexander Lebed, the third place finisher with 14.7 per cent of the vote, had been appointed by Yeltsin to head the National Security Council. To solidify Lebed's support in the second round of the election Yeltsin then proceeded to fire the inner-circle of hard-line advisors which had vocally promoted the bloody Chechen intervention. By these adroit tactical moves Yeltsin effectively neutralized the possible merger of Lebed's nationalists and the communists while simultaneously giving the democratic reformers a reason to vote for him. In the second round Yeltsin's momentum became unstoppable, on 3 July he soundly defeated Zyuganov by a margin of 54 per cent to 40 per cent.[28] Russia had freely re-elected its first post-Soviet President, showing that the new order is possibly more stable than many had imagined. Caution is warranted for any liberal democratic-enthusiasts. If recent history is any guide, Yeltsin's apparent swing back to the liberal direction between the first and second rounds of voting may be temporary. However, Yeltsin has defied prediction in the past and may also choose to use the early post-electoral period to push forward economic and political reforms. Whatever path he chooses, the country is still faced with the same potentially explosive economic and social problems that gave rise to the remarkable resurgence of the communists in 1995–96.

## EURASIANISM: THE 'RUSSIAN WAY' IN THE PACIFIC CENTURY

A mixture of autocratic and democratic characteristics is a prevalent leadership attribute in Asia. With the exception of Japan (whose present governing structure was dictated by US military rule from 1945 to 1952), military intervention in domestic politics is one widely shared characteristic in post-1945 Asian politics. In capitals from Beijing to Djakarta, coercive police power has been and continues to be used (in varying degrees) to control politics, to stifle opposition, and to manage elections. Even Francis Fukuyama seems to question his own 'end of history' thesis by conceding that there is the possibility of an 'Asian alternative' that might invalidate the link between economic development and Western-style democracy as postulated by modernization theory. According to Fukuyama, there may now exist an 'Asian way' of political development which combines 'soft' authoritarianism, limited democracy and advanced capitalism.[29]

In Russia, a similar process is also clearly at work. There is an emerging consensus among many Russian elites that the state must follow its own 'Eurasian' form of political development, or what can be described as the 'Russian way.' Russia's policy-making circles have been characterized by discord, and they mirror post-Cold War soul-searching in the United States by those seeking a new foreign policy *raison d'être* to replace containment. After 1991, Russian policy intellectuals began searching for a philosophical rationale to explain their role in the new world order, with emphasis on a 'special' responsibility for the 'near abroad' states of the post-USSR space. 'Eurasian' thinking began to coalesce in 1992 as a mixture of traditional Russian romantic-nationalist perceptions of a shared Slavic ethnic history, culture and experience, juxtaposed with geo-political concerns over Russia's sphere of influence and security.

Contemporary Eurasianism is rooted in a version of the concept which was first developed in the 1920s by Nikolai Trubetskoy, Pyotr Savitsky and Georgy Vernadsky. According to one of today's leading Eurasianist scholars, Lev Gumilyov, these authors stressed that: 'the territory of the former Russian Empire or USSR is a specific historical and geographical universe, belonging neither to Europe nor to Asia, being a specific unique phenomenon.' Trubetskoy declared, 'I deny any possibility of a universal human culture'. Gumilyov explains that in the post-Soviet era,

[a] universal human culture equal to any ethnos is impossible as every ethnos has [a] different encompassing and [a] different past forming their present both in time and space. The culture of every ethnos is specific and this mosaic nature of humans as specimen gives them [the] adaptivity due to which *Homo Sapiens* have survived on Earth.[30]

In 1993, the Russian press began publishing reviews of the writings of early Eurasian scholars; for example, the right-wing publication *Den* reprinted portions of B. Y. Vladimirtsov's 1922 essay, which stressed the major impact that Genghis Khan had on Russian development. Vladimirtsov claimed, 'Russia will be transformed only when it realizes that its sun really does rise in the east and not the other way around.' The *Den* reporter Brontoi Bedyurov concluded that for Russians in the post-Soviet period:

> *We are indeed an integral state-political and cultural-historical continent, a distinctive Eurasian cosmos. We are neither Europe nor Asia; we are both of them together.* . . . . We are fated to be joined together in world history, to exist in pan-Eurasian symbiosis in one combination or other.[31]

Other variations on this theme are also pervasive. Probably the best-known author who can be included in the 'Russian way' school is Nobel Prize winner Alexander Solzhenitsyn. Solzhenitsyn has long been known for his anti-modernist, romantic-nationalist views of Russia. In 1990 and 1991, he began denouncing the pro-Western, democratic elements in Russian society and urged Russians to seek spiritual clarity, claiming that free elections and multi-party politics were negative forces which harmed the organic Russian polity. Differing from other romantic-nationalists, however, Solzhenitsyn actually supported the separatist claims of ethnic groups in predominantly non-Russian areas such as Chechnya and outer Kazakhstan. He proposed the limited redrawing of some borders to fit ethnic populations. However, Solzhenitsyn alarmed Ukrainian and Belarussian nationalists by denying that they were ethnically different from Russians, and he called for the territorial reunification of Russia, Ukraine, Belarus, and those large sections of Kazakhstan populated by Russians.[32]

Yeltsin and his advisers display a sometimes contradictory mixture of 'Western-liberal', 'nationalist' and 'Eurasian' political characteristics, initially expressing a more liberal approach, but with the conservative elements of nationalism and Eurasianism becoming more prominent over time. Vladimir Lukin, Chairman of the Duma Foreign Affairs Committee, recently stated that Russia may take the 'Central Asian' path of using referendums to extend presidential terms, deferring parliamentary elections and restricting civil rights.[33] In Russian foreign policy, the Eurasianist claim that Russia has a special geo-political role to play in the post-Soviet space is now shared by a wide spectrum of elites. Even Russia's Foreign Minister, Andrei Kozyrev, often under attack as a 'Western lackey' by critics for his openly pro-European, pro-US policies, moved closer to the Eurasian/nationalist position before his dismissal in early 1996. While stopping far short of Vladimir Zhirinovsky's aggressive calls for a new Russian empire, Kozyrev made numerous public statements in March and April 1995 reiterating that Russia had the right to use military force to protect Russians living in the 'near abroad', and he was sharply critical of NATO plans for expansion into Eastern Europe.[34]

Perhaps the most accurate early vision of Russia's evolving Eurasian path to development in the coming Pacific Century was expressed in April

1992 by Sergei Stankevich, one of Yeltsin's advisers. Stankevich saw the evolution of two coexisting trends, Alanticism and Eurasianism:

Today's Russia cannot escape the combination of old and new realities. For example there is no escaping the fact we are now separated from Europe by a whole chain of independent states. We have moved farther away from it geographically and geopolitically, which will inevitably entail a rather significant redistribution of our resources, our possibilities and ties and our interests in favor of Asia, in an eastward direction. In addition, the development of the domestic political situation in Russia, which will unavoidably have an effect on foreign policy, is also pushing us toward this.[35]

With the majority of political elites from both the left and right accepting the basic vision of Eurasianism, Russia's future presence as an Asia-Pacific actor remains certain. Having been a political culture controlled through coercive state violence under both the czars and the communists, now a society that is experimenting with legal, constitutional and democratic forms of legitimacy, Russian civic society in the later 1990s remains in a state of unstable transition. Boris Yeltsin's attacks on Parliament in 1993 and on Chechnya in 1994 are perhaps Russia's version of China's Tiananmen Square. Political opposition will be tolerated to a degree, but when the state reacts to perceived challenges to its sovereignty, it may still do so with deadly force reminiscent of the past.

Whether or not a neo-authoritarian, neo-democratic Russia will actually achieve economic prosperity similar to East Asia's is an unfathomable question. If neo-imperial politicians gain power and attempt to control and/or dictate regional politics to a degree that is beyond Russia's economic means to sustain, they will be repeating the mistakes of the czars and communists, and failure is the likely outcome. However, if Russia does not overextend itself, and it focuses its energy on both political stability and economic revival, it may be able to emulate its East Asian neighbours. According to retired army general, presidential candidate, and outspoken Yeltsin critic Alexander Lebed, Russia has yet to abandon its traditional political culture and historic ambitions:

We don't have any democracy because Russia's mentality remains imperial. Pre-revolutionary czars were replaced by post-revolutionary ones, like Gorbachev and Yeltsin. Nothing has changed, and now we are trying to leap from totalitarianism to democracy. It doesn't work, there must be a transition period.[36]

Lebed's views on political, economic, military and foreign policy issues are authoritarian-statist and hard-line nationalist. He was Russia's most popular politician in 1995, and at the beginning of 1996 he was seen as one possible successor to Yeltsin as President. Lebed speaks of his admiration for one of the countries often described as Latin America's version of Asia's 'tigers' – Chile under General Augusto Pinochet:

> during his 16 years in power he killed 3,500 people. We kill more in a single day. But Pinochet's so-called bloody regime lifted Chile from the ruins, forced everybody to work, revived the economy, restored a feeling of ownership among the people and then legally turned power over to a civilian government.[37]

Lebed has criticized Yeltsin, especially over his military intervention in Chechnya. However, his criticism is focused on what he perceives as lack of competence and effective leadership by Yeltsin, not on the civil or human rights of the population. It is also clear that Lebed's views on the use of state violence to maintain order are even more traditional than Yeltsin's, and none of Yeltsin's potential successors, whether nationalists or communists, are different in this regard. Over the years many of Yeltsin's previous supporters in the West and in Russia have grown alarmed by his apparent evolution from democratic hero to neo-czar. However, as the year 2000 approaches, a mixture of autocratic and democratic characteristics constitutes the prevalent leadership attributes in Asia. Yeltsin and the conservative Eurasianists have clearly grafted the politics of the 'Russian way', more from their Asian-authoritarian than European-liberal roots.


## CONCLUSION: THE NEW EURASIAN STATE

As Asian economies grow and compete for dwindling supplies of global resources, Russia's place in the Pacific Century, first as a source of raw materials, energy and weapons, and later as a market for goods and venture capital seems assured. For instance, in 1994 Russia and Western oil companies signed a hydrocarbon development project for the Sakhalin Oblast worth an estimated US$15 billion. Located only 50 miles north of Japanese territory, its attractiveness to international oil companies is enhanced by its overall geographic accessibility and proximity to the Japanese and other East Asian markets.[38] Despite economic statistics showing that overall industrial output has declined by approximately 50 per cent during Yeltsin's presidency, from 1992 to 1994 the export of raw materials from the Russian east has increased significantly, ranging from a 24 per cent increase in natural gas, to a 180 per cent in copper, and an astounding 303 per cent in newsprint.[39] According to Demosthenes Peterson,

> a large share of Russia's primary products output now has been diverted from domestic to global markets, a trend that strengthened in 1994. . . . In sum, what is taking place is a realignment of the Russian economy away from manufacturing toward the increasing dominance of the service sector, agriculture, and natural resources development, and this is being facilitated by greater integration into the world economy.[40]

Due to its geographical isolation from European Russia, and to a lack of financial support and political interest from Moscow, the Russian Far East has been the region most dramatically affected by market forces and integration into the global economy. Since 1992 Russia's international trade has shifted significantly away from the former Soviet bloc, which cannot afford to pay market prices for Russian commodities, towards the dynamic economies of Asia, namely China, South Korea and Taiwan, which can pay with hard currency.[41]

Russian trade officials have increasingly turned their attention to the importance of looking east as a source of economic revival. Shortly before attending the second general session of the Pacific Economic Co-operation Council in Beijing in September 1995, Oleg Davydov, Deputy Prime Minister for Foreign Economic Relations, told a Moscow news conference that Russia's strategic priority for the next decade would be to widen business cooperation with Asia-Pacific countries. According to Davydov, 'Moscow's turn to the Asian Pacific region is dictated by its firm conviction that the center of world trade in the 21st century will move to this region, which already accounts for 40 per cent of global turnover'. Russia hopes that massive capital investments in Siberia and the Russian Far East will follow upon closer business ties with China, Japan and South Korea. Russia has indicated interest in creating a free trade zone in the region and Moscow hopes to join the Asia Pacific Economic Cooperation organization in 1996, when the moratorium on admission of new members expires. Russia's trade with Asia-Pacific countries now exceeds $20 billion, or more than a quarter of its total foreign trade turnover.[42]

In March 1996, a Russian delegation headed by Arkady Volsky, a leading industrialist, presented to Japanese business leaders in Tokyo a long-range programme of development for the Russian Far East. The major goals of Volsky's plan, which is to unfold in three stages between 1996 and 2005, are to hold down the region's energy and transportation prices, to develop export-oriented industries, and to integrate the Russian Far East into the world economy. Special attention is also to be given to re-orienting Russian machine-building and defence enterprises. The total cost of the programme was estimated at 371 trillion roubles (over $70 billion), of which the Russian government is expected to contribute only a small portion, the balance being supplied by Asian (primarily Japanese) investors.[43]

Also in March 1996 Oleg Davydov announced that the Kremlin had designated markets in the Asia-Pacific region as a priority target for Russian exporters and that Moscow's emphasis would be on promoting 'engineering and research-intensive products'. Davydov suggested that the Russian government would be more active in offering assistance to promote trade and economic cooperation with Asia-Pacific countries, including implementing large-scale investment projects, technical exchanges and co-production arrangements. Davydov identified China as Russia's main strategic partner in the region.[44]

The vast majority of Russia's natural resource base is located east of the Urals. Thus, from a Russian perspective, there are distinct advantages in turning away from Europe and towards the Asia-Pacific. Divergent levels of economic development and differing economic structures are the norm in the region's diverse national economies. This diversification contributes to economic growth as each country performs functions in the regional economy best suited to its existing development, but with the prospect of achieving growth, modernization and development through trade, investment and technology transfer.[45]

However, the process will not be an easy one. Potentially explosive political restraints, such as territorial claims on the Amur River basin and Kurile Islands, remain as historic reminders of Russia's long competition in the region with China and Japan.[46] Furthermore, the immutable realities of the region's geographic isolation and inclement weather increase the costs and decrease the rewards of foreign and internal investment. As shown recently by a report from Kamchatka, the people of the Pacific regions of Russia are increasingly dissatisfied with Moscow's unreliable interest; residents described themselves as the 'Chechnya of the Far East' because of the enormous destruction that earthquakes and other disasters have visited upon them and because of the failure of Moscow to help. As a result, the residents, citing high costs, have refused to send local ships to European Russia via the Arctic Sea route, suggesting that the most reasonable shipping links are 'not with Russia but with America'.[47] Residents have also shown their dissatisfaction with Moscow at the ballot box. In December 1995, in the Maritime Region in the Far East, the strong-willed incumbent, Yevgeny Nazdratenko, won election as Governor with over 60 per cent of the vote. This popular mandate has strengthened Nazdratenko's hand in his continuing struggle with Moscow for greater autonomy for his region, which is increasingly looking away from Moscow and towards markets on the Pacific Rim.[48]

In the near future, post-Yeltsin Russia will come, as a result of either his failing health, or constitutional term limits. Regardless of what precipitates the transition, history will show that Yeltsin was successful in establishing the constitutional foundations of the new Russian state and the rudimentary beginnings of a new Russian political economy, and that he has most probably charted the leadership model for the future – a combination of tradition and modernity, both autocracy and democracy. If in the future Russia is rebuffed when looking West, it will be better received by a less critical, less liberal East. Russia may be a forgotten Pacific player in the international power game as perceived in the West. However, as time goes on, it becomes increasingly apparent that Russia will play an important economic role in the Asia-Pacific, and that it will painfully chart its own unique path into the Pacific Century.

## NOTES

1 Gerald Segal, *The Soviet Union and the Pacific* (London: Royal Institute of International Affairs, 1990), pp. 5–8. If separated from Russia, this region would still be the largest state in the world (approximately 6 million square miles). However, if defined as only the Far East administrative area, it would make up 29 per cent of the nation's territory with 8 million inhabitants. See Allan Rodgers, ed., *The Soviet Far East: Geographic Perspectives on Development* (New York: Routledge, 1990), pp. 1–4.
2 Segal, *The Soviet Union and the Pacific*, pp. 15–16 (emphasis added).
3 ibid., pp. 16–17.
4 Paul Kennedy, *The Rise and Fall of the Great Powers* (New York: Random House, 1987).
5 F. A. Goulder, *Russian Expansion on the Pacific 1641–1850*, 1960, p. 65. For a copy of the treaty in both the original French and with an English translation, see Appendix C.
6 Benson Bobrick, *East of the Sun: The Epic Conquest and Tragic History of Siberia* (New York: Poseidon Press, 1992), pp. 211–242.
7 Gary Hausladen, 'Settling the Far East: Russian Conquest and Consolidation' in A. Rodgers, *The Soviet Far East: Geographic Perspectives on Development*, p. 8. See also Segal, *The Soviet Union and the Pacific*, p. 17–20; Bobrick, *East of the Sun*, pp. 242–266.
8 Peter S. H. Tang, 'Sino-Soviet Border Regions: Their Changing Character' in Kurt London, ed., *Unity and Contradiction: Major Aspects of Sino-Soviet Relations* (New York: Praeger, 1962), p. 268.
9 Segal, *The Soviet Union and the Pacific*, pp. 23–24.
10 Japan was interested in carving up Russia's holdings in North Asia, while the United States and other allied states intervened with the intent of installing the White Russian generals who supported re-establishing the eastern front against Germany. See George F. Kennan, *The Decision to Intervene* (Princeton, NJ: Princeton University Press, 1961).
11 Walter C. Clemens, Jr., *Can Russia Change: The USSR Confronts Global Interdependence* (Boston, Mass.: Unwin Hyman, 1990), p. xix.
12 Douglas A. Borer, 'The Afghan War: Communism's First Domino' *War and Society* vol. 12, no. 2, 1994, pp. 128–130.
13 ibid., pp. 130–142.
14 Francis Fukuyama, 'The End of History?' *The National Interest* vol. 16, no. 8, 1989, pp. 3–4, 15. See also Francis Fukuyama, *The End of History and the Last Man* (London: Hamish Hamilton, 1992).
15 Francis Fukuyama, 'Capitalism and Democracy: The Missing Link' *Journal of Democracy* vol. 3, no. 3, 1992, p. 104 (emphasis in original).
16 Renee De Nevers, *Russia's Strategic Renovation* Adelphi Paper 289, July 1994, pp. 8–10.
17 *Foreign Broadcast Information Service, Daily Report* FBIS-SOV-91-203, 21 October 1991, p. 60. Hereafter cited as *FBIS*.
18 De Nevers, *Russia's Strategic Renovation*, pp. 11–12.
19 ibid., pp. 10–14.
20 For statements supporting Yeltsin, see the following stories in *Current Digest of the Post-Soviet Press (CDPSP)* vol. 45, no. 38, 1993, pp. 8–9: *Rossiiskiye Vesti* 23 September 1993. *Pravda* 23 September 1993; *Sevodnya* 23 September 1993; *Megapolis-Express* 29 September 1993. The official death toll in the attack on the White House was forty-six. Many eyewitnesses estimate that several hundred were killed. See Jonathan Steele, *Eternal Russia: Yeltsin, Gorbachev and the Mirage of Democracy* (London: Faber & Faber, 1994), p. 382.

21 Lev Bruni and Pyotr Zhuravlyov, 'A New Duma, A New Constitution, But the Old President' *Sevodnya* 14 December 1993, in *CDPSP* vol. 45, no. 50, 1994, pp. 2–3.
22 See Jeffrey Lilley, 'Far Eastern Satraps' *Far Eastern Economic Review* 13 January 1994; and Nikolai Troitsky, 'New Parliament Viewed as Antagonistic to Reform' *Megapolis-Express* 5 January 1994, in *CDPSP* vol. 46, no. 1, 1994, pp. 1–2.
23 Reuters, 17 April 1995, interview with Vyacheslav Bobkov, head of the All-Russian Center for Living Standards, cited in *OMRI Daily Digest* vol. 1, no. 76, 1995.
24 John Thornhill, 'Liberal Faction Abandons Yeltsin' *The Australian* 14 March 1995, p. 11.
25 Michael McFaul, 'Eurasia Letter' *Foreign Policy* Summer 1995, pp. 153–155.
26 *Washington Post* (7 July, 1996).
27 *OMRI Daily Digest* vol. 2, nos 50–130 (March–June, 1996).
28 *OMRI Russian Presidential Election Survey*, no. 13 (July, 1996).
29 Fukuyama, 'Capitalism and Democracy: The Missing Link', pp. 108–110.
30 L. N. Gumilyov, *Ritmy Yevrazii* ('Eurasian rhythms') (Moscow: Ekopross, 1993), p. 9, cited in Alexei Zagorsky, 'The Post-Cold War Security Agenda of Russia: Implications for Northeast Asia', paper presented at the International Studies Association Convention, Washington, DC, 28 March 1994, pp. 18–19. See also N. S. Tubetzkoy, *The Legacy of Genghis Khan* (Ann Arbor: Michigan Slavic Publications, 1991).
31 Brontoi Bedyurov, 'Who Enjoys the Protection of the Spirit of the Universe?' *Den* 9–15 May 1993, in *CDPSP* vol. 45, no. 21, 1993, pp. 10–12 (emphasis in original).
32 Alexander Solzhenitsyn, *Rebuilding Russia: Reflections and Tentative Proposals*, translated by Alexis Klimoff (London: Harvill, 1991).
33 See *OMRI Daily Digest* vol. 1, no. 79, 1995.
34 See *OMRI Daily Digest* vol. 1, nos. 60–80, 1995.
35 Sergei Stankevich, 'A Power in Search of Itself' *Nezavisimaya Gazeta* 28 March 1992, in *CDPSP* vol. 44, no. 13, 1992, pp. 1–4 (emphasis added).
36 Cited in Stephen F. Cohen, 'If not Yeltsin: Four Voices of the Russian Opposition' *Washington Post* 3 December 1995, p. C3.
37 ibid.
38 Matthew J. Sagers, 'Prospects for Oil and Gas Development in Russia's Sakhalin Oblast' *Post-Soviet Geography* vol. 36, no. 5, 1995, p. 274.
39 Demosthenes James Peterson, 'Russia's Environment and Natural Resources in Light of Economic Regionalization' *Post-Soviet Geography* vol. 36, no. 5, 1995, p. 294.
40 ibid., pp. 292–294.
41 ibid., p. 295.
42 *Monitor* vol. 1, no. 104, 27 September 1995.
43 *Monitor* vol. 2, no. 63, 29 March 1996.
44 *Monitor* vol. 2, no. 63, 29 March 1996.
45 Peterson, 'Russia's Environment and Natural Resources in Light of Economic Regionalization', p. 295.
46 David Kerr, 'The New Eurasianism: The Rise of Geopolitics in Russia's Foreign Policy' *Europe-Asia Studies* vol. 47, no. 6, 1995, p. 984.
47 *Monitor* vol. 1, no. 78, 21 August 1995.
48 *Monitor* vol. 1, no. 160, 18 December 1995.

# 5 Fragmented visions of Asia's next Tiger: Vietnam in the Pacific Century*

*Gerard Greenfield*

## INTRODUCTION: VIETNAM IN THE PACIFIC CENTURY

A decade after the reform process was institutionalized in the 'renovation' (*doi moi*) programme of 1986, a renewed optimism pervades commentaries on Vietnam. Armed conflict with Cambodia and China, the failed experiment of Soviet-style command planning, and – for some – the Vietnam War have been relegated to a distant past. The future has become inextricably tied to the shift in the locus of global economic power to the Asia-Pacific that signifies the beginning of the so-called 'Pacific Century'. For many the fact that Vietnam will be a part of this Pacific Century seems beyond doubt. The World Bank concludes that despite facing 'a long transition from its low-income status to being another East Asian Tiger', continued economic liberalization, the expansion of the private sector, and dissolution of the last remnants of state socialism guarantee that Vietnam 'will be well on its way to joining the other successful tigers'.[1] The metaphor of the 'Tiger economy' has become central to the ever-widening consensus about developing capitalist societies in the Asia-Pacific which has taken shape among bureaucrats and scholars inside and outside Vietnam.

## ELITE VISIONS OF ASIA'S NEXT TIGER

At the same time, for marxist and liberal observers, the symbolic power of the Vietnamese revolution has by no means diminished: 'renovation' is seen as an extension of its nationalist and democratic aspirations. This new orthodoxy is expressed by Tuong Lai, the director of the Institute for Sociology in Hanoi, who argues that the reform process has 'gradually set loose people who had become fastened to a fixed and centralised model'.[2] Market forces have, according to the Prime Minister, Vo Van Kiet, inspired 'motivation and initiative among the people'.[3] Ultimately, the political leadership's sustained commitment to reform is interpreted as the end of ideology itself, as 'theoretical conceptualism has given way to pragmatism'.[4] While for many, an enlightened leadership and their entourage of liberal economists underlies such pragmatism, others have argued that market reforms are an objective necessity in the era of global capitalism. According to Tran Phuong, editor-in-chief of the newspaper *Thoi Bao Kinh Te Viet Nam* ('Vietnam economic times'), the market economy, once seen as a source of 'disorder' induced by competition, class differentiation and the spontaneous development of capitalism, is now praised for its flexibility, autonomy, egalitarianism and freedom. Debates over the market economy as 'good' or 'bad' are dismissed as mere subjectivism:

> Human beings have no right to choose which is better for them – the market economy or the planned economy, like choosing a green shirt or a pink shirt. Only existing objective economic conditions can determine which system is fit for them. This objective necessity explains why slavery once presented a motive force for human society in spite of its inhumanity.[5]

Citing Marx, Tran Phuong argues that the existing division of labour and private ownership made the emergence of the market under socialist systems inevitable. Hence the market has become a natural law where flexibility and competition 'eliminate backwardness', but also generate 'disorder, imbalances and waste of productive resources', and occasionally 'economic crisis'. Finally, it is inevitable that 'the market economy, according to its own laws, leads spontaneously not to socialism, but to capitalism'.[6]

In the context of this vision of Vietnam as 'Asia's next Tiger' there is an easy convergence of disparate political commitments whereby the rationalist teleology of modernization in liberal and marxist narratives on Vietnam's transition to a market economy articulates once more the promise of development, whether viewed as market socialism or capitalist revolution.[7] Market-socialist approaches reproduce much of the hegemonic vision of Anglo-American liberalism, with a unilinear trajectory of modernization and development, and an emphasis on the liberating power of market forces which generate material rewards for the 'people' (the purported beneficiaries of reform). This signals a new stage in Western socialist utopias – the remaking of socialism at the very centre of the Pacific Century. The diminished number of revolutionary states which can still be considered 'heroes' in marxist narratives has made the Vietnamese claim to market socialism all the more acceptable. It seems that the need to retain this hero, along with Cuba, has produced a commitment among Western socialists that binds them to the political imagination and interests of national elites and transcends a more fundamental concern for subaltern social groups and classes.[8]

The mystification of capitalism and the rhetoric of market economics in the market-socialist paradigm facilitates the Anglo-American liberal project of reifying the market and restoring rationality to the periphery of global capitalism, while East Asian triumphalists in Tokyo and Kuala

Lumpur welcome yet another developmental state to the East Asian club.[9] The East Asian model replaces the rhetoric of the market with a strong state and a common 'Asian culture' which belies the need for democracy.[10] This idea has gained currency in the modern imaginings of Vietnam's elites as they remake themselves into an authoritarian regime presiding over a strategy of capitalist industrialization. Recently the trade union leadership has looked to Singapore for its more effective (and repressive) regime of labour control.[11] Furthermore, the danger of *not* adopting the East Asian model of development and falling behind Vietnam's regional neighbours economically was specified in a report to a meeting of the Central Committee of the Communist Party in early 1994. The report concluded that industrialization based on the country's comparative advantages – cheap labour and agriculture – offered the only rational response to this danger.[12] This rhetoric on the new dangers faced by the nation serves to justify the turn to capitalism while producing an economic-nationalist agenda common to what Alexander Woodside has called the 'mobilization myth' of the Asia-Pacific which 'mobilises the poor of the region for economic production without representing or encouraging their political and social claims'.[13]

The early 'success' of economic liberalization lies in the government's gradualist approach to market reform which has prevented a decline into the social disorder and crisis witnessed in the former Soviet Union and Eastern Europe in the wake of 'shock therapy'.[14] While price and interest rate reforms and massive reductions in state subsidies in Vietnam in 1989 are considered a 'small shock therapy', liberal and neo-liberal commentaries on the transition view the overall impact on society as positive.[15] Despite this rhetoric of gradualism, economic liberalization has devastated social welfare services and loosened controls over diminishing state resources. The number of state enterprises was reduced from 12,500 to fewer than 4000 in three years, with less than six formal privatizations.[16] The other side of the 'small shock therapy' of 1989 was the 'surplus labour redistribution programme' (Decree 176/HDBT) under which 1 million workers were sacked from the state sector.[17] In the surge of lay-offs that occurred in the late 1980s an average of 30–40 per cent of workers were dismissed from state enterprises, and in some state economic units the power vested in directors under the new managerialist regime led to the sacking of 80–90 per cent of the workforce.[18] This was the culmination of growing managerial autonomy from bureaucratic control in the state enterprise sector in the early 1980s, which increased the power of directors to hire and fire freely. Well before its institutionalization as an official policy of the state in 1989, directors had begun laying off workers as a way of reducing production costs. The new politics of production which has emerged in these (quasi-)state enterprises is characterized by authoritarian regimes of production which seek to emulate the logic of rapidly expanding private capitalist enterprise.

The vision of Vietnam as an emerging Asian Tiger articulated by Vietnamese political leaders, state officials, intellectuals and policy advisers is due as much to their nationalist aspirations and an ongoing nation-building project as it is to the fact that they, more than anyone else, are benefiting from linkages to a resurgent indigenous capitalist class and to transnational capital, and the looting of state resources under economic liberalization.[19] Furthermore, with the enmeshment of government agencies, research centres, policy groups, universities, and private consultancy groups formed by state officials with the World Bank, IMF, UN Development Programme and a myriad inter-governmental organizations, this 'Pacific vision' is very much the product of a globalized site of knowledge production, intertwined with the pathways of global capital and drawing into it the expertise of overseas scholars and consultants whose ideas reinforce and are reinforced by elite discourses on 'renovation'. In effect these institutions are universalizing the rationality of development and modernity, creating what Arturo Escobar has called 'a whole new political economy of truth'.[20] However, this new political economy of truth is not unchallenged. There are an increasing number of critics of this imaginary of development, such as Nguyen Tri Dung who argues that 'between the lines of praise for Asia's newest "tiger", lies the stark reality of a widening gap between rich and poor'.[21] It is not just the transparent disparity of wealth that has led to the contestation of the dominant vision of Asia's next Tiger. The wave of wildcat strikes and what the Party-state has identified as 'social disorder' among subaltern groups and classes have challenged not only the prospects of such a vision being realized, but the very process by which such a social vision is manufactured and maintained. In particular, this process is contested not at the national level but within particular localized sites of struggle. To illustrate the way in which subnational struggles challenge the 'Pacific vision' in elite narratives on 'renovation', this article focuses on the process of fragmentation in the coal-mining areas of the northern province of Quang Ninh.

## NATIONAL UNITY AND ORDER: THE MYTHS OF HOMOGENEITY

Maintaining national boundaries in the transition to capitalism has involved significant shifts in the social and political actors authored and authorized by national elites. In particular, 'the working class' as a collective identity within the space of the nation-state is rapidly being replaced by the national citizen. This is apparent in the annual political-ceremonial visit to the coal mines in 1993, by Party General Secretary Do Muoi, who brought a very different message to that which he had delivered a decade earlier. Then he had addressed coal miners as members of the working class. Now for the first time the collective identity of workers was fragmented, with Do Muoi asserting that there had been 'improvements noted in the lives of a *segment* of the workers'. There is also an indication that there had been some form of protest by workers, as he confirmed that '[t]he employment-related worries of a large number of workers are well-founded and legitimate'.[22] Yet they were also reminded that they no longer hold a privileged position as the politically constituted 'ruling class' in a working-class state. Instead, the new social order is governed by 'a state based on the rule of law' under which the rights of citizens are subordinated to 'the requirements of national development' and 'the struggle of the entire nation'.[23] A senior member of the Party Central Committee, Vu Oanh, later developed this theme, calling for 'national unity' (*doan ket dan toc*) and an end to social disorder. Accordingly, '[t]he settlement of sectional interests must be in harmony with national interests'[24] and 'Vietnamese citizens should realize their historic duty towards the nation'.[25] What this suggests is that 'sectional interests' such as the working class are not only subordinated to the project of national unity, but are replaced by a collective identity centred on the *national citizen*. This discursive reconstruction of the working class is enmeshed in the commodification of labour under the creation of a capitalist labour market – a process by which the working class is being remade. The subsumption of the masses into the homogeneous entity of the nation is part of a wider political process through which the propertied classes and political power holders are able to consolidate their positions.

Though conceived in ahistorical terms, the extension of this homogeneity into the past in the form of a 'national consciousness' serves to legitimate the project of Vietnamese elites in the present. The subordination of sectional interests to the national interest and national consensus in the process of market reform and global integration is presented as inherent to the Vietnamese people and hence natural. The argument, it seems, is that the longer the history of this nation-idea the greater its significance as a genuine source of the aspirations and visions of subaltern groups and classes. Moving within this hegemonic discourse of nationalist elites and Party historians, Craig Lockard attributes the 'miracle' of Vietnamese nationalism to this very same pre-colonial national consciousness. Lockard writes that: 'Unlike most premodern peoples the Vietnamese seem to have long enjoyed a well-developed sense of "nation", of the difference between "us" and "them", in other words something similar to nationalism.' And despite the transformative power of Chinese colonialism (which lasted until the tenth century), he argues that an 'indigenous core of "Vietnameseness" survived', though 'not unscathed'.[26] The homogeneity implied by this Vietnameseness is understood as a force which brought together peasants and their rulers alike as 'us', rather than the possibility that it constituted part of the very system of domination and exploitation of subaltern peoples by nationalist elites. As Serge Thion's study of the formation of the Vietnamese nation shows, far from being homogeneous the anti-

Chinese nationalists were made up of a creole elite who initiated an imperialist project of their own against the stateless peoples of the West and the Cham in the south.[27] This recalls the link between creole elites and the imagined community of the nation drawn by Benedict Anderson whose concept of 'imagined communities' is dismissed at the outset in Lockard's essay.[28]

Drawing on Truong Buu Lam's study of rebellion and popular resistance in Vietnamese history, Lockard interprets peasant rebellions as primarily nationalist movements. Yet it is recognized that (in Lockard's words) 'foreign attackers soon enmeshed in the intricacies of local struggles that divided the Vietnamese population'.[29] The assertion that by the eleventh century, unlike other Southeast Asian countries with 'fluctuating, porous borders', Vietnam had a 'permanent territory with fixed borders'[30] also fails to take into account the way in which diasporic communities of sojourners and migrants cut across these borders and reshaped the 'nation', 'us' and 'them'.[31] I am not arguing that national consciousness or nationhood did not exist in any form prior to Chinese colonialism, but that there are *nationhoods* in the social imagination of subalterns, where the struggles by peasants against foreign oppressors involve aspirations and visions which often contest those of elites. Also, in his focus on pre-colonial national consciousness and nationhood, Lockard has not taken into account the way in which the technologies of state power appropriated and redeployed by the national elite in the aftermath of colonialism continued to construct ethnicity and national identity, and inscribe subaltern groups.[32] In both past and present the subaltern imagination is extinguished and hegemonic notions of national identity and 'ethnocultural homogeneity' marginalize those subordinated to this homogeneity.[33]

Legitimation of this marginalization under the guise of homogeneity is illustrated by Nguyen Tu Chi's study of tradition and the nation in Vietnam in which it is argued that '[t]he "major ethnic group" of all countries in continental Southeast Asia has played a primary role historically in the management of the state'.[34] There is no mention of the violence systematized within the state that ensures this dominance. Rather, it becomes a natural order in which the distribution of social and political power among different ethnic groups is attributed to demographic factors. The dissolution of difference in localized social and cultural spaces is central to the discourse on national unity, as in Nguyen Khac Tung's study of architecture in the villages of northern Vietnam in which he concludes, 'there are many types of settlements according to local conditions, but generally speaking their main features are identical, showing unity in the cultural tradition of the Vietnamese people.'[35] But such unity is manufactured through the relocation of 'minority' ethnic groups[36] and the saturation of their communities with ethnic Vietnamese in a process Grant Evans has described as 'internal colonialism'. The modernizing authoritarian regime sought to construct a nation-state with an 'organized' population living within specially administered territories, with some 10 million people to be resettled in New Economic Zones (NEZs). Securing national borders was an important objective. Amid heightened conflict with China and Cambodia, 'the state wished to gain stronger control over its border areas which the minorities overlapped, and for this reason were considered less reliable than ethnic Vietnamese.' Many of the families resettled in NEZs eventually abandoned them and returned to their villages or migrated to urban centres.[37] This opens up the possibility of *que* (home-lands) as a more powerful imaginary than the concept of *dan toc* (nation) used uncritically by Lockard.[38] The place of *que* in subaltern historical consciousness and the way in which it informs collective identities contests the nation-idea of Vietnam in some way. Resistance to resettlement forms part of that subaltern social space in which systems of labour control have been and continue to be contested. One response to this by national elites was a new official discourse on *que* which emerged at the height of the resettlement programme in the 1970s. In an attempt to appropriate the powerful imaginary of homelands, the Party newspaper, *Nhan Dan*, claimed that: 'For a rich, attractive homeland, everywhere is a home area.'[39]

There is also a spatial-temporal subversion of representations of East Asia which has contributed to local discourses on an imagined future beyond national borders. In the 'mobilization myths' of Vietnamese indus-trialization and development, East Asia – particularly Japan – is framed as the future. The social costs of the transition to a market economy are largely justified in terms of the sacrifices that must be made to attain this imagined future. Subsequently there has been a growing number of Vietna-mese emigrating to Japan illegally. In 1993, for example, several hundred people left for Japan from Quang Ninh at a time when the international programme for the repatriation of Vietnamese refugees was being intensified.[40] In a sense illegal emigration to Japan is partly a consequence of these modern imaginings, where subaltern groups have sought to reach that future through space rather than time. In the coastal provinces of Quang Ninh and Hai Phong this has contributed in some way to Vietna-mese workers and petty traders paying up to US$2000 to become guest workers in Taiwan and South Korea. These destinations are often seen as stepping-stones to Japan. While Vietnamese workers seek out this imagined future, growing unemployment and poverty in Vietnam, the crisis of East Asian capitalism and the dynamic of the global capitalist labour market draw cheap Vietnamese labour to replace relatively more expensive and 'militant' Filipino labour, particularly in Taiwan.[41]

## REIMAGINING THE VIETNAMESE WORKING CLASS

The fact that Vietnamese workers are perceived as 'cheaper' and more disciplined than their Filipino counterparts is indicative of how the

Vietnamese working class is being remade. In an article in the newspaper *Thoi Bao Kinh Te Viet Nam*, An Yen, a commentator on economic and social issues, quotes a foreign manufacturer as describing the women workers in the clothing industry as 'the cheapest manpower in the world'.[42] However, rather than seeing this as the natural outcome of Vietnam's low level of economic development, An Yen points out that the lack of investment in technology and training, and the tendency for Vietnamese firms to reduce wage rates to gain export contracts and form joint ventures with foreign capital, underlie 'the dirt-cheap labour in this business'.[43] Late or non-payment of these dirt-cheap wages, combined with unpaid shift-work, physical abuse and mistreatment, and poor health and safety conditions, has led to a series of strikes by women workers in the clothing industry.[44]

These workers form a significant proportion of the total number of workers employed by foreign capital and hence – in the new political economy of truth – they are at the forefront of those purported to be beneficiaries of integration into the global economy. Yet these are the very same workers who have been engaged in strikes to protest against the conditions of their exploitation. This is not simply a matter of inadequate material rewards – which would be easily dismissed as premature in the narratives of national development and modernization. Despite attempts by Vietnamese economists and policy makers to define these collective protests in terms of basic economic claims, the most important issues expressed by workers have concerned the abuse of their dignity and the 'lack of democracy' in the workplace, as well as the failure of the state and trade unions to protect them.[45] Yet as Do Muoi articulated in his speech to the coal miners in 1993, national unity and order require that the state only 'guarantee the legitimate interests of the labouring people such as being treated equally before the law'.[46]

The interpretation of what may constitute 'legitimate interests' lies with those state and Party institutions which control labour by representing it, while the positioning of workers as legal subjects further diminishes the power of the language and practice of class. Recognition of the rights of capital emerges as the logical consequence of this notion of equality before the law, while legitimizing attempts by the state and trade unions to suppress the disorder caused by spontaneous strikes. Ha Ngoc Que, a Labour Ministry official who was involved in writing the new labour laws, argues that, '[l]abourers have protection, why not employers? They should be given the right to voice their opinions.'[47] Hence capital is attributed rights on an equal footing with workers. Implicit in such a view is the two-fold assumption that on the one hand the capital–labour relationship is an equal one and therefore both sides require equal protection, and on the other, that the exploited can somehow infringe upon the legitimate rights of global capital.

The non-antagonistic role of trade unions towards transnational and multinational capital is expressed in the reassurance given by the President of the Vietnam General Confederation of Labour (VGCL), Nguyen Van Tu, on whether attempts to organize unions in foreign joint ventures might be seen as provocative: 'Although we are the hosts and owners of this country, a factory is still considered a private house. Whenever we enter that house we should ask the approval of the host.'[48] Subsequently, by 1995 only 15–20 per cent of workers in foreign joint-venture enterprises had been granted the right to union membership.[49] Recent plans to construct Export Processing Zones (EPZs) throughout the country suggest that this 'house' will have a garden.[50] Despite the rhetoric of technology acquisition and the skilling of workers by foreign capital, the Chinese model of EPZs actively pursued by Vietnamese policy makers and economists is designed precisely to ensure the non-interference of trade unions and a slimming-down of workers' rights.[51] This is based on the special 'incentives' and 'breaks' offered by the state. These special conditions include the construction of workers' dormitories in these zones, creating new social spaces within which global capital is free to extend the regime of labour control beyond the factory floor.

Rather than taking up the issues raised by striking workers there is a tendency for state and trade union officials to promote the passivity of Vietnamese labour. Given the importance of transnational and multinational capital to the national industrialization strategy, the industrial militancy manifested in spontaneous strikes has been played down as somehow out of character for Vietnamese workers. This also supports the interests of government ministries, state enterprises and trade unions involved in the export of labour for profit.[52] The director of the international relations department of the Ministry of Labour, Invalids and Social Affairs, Tran Luc, promoted the 'versatility' of Vietnamese workers, quoting the general director of a construction project in Iraq as having said: 'Vietnamese workers are like tomatoes, tasty when cooked with chicken, delicious with beef and even nutritious when eaten raw.'[53] The same department was later forced to investigate the abuse of Vietnamese women sent to Lebanon, when the labour service company in Ho Chi Minh City which had originally contracted the women was accused of exporting them into slavery.[54]

In the new political economy of truth these 'human resources'[55] are being redefined, radically transforming the position of the working class in the national polity. The policies and studies on labour produced by those institutions of the Vietnamese state concerned with the control of labour – the Ministry of Labour and its various branches and research institutes, Party organizations, trade unions and international organizations such as the ILO – inform the political, economic and cultural process of reconstructing labour as a commodity as well as engineering the creation of a labour market. These institutions are also engaged in the project of 'knowing labour' where knowledge of the working class continues to be an important element of hegemonic power and, necessarily, a source of subaltern subversion. While remaining integral to the process of national industrialization, the new position of the working class involves politico-legal redefinition. According to the political theorist Le Minh Chau – a senior member of the Ho Chi Minh Political Academy's Institute of Mass Media and Propaganda – the interests of the working class and the national interest are inseparable precisely because of the challenge posed to workers by the decline of the state sector and the rise of an unregulated private sector.[56] Under these reforms certain segments of the working class are 'fading away', and while workers are 'masters in terms of dignity and spirit . . . they are still hired workers'.[57] Accordingly, only legal-institutional arrangements guaranteed by the state will protect workers' interests and dignity as *employees and citizens*, not as a collective political entity. The link between modernization and proletarianization drawn in orthodox marxist narratives is reasserted: industrialization initiated by market reforms will 'develop the quantity and quality of the working class'. However, working-class consciousness is measured not in terms of class antagonism or social conflict, but in workers' 'traditional patriotism, self-reliance and self-advancement'.[58] The homogenizing dialogue of national unity resurfaces here, with Chau concluding that the Vietnamese working class is characterized by a 'culture of discipline' which is founded on obedience to the laws of the Party and state and individual responsibility.[59] Like national consciousness, this culture of discipline and obedience to the Party is projected into the past. The Party and its revolutionary antecedents are situated as far back in the history of national struggle as possible, thus defining the limitations of a self-constituted working class that existed prior to the founding of the Party. Ultimately workers are denied a collective identity formed outside the Party-state.

The historical construction of Vietnamese marxism and its embeddedness in nationalism is critical for our understanding of the way in which the Vietnamese working class is presently being remade. The Vietnamese working class was intertwined with nationalist aspirations, both as an agent of social change and as a political identity constructed by nationalist elites. Zachary Lockman has argued in his study of the formation of the Egyptian working class that this 'making' of the working class is as much a discursive as a material process. Intellectuals in the anti-colonialist movement 'discovered' workers and the working class, and configured them as an indigenous social category inextricably bound up in the 'nation'. It is in this sense that Lockman asserts that the imagining of the working class as a 'vision of society, and the practices with which it was bound up, constituted an intervention, a political project, on the part of a specific social political group operating within a larger field of cultural, social, and political contestation'. Lockman adds that this does not deny the role of workers in making themselves as a class; rather, it identifies an important site of contestation in this process. Subaltern classes engaged in social practices which shaped and continue to shape collective identities and produced social visions which to be understood must be read (if possible) outside 'the history that nationalism gives itself'.[60]

With over a hundred spontaneous strikes in five years (1989–1994) the possibility of workers taking collective action autonomously of the Party and official trade unions has challenged this discourse on unity and discipline and the whole system of labour control. In particular, the wave of wildcat strikes in the southern province of Song Be emerged as a major crisis for the Party-state in the early 1990s. Obviously the outbreak of strikes, particularly in the state sector, challenged the legitimacy of the Party and its mass organizations as well as the programme to attract foreign capital. But what made the Song Be strikes such a dilemma for the Party-state was that this well-organized resistance echoed a tradition of working-class radicalism in Song Be under French colonialism. Some of the most highly organized strikes of the late 1920s and 1930s occurred in the rubber plantations in this province. There were also strong parallels in the issues raised by workers. In two incidents in 1994 over 800 workers at a state-run cashew-processing plant and workers at the Song Be Export Garment Company went on strike in protest against the new piece-rate system of wage payments and the authoritarian behaviour of managers.[61] One of the key demands of striking workers at the Michelin plantation in Dau Tieng in the 1930s, according to Martin Murray, was 'a reduction of the pace of work required by the daily quota system' and an end to mistreatment by overseers.[62]

Despite the importance of resistance and change initiated by workers and peasants within the subaltern domain of politics and culture in the overthrow of French colonialism and the establishment of North Vietnam in 1954, in the course of the first five-year plan (1961–1965) soon afterwards they were to experience a new sense of subordination.[63] The knowledge of workers and the working class constructed by those institutions of the Vietnamese state whose function it was to control labour, combined with proletarian literature and the arts, formed a new regime of representation of the social order in which the historical agency ascribed to the working class was intertwined with the Party and the struggle for national liberation. Reconfigured as an agent of modernity and a force for national economic development, the collective identity of 'the working class' became a category of social control. The initiation of the heavy industrialization drive in the early 1960s saw the emergence of the skilled, disciplined technical worker (of whom managers and engineers were but advanced forms) as the model worker within a broader version of technicist-managerialism.[64] According to Arif Dirlik, the objectives of 'change and progress' as national goals led state-socialist regimes 'to mimic the economic achievements of capitalism, goals that not only distorted socialism but, because capitalism is obviously much better equipped than socialism to achieve capitalist goals, undermined the legitimacy of the system as well'.[65] The economic criteria of efficiency and cumulative growth were inspired largely by the centrality of the national economy in the construction of Vietnamese marxism and the adoption of what Steve Smith labels 'technicist Bolshevism' – a version of Taylorism which underpins the regime of labour control in the Stalinist model of industrialization.[66] Workers' resistance to the pace and intensity of the production regime and their diminishing bargaining power at the point of production coincided with campaigns against the failure of workers to fulfil their role as members of a modern working class. This failure was further justification for the increasing concentration of control over the production process by managers.

By 1988 the Vietnamese trade union leadership attributed the crisis in production and distribution to 'laziness, indiscipline, violation of socialist property, wastage, shoddy work [and] social vice' as manifestations of workers' 'negativism', and the failure to reach maturity as a modern working class.[67] However, if the master concepts of productivity and industrial discipline are problematized rather than the worker, what emerges is an alternative discourse of reconstructed and self-constructed social identities (gender, ethnicity, place) and the different forms in which the power of the dominant classes is contested. Most visible are everyday acts of resistance.[68] Indiscipline as social protest appears in the text of the trade union leadership's report to the national congress as silence, where it is stated that 'it is not necessary to have recourse to the forms of action as made under the capitalist regime'.[69] Ironically it was at this historical juncture that capitalist organizational principles and regimes of production came to be institutionalized in 'managerial autonomy' and 'experimental' reforms in labour management. As part of the wider process of economic liberalization these reforms signify attempts by state managers to overcome the impediments generated by workers' resistance. After less than a decade of market reforms the state had constructed the disciplined, modern worker as a commodity in a labour market. At the Seventh National Congress of Vietnamese Trade Unions in November 1993, the trade union leadership stated that 'the market mechanism, with labour turned into a commodity, has infiltrated deeply into all social relations and directly impacted on the working class.'[70]

## 'PEASANTS DOING COAL' IN MINING COUNTRY

During the local elections of September 1994 a 15-foot billboard stood above the post office in Ha Long, the provincial capital of Quang Ninh, urging people to vote. The painting depicted four people lined up in front of a ballot box holding ballot cards: a scholar, a nurse, a coal miner and a soldier. In one sense this particular representation of citizens engaged in a modern political ritual is powerful in its display of the ordering of popular participation and the technologies of state power (registration and citizenship), as well as localizing the Communist Party and instilling a sense of the nation through a collectively practised political ritual. In another sense local social practices and material conditions contest the symbolic power of the billboard since the subaltern realities beneath it are characterized by the closure of hospitals and schools, the gradual dissolution of free public health and education services, massive lay-offs of teachers and nurses, and the demobilization of soldiers in their tens of thousands.[71] The professional coal miner wearing safety equipment has been replaced by barefoot children, retired miners and peasants employed in illegal private coal mines. Bandit coal mining, smuggling from China and sex tourism in Ha Long Bay now sustain the local economy.

In the state-run coal mines at Thong Nhat, Mong Duong and Khe Cham there is a shortage of 350 to 400 skilled miners as a result of economic rationalization policies which abolished training funds and closed technical schools at the mine sites.[72] The wider impact of these reforms is evident in the deterioration of health and safety conditions as the logic of profit maximization and competition with bandit mines has led to changes in the intensity and nature of exploitation. Contrary to economists' claims that market forces would lead to modernization of the production process and the acquisition of new technologies, machinery and equipment are being replaced by cheaper child and female labour. In the bandit mines themselves hundreds, possibly a thousand, are killed every year.[73] According to Huynh Thai, mine owners try to avoid the cost of recovering bodies and 'in some cases the employer makes the pit cave in to cover any trace'. Given these conditions, Huynh Thai notes that the film-maker Nguyen Khac Loi – who made a film in 1985 about the 1936 coal miners' strikes against French coal companies – need only have waited a few more years and he would have had a ready-made set for the film. There would have been no need for the made-up extras and the creation of pre-industrial settings which were necessary on the eve of *doi moi* in 1985.[74]

There is considerable resistance to lay-offs in the state mining companies under Decision 176 (1989), which has led to an uneasy compromise whereby workers are able to keep their jobs, but are not paid. After three months of unpaid work, miners at one of the state mines in Ha Tu sold everything at the site. In one of the oldest mines, run by the Hong Gai Coal Company, the director insisted that economic rationalization required a reduction of the workforce from 13,500 to 7000, though such a policy could not be carried out.[75] In emphasizing the need for these reductions if the coal industry is to become an efficient exporting sector, the World Bank recognized that in the interim, 'Laying off surplus labour creates a conflict with the mining companies' perceived social obligation of maintaining employment.'[76] The response of managers of state coal companies has been to withdraw from production altogether, focusing on trading and financial activities, while buying coal from the bandit mines and their intermediaries. The 'black gold rush' of the late 1980s saw the influx of 20,000 bandit coal miners,[77] who extract, sort and transport coal more cheaply than state sector workers as well as working 12–16 hour shifts under any conditions. The formation of the new state conglomerate Vinacoal, through a merger of the management of the four state coal companies, the export company Coalimex and local coal enterprises, centralized the purchase of coal from bandit mines but did not alter production. Vinacoal was able to double coal exports in 1995, while employing only 10,000 of the estimated 70–90,000 workers in the industry.[78] Another 7000 soldier-labourers are employed in over twenty mines operated by units of the People's Army (though these are not considered 'bandit' mines).[79]

The origins of this crisis lie in the response of state sector managers to stagnation in production in the 1970s and the reforms of the 1980s. It should be noted here that one of the fundamental problems with economic studies of the coal-mining industry under 'renovation' is that the impact of war on the coal mines and villages, both in the sense of the destruction of infrastructure and industrial capacity and the militarization of the production process, is neglected. In his critique of the neo-liberal analysis of the political economy of North Vietnam by Adam Fforde and Suzanne Paine, Gabriel Kolko has argued that history, particularly the experience of war and its impact, should be brought back into studies of the perceived crisis in the Vietnamese economy.[80] The importance of this is expressed in an editorial in *Nhan Dan* in 1979 which warned of a crisis in the coal-mining industry: 'In 1978 and 1979, coal production had encountered many difficulties due to lack of vehicles, machinery, spare parts and raw and other materials and as a result of the destruction caused by the enemy and prolonged bad weather.'[81]

This crisis in coal production led to so-called 'experimental' reforms in the Deo Nai and Mao Khe mines in 1980–1981, which were later to be generalized and implemented in all mines by the mid-1980s.[82] What is most significant about these reforms – as with reforms in other industries in other parts of Vietnam at this time – is that they were based on changes to the labour regime by managers, where the problem of low productivity was attributed to constraints on their control over labour and workers' laziness and unwillingness to work reflected in continuous 'go-slows' (*lan cong*). Consequently, the introduction of piece-rate wages and wider wage differentials, greater power over the reallocation of labour at the level of production, and the rationalization of work practices were integral to the enforcement of capitalist time-work discipline. Despite these experimental reforms – or because of them – the coal mines suffered from a rapid decrease in the number of highly skilled miners in the early 1980s. Replacing them proved impossible. The Ministry of Energy and state mining companies organized labour recruitment campaigns in the neighbouring province of Hai Hung, and the provinces of Nghe An, Thanh Hoa and Thai Binh. (These were also the provinces from which labour was brought to the mines under French colonialism.) Flags and slogans in the mobilization campaign urged peasants and workers to go to the Quang Ninh coal mines, promising exemption from military service. People were encouraged to go with their children, build houses and stay there. But in the end, according to Huynh Thai's account, only about 10,000 were brought to the mines and those who came deserted after only ten days.[83] The National Union of Energy Workers estimates that more than 20,000 deserted the mines in the 1980s.

In elite representations of economic crisis, workers came to be constituted as the problem just as narratives on development define peasants as the problem in the linear journey from tradition to modernity.[84] Coal workers were a 'problem' in that they were not workers in the true sense, but 'peasants doing coal' (*nong dan lam than*). This implies a lack of skills, technical expertise and an appropriate work culture that was exacerbated by their lack of commitment to the long-term development of the mining industry. Yet the notion of peasants doing coal was not simply a dismissal of their capacity as agents of modernity, but part of a wider critique of working-class culture by national elites. The shortcomings of miners as constructed by Le Dai, the secretary of the Standing Committee of the Quang Ninh Provincial Party Committee, in 1969 still have a resonance in elite discourses on labour. Le Dai referred specifically to the failure to realize the 'models' for creating 'new workers' as part of a broader failure in achieving 'consciousness of being masters of the community'.[85] A new culture of work embodied in these new workers would be necessary to 'overcome the manifestations of subjectivism, simplism, lack of a sense of organization and discipline and regionalism'.[86] The tendency of workers to leave the mines to eat and to fail to return to work on time, or at all, were targeted in the strategy to reorganize eating houses at mining sites and arrangements for workers to be transported to and from work. Implicit in Dai's criticism is the failure of the state to engineer this new worker.

The loss of skilled miners in the late 1970s was not solely the outcome of desertions by workers returning to their home provinces. Another homeland, China, also framed this exodus. The most highly skilled miners and those who were from third- and fourth-generation mining families were predominantly ethnic Chinese or Hoa. Among the hundreds of thousands who crossed the border into China in 1978–1979 in the mass exodus of ethnic Chinese were thousands of workers from the coal-mining districts. Though Vietnamese trade union officials now recognize this phenomenon, the precise number of those who left remains unclear. According to provincial trade union officials, some 3000 highly skilled Hoa miners had left in 1978 and 1979.[87] However, this did not enter public discourse on crisis and stagnation at the time. Instead a new silence emerged in the narratives on workers in mining country in which ethnic Chinese workers were forgotten. This collective forgetting was particularly difficult because of the critical role of the *chu khach* (Chinese sojourners) in the workers' uprisings of the 1930s.[88] Yet the amnesias of nationalism were to remove them from the struggle against US imperialism and the post-revolutionary development of the mining industry. Only in the late 1970s did the Chinese miners re-emerge in official discourse – as saboteurs and deserters. This posed a serious dilemma for labour managers since ethnic Chinese miners conformed most closely to the work ethic sought in the 'new worker'. As sojourners they were more inclined to live in towns near the mines and not leave for several years (particularly since they would not return to their homelands for harvests and the Lunar New Year). But they were precluded from the nationalist discourse on the Vietnamese worker, particularly in the context of the deterioration of relations with China and the conflict which followed. If we return then to the election billboard (mentioned on pp. 135–136), the significance of its particular representation of the miner lies not in its failure to keep up with the times, but in the fact that the professional Vietnamese miner was extremely rare, if 'he' has existed at all.

In addition to being 'peasants doing coal', the coal miners came to be known as 'the ghost army from hell' (*quan doi am phu*) because of the uncertainty of the number of workers in the coal industry.[89] When workers had deserted the mines for their villages or other jobs only their names remained on the records of the state mining companies. It was impossible to work out how many were working in the mines at any point in time. Desertion of the mines was a widespread practice prior to the Vietnamese revolution. Under French colonialism the mines suffered an ongoing crisis in labour supply as a result of workers returning to their villages at the Lunar New Year and during harvesting months. Though a system of indentured labour organized by labour contractors brought workers from distant provinces, E. Willard Miller, writing in 1946, noted that '[t]his method has not developed a permanent mining class'.[90] The project of creating this class continued under the post-colonial state, for in spite of the system of labour control which relied on trade unions and the discourse on the revolutionary national working class, mine workers continued to desert the mines and return to their villages (*bo ve lang*). In fact the policy of the provincial trade union of Quang Ninh to get miners to settle near the mines and stop returning to their villages involves a logic similar to the policy of French coal companies of constructing permanent settlements and towns near the mines.[91] Obviously the latter was a violent process involving the destruction of villages and forced labour, in contrast to the programmes of Vietnamese trade union officials in the 1980s.

The concept of the 'ghost army from hell' is part of an elite narrative on the indiscipline and backwardness of mine workers, though it can also be read as workers' resistance to capitalist time-discipline which conflicts with the work rhythm which they were accustomed to in their villages.[92] The social practices which generate this 'backwardness' constitute a form of engagement with the system of domination and exploitation. Thus 'peasants doing coal' and the 'ghost army from hell' are elements of the social practice of mine workers which ruptured not only national boundaries but social categories of class and community. The majority of mine workers considered themselves to be 'peasants doing coal', in the sense that they were transient labourers soon to return to farming in their villages. As such the distinct categories of the peasantry and the working class which were central to the political project of national elites were subverted by the fusion of peasants and workers as they resisted the historical and cultural division of town and village and the dictates of modernization. Ultimately new social and cultural spaces were created in which resistance to the material conditions of exploitation and counter-hegemonic local discourses undermined (and continue to undermine) the knowledge of workers and the working class produced by the state. Subaltern practices such as these also suggest an alternative interpretation to the causes of economic stagnation and reform.

In another sense, workers were reacting to the technicist-managerialism introduced into the mines at different stages of the modernization process in which elite knowledge came to be privileged over workers' experience or what was called 'innovation' in official rhetoric. Innovation, considered a peasant characteristic, was antithetical to the scientific knowledge of professional miners. This is a recurring theme in the short stories of Nguyen Son Ha, written in 1975–1985.[93] 'The Newcomer' deals explicitly with the confrontation between a highly skilled miner who is both patriotic and the bearer of expert knowledge, and the older miners whose backwardness threatens production despite their obvious patriotism.[94] The message carried in Nguyen Son Ha's story is that modernization of the nation can only be carried out by this new worker, and that resistance to progress and change must be overcome. The abandonment of 'primordial pasts', particularly village ties, is a necessary step in the pursuit of progress. In 'In a Mining Village', Nguyen Son Ha articulates the official discourse on the modern worker by demonstrating the futility of resurrecting primordial pasts: an old miner deserts the mines and returns to his village in protest against the arrival of the 'new worker', only to find that he can no longer be integrated back into a tradition and culture he no longer understands.[95]

In the 1990s desertion as a subaltern practice has been demolished by the imperatives of the market. Rather than deserting, the thousands of workers in state-run mines who were declared redundant in 1989 were transported back to their villages. Under the new coercive regime of the capitalist labour market, 'cheaper' labour is drawn to the mines from villages and towns faced with massive unemployment. As Huynh Thai points out, there are no longer any campaigns to recruit workers for the mines, and in the absence of flags and slogans tens of thousands come to work there for starvation wages. The fact that migrant workers beg for work in the mines means that wages and conditions are negotiated briefly (if at all), leading Thai to conclude: 'It's easy. Labour is bargained more quickly than any other commodity.'[96] And for those mine workers who remain in the formal state sector, the particular forms of resistance which allowed miners to renegotiate the labour process and the intensity of exploitation in the past have been undermined by a more authoritarian regime of production and the threat of unemployment.

## CONCLUSION: FRAGMENTED VISIONS OF ASIA'S NEXT TIGER

This chapter has made clear that a decade of *doi moi* (renovation) has been complemented by an optimistic vision of Vietnam as Asia's next Tiger in the context of the coming of the so-called Pacific Century. Against the backdrop of the vision of Vietnam as 'Asia's next Tiger' there is a growing convergence of political outlooks and interests. The rationalist teleology of modernization in Anglo-American narratives on Vietnam's capitalist transition once more promises economic development. At the same time triumphant East Asian observers see Vietnam as having embarked on a development trajectory which is following the 'Asian way' already charted by a number of its neighbours. It is this latter vision which increasingly encapsulates the contemporary imaginings of Vietnam's elites as they reposition themselves at the helm of a capitalist developmental state. This chapter has argued that while the vision articulated by Vietnam's political and economic elites flows from nationalist sentiments it is also grounded in the spectacular benefits for them which flow from the privatization of state assets in the context of growing connections to both transnational capital and a resurgent indigenous capitalist class. At the same time, the growing 'social disorder' among the subaltern classes has challenged both the possibility of the elite vision of Vietnam as 'Asia's next Tiger' ever coming to fruition, and also the very mechanisms by which such a vision is produced and sustained. As we have seen, the dominant nationalist vision in Vietnam is challenged, and the roots of its fragmentation can be found, at localized sites such as in the mining areas of Quang Ninh.

## NOTES

*I would like to thank Mark Berger, Stephen Frost and Carol Warren for their comments on an earlier draft. I would also like to thank two Vietnamese colleagues (who wish to remain anonymous) for their helpful comments on translations from the Vietnamese. Any errors in translation are my own.

1 World Bank, *Viet Nam: Transition to the Market* (The World Bank Country Operations Division, Country Department 1, East Asia and Pacific Region, September 1993), pp. 223, 229.

2 Quoted in Nguyen Tri Dung, '"Renovation Hits New Heights", says Do Muoi' *Vietnam Investment Review* 31 January–6 February 1994, pp. 1–2.

3 Speech by Vo Van Kiet to the fourth session of the ninth National Assembly, Hanoi, 6 December 1993, BBC Summary of World Broadcasts, Far East, 1868 B/4, 10 December 1993.

4 Nguyen Xuan Oanh, 'Vietnam: Recent Developments and the World Economy' in Seiji Naya and Akira Takayama, eds, *Economic Development in East and Southeast Asia: Essays in Honour of Professor Shinichi Ichimura* (Singapore: Asean Economic Research Unit, ISEAS, 1990), p. 96.

5 Tran Phuong, 'Nhung van de kinh te cua thoi dai: Kinh te thi truong vi sao thang te?' ('Economic issues of the time: why has the market economy gained ascendancy?') *Thoi Bao Kinh Te Viet Nam* ('Vietnam economic times') no. 13, 31 March–6 April 1994. p. 2.

6 ibid.

7 Nguyen Xuan Oanh, the economic adviser to the incumbent Prime Minister, Vo Van Kiet, stated: 'At last I feel part of a revolution – the capitalist revolution:' (Quoted in David Devoss, 'Deja Vu for the Viet Kieu' *Asia Inc.* January 1995, p. 44.) Nguyen Xuan Oanh, a Harvard-trained economist and former IMF official, was Prime Minister of South Vietnam in 1965. See Gareth Porter, 'Vietnamese Communism: Internal Debates Force Change' *Indochina Issues* no. 31, December 1982, pp. 5–6; and Michel Chossudovsky, 'Vietnam's New War' *Third World Resurgence* no. 47, July 1994, p. 15.

8 Melanie Beresford, 'The Vietnamese Economy 1979-1993: Reforming or Revolutionising Asian Socialism?' *Asian Studies Review* vol. 17, no. 2, 1993, pp. 33–46; James Elliott, 'The Future of Socialism: Vietnam, The Way Ahead?' *Third World Quarterly* vol. 13, no. 1, 1992, pp. 131–142; Martin J. Murray and Steve Vieux, 'The Struggle for Socialism in Vietnam' *Humanity and Society* vol. 15, no. 2, 1991, pp. 202–222. In contrast see James Petras and Morris Morley, *Latin America in the Time of Cholera: Electoral Politics, Market Economics, and Permanent Crisis* (London and New York: Routledge, 1992), pp. 93–127.

9 Pham Khiem Ich and Nguyen Dinh Phan, eds, *Cong Nghiep Hoa va Hien Dai Hoa o Viet Nam va cac Nuoc Trong Khu Vuc* ('Industrialisation and modernization in Vietnam and the Asia-Pacific region') (Ha Noi: Nha Xuat Ban Thong Ke, 1994), Dao The Tuan even argues that the Taiwanese and South Korean models have prioritized social equity over economic growth. See Dao The Tuan, 'Economic Growth and Social Equity' *Vietnam Social Sciences* vol. 36, no. 2, 1993, p. 6.

10 Nguyen Cong Nghiep, Dinh Van Nha and Le Hai Mo, *Viet Nam: The Blazing Flame of Reforms* (Hanoi: Statistical Publishing House, 1993), p. 75; Elliott, 'The Future of Socialism', p. 141. See also Keizo Nagatani, 'The Asian Economic Culture and the Role of the State in Economic Development' in Vu Tuan Anh, ed., *The Role of the State in Economic Development: Experiences of the Asian Countries* (Hanoi: Social Science Publishing House, 1994).

11 Nguyen Van Dung, 'Vi sao cac doanh nghiep cong doan Singapore thanh cong?' ('Why are the Singaporean enterprise unions successful?') *Lao Dong* ('Labour') 15 September 1994.

12 Phuong Thao, 'Chien luoc cong nghiep hoa moi' ('A new industrial strategy') *Thoi Bao Kinh Te Viet Nam* ('Vietnam economic times') 27 January–2 February 1994, p. 1.

13 Alexander Woodside, 'The Asia-Pacific Idea as a Mobilization Myth' in Arif Dirlik, ed., *What is in a Rim? Critical Perspectives on the Pacific Region Idea* (Boulder, Colo.: Westview, 1993), p. 24.

14 Nguyen Cong Nghiep *et al., Viet Nam*, pp. 72–75; Le Hong Nhat, 'Vietnam's Market Economy During the Transition Stage to Market Mechanisms: Advantages and Inconveniences of Gradual Reforms' *World Economic Problems* (Hanoi) vol. 19, no. 1, March 1993, pp. 11–19. On 'shock therapy' in the former Soviet bloc see Peter Gowan, 'Analysing Shock Therapy: Neo-Liberal Theory and Practice for Eastern Europe' *New Left Review* no. 213, 1995.

15 See Le Dang Doanh, 'May van de ve doi moi kinh te o Viet Nam' ('Some problems of economic renovation in Vietnam') *Nghien Cuu Kinh Te* ('Economic studies') vol. 194, no. 4, August 1993, p. 4.

16 Gerard Greenfield, 'The Development of Capitalism in Vietnam' in Ralph Miliband and Leo Panitch, eds, *Between Globalism and Nationalism. Socialist Register 1994* (London: Merlin Press, 1994), p. 218.

17 World Bank, *Viet Nam: Transition to the Market*, p. 66.

18 Greenfield, 'The Development of Capitalism in Vietnam', p. 209.

19 Benedict J. Tria Kerkvliet, 'Politics and Society in the Mid 1990s', in Benedict J. Tria Kerkvliet, ed., *The Dilemmas of Development in Vietnam*, Political and Social Change Monograph 22 (Canberra: Australian National University, 1995), pp. 20–28.

20 Arturo Escobar, 'Imagining a Post-Development Era? Critical Thought, Development and Social Movements' *Social Text* nos 31/32, 1992, pp. 23–24.

21 Nguyen Tri Dung, 'Social Stratification and Market Reform' *Vietnam Investment Review* 13–19 June 1994, p. 9. Also see Nguyen Tri Dung, 'Urbanisation and Polarisation' *Vietnam Investment Review* 20–26 June 1994, p. 16.

22 Emphasis added. BBC Summary of World Broadcasts, Far East, FE/1597 B/12, 27 January 1993.

23 Excerpts of the speech by General Secretary Do Muoi to the eleventh session of the eighth legislature of the National Assembly, 24 March 1992. Published in English as 'Towards a State Based on the Rule of Law' in *Vietnam: One Year After the 7th National Party Congress* (Hanoi: The Gioi Publishers, 1992), p. 14.

24 *Nhan Dan*, 1 February 1994, p. 3.

25 *Nhan Dan* 2 February 1994, p. 3.

26 Craig A. Lockard, 'The Unexplained Miracle: Reflections on Vietnamese National Identity and Survival' *Journal of African and Asian Studies* vol. 29, nos. 1–2, 1994, p. 12.

27 Serge Thion, 'Remodelling Broken Images: Manipulation of Identities Towards and Beyond the Nation, an Asian Perspective' in Remo Guidieri, Francesco Pellizi and Stanley J. Tambiah, eds, *Ethnicities and Nations: Processes of Interethnic Relations in Latin America, Southeast Asia, and the Pacific* (Houston, Tex.: Rothko Chapel, 1988), p. 235.

28 Lockard, 'The Unexplained Miracle', p. 11; see Anderson, *Imagined Communities*, pp. 47–66.

29 Lockard, 'The Unexplained Miracle', p. 16; see Truong Buu Lam, *Resistance, Rebellion, Revolution: Popular Movements in Vietnamese History*, Occasional Paper no. 75. (Singapore: Institute for Southeast Asian Studies, 1984).

30 Lockard, 'The Unexplained Miracle', p. 16.

31 Frederick Cooper, 'Conflict and Connection: Rethinking Colonial African History' *American Historical Review* vol. 99, no. 5, 1994, p. 1542.

32 Bernard S. Cohn and Nicholas B. Dirks, 'Beyond the Fringe: The Nation State, Colonialism and the Technologies of Power' *Journal of Historical Sociology* vol. 1, no. 2, 1988, pp. 224–229; Nicholas Dirks, 'The Invention of Caste: Civil Society in Colonial India' *Social Analysis* no. 25, 1989, pp. 42–52.

33 Jean-François Bayart, *The State in Africa: The Politics of the Belly* (London and New York: Longman, 1993), pp. 41–59.

34 Nguyen Tu Chi, 'Traditional Nation and Village in Vietnam' *Vietnamese Studies* vol. 106, no. 4, 1992, p. 8. Obviously Nguyen Tu Chi has not considered the case of Malaysia.

35 Nguyen Khac Tung, 'The Village: Settlement of Peasants in Northern Vietnam', in Phan Huy Le, ed., *The Traditional Village in Vietnam* (Hanoi: The Gioi Publishers, 1993), p. 41.

36 As Gehan Wijeyewardene suggests, the term 'minority' is problematic since it is 'often the result of exigencies of time and place'. See Gehan Wijeyewardene, 'Introduction: Definition, Innovation, and History' in Gehan Wijeyewardene, ed., *Ethnic Groups Across National Boundaries in Mainland Southeast Asia* Singapore: Institute for Southeast Asian Studies, 1990), p. 12, footnote 4.

37 Grant Evans, 'Internal Colonialism in the Central Highlands of Vietnam' *SOJOURN: Social Issues in Southeast Asia* vol. 7, no. 2, 1992, pp. 283, 298.

38 Lockard, 'The Unexplained Miracle', p. 17.

39 *Nhan Dan* 5 March 1977, quoted in Jacqueline Desbarats, 'Population Relocation Programs in Socialist Vietnam: Economic Rationale or Class Struggle?' *Indochina Report* no. 11, April–June 1987, p. 17.

40 This is based on interviews with returnees and labour export organizers in Ha Long and Hai Phong in September 1994.

41 *Migration News* vol. 1, no. 1, February 1994.

42 An Yen, 'Tho may an chi' *Thoi Bao Kinh Te Viet Nam* ('Vietnam economic times') 8–14 December 1994, p. 13.

43 ibid.

44 See Greenfield, 'The Development of Capitalism in Vietnam', pp. 226–228.

45 'Van de dinh cong' ('The problem of strikes') *Lao Dong va Xa Hoi* ('Labour and society') 10–25 September 1993, p. 11.

46 BBC Summary of World Broadcasts, Far East, FE/1597 B/12, 27 January 1993.

47 Phu Vinh, 'The Right to Strike Worries Employers' *Vietnam Investment Review* 9–15 May 1994, p. 8.

48 'Striking a Balance' (Interview with VGCL President, Nguyen Van Tu) *Vietnam Economic Times* Issue 2, May 1994, p. 24.

49 Gerard Greenfield, 'Strikes in Vietnam: Between Discipline and Dignity' *Asian Labour Update* Issue 19, August–October 1995, pp. 25–27.

50 On the first EPZ in Vietnam, see Khanh Tran, 'Khu che xuat tan thuan' ('The Tan Thuan Export Processing Zone') *Thoi Bao Kinh Te Viet Nam* ('Vietnam Economic Times') 12–18 May 1994.

51 See Nguyen Quang Lan, 'May van de ve khu che xuat tren the gioi va viec hinh thanh cac khu cong nghiep, khu che xuat tai Ha Noi' ('On Export Processing Zones in the world and the formation of industrial areas and export processing zones in Hanoi') *Nghien Cuu Kinh Te* ('Economic studies') no. 2, 1994, pp. 62–64. Also see Hoa Huu Lan, 'Some Features of Export Processing Zones in South-East Asian Countries and Their Relevance to Vietnam' *World Economic Problems* vol. 20, no. 2, June 1993, p. 20.

52 Greenfield, 'The Development of Capitalism in Vietnam', pp. 224–225.

53 Tran Luc, Director of the Department for International Relations, Ministry of Labour, War Invalids and Social Affairs, Speech to the National Seminar on the Role of Labour Administration in the National Economy, Hanoi, 10–14 July 1989.

54 Manh Hung, 'Ministry Probes Lebanon "Slave Trade"' *Vietnam Investment Review* 20–26 March 1995, p. 7.

55 See Nguyen Huu Dung, *Human Resource Development in the Transformation Process to Market-Oriented Economy in the Socialist Republic of Vietnam* (Hanoi: Department of Social and Labour Policies and National Centre for

Employment, Ministry of Labour, Invalids and Social Affairs, September 1994); Vali Jamal, 'Macroeconomic Context of Employment and Human Resources Development in Vietnam', paper presented at the subregional seminar: Employment and Labour Market Policies in Transitional Asian Economies, Hanoi, 7–10 December 1994, held by the International Labour Office East Asia Multidisciplinary Advisory Team (ILO/EASMAT); and Geoffrey B. Hainsworth, 'Human Resource Development in Vietnam' in Mya Than and Joseph L. H. Tan, eds, *Vietnam's Dilemmas and Options: The Challenge of Economic Transition in the 1990s* (Singapore: ISEAS, 1993).

56 Le Minh Chau, 'Van de ve xay dung giai cap cong nhan Viet Nam trong giai doan cong nghiep hoa, hien dai hoa dat nuoc' ('On building up the Vietnamese working class in the period of national industrialization and modernization') *Tap Chi Bao Chi va Tuyen Truyen* ('Media and propaganda review') September–October 1994, pp.12–13, 14.

57 ibid., p. 13.

58 ibid.

59 ibid.

60 Zachary Lockman, 'Imagining the Working Class: Culture, Nationalism, and Class Formation in Egypt, 1899–1914' *Poetics Today* vol. 15, no. 2, 1994, p. 161.

61 '"Epidemic" of Rolling Strikes Continues to Hound Song Be' *Vietnam Investment Review* 2-8 May 1994, p. 14; *Thoi Bao Kinh Te Viet Nam* ('Vietnam Economic Times') 24-27 April 1994, p. 2; *Lao Dong* ('Labour') 19 April 1994; and '"Rude and Indecent" Behaviour Cause of Song Be Stoppage' *Vietnam Investment Review* 25 April-1 May 1994, p. 4.

62 Martin J. Murray, *The Development of Capitalism in Colonial Indochina (1870–1940)* (Berkeley: University of California Press, 1980), pp. 295–307; 313.

63 The concept of the 'subaltern domain of politics and culture' used here is drawn from Subaltern Studies. See Ranajit Guha, *Elementary Aspects of Peasant Insurgency in Colonial India* (Delhi: Oxford University Press, 1983); and Ranajit Guha and Gayatri Chakravorty Spivak, *Selected Subaltern Studies* (Oxford: Oxford University Press, 1988).

64 A summary of this argument can be found in Thanh Le, 'May su nghi ve giai cap cong nhan trong cong nghiep hoa, hien dai hoa' ('Some ideas about the working class in the cause of industrialization and modernization') *Tap Chi Cong San* ('Communist review') no. 1, 1995, pp. 44–46.

65 Arif Dirlik, *After the Revolution: Waking to Global Capitalism* (London: University Press of New England, 1994), p. 44.

66 Steve Smith, 'Taylorism Rules OK? Bolshevism, Taylorism and the Technical Intelligentsia in the Soviet Union, 1917–41' *Radical Science Journal* no. 13, 1983, pp. 3–27. This is not to argue that the Soviet model of managerial-technicism was actually implemented, but rather, as Rajnarayan Chandavarkar argues in the case of Bombay in the 1920s, Taylorist principles were 'primarily a discourse of industrial management' which was not applied in practice. See Rajnarayan Chandavarkar, 'Workers' Resistance and the Rationalisation of Work in Bombay Between the Wars' in Douglas Haynes and Gyan Prakash, eds, *Contesting Power: Resistance and Everyday Social Relations in South Asia* (Berkeley: University of California Press, 1991), p. 111.

67 Report on the Situation and Tasks of the Trade Unions, presented by Duong Xuan An, General Secretary of the Vietnam General Confederation of Labour at the Sixth National Congress of Vietnamese Trade Unions, October 1988.

68 James C. Scott, *Weapons of the Weak: Everyday Forms of Peasant Resistance* (New Haven, Conn.: Yale University Press, 1985), p. 29.

69 Report on the Situation and Tasks of the Trade Unions, Sixth National Congress of Vietnamese Trade Unions, 1988.

70 Political report of the Executive Committee of the Vietnam General Confederation of Labour (VGCL) to the Seventh National Congress of Vietnamese Trade Unions, Hanoi, 10 November 1993.

71 Dam Minh Thuy, 'Dieu chua biet o Vinh Xanh' ('Green Bay – what remains unknown') *Lao Dong* 15 December 1994; also see the report by Truong Thanh Dam, 'Human Resources: Labour and Employment, Training and Education, Public Health and Social Security', Report no. 5, United Nations Development Programme (UNDP) Human Development Country Initiative, 29 January 1991.

72 Tran Ngoc Tao, 'Thieu tho lo – dang la moi lo cua nghanh than' ('The lack of miners is a concern for the coal industry'), *Quang Ninh*, 7 July 1994, p. 3.

73 Interview with Professor Nguyen Van Hoai, National Institute for Labour Protection, Vietnam General Confederation of Labour, Hanoi, 9 November 1994.

74 Huynh Thai, 'Than Lau' ('Illegal coal'), *Van Nghe* ('Literature and art'), 19 September 1992, p. 3.

75 Minh Tam, 'Than phan nguoi tho mo' ('The fate of miners') *Lao Dong va Xa Hoi* ('Labour and society') 5–11 August 1994.

76 World Bank, *Viet Nam Energy Sector Investment and Review. Volume 1 – Annexes*, Industry and Energy Operations Division, Country Department 1, East Asia and Pacific Region, 6 October 1993, p. 32.

77 *Vietnam News* 4 September 1994, p. 5.

78 *Vietnam Investment Review* 6–12 March 1995, p. 6. Do Hoang, 'Quang Ninh sap xep lai lao dong' ('Rearrangement of the labour force in Quang Ninh') *Lao Dong Xa Hoi* ('Labour and society') 27 October–2 November 1994; 'Lap lai trat tu trong khai thac va kinh doanh than' ('To restore order in coal exploitation and business') *Quang Ninh* 14 July 1994.

79 This forms part of several new business activities undertaken by the military in the transition to the market. Interview with Xuan Cang, Research and Information Centre, Vietnam General Confederation of Labour, Hanoi, 21 November 1994.

80 Adam Fforde and Suzanne Paine, *The Limits of National Liberation: Problems of Economic Management in the Democratic Republic of Vietnam* (London: Croom Helm, 1987); reviewed in Gabriel Kolko, 'The Structural Consequences of the Vietnam War and Socialist Economic Transformation' *Journal of Contemporary Asia* vol. 18, no. 4, 1988, pp. 473–482. See also Ngo Vinh Hai, 'Postwar Vietnam: Political Economy' in Douglas Allen and Ngo Vinh Long, eds, *Coming to Terms: Indochina, the United States and the War* (Boulder, Colo.: Westview Press/Bulletin of Concerned Asian Scholars, 1991), pp. 65–88.

81 Nhan Dan 12 November 1979, in BBC Summary of World Broadcasts, Far East, FE/W1059/A/26, 28 November 1979.

82 *Quang Ninh* 18 September 1984, 10 November 1984; *Nhan Dan* 6 March 1981.

83 Huynh Thai, 'Than Lau'.

84 Stacy Leigh Pigg, 'Unintended Consequences: The Ideological Impact of Development in Nepal' *South Asia Bulletin* vol. 13, nos. 1–2, 1993, pp. 53–54.

85 Hanoi Home Service 04.30 GMT 12 November 1969, translated in BBC Summary of World Broadcasts, Far East, FE/W546/A/14–15.

86 Song Thanh, 'Ho Chi Minh's Thoughts on the Way to Socialism in Vietnam' *Vietnam Social Sciences* 2, 1992, pp. 3–9.

87 This is based on interviews with coal miners and their families in Ha Long City and Cam Pha, Quang Ninh Province, in August and November 1994.

88 *Chu khach* carries the same meaning as Hoa (Chinese), though it encompasses the notion of Chinese as guests, as it is derived from *tru khach*, which means sojourner.

89 Interview with Nguyen Dinh Thua, President of the National Union of Energy Workers, Hanoi, 25 November 1994.

90 E. Willard Miller, 'Mineral Resources of Indochina' *Economic Geography* October 1946, no. 22, p. 277.

91 ibid.

92 This argument is made by Frederick Cooper in 'Colonizing Time: Work Rhythms and Labor Conflict in Colonial Mombasa' in Nicholas Dirks, ed., *Colonialism and Culture* (Ann Arbor, Mich.: University of Michigan Press, 1992).

93 Nguyen Son Ha, *Nguoi moi den* ('The newcomer') (Tap truyen, Quang Ninh: Hoi van hoc nghe thuat, 1985).

94 'Nguoi moi den' ('The newcomer') in *The Newcomer*, pp. 92–105.

95 'O lang mo' ('In a mining village') in *The Newcomer* pp. 1–12.

96 Huynh Thai, 'Than Lau'.

# 6 The politics of ethnicity and post-Cold War Malaysia: the dynamics of an ethnic state*

*Steve Majstorovic*

## INTRODUCTION: THE DYNAMICS OF AN ETHNIC STATE

The combined impact of the collapse of the Soviet empire in 1989 – which marked the end of both the Cold War and of the dominant ideological debate of the twentieth century – and of the approaching millennium has predictably launched an array of millennial theories which claim to predict the future of the international order. This foray into macro-level speculation also occurred as the year 1000 approached and a host of dire predictions about the end of the world or of the coming new age abounded. The concern here, however, will be with recently articulated theories that address future socio-political, economic and cultural possibilities. An examination of ethnopolitics and ethnopolicy in Malaysia over the past three decades will illustrate the salience of ethnocultural identity in Asia and will question the somewhat premature assumptions about a 'new world order', the coming 'clash of civilizations', and the 'end of history'.

The discussion below contends that the persistence of strong ethnic consciousness calls into question the liberal-democratic notion that ethnicity and its politicization will fade with the advent of modernity and political-economic development. Politicized ethnic groups also contradict marxist arguments about false consciousness as they pursue strategies that stress non-material cultural interests over economic/class considerations. In confronting the modern state and in conflict with each other, and by identifying along vertical ethnic cleavages instead of horizontal economic categories, ethnonational groups transcend class-based analyses and liberal-democratic assumptions that democracy and capitalism will erode cultural identities and antagonisms. The examination of the Malaysian case will address these contentions and will also suggest that Francis Fukuyama's 'end of history' pronouncement downplays the cultural dimensions of the historical dialectic.[1] In particular, Fukuyama's vision is really one that sees a triumph of capitalism more than the development of liberal-democratic systems. This political economic vision privileges economic variables over cultural ones; many Asian states, though capitalist in their economic arrangements, are not bastions of liberal democracy and are often fragmented along ethnic lines. Moreover, the 'Confucian' model of capitalist development, which suggests that Confucianism and capitalism are inherently compatible, glosses over important variants of Confucianism.[2]

Samuel P. Huntington's thesis that the future world order will be a 'clash of civilizations'[3] focuses on culture but his level of analysis misses the divisive effects of ethnonationalism and identity politics within and among the member states of any particular civilization. Huntington's scenario creates religious 'fault lines' among Islamic, Slavic-Orthodox, Western, Japanese, Confucian, Hindu and, possibly, Latin American civilizations. His argument erodes the primacy of the state without clearly explicating the process of this apocalyptic shift in the international order. Matters of cultural identity cannot, however, be reduced into a 'fault line' of civilization. Kishore Mahbubani, Singapore's permanent Secretary of the Foreign Ministry, seems to accept Huntington's perspective and is a vocal proponent of the 'Asian way'. He contends that Asian interests and methods are different and must be decoupled from the West.[4] Recently, Mahbubani has expanded his conception to call it the 'Pacific way'. But his vision remains the same. Asia's common culture has a separate agenda and differences can be transcended or controlled through an economic, cultural and security framework that is on an equal footing with and separate from the West.[5]

In an interview in 1992 Malaysia's Prime Minister Mahathir seemed to agree with Mahbubani's view that Asia needs to turn to the East. In the same interview, Malaysia's Minister of Finance agreed with the essence of the Mahbubani analysis but also insisted that 'if the new world order means a mutilation of self-identities and new barriers to cultural expressions then it is not an improvement over the old order'.[6] Thus it should be clear that any formation of 'civilizations' for a coming 'clash' will always be cross-cut by identity maintenance at the national or ethnonational level. Moreover, Huntington's thesis quickly precipitated numerous responses that made the case for state sovereignty as an almost eternal entity. Fouad Ajami tells us to 'be clear: civilizations do not control states, states control civilizations. . . . We remain in a world of self-help. The solitude of states continues'.[7] The process of modernity is irresistible, suggests Liu Binyun, and religious fault lines are constantly breached in a communicative process in which 'no culture is an island'.[8]

The state, however, is not always the final word in the international order. Thomas Friedman contends that the principal threat to international stability and the structure of the modern state is not conflict between nation-states but ethnic turmoil within nation-states, particularly since the decline of the Cold War and the resultant erosion of superpower hegemony. Friedman quotes Stanley Hoffmann who suggests that:

[T]he new world order, or whatever there is of it, is still very much based on state sovereignty, and that is quite inadequate, and indeed dangerous when you consider that many of the most destabilizing troubles are likely to come from within states . . . because of ethnic strife.[9]

Despite the virulence with which ethnopolitical conflict is metastasising world-wide, the problem requires approaches that are not yet evident to state policy makers. Ted Robert Gurr contends that this problem defies policy solutions based on economic reform or counter-insurgency because neither approach can satisfy or suppress the need for ethnic groups to maintain and protect collective identity. Gurr also identifies perhaps the most critical area of intractability for political leaders who address ethnic conflict. He asserts that policy solutions are fundamentally confounded when political decision makers are confronted with the disturbing actuality that '[t]he disconcerting intensity and persistence of ethnopolitical conflicts derives largely from the fact that they are driven by the clash of non-material interests'.[10]

The notion of 'nonmaterial interests' implies that human affairs cannot be reduced to matters of economic interest. In his controversial essay about the 'end of history' which celebrates the triumph of liberal democracy and market economics, Fukuyama prioritizes the importance of ideas and consciousness as driving forces in history, forces which shape and create economic systems.[11] But what he finally does articulate is that his end of history is more of a free-market model than a liberal-democratic one. Gabriel Almond makes the clear point that capitalism is a 'necessary but not sufficient condition' for liberal democracy.[12] The Asian experience has shown that some of Weber's 'Protestant ethic' is reproduced in Confucianism – hard work, delayed gratification, respect for authority, order and harmony – but the Western liberal-democratic notions of individualism and a limited state are not reproduced.[13] In much of Asia, a state-driven neo-corporatist model of capitalist development with limited social space for liberal-democratic levels of individual and minority rights is the norm and not the exception.[14]

Benedict Anderson's concern with ethnic and nationalist identity, particularly in the development of West European states, is a welcome alternative to the macro-level analyses depicted above. Anderson has contributed greatly to the understanding that cultural identity is a critical variable for examining politics within and among nation-states.[15] Anderson, however, sees ethnocultural identity as a malleable entity which is amenable to social construction in myriad patterns. The discussion below, however, suggests that ethnic identity, though not fixed as scholars with a primordialist perspective intimate, is also not so simply changed and adapted as scholars with a constructionist or elite/instrumentalist orientation contend.[16] Anderson also succumbs to political economy by contending that in the future ethnic and national conflicts will be driven by uneven capitalist development in the context of permeable boundaries and the world-wide communication and information revolution.[17] Economic variables are of course critical for political analysis. But the perspective presented below argues that the forces of ethnic and national identity cannot be reduced to matters of economic inequality and political economy. This perspective does not privilege cultural over material variables, or present a non-material/material dichotomy. Instead it is suggested that ethnocultural identity is a critical component of political analysis and within the Asian context needs to be considered as seriously as economic issues.

## POLITICIZED ETHNICITY AND A SUBJECTIVE PERSPECTIVE

The transformation process of ethnic groups into modern politicized and conflictual ethnonational actors is traceable to three periods in recent history:

> eighteenth century conceptions of popular sovereignty flowered with the burst of nationalism in nineteenth century Europe and the building of states like Germany and Italy out of more parochial units. The twentieth century, on the other hand, entailed the dismemberment of empires and large states in favor of smaller units, beginning after World War I, when the Wilsonian espousal of self-determination helped remake the map of Eastern Europe. The process was repeated after World War II, with the termination of colonial control in Asia and Africa. Decolonization set in motion a chain reaction, the ultimate impact of which has yet to be felt.[18]

Nineteenth-century nationalism in Europe and twentieth-century nationalism in the post-World War II decolonized Third World has generally produced multiethnic nation-states. These states are almost inevitably dominated by a single ethnic group.[19] In reaction, ethnic groups outside the state apparatus have become politicized and highly aware of their collective interests. 'Within these boundaries, the question was to whom the new states belonged.'[20]

Thus the context within which ethnonational conflict occurs is a nation-state system which is the product of European history and now in the post-colonial period encompasses the entire planet. 'In consequence of all these developments, ethnic conflict possesses elements of universality and uniformity that were not present at earlier times.'[21] Furthermore, it is this 'universality' and 'uniformity' in ethnopolitical behaviour which allows comparative inquiry. Cynthia H. Enloe and Joseph Rothschild also generally contend that not only have ethnic groups politicized and transformed themselves in reaction to the modern state, but that the alienation and dislocation caused by the industrial revolution and the nation-state have not precipitated a bonding along class lines but has instead fostered a reaffirmation of ethnonational identity.[22]

The problem of dualism also creates ethnopolitical conflict in the nation-state. There is a significant ambiguity in the relationship between the state and the various ethnonational groups which are incorporated into it. The state disseminates a picture of a nation which can transcend and subsume the differences between political allegiance to the state and ethnonational identity. However, very few states have succeeded in making the state and nation congruent.[23] This dualism also results in an ideological conflict between the political ideal of the nation-state and the historical reality of the nation.

Walker Connor strongly asserts that ethnicity is generally an independent variable and social formation whose behaviour can be manifested by the dimensions of language, religion and class.[24] But these dimensions are themselves not the essence of ethnicity and of the forces which drive ethnic politics to such intense levels of political conflict over the issues surrounding these dimensions. Connor advances the proposition that ethnicity is a form of shared identity which is subjectively defined.[25] It is the intangibility of this subjective bond which leads Connor to conclude that language, religion and economics/class are epiphenomenal and that the essence of ethnicity and its relationship to politics will remain amorphous and resistant to analyses which depend upon objective categories in order to explain ethnopolitical behaviour and conflict.

Clearly, Walker Connor presents a subjectivist position. He laments that few scholars have confronted the nature of the ethnonational bond and criticizes others who have little appreciation for the emotional and psychological hold that ethnonational identity has upon the members of the group.[26] He contends that one critical issue which many scholars miss is that the objective history of an ethnonational group is irrelevant for understanding the critical subjective essence of ethnic identity:

> it is not *what is*, but what people *believe is* that has behavioral consequences. And a subconscious belief in the group's separate origin and evolution is an essential ingredient of ethnonational psychology. A nation is a group of people characterized by a myth of common descent. Moreover, regardless of its roots, a nation must remain an essentially endogamous group in order to maintain its myth.[27]

As mentioned above, Connor also suggests that scholars misunderstand ethnonationalism because they have tended to comprehend it in terms of its objective characteristics or manifestations, in particular language, religion and class.[28] Instead, scholars should recognize, Connor insists, the sense of common kinship which is the essence of ethnonational identity. Such a recognition distinguishes ethnonational identity from non-kinship identities which are predicated upon membership in a religion, a linguistic group or an economic class.[29] Stating that language, religion and class are manifestations of ethnonational identity but not its essence is an argument which may be difficult to accept. This subjectivist perspective does not argue that there are differences among ethnonationalisms. But it does suggest that although Irish, Chechen, Kurdish and Malaysian nationalisms differ on the objective manifestations of their various ethnopolitical expression, the underlying reality is the ubiquity of identity maintenance and survival across various ethnocultural formations. And it is this ubiquity that facilitates comparison.

Joseph Rothschild notes that it would not be useful, or even possible, to separate ethnonational identity from religious, linguistic or other dimensions. He feels that if these dimensions were peeled off it would be difficult to see what would be left to examine and understand.[30] Rupert Emerson, however, would disagree with Rothschild and presents the subjectivist position in an elegant statement:

> The simplest statement that can be made about a nation is that it is a body of people who feel that they are a nation; and it may be that when all the fine-spun analysis is concluded this will be the ultimate statement as well. To advance beyond it, it is necessary to attempt to take the nation apart and to isolate for separate examination the forces and elements which appear to have been the most influential in bringing about the sense of common identity which lies at its roots, the sense of existence of a singularly important national 'we' which is distinguished from all others who make up an alien 'they'. This is necessarily an overly mechanical process, for nationalism, like other profound emotions such as love and hate, is more than the sum of the parts which are susceptible of cold and rational analysis.[31]

Of course Emerson described a world which existed fifty years ago. However, his use of the word 'nation' is a cultural one and implies a state that is dominated by an ethnic nationalism such as we find in Germany, Japan, Malaysia and Indonesia. The United States and most Western European countries claim to be states with a civic nationalism in which all ethnic groups are equal. But the fact remains that most states are dominated by a particular ethnonational formation. Moreover, some states like France are now engaged in a debate over which variant of nationalism really represents the national identity.[32]

If Connor and Emerson are correct, then why would so much of the literature on ethnonationalism disregard the persuasive power and intuitive logic of the subjectivist perspective? Connor considers seventeen reinforcing and overlapping reasons. However, there are perhaps five reasons which are most relevant to this chapter:

1 a misunderstanding of the nature of ethnic nationalism resulting in a tendency to underestimate its emotional power;
2 an unwarranted exaggeration of the influence of materialism upon human affairs;

3 unquestioned acceptance of the assumption that greater contacts among groups lead to greater awareness of what groups have in common, rather than of what makes them distinct;

4 over-exclusive concentration upon the state;

5 the tendency of many scholars to favour explanations based on class.[33]

A recent cross-national statistical analysis asserts that economic inequality has an only weak to moderate relationship with political conflict while the subjective forces of politicized ethnicity are strongly correlated with political conflict. And perhaps most importantly, the relationship between economic inequality and ethnicity is very weak. This cross-national analysis argues that economic and cultural forces have large autonomous spaces which cannot be reduced to each other and that prioritizing political-economic analysis over the issues of ethnocultural identity in multiethnic states misses much of the essence of what must be understood for useful explanation.[34]

## POLITICIZED ETHNICITY AND POLITICAL ECONOMY IN MALAYSIA

Ethnic relations in Malaysia have been shaped by 150 years of British colonization and then by the subsequent difficulties of state building after independence in 1957.[35] Despite a colonial history which imposed an ethnoclass structure on Malaysian society, political developments since independence reflect a pattern in which concerns over ethnonational identity determine state policies – cultural policies drafted to benefit a particular ethnonational formation – and class considerations are of secondary importance. This contention will be supported by examining Malaysian ethnic politics in relation to the crucial role of policies which have been formulated by the native Malays who dominate the political system.

Contemporary Malaysia has evolved into what can usefully be described as an ethnic state. That is, the state apparatus is captured by and is beholden to a particular ethnonational formation. Consequently this ethnic state conceptualizes its role as one in which the interests of the native Malays (the bumiputra)[36] are prioritized in socio-political, cultural and economic policy making. The outcome of the policies pursued by this ethnic state is that policy making not only politicizes Malay ethnonational identity but through a reactive process also politicises and sharpens the ethnonational identities of non-Malay segments of the population, and in particular the Chinese.[37] This state is of course capable of having autonomous interests and can behave accordingly. However, the autonomous capability of the ethnic state is always constrained by its cultural allegiance.

In Malaysia the Malays and Chinese comprise 90 per cent of the total population (58 per cent Malay and 32 per cent Chinese), with the remainder of the population, primarily Indians, being politically weak.[38] Peninsular Malaysia constitutes over 84 per cent of the total population and it is overwhelmingly important as the centre of socio-economic and socio-political life. Almost all the indigenous peoples of Malaysia are concentrated in East Malaysia – Land Dayaks, Sea Dayaks and the Kadazans. Their total population numbers slightly less than 1 million and they represent minimal political power. Moreover, the indigenous population in East Malaysia overwhelmingly supports the policies of the Malaysian state, and this support only reinforces the political paramountcy of the Malays.

In 1957 the independent Federation of Malaysia was created within a constitutional framework that institutionalized the special position of the bumiputra.[39] The constitution was essentially a compromise which guaranteed the Malays political supremacy while assuring the Chinese continued opportunities to pursue their economic interests.[40] Chinese support for the constitution was, however, much less enthusiastic than bumiputra support. Also incorporated within the constitutional framework were preferences for helping Malays with economic development, obtaining business and professional licences, appointments to civil service positions, and receiving educational scholarships. All these preferences were already in practice but the new constitution guaranteed them in Article 153.[41] The special preferences accorded to the bumiputra were supposed to be temporary until they had caught up with the Chinese and the Indians, especially in the economic sphere.

The 1957 constitution allowed that English would remain along with Malay as the official languages, but that in 1967 Malay would become the official language unless there was parliamentary opposition. Non-Malay languages were not recognized as official but the constitutional framework did allow for certain important announcements and documents to be published in Chinese and Tamil.[42] The Constitutional Commission recommended that Islam not be specified as the official state religion. The bumiputra forces contended that not specifying a state religion would infringe upon their authority in religious matters within the various federal units. At the same time it was strongly suggested to the Constitutional Commission that non-Muslims would still be free to pursue their own religious beliefs and denoting Islam as the religion of Malaysia did not necessarily indicate that the Malaysian state was not a secular state.[43] This line of reasoning was, however, lost on the non-Malays.

Ethnonational politicization and tensions continued throughout the 1960s. Malay and non-Malay parties and interest groups launched political offensives to influence legislation on the constitutional question of whether Malay would become the only official language in 1967. As it was a decade before, the language issue was settled rather ambiguously. In 1967 Malay did indeed become the official language of Malaysia but the 1967 decision also allowed for numerous exceptions in court, legislative and official business. Needless to say, neither the non-Malays nor the bumiputra were satisfied.[44] While the political parties in Malaysia were aligning along ethnonational lines, interest groups and professional associations were also following the ethnic pattern of association and allegiance. An examination of trade unions in Malaysia provides a typical example of ethnonational segmentation.

Historically, trade union activity in Malaysia was not very significant. Until recently the bumiputra were concentrated in agriculture and unionization was almost non-existent. The Chinese were somewhat more active but the government, fearing communist penetration of Chinese trade unions, maintained a close watch, especially with the recent experience of the emergency period. After independence the government relaxed somewhat its monitoring of union activity. Trade unions did not, however, form alliances with political parties and one explanation, other than government monitoring, is that the period of the Alliance (1954–1969) was to a degree transethnic but the unions were organized along ethnic lines. It could be argued that the ethnic make-up of the unions is a result of the ethnic division of labour produced during the colonial period. Some economic sectors are still unionized according to ethnicity. The National Union of Plantation Workers is predominantly Indian, but in other situations there are separate ethnically based unions for the same functional category. The Chinese and Malay teachers' unions have different opinions and interests on education policy. These unions do not compete with each other for government services but lobby for policies which maintain or extend opportunities for instruction in Malay or Chinese.[45]

In a case study of a Malaysian Shoe Workers' Union, Ackerman states in her introduction that:

> Though the Malaysian government's development policies, which emphasize rapid industrialization, are eroding the ethnically based colonial division of labor, consciousness of ethnic identity persists as a salient feature of the trade union movement. . . . [O]rganized labor in Malaysia is constrained by a political context . . . that heightens ethnic rather than class consciousness among trade union members.[46]

However, Ackerman fails to mention the fact that the political context itself represents an ethnonational structure when Malaysia is considered as an ethnic state. The trade union leadership in Malaysia would be expected to make some type of appeal to class solidarity over the divisive forces of 'false' ethnic consciousness. But the trade union leadership itself is overwhelmed by cultural forces:

> The workers do not unambiguously distinguish ethnic and economic interests. They prefer to support leaders from their own ethnic group and to pressure these leaders to promote ethnic interests. The workers' assertion of ethnic claims challenges the class ideology professed by

trade union leaders. Both grass-roots union members and the wider political arena [the ethnic state] exert pressures that trade union leaders cannot convincingly dismiss with appeals to the rhetoric of class.[47]

Capitalist interest organizations in Malaysia follow the same ethno-national distribution patterns as do the unions. The Malays, Chinese and Indians each have their own Chamber of Commerce. The Chinese Chamber of Commerce is the most politically active and is loosely associated with the Malay Chinese Association (MCA), although the MCA keeps its distance since it is illegal in Malaysia to hold a party and union position at the same time.[48] Since Chinese business associations are powerful and well organized, it comes as no surprise that the Malaysian ethnic state is wary of any official cooperation between Chinese politicians and business leaders.

The elections of 1969 and the subsequent interethnic riots were watersheds in Malaysian ethnonational relations. The reaction by the government to the election and the riots signalled the coming of age of a self-conscious ethnic state increasingly devoted to policy making dictated by the ethnic interests of a particular segment of society over the interests of all the other segments. The 1969 election pitted the Alliance party, which had become almost completely Malay-dominated, against three non-Malay parties. The opposition parties were particularly concerned with the emotional issues of language and education, and of the future interests of non-Malays in a country in which they determined that bumiputra interests were encroaching on the interests of the non-Malay population. The results of the election shocked the Alliance. Despite capturing a majority of seats in the Parliament the Alliance majority had dropped below the two-thirds necessary for a smooth constitutional amendment procedure. In the popular vote the Alliance declined from 58.4 per cent in 1964 to 48.8 per cent.[49]

On the day following the elections, 13 May, opposition supporters took to the streets of Kuala Lumpur for 'victory marches'. The bumiputra felt threatened and responded by attacking non-Malays, especially Chinese. The scale of the violence was reminiscent of World War II and the emergency period. After four days of bloody fighting the constitution was suspended and a national emergency was declared. Even then, sporadic ethnonational violence continued for the next two months.[50] The 13 May riots are now irrevocably imprinted upon the Malaysian population as collective memory, albeit a different memory for Malays and for non-Malays.[51] The riots symbolized, particularly for the Chinese, the end of any real political representation. The Malays interpreted the May 1969 events as a 'collective symbol of the political sanctity of Malay nationalism'.[52] This symbol of the Malayan struggle was institutionalized with the inauguration of the New Economic Policy (NEP). The NEP forecast 1990 as the target date for a transformation of the Malaysian socio-economic system to the point where the bumiputra would enjoy a 30 per cent share in commerce and industry. The NEP signalled the beginning of almost parasitic intrusions by the bumiputra into Malaysian economic life at the expense of the non-Malays, especially the Chinese.

The most critical dimension of the NEP, which continues to this day in five-year plans, is the active participation of the state in corporate owner-ship via state enterprises. In order to realize the 1990 goal (which has not been met) of 30 per cent Malay ownership of the economic sector, mone-tary allocations for new and existing government enterprises were consider-ably increased after 1969. But by the mid-1970s, of the $353 million of share capital reserved for bumiputra investment, only half was appro-priated for investment. And by 1973, only 6 per cent of the shares in new companies were owned by bumiputra.[53] These figures were unacceptable to the state and the Bumiputra Investment Foundation was established in 1974 to increase bumiputra investment steadily over the decade of the 1970s and by 1981 it was estimated that over 350,000 bumiputras had participated.[54]

As part of the NEP, Malaysian banks were required to boost lending to Malay entrepreneurs. In August 1974, Malaysian banks were directed to grant at least 12 per cent of their loans to the bumiputra and by October 1976 the credit share guarantee for Malays was increased to 20 per cent.[55] There was no end to the various schemes, enticements and entitlements which the state devised in order to create an entrepreneurial bumiputra juggernaut. Moreover, there has never even been a hint by the Malaysian state that if the NEP was ever to succeed then the government would eliminate the policies of ethnic favouritism.[56] Gordon Means suggests that while the NEP tries to reduce interethnic economic disparities, it could also reduce ethnic conflict by devolving the affirmative action policies of the NEP from a focus on ethnicity to smaller pluralized target groups based on economic disadvantage.[57] The problem with this solution is that class-based politics have been shown above to be ineffective. A devolution to smaller pluralized groups also suggests an eventual constitutional arrangement in which rights are understood in an individual context. But in Malaysia identity and rights are understood in a collective sense and the problem remains that the transition to liberal democracy must come from cultural change and not economic policy.

The ethnic state also launched an effort to increase the ranks of the bumiputra in higher education. In 1970 the Malay percentage of university students was 40 per cent (3237 students). By 1975 the percentage had risen to 57 per cent (8153 students), and in 1980 the percentage had further increased to 67 per cent (13,857). Clearly the bumiputra portion of univer-sity students had risen to a level far beyond the percentage of Malays in the population.[58] The Malaysian government was expressly attentive to the need for bumiputra education in business, science and technology in order to help train a vigorous future bumiputra industrial and commercial community. But the government has been less successful in this area. For example, in 1970 only 12 per cent (384) of Malay students pursued degrees in science compared to 49 per cent (2430) non-Malays in science fields. By 1975 the percentage of Malays in science education had changed to 29 per cent (2342) while the percentage of non-Malays had increased dramatically to 65 per cent (4004) of non-Malay students.[59] The success of non-Malays in the science fields had been a thorn in the side of the ethnic state and officials are sensitive to bumiputra demands that perhaps the access of non-Malays to science education should be limited. Moreover, bumiputra students still gravitate to fields where they can enter the civil service and receive a secure job after graduation.

Education policies aimed at creating a considerable professional and middle class were only a partial success. In 1957 only 3 per cent of the bumiputra were in the professional/technical and administrative/managerial occupational categories. The combination of these classifications grew to 4.8 per cent Malay by 1970 and to 6.1 per cent Malay in 1980. In other occupational classifications the bumiputra percentages also increased. The outcome of this growth, however, was a relatively low impact upon the Malay/non-Malay balance in the occupational categories that the government was attempting to effect. Even though non-Malay growth in this period slowed down, the Chinese percentage in the first two occupational classifications is still appreciably higher than the bumiputra. Furthermore, during the decade of the 1980s, bumiputra growth in these categories had slowed.[60]

In the corporate sector the economic growth of non-Malays has slackened compared to the bumiputra, but the non-Malayan share of the corporate sector is still over three times that of the Malays. Changes in corporate ownership from 1971 to 1980 have favoured the Malays but their relative impact is still not overwhelming. The bumiputra have gone from a 4.3 to a 12.4 per cent share of the corporate sector while the non-Malays (in this context the Chinese) have gone from 34 to 40.1 per cent of the corporate sector. Moreover, in the context of household income, the median income of the Chinese is still almost twice that of the bumiputra (as of 1981 with similar trends extending into the mid-1990s).[61]

The Chinese in Malaysia are also confronted by the choice between Confucian civilization and more particularistic identities. There is a strong Chinese trading arrangement that links the Chinese mainland with the Chinese in Malaysia through the vehicle of Chinese multinational corporations. This connection, however, also has to contend with the different clan, regional and religious ties that the Chinese in Malaysia still maintain with mainland China.[62]

Although the bumiputra seem to be catching up somewhat in the corporate sector, even the statistics can be misleading. Almost all successful bumiputra businessmen have joint ventures with non-Malayan partners, whether local or foreign.[63] One explanation for the bumiputra predilection

for partnership with non-Malayans, and unwillingness to engage in bumiputra entrepreneurship, relates to what is referred to as the 'Ali-Baba'
phenomenon:

> Statistics in the various industries seem to indicate considerable success
> in Malay participation; but the reality is less comforting. It is revealed
> time and time again, in almost every Malay economic conference, that
> most Malays resell their licenses or corporate control to non-Malays
> for a lucrative fee and allow their names to be used as fronts for non-
> Malays who run the enterprise and pay a tribute to the Malays. This
> problem of sleeping partnership, termed Ali-Baba . . . is as intractable
> as it is ubiquitous . . . the Malays who are granted licenses or have
> corporate ownership find it easier to sublease or relinquish corporate
> control for a lucrative fee than to operate the business themselves.[64]

Mah Hui Lim suggests that the Ali Baba phenomenon is essentially a
cultural disposition in which the bumiputra would rather profit less and
not have to work with non-Malayans. It is a subjective ethnic prejudice
that contends with the rational economic decision to control one's own
venture and reap the monetary benefits. Thus, the ethnic state has to contend with bumiputra resistance to certain ethnic affirmative action programmes which do not redistribute wealth but instead attempt to foster a
culture which will itself grow into economic dominance. Furthermore,
despite abundant natural resources, Malaysia's industrial development
strategy hinders economic transformation. Developmental expenditures
are used to mollify distributional ethnic demands instead of to attain developmental goals.[65] Ethnic considerations vitiate assumptions about economic rationality.[66]

The language policies of the Malaysian ethnic state have been a failure
compared to the very limited success of the economic policies. The state
has legislated a single official national language (Malay) in order to overcome the difficulties of ruling a multilingual state. These policies have
served to assuage the intense feelings of the bumiputra but they have also
served to solidify the ethnopoliticization of the non-Malayan communities.
Statistical surveys indicate that from 1972 to 1978, knowledge of Malay by
non-Malays has decreased while intraethnic communication has continued
to decline into the 1990s.[67] The language statistics suggest that the politicization of ethnicity among non-Malays is a reaction to the attempts by
the Malayan ethnic state to rationalize administration in a particular direction. The non-Malay ethnonational actors are politicized and their ethnic
consciousness is crystallized. In addition, the ethnic state of Malaysia is
itself a hostage to subjective ethnonational concerns and could not pursue
different policies even if it attempted to change course. But of course, the
Malaysian ethnic state is not likely to change its course. The present
Prime Minister, Mahathir Mohammad, writes that:

Malay is truly the indigenous language. . . . As the language of the first people to settle and form effective governments . . . it has priority over other languages as the definitive language of the country. . . . To be identified with the definitive people is to accept their history . . . their language . . . and to reject anything else. . . . Their language distinguishes them from other nationals, and, when adopted by new non-Malay citizens, would similarly distinguish them.[68]

The language polices have created an unintended outcome, however. Among non-Malays the knowledge of the Malay language eroded over 7 per cent in just the six years between 1972 and 1978.

In August 1985 the government announced that it intended to close Tamil and Chinese primary schools since they were an obstacle to national integration. This pronouncement produced an intense reaction from Chinese and Indian educators. The government also decided to phase out English-language schools as another method to achieve integration. Non-Malays felt frustrated since English was the medium for conducting international business and for functioning within the English Commonwealth. The government also planned to phase out Mandarin instruction in Chinese high schools. The inevitable reaction only furthered ethnonational friction and solidified subjective perspectives of one's own ethnic identity and of the ethnic identity of others.[69] The anti-English campaign finally ended in December 1993 when Prime Minister Mahathir took a pragmatic turn and admitted that English was indispensable for Malays to become competitive and that most scientific publications are in English. But he also noted that: 'Once we have become a successful race, our language will become successful also.'[70] In fact, there are now indications that merit is being considered in higher education and the turn to English is gathering steam. Mahathir feels that perhaps the emerging Asian economies are ones in which 'tigers need brains as well as brawn'.[71]

Religious policy in Malaysia also took a stronger pro-bumiputra turn after the 1969 violence. The emergence of an Islamic revivalist movement (*dakwah*) during the 1970s had a profound effect on Malaysian ethnonational relations. The bumiputra state not only made the Malay language the official tongue of Malaysia but Islam was further reinforced as the state religion after 1969. As mentioned above, the ethnic state quickly acceded to many of the demands of the *dakwah* movement in order to outflank bumiputra Islamic parties. One of the most inflammatory issues was land allocation for religious buildings. Before independence non-Malays were able to erect churches and temples on property received from the British colonial government. But after independence and particularly after 1969, the pressure for Islamization grew and non-Muslims experienced ever increasing obstacles in acquiring land and building permits. Non-Muslims were reduced to congregating and worshipping in rented houses and storefront facilities.[72]

Non-Muslims have formed organizations to air their grievances over real and imagined cases of religious persecution. Although these organizations have been somewhat vocal in public, their role seems limited to presenting seminars and giving out press statements. The ethnic state will only negotiate with individual religious organizations and non-Malay politicians, and will not recognize the legitimacy of any transethnic non-Muslim organizations.[73] Christian denominations which have a very pan-ethnic character have been particularly singled out by the Malaysian government for close scrutiny.

Hussein Mutalib has suggested that Islam could prove to be a divisive force among the Malays because the symbol of Islam has been politicized so often by the Malay government that it has become ambiguous and consequently ethnic identity is more central to Malays than religious identity.[74] As if to reinforce this suggestion, Prime Minister Mahathir ordered a crackdown on the growing influence of Al Arqam, a powerful Islamic fundamentalist group. Ashaari Muhammed, the leader of Al Arqam, was arrested as a threat to national security. Al Arqam has 10,000 hard core followers and as many as 200,000 sympathizers.[75] It is clear that Malaysia's ethnic state will not bow to Huntington's higher level of analysis which sees Islam as an underminer of ethnic identity.

Raymond Lee portrays state policies in Malaysia as a process of ethnic rationalization.[76] He follows Anthony Smith's argument that 'the resurgence of ethnic nationalism and the growth of the scientific state cannot but become locked into a vicious cycle of conflict'.[77] The Malaysian state, however, reduces some of this conflict by policy rationalization which incorporates the cultural essence of the dominant ethnonational formation within the state apparatus. Lee contends that such a state is 'characterized by a rationalism that is influenced by nationalist ideals'.[78] Whenever this type of state has its rationality challenged by competing forces such as the *dakwah* movement (or Al Arqam), the state (since it is an ethnic state) easily incorporates the religious movement within the 'iron cage' of the state.[79]

Margaret Scott posits that the Malaysian ethnic state has gone even beyond the politics of ethnonational privilege and now 'discrimination is the law of the land and segregation the way of life'.[80] She suggests that there is a feeling of hopelessness among a non-Malay population that has become fatalistic about life in Malaysia for a non-bumiputra. In contrast, the Malays have gone from a perspective after the 1969 riots where they demanded temporary ethnonational privileges to an outlook where the special preferences are considered inviolable and permanent. From her observations of the socio-economic environment, Scott contends that without the endless reams of statistics which prove that the bumiputra are victims, the Malays would be hard pressed in justifying the retention of their privileges. Scott does conclude with a bit of optimism when she suggests that some of the young bumiputra intelligentsia are having second thoughts about the practicability and ethical dimensions of the constitutional guarantees for the Malays.

Whether the present arrangement in Malaysia will continue unchanged is not clear, but the possibility of severe political upheavals is conceivable. In a pessimistic evaluation, Cait Murphy concludes that Malaysia is 'the grandest affirmative action failure of all' and that:

> In the wake of India's caste riots, Sri Lanka's civil war and Fiji's political mess, one might expect Asian policy makers to have wised up to the dangers of racial number-crunching. That is not the case. In Malaysia, in particular, the arithmetic of race is calculated in education, in business and in every part of the political system. The country's wide-ranging efforts of social engineering have only widened ethnic divisions and have dampened economic growth. They have also undermined any chance of creating a national identity to which all Malaysians can claim a connection. Malaysia is a lesson with implications for any society tempted to believe that racial formulas can be allocated with justice and imposed without rancor.[81]

Clearly, Ms Murphy's warning is applicable to a myriad nation-states within and beyond the Pacific arena. Of the 185 states in the world, over 80 per cent are multiethnic, and in the fallout associated with the end of the bipolar arrangement of the Cold War, the tendency of many states to pursue policies that favour the dominant ethnonational formation (the ethnic state scenario) will eventually only protract ethnopolitical conflict within states and across regional borders.

## CONCLUSION: THE POLITICS OF ETHNICITY AND POST-COLD WAR MALAYSIA

The debate over whether material or non-material forces – perhaps best depicted in the endless struggle between Marx and Hegel – are the determining engines of history can never be answered. However, the examination of Malaysia illustrates that both forces are important for understanding the socio-political environment. Although ethnonationalism and ethnic identity have been the focus in this analysis, it should not be construed as a case for some type of ethnic determinism. That would be as mistaken as theories of economic and structural determinism. Perhaps ethnocultural identity is so pervasive because in the age of rationality the focus has been on rational economic solutions for societal ills. The policy formulations and analyses of the capitalist, former marxist, and developing world are all generally concerned with material approaches while cultural policies are marginalized. If ethnonationalism were a dependent variable and a pre-modern phenomenon, then the process of modernization and industrialization would only produce the type of conflict associated with the normal economic and social displacement precipitated by rapid social change.[82]

Modernity itself, however, has not weakened or dissolved the supposedly primordial ethnonational bond. Instead, ethnonational identity has transformed and politicized itself in the modern age. In fact, the alienation and dissociation of modern industrial societies or developing societies have only served to reinforce the already pre-existent ethnonational formations. It could be that in the ideal world the influence of material forces and cultural forces would be approximately equal. Thus Fukuyama's attempt to conceptualize an 'end of history' with a balance between liberal-democratic and capitalist triumph could be successful. But whether the arena is the Asia-Pacific or Europe, an emerging contradiction in the dialectic of the development of the nation-state and modernity, and its focus on rational economic man, is the continual effort to maintain and assert cultural identity. In a rebuttal of Fukuyama, Gertrude Himmelfarb suggested that Hegel was not known for his modesty but he did concede that 'The owl of Minerva spreads its wings only with the falling of dusk'. In other words, 'we know, at best, only what was, not what will be'.[83]

## NOTES

*The work for this study was supported by a postdoctoral fellowship at the Hoover Institution – Stanford University (1992–1993) under the auspices of the US Department of State's discretionary grant programme, Public Law 98-164, Title VIII, 97 Stat. 1047-50 and by a National Endowment for the Humanities grant to attend a seminar on Cultural Pluralism and the Nation-State: Comparative Perspectives, which was directed by M. Crawford Young at the University of Wisconsin-Madison, 12 June–29 July 1994.

1 See Francis Fukuyama, 'The End of History' *The National Interest* vol. 16, no. 8, 1989, pp. 3–18.
2 Winston Davis, 'Religion and Development: Weber and the East Asian Experience' in Myron Weiner and Samuel P. Huntington, eds, *Understanding Political Development* (Boston, Mass.: Little, Brown & Company, 1987), pp. 221–280.
3 Samuel P. Huntington, 'The Clash of Civilizations?' *Foreign Affairs* vol. 72, no. 3, 1993, pp. 22–49.
4 Kishore Mahbubani, 'Why Asia's Balkans Are at Peace' *New Perspectives Quarterly* vol. 12, no. 1, 1995, pp. 51–53.
5 Kishore Mahbubani, 'The Pacific Way' *Foreign Affairs* vol. 74, no. 1, 1995, pp. 100–111.
6 Datuk Seri Mahathir bin Mohammed, 'Look East' *New Perspectives Quarterly* vol. 9, no. 1, 1992, pp. 16–19.
7 Fouad Ajami, 'The Summoning' *Foreign Affairs* vol. 72, no. 4, 1993, pp. 2–9.
8 Liu Binyun, 'Civilization Grafting: No Culture is an Island' *Foreign Affairs* vol. 72, no. 4, 1993, pp. 19–21.
9 Thomas L. Friedman, 'Nations at War With Themselves' *New York Times* 2 June 1991, p E3. Stanley Hoffmann is a leading international relations theorist and noted scholar of US foreign policy at Harvard University.

10 See Ted Robert Gurr, 'Ethnic Warfare and the Changing Priorities of Global Security' *Mediterranean Quarterly* no. 1, 1990, pp. 82–98.

11 Fukuyama, 'The End of History?'.

12 Gabriel Almond, 'Capitalism and Democracy' *Political Science and Politics: PS* vol. 24, no. 3, 1991, pp. 467–474.

13 Davis, 'Religion and Development: Weber and the East Asian Experience', pp. 221–280.

14 Samuel P. Huntington, 'Democracy's Third Wave' *Journal of Democracy* Spring 1991, pp. 12–34.

15 Benedict Anderson's influential work on national identity, *Imagined Communities. Reflections on the Origins and Spread of Nationalism* (London: Verso, 1991; 2nd edn) is particularly useful on how ideas and myths can drive ethno-national mobilization.

16 For a discussion of the ethnohistorical antecedents of nations and states see Anthony D. Smith, *The Ethnic Origins of Nations* (Oxford: Basil Blackwell, 1986).

17 Benedict Anderson, 'The Last Empires: The New World Disorder' *New Left Review* no. 193, 1992.

18 Donald L. Horowitz, *Ethnic Groups in Conflict* (Berkeley: University of California Press, 1985), p. 4.

19 See Joseph Rothschild, *Ethnopolitics: A Conceptual Framework* (New York: Columbia University Press, 1981), p. 216.

20 Horowitz, *Ethnic Groups in Conflict*, p. 4.

21 ibid., p. 5.

22 See Cynthia H. Enloe, *Ethnic Conflict and Political Development* (Boston, Mass.: Little, Brown & Company, 1973); and Rothschild, *Ethnopolitics*.

23 Japan, Iceland and, until recently, Germany are exceptions to the general incongruence between the state and nation that is characteristic of the majority of nation-states.

24 Describing ethnicity as an independent variable does not imply a simplistic causal assumption. It is clear that no socio-political variables are completely independent or dependent. It is being argued here, however, that the force of politicized ethnicity is powerful enough to shape political outcomes in a manner which is largely independent of class structures.

25 For a representative survey of Walker Connor's perspectives on ethnicity see Walker Connor, 'Ethnonationalism' in Weiner and Huntington, eds, *Understanding Political Development*; Walker Connor, 'Eco- or Ethno-Nationalism' *Ethnic and Racial Studies* vol. 7, no. 3, 1984, pp. 342–359; Walker Connor, 'A Nation is a Nation is a State, is an Ethnic Group, is a . . .' *Ethnic and Racial Studies* vol. 1, no. 4, 1978, pp. 377–400; Walker Connor, 'Nation-Building or Nation-Destroying?' *World Politics* no. 24, 1972, pp. 319–355.

26 Connor, 'Eco- or Ethno-Nationalism', pp. 204–205.

27 ibid., p. 206.

28 Connor, 'Nation-Building or Nation-Destroying?', pp. 337–341.

29 Connor, 'Eco- or Ethno-Nationalism', p. 204.

30 Rothschild, *Ethnopolitics*, pp. 8–9.

31 Rupert Emerson, *From Empire to Nation: The Rise to Self-Assertion of Asian and African Peoples* (Boston, Mass.: Beacon Press, 1962), p. 102.

32 For a clear discussion of the differences between civic and ethnic nationalisms see Christian Joppke, *East German Dissidents and the Revolution of 1989: Social Movements in a Leninist Regime* (New York: New York University Press, 1995). For a complete discussion of the problems of a state in debate between espousing ethnic versus civic nationalism, see William Safran, 'France

and the Problem of National Identity: Old Ideologies and New Challenges' *International Political Science Review* vol. 12, no. 3, 1991, pp. 219–238; and William Safran, 'Ethnic Mobilization, Modernization, and Ideology: Jacobinism, Marxism, Organicism, and Functionalism' *The Journal of Ethnic Studies* vol. 15, no. 1, 1987, pp. 1–31.

33 Connor, 'Eco- or Ethno-Nationalism', pp. 197–198.

34 This is a cross-national analysis of sixty-six states: Steven Majstorovic, 'Politicized Ethnicity and Economic Inequality: A Subjective Perspective and a Cross-National Examination' *Nationalism and Ethnic Politics* vol 1, no. 1, 1995, pp. 33–53.

35 R. K. Vasil, *Ethnic Politics in Malaysia* (New Delhi: Radiant Publishers, 1980).

36 The term 'bumiputra' means 'sons of the soil' and is a politically potent term because it represents the paramount political position of the indigenous Malays over the non-Malay population.

37 For an extensive discussion of the 'ethnic state' in Malaysia see Steven Majstorovic, 'Malaysia: The Evolution of an Ethnic State' *The Journal of Pacific Studies* vol. 17, nos. 1–2, December 1993, pp. 161–189.

38 Cait Murphy, 'The Grandest Affirmative Action Failure of All' *Wall Street Journal* 27 December 1990.

39 R. S. Milne and Diane K. Mauzy, *Politics and Government in Malaysia* (Vancouver: University of British Columbia Press, 1980), pp. 36–42.

40 Vasil, *Ethnic Politics in Malaysia*, p. 9.

41 See Gordon P. Means, 'Special Rights as a Strategy for Development' *Comparative Politics* no. 5, 1972, pp. 29–61; Vasil, *Ethnic Politics in Malaysia*, p. 42.

42 Vasil, *Ethnic Politics in Malaysia*, pp. 38–39.

43 ibid., p. 40.

44 William R. Roff, *The Origins of Malay Nationalism* (New Haven: Yale University Press, 1967), pp. 316–328.

45 R. S. Milne, *Politics in Ethnically Bipolar States: Guyana, Malaysia, Fiji* (Vancouver: University of British Columbia Press, 1981), p. 55.

46 See Susan E. Ackerman, 'Ethnicity and Trade Unionism in Malaysia: A Case Study of a Shoe Workers' Union' in Raymond Lee, ed., *Ethnicity and Ethnic Relations in Malaysia* (DeKalb: Center for Southeast Asian Studies Northern Illinois University, 1986), p. 145.

47 Ackerman, 'Ethnicity and Trade Unionism in Malaysia', p. 166.

48 Milne, *Politics in Ethnically Bipolar States*, pp. 55–56.

49 Barbara Watson and Leonard Y. Andaya, *A History of Malaysia* (London: The MacMillan Press, 1982), p. 280; Vasil, *Ethnic Politics in Malaysia*, pp. 185–186.

50 See William C. Parker, *Communication and the May 13th Crisis* (Kuala Lumpur: University of Malaya Press, 1979); Karl von Vorys, *Democracy Without Consensus* (Princeton, NJ: Princeton University Press, 1975), pp. 11–13.

51 See Raymond L. M. Lee, 'The State, Religious Nationalism, and Ethnic Rationalization in Malaysia' *Ethnic and Racial Studies* vol. 13, no. 4, 1990, pp. 491–492.

52 ibid., p. 491.

53 Malaysia, *Mid-Term Review of Second Malaysia Plan* (Kuala Lumpur: Government Printers, 1973).

54 See Mah Hui Lim, 'Affirmative Action, Ethnicity and Integration: The Case of Malaysia' *Ethnic and Racial Studies* vol. 8, no. 2, 1985, p. 264.

55 ibid., p. 265.

56 For a comprehensive discussion of the NEP see Just Faaland, J. R. Parkinson and Rais Saniman, *Growth and Ethnic Inequality: Malaysia's New Economic Policy* (New York: St Martin's Press, 1991).

57 See Gordon P. Means, *Malaysian Politics: The Second Generation* (London: Oxford University Press, 1991), p. 314.

58 Malaysia, *Fourth Malaysia Plan 1981–1985* (Kuala Lumpur: Government Printers, 1980), p. 352; Malaysia, *Third Malaysia Plan 1976–1980* (Kuala Lumpur: Government Printers, 1976), p. 401.

59 Malaysia, *Third Malaysia Plan 1976–1980*, p. 403.

60 Lim, 'Affirmative Action', 1985, p. 259.

61 ibid., p. 268; 'Malaysia: the Language of Progress' *The Economist* 15 January 1994.

62 For a close look at the Chinese connection see Eddie C. Y. Kuo, 'Ethnicity, Polity and Economy: A Case Study of Mandarin Trade and the Chinese Connection', a working paper published by the Department of Sociology – National University of Singapore, 1990.

63 Lim, 'Affirmative Action', p. 268.

64 ibid., p. 259.

65 For an interesting analysis of how Malaysian economic policies are often counter-productive see Alasdair Bowie, 'Redistribution with Growth? The Dilemmas of State-sponsored Economic Development in Malaysia', in Cal Clark and Jonathan Lemco, eds, *State and Development* (New York: E. J. Brill, 1988).

66 James V. Jesudason, *Ethnicity and the Economy: the State, Chinese Business and Multinationals in Malaysia* (Singapore and New York: Oxford University Press, 1989), p. 6.

67 See Martina Ting and Lee Yong Leng, 'Language and National Cohesion in Malaysia' *Asian Profile* vol. 14, no. 6, 1986, p. 522; 'Malaysia: the Language of Progress' *The Economist* 15 January 1994.

68 ibid., p. 525.

69 ibid., p. 526. For a compelling discussion of the construction of Malay identity and of the subjective nature of identity choice see Joel S. Kahn, 'Class, Ethnicity and Diversity: Some Remarks on Malay Culture in Malaysia' in Joel S. Kahn and Francis Loh Kok Wah, eds, *Fragmented Vision: Culture and Politics in Contemporary Malaysia* (Honolulu: University of Hawaii Press, 1991), pp. 158–178.

70 'Malaysia: The Language of Progress' *The Economist* 15 January 1994, pp. 37–38.

71 'Who's Nicest?' *The Economist* 13 August 1984, pp. 31–32.

72 Raymond L. M. Lee, 'Patterns of Religious Tension in Malaysia' *Asian Survey* vol. 28, no. 4, 1988, p. 410.

73 See Ameer Ali, 'Islamic Revivalism in Harmony and Conflict: The Experience in Sri Lanka and Malaysia' *Asian Survey* vol. 24, no. 3, 1984, pp. 306–309; Lee, 'Patterns of Religious Tension in Malaysia', pp. 413–414.

74 See Hussein Mutalib, *Islam and Ethnicity in Malay Politics* (Singapore: Oxford University Press, 1990).

75 See 'Holier Than Them' *The Economist* 23 July 1994, pp. 33–34; 'A Butterfly Upon a Wheel' *The Economist* 10 September 1994, pp. 35–36; and 'Malaysia's Dangerous Brew' *The Economist* 10 September 1994, pp. 17–18.

76 Lee, 'The State, Religious Nationalism, and Ethnic Rationalization', pp. 482–502.

77 For a complete historical examination of ethnic identity see Anthony D. Smith, *The Ethnic Revival* (London: Cambridge University Press, 1981), p. 184.

78 Lee, 'The State, Religious Nationalism, and Ethnic Rationalization', p. 499.

79 ibid.

80 See Margaret Scott, 'Where the Quota is King' *New York Times Magazine* 17 November 1991, pp. 62–67, 111.

81 Murphy, 'The Grandest Affirmative Action Failure of All'.
82 See for example Harry Eckstein, 'Theoretical Approaches to Explaining Collective Political Violence', and Ekkart Zimmermann, 'Macro-Comparative Research on Political Protest' in Ted Robert Gurr, ed., *Handbook of Political Conflict* (New York: The Free Press, 1980).
83 See Gertrude Himmelfarb in *The National Interest* vol. 16, 1989, pp. 24–26.

# 7 Post-Cold War Indonesia and the revenge of history: the colonial legacy, nationalist visions and global capitalism*

*Mark T. Berger*

## INTRODUCTION: THE COLONIAL LEGACY, NATIONALIST VISIONS AND GLOBAL CAPITALISM

While the demise of state socialism has been heralded as a triumph for capitalist democracy (and even as the 'end of history'), there are a growing number of observers who see the collapse of Soviet imperium as a warning to the world. Certainly the resonance between the ethnonationalist resurgence in the former Soviet Union and trends in Latin America, Africa and parts of Asia have been noted by many commentators. For example, a 'Voice of America' (VOA) report on the final day of the APEC meeting in Bogor, Indonesia, in mid-November 1994, clearly reflected the tendency to look to the struggles in the one-time Soviet empire as reminders of the continued potency of ethnic and religious loyalties around the globe. The VOA noted that Soeharto's New Order (a 'less than perfect democracy') boasted 'one of the fastest rates of economic growth in the world' and this had not only 'lifted millions out of poverty and greatly increased health and literacy', but had 'also helped to bind together' the ethnically diverse country of more than 180 million people. The VOA report quoted Robert Hefner who argued that, unlike the former USSR, Indonesia had 'the solid foundation for a national culture'. He conceded that 'there are regional tensions, but Indonesia has achieved a shared national language, which virtually the entire young generation of Indonesians speak'. On the question of Islam (90 per cent of Indonesians are nominal Muslims) the VOA report cited Benedict Anderson who noted that there was a 'possibility not so much of ethnic conflict but of conflict between committed Muslims and everybody else'. However, Hefner argued that in Indonesia, the 'most prominent' Muslims and the 'most prominent' Islamic movements 'are remarkable for the verve with which they declare their allegiance to principles of democracy, human rights and religious tolerance and pluralism'. The report concluded with the anticipation by Hefner that as long as economic growth continued tolerance and social stability would predominate.[1]

In the context of increasing concern about ethnic conflict and social instability, the VOA report reflected the continued reach of powerful Anglo-American theories of modernization which emerged during the Cold War and remain central to post-Cold War visions of an increasingly integrated and prosperous Asia-Pacific.[2] Against this background, much of the recent analysis of Indonesia continues to rest on an elite-oriented and evolutionary conception of history, assigning a major role in political and social transformation to the middle class.[3] This results in an analysis of Indonesia in which it is assumed that the country is headed towards, or at least ought to be headed towards, the continued rationalization of government–business relations, in the context of the emergence of a politically significant middle and business class. This perspective fails to give sufficient weight to the wider social changes that have been part of the uneven process of capitalist development of the past thirty years. The approach taken in this chapter assumes that capitalist development contributes as much to social and ethnic fragmentation as it does to unity and stability. What will be highlighted here is the specific history of the state in the context of the emergence of capitalism in what became Indonesia. As a result of the country's particular historical trajectory a key aspect of New Order Indonesia has been the way in which the power of the dominant elite originated primarily from within the bureaucratic structures of the state.[4] At the same time, the perspective on New Order Indonesia being outlined here seeks to go beyond the often culturally empty usage of the categories of class and state associated with structuralist political economy. The view taken here is that there is more to historical analysis than an emphasis on class structure and/or class struggle, at the same time as class remains a relevant, albeit not necessarily a foundational, category of analysis. Attention is drawn to the culturally specific bases of the exercise of power, the particular forms of domination and the complex contours of subaltern accommodation and resistance in the context of the long and uneven deepening of the capital accumulation process during the colonial and national periods. At the broadest level, the emergence and survival of the New Order flows from the history of the rise and fall of the Netherlands East Indies, an uneven process of capitalist development and the dynamics of Indonesian nationalism. While nationalism represented the main site of anti-colonial resistance, the new nations which emerged from the nationalist struggle have increasingly demonstrated the ability of colonialism to reproduce itself. At their 'moment of arrival' nationalist movements turned the 'state' into the embodiment of the national struggle; and the many contradictions and tensions of the national struggle were given a unity by the 'state' erected on the foundations of colonial power.[5] The limits built into the nationalist struggle and the wider legacy of colonialism have meant that decades later the colonial era continues 'to haunt "new nations" where shifting identities and precarious polities are anchored against the modern by the reinvention of forms of tradition that too often clearly betray the traces of a colonial past'.[6]

In Indonesia since World War II politico-economic hierarchies and ethnic, religious and national identities have been created and reconfigured against the background of the wider process of uneven capitalist development. This has taken place in the context of both efforts by the Java-centred elite to gain or maintain hegemony and the complicated processes of accommodation and resistance of the rural and urban poor. Central to the hegemony of the Java-centred elite and the New Order state has been the production of a powerful development discourse, which has exhorted Indonesians to work together to develop the 'nation' and bring about economic 'take-off'. The state-sponsored ideology of economic development (*pembangunan*) has emerged as a key element in wider efforts to legitimate the New Order, and Soeharto himself is proudly styled the 'father of development' (Bapak Pembangunan).[7] Although powerful New Order rhetoric about national development and national identity, which built on twenty years of 'nation building' under Sukarno, has certainly ensured that national consciousness has expanded since 1945, national identity in Indonesia (as elsewhere) has continued to be informed by historically specific ethnic, regional, religious and class consciousness. While the nation-state of Indonesia emerged out of the forcing ground of the intensified nationalist mobilization of the Japanese occupation and its aftermath, neither World War II nor the national 'revolution' (1945–1949) was as transformative as the latter term implies. By the mid-1990s Indonesia has become a tension-ridden Java-centred empire, which owes as much to the complex legacy of Dutch colonialism as it does to the promise of Indonesian nationalism. Soeharto's New Order has increasingly incorporated the people of the archipelago into a Java-centred imperium dominated by an elite whose hegemony is legitimated by a powerful national development discourse, as well as considerable coercion, and the selective appropriation of the symbols of the 'Javanese' and 'Indonesian' past. This is occurring in the context of the end of the Cold War, a major trend in international political economy towards globalization, and the rise of new social forces in Indonesia (epitomized by growing labour unrest in a number of key urban areas, most notably in Medan in April 1994), all of which represents a serious set of challenges to the Java-centred imperium and the New Order state.

## THE LINEAGE OF THE NEW ORDER STATE: DUTCH COLONIALISM AND THE INDONESIAN TRAJECTORY, 1600–1965

Soeharto's New Order state can be understood in key ways as the successor to the complex historical amalgam which was the Dutch colonial state. East Timor aside, Indonesia continues to lay claim to the former Dutch colonial boundaries as they were consolidated by the beginning of the twentieth century.[8] Apart from the same boundaries, the historical connection between the New Order and the colonial era is apparent in socio-ethnic terms insofar as the Javanese priyayi (the hereditary aristocracy of Java who became the backbone of the emergent Dutch colonial state) has continued to reproduce itself and play a central role in the bureaucratic (and military) structures of the modern Indonesia state.[9] The Javanese, ostensibly under priyayi leadership, represent the 'ethnic core' of, and in many ways provide the cultural basis for, the New Order in Indonesia.[10] This flowed from the history of Dutch colonialism and the overall character of the archipelago's pre-colonial social formations, particularly on Java, which was heavily populated, agriculturally significant and a regional power centre. In the context of Dutch colonial expansion the Javanese aristocracy was transformed into a bureaucratic elite and coopted into the colonial state apparatus.[11] Already well entrenched in the colonial system, the priyayi benefited the most from the expansion of colonial education which gained momentum at the end of the nineteenth century. As a result, the Javanese elite took up most of the administrative jobs in the growing colonial state at the same time as a number of the Dutch-educated leaders of the Indonesian nationalist movement also came from priyayi backgrounds. In this period the number of priyayi grew dramatically, through both birth and recruitment, as they reproduced and consolidated themselves as a relatively distinctive social class. Their enlargement in numbers and an increase in administrative positions within the colonial state were part of a shift from being a group of officials dependent on the variable patronage of the Javanese kings to being salaried officials in a broader colonial political economy.[12] By the end of the colonial period a large and variegated colonial state had emerged, staffed primarily by members of the priyayi-centred Javanese elite. But, while they dominated the lower and middle ranks of the colonial state, their influence was much weaker in the emerging nationalist movement.[13] Anti-colonial nationalism did not take hold in the Netherlands East Indies until the early twentieth century, but throughout the colonial period local and regional rebellions and acts of resistance had shaped the wider historical trajectory in important ways.[14] However, they rarely threatened Dutch colonial rule as a whole. Even the emergent nationalist movement of the 1920s, over which the colony's nascent labour movement and the Indonesian Communist Party (PKI) exercised considerable influence, was unable to overcome the myriad forms of accommodation and cooptation, or the repressive capacity deployed by an increasingly powerful colonial state.[15]

In 1934, by which time the nationalist movement was dominated by urban intellectuals, Sukarno and many other major nationalist leaders were banished to remote islands where they languished until the Japanese invasion in 1942. The Japanese advance into Southeast Asia dealt a blow to European colonialism in Asia generally, while their occupation of the Netherlands East Indies led to the release and encouragement of the gaoled nationalist leaders. At the same time, the Japanese occupation and the end of Dutch colonial rule threatened the historical dominance of the bureaucratic priyayi. The Japanese era marked the beginning of widespread rivalry between the Javanese elite and other social classes for control of the emergent Indonesian state.[16] An important element in this rivalry was the struggle between the syncretized Islam of the Javanese aristocratic-administrative elite and the more strident Islam of non-priyayi and non-Javanese nationalists. The Japanese gave Sukarno and Hatta, as well as other Indonesian nationalists, important opportunities in the form of various mass-based political organizations to reach out to the people in the rural areas. Japan also set up auxiliary armies in Sumatra, Java and Bali, using Indonesian officers, thus providing the nationalists with a future source of military power. They encouraged the use of 'bahasa Indonesia' as a national language as well as providing jobs in the bureaucracy for an increased number of 'Indonesians'. On the eve of Japanese defeat a plan was promulgated by Sukarno and Hatta and the Japanese high command for Southeast Asia which laid the groundwork for an independent republic of Indonesia. On 17 August 1945, just after the Japanese surrender, Indonesia declared its independence. The new government, with Sukarno as the first President and Hatta as Vice-President, had been somewhat reluctantly 'elected' by the recently created Committee for the Preparation of Indonesian Independence. The government of independent Indonesia received wide support from many important political sectors of the new nation. But what followed was a four-year battle for control of the archipelago.[17] Furthermore, as Paul Stange has emphasized, 'the phase of military engagement and diplomatic transition, from August 1945 to December 1949, conventionally delineating "the revolution", marked the beginning of a cultural transition that is still contentious'.[18]

Between 1945 and 1949 there were two states effectively operating in what remained of the Dutch colony: the apparatus of the new republic and the old Dutch colonial administration. By the end of 1948 most of the former colonial administration was in Dutch hands, as were all the main urban centres while Sukarno, Hatta and other leading nationalists had been detained. At the same time, the Dutch still faced highly localized popular military resistance, especially on Sumatra and Java. This, combined with strong US diplomatic and financial pressure and Dutch warweariness, led to a breakthrough at the end of 1949 at which time the Netherlands formally transferred power to the independent United States of Indonesia. By 1950 the initial decentralized federal system had been replaced by a unitary republic which fell much more under direct Javanese control. Between 1950 and 1957 this fragile entity (fragile as a 'state' and as a 'nation') was governed by a number of elected administrations which sought to stabilize and unify the 'nation' and reintegrate a state structure whose 'collective memory' kept the pre-1949 struggles alive. The bureaucratic structures were also undermined by the way various administrations dramatically expanded the size of the civil service and turned it into a system of party patronage. At the same time, between 1950 and 1957 all governments were coalition administrations, further facilitating departmental fragmentation.[19] From 1950 to 1957 the Indonesian state sought (under the overall supervision of Sukarno) to escape the economic structures of Dutch colonial rule via the encouragement of 'indigenous' capitalists. By the second half of the 1950s, as the republic lurched from constitutional democracy to guided democracy, it was apparent that Indonesian capitalists were unable to compete effectively with Dutch and other foreign corporations, not to mention the powerful Indonesian-Chinese business groups. Many of the new 'indigenous' capitalists increasingly cooperated with and were coopted by established Indonesian-Chinese businesses, with the former providing the political linkages rather than anything resembling business acumen. As of 1957, at least 70 per cent of the plantation agriculture on Sumatra and Java remained foreign-controlled, while another 19 per cent was run by Indonesian-Chinese companies. In most instances where foreign capital had left Indonesia it was Indonesian-Chinese capital which had taken its place. At the same time, very little expansion of the industrial sector had occurred, and the share of the GDP which flowed from manufacturing actually fell from 12 per cent in 1953 to 11 per cent in 1958.[20]

Between independence and the late 1950s a series of increasingly weak coalition governments grappled unsuccessfully with the new nation's economic problems, while military and civilian officials increasingly sought to integrate their bureaucratic authority with wider political power.[21] By 1957 Indonesia had clearly turned to an 'intensified nationalist strategy' which involved increased state intervention to restructure the economy and the takeover of a great deal of Dutch-owned property. At this point, more than 90 per cent of the productive plantation sector, 60 per cent of the previously foreign-controlled export trade, along with almost 250 factories, numerous banks and mining companies, not to mention shipping business and various service industries, came under the direct control of the Indonesian state.[22] By the second half of the 1950s the central government was also confronting serious rebellions in the Outer Islands, which were often coloured by ethno-religious opposition to Javanese dominance.[23] By the early 1960s, although the Outer Islands rebellions had been contained, they had resulted in further increases in power for the Indonesian Army (ABRI) and the enhancement of their ability to stifle political opposition under the umbrella of Sukarno's 'Guided Democracy'. ABRI also assumed a dramatically expanded economic role with direct control of large sectors of the economy after 1957. Apart from the military, Sukarno's 'Guided Democracy' rested on a complex web of political alliances which revolved around the nationalist party (PNI), the PKI and a major Muslim party. He played these parties off against each other, at the same time as he pitted the mainly anti-communist military against the PKI.[24] 'Guided Democracy' (underpinned by Sukarno's strident anti-Western nationalism and idiosyncratic socialism) represented an explicitly state-led attempt at capitalist development. The Indonesian state directed earnings from the primary export sector into the primarily state-owned and state-operated manufacturing sector. Export earnings were also directed towards public works, health, food production, education and transportation, not to mention payment on foreign debts. At the same time the state sought to attract new foreign loans in an effort to expand further the country's industrial base and infrastructure. By the early 1960s, however, stagnation and decline in the sugar and rubber sectors, combined with falling commodity prices, had resulted in a shortage of funds and a serious balance of payments problem. Furthermore, the nationalization of large parts of the economy had done little to attract foreign investment. By the first half of the 1960s Indonesia's economy was on the brink of collapse. Inflation was hitting 600 per cent annually, foreign debt was climbing rapidly and statistics on income and food intake per capita rivalled some of the poorest countries in the world.[25] At the same time Sukarno had become very ill by mid-1964. By early 1965 it was increasingly apparent that the country's fragile power structure was in crisis and rumours of military coups and/or a PKI-led putsch became regular occurrences. The sequence of events during the fateful years of 1965 and 1966 are complex and many aspects are hotly debated.[26] What is beyond dispute, however, is that by 1967 Soeharto had emerged as paramount leader, and was presiding over a major shift in Indonesia's trajectory.

## SOEHARTO'S NEW ORDER: (RE)COLONIZATION AND JAVA-CENTRED IMPERIUM 1965–1985

While 1945 to 1965 was an era of escalating crisis, in the context of the overall failure of a state-led capitalist development strategy, too tight a focus on the transition from constitutional democracy to guided democracy or on the crisis of import-substitution industrialization neglects another important dynamic. The period prior to 1965 can be seen as one in which the Javanese bureaucratic-aristocratic elite eventually reconsolidated their position within the wider post-colonial social formation. Throughout the national revolution period from 1945 to 1949 there were a number of social revolutionary tendencies led by non-priyayi radical intellectuals against the bureaucratic priyayi. And, while independence in 1949 left the position of the bureaucratic priyayi within the post-colonial state more or less intact, up to the early 1960s various Indonesian political parties and their leaders made serious efforts to displace the priyayi as 'the' bureaucratic class. The priyayi-centred Javanese elite maintained its relative predominance as a result of its control over the new Indonesian Army set up in the early 1940s. Most army officers were of priyayi origin, and up to the 1960s most were also products of the PETA, the armed forces set up by the Japanese in 1943–1945. Officers and soldiers who had been trained by, and/or served the Dutch in, the Royal Netherlands East Indies Army (KNIL) were also integrated into the Indonesian Army (of course many thousands also went into exile in the Netherlands after 1949). For example the Army Chief of Staff by the late 1950s, General A. H. Nasution, was a product of the KNIL (his career is a good example of the dynamic and accommodative character of priyayi-centred Javanese hegemony, insofar as he himself did not come from a priyayi background although he was married to a priyayi). Although the officers who entered the PETA during the Japanese occupation were perceived as priyayi they had often embarked on a military career at a young age and had limited education. While they shared with the more educated priyayi a commitment to Javanese cultural tradition, they also cleaved more to a Javanese cultural nationalism that emphasized the Javanese traditional state over the modern state, at the same time as they articulated a virulent anticommunism and a marked hostility to the political Islam which was particularly prevalent outside Java. The Indonesian Army went on to preserve priyayi dominance in the Islamic revolts in the Outer Islands in 1958–1959, and by 1960 ABRI, in the specific context of the expansion and deepening of its commitment to the politico-economic management of Indonesia under Sukarno, was already central to the state-building process. Of course, it was the Indonesian Army which eventually guaranteed wider priyayi dominance when the Java-centred New Order emerged after 1965.[27]

In this light, the events of 1965, which saw the massacre of at least 1 million PKI members and their supporters (80 per cent of whom were from the provinces of central and eastern Java), have a particular cultural resonance. From one perspective the massacres were the culminating battle in an escalating Javanese civil war. The elite interpretation, which was offered to the Javanese lower classes and the peasantry, emphasized that the era of civil war on Java had precipitated social polarization between classes, and by ending class conflict and returning to their 'cultural heritage', the peasants of Java could successfully avoid a recurrence of 1965.[28] The violence of 1965 certainly served to anchor a dramatic shift from a resistance-oriented to a more accommodation-oriented mode of existence in many parts of Java and beyond. However, as more than one observer has emphasized, the levelling of radical movements and parties in the wake of 1965 did not mean that socialist, populist and democratic ideas, which had gained great currency between 1945 and 1965 (but can be traced to the first three decades of the twentieth century), vanished from popular discourses and the wider political culture. In Java, and on other islands such as Bali, the PKI and Sukarno-style radicalism had put down deep roots. For example, as Carol Warren has argued in the case of Bali, the idiom and concepts of pre-1965 political discourse continue to echo with considerable regularity in contemporary Balinese village life in the context of everything from local political disputes to shadow puppet plays.[29]

While the radical ferment of the previous twenty years or more had left powerful traces, the successful imposition of Soeharto's New Order after 1965 still represents the victory of the historic state which had emerged in the Dutch colonial period. Although the consolidation of the New Order flowed from the elimination of the PKI and its supporters inside and outside the apparatus of the state, and from Sukarno's relatively rapid passing from the political stage, the overall 'character' of the rise of the New Order is symbolized by the way that Soeharto's career trajectory (unlike that of his predecessor) had evolved inside the state, especially the security branch of the state. While the key factor in this was the priyayi, which was the hegemonic class in Java from the 1950s to the 1970s, there was an important difference between the 1950s and the 1970s as a result of the consolidation of the New Order. While the old PNI (which was the country's most successful political party in the mid-1950s when open elections occurred) had been strongly led by, and rooted in, the priyayi class, the support of this group was increasingly taken over by the state, and later by the state party Golkar, which had its origins in the Sukarno era (it was set up by the military in 1964), but emerged full-blown by the time of the 1971 elections. The main difference between the old PNI and Golkar is that the former reflected the class interests of many state functionaries, while the latter articulated the interests of the historic state.[30] After 1965, priyayi officers represented the vanguard in the wider process of building the New Order state, while civilian priyayi bureaucrats oversaw the consolidation of a more centralized bureaucratic administration.[31]

At the same time, Soeharto's elimination of the PKI and his decisive victory in the war against communism in Southeast Asia and beyond after 1965 provided the circumstances under which the US and its allies quickly embarked on a major effort to reincorporate Indonesia into the world economy. This included generous quantities of aid and a considerable amount of debt rescheduling.[32] At the centre of this new orientation in macroeconomic policy was a group of US-trained 'technocrats' who became known as the 'Berkeley Mafia'.[33] Under their guidance the New Order solicited foreign investment, particularly from the US and Japan. From the mid-1960s to the mid-1970s the New Order regime pursued an import-substitution industrialization strategy financed by growing foreign investment, as well as by foreign aid and some domestic investment. Between 1967 and 1985, 65 per cent of Indonesia's total manufacturing investment came from Japanese corporations, while US investment in the oil sector was 58 per cent. Between 1967 and 1975 the manufacturing sector grew at an average annual rate of 16.5 per cent, and, as in the colonial period, it remained concentrated on Java. Mining, oil, primary agriculture and timber all boomed in the 1970s and early 1980s. And, after the dramatic rise in the price of oil in 1973 and then 1979, the oil industry became increasingly important: 70 per cent of all foreign investment in Indonesia was in the oil industry by 1979, rising to 85.5 per cent in 1982.[34] During the late 1960s and early 1970s, in the context of a continuing commitment to an import-substitution industrialization strategy, an increasingly coherent Indonesian capitalist elite appeared, based on privileged access to the state-controlled network of credit, contract distribution and trade monopolies, in the context of strict regulations requiring that foreign investors work with local capitalists, and a tightly controlled manufacturing licensing process. These rising capitalists had close, often very close, links to officials who were well placed in the state, at the same time as a growing number of state officials emerged as capitalists in their own right: the most famous 'bureaucratic capitalist families' to rise out of the state capitalism of the New Order have been the Soehartos and the Sutowos. However, the general cohesiveness of an emerging capitalist elite, based on preferential access to state power, was still relatively narrow because many of them were Indonesian-Chinese, whose growing economic power remained dependent on the socio-political power of the mostly Javanese members of the Java-centred elite.[35]

Despite the emergence of an increasingly powerful layer of domestic capitalists under the umbrella of the New Order state, 'economic nationalism' (state capitalism) was in retreat in Indonesia from the mid-1960s to the mid-1970s. Until the mid-1970s, Soeharto was indebted to the various US-backed international agencies particularly, and to a range of foreign investors more generally, for both the alacrity with which they had moved to support his regime and the quantity of their assistance. And this meant adopting an economic stance that was receptive to the interests of foreign capital. However, the dramatic increase in oil prices in the 1970s provided the New Order with the means to return to an even more state-centred capitalist model within a decade of its inception. In the first years of the 1980s, gas and oil sales were over 80 per cent of export earnings and brought in 70 per cent of the regime's total revenue. From the middle of the 1970s, surging oil prices, combined with increased state investment in import substitution under the direct control of the military and Soeharto, served to bring about a dwindling of the regime's reliance on foreign capital and foreign aid. At the same time, renewed restrictions were placed on foreign capital, and overall foreign investment reached a plateau in the mid-1970s. By the 1980s state-guided industrialization was financed primarily by oil money.[36] However, as oil prices dropped in the 1980s the whole system came under pressure. This resulted in increasing debt and a decreased capacity on the part of the state to facilitate local capital accumulation, while greater use of foreign loans and foreign aid led to greater leverage on the part of the World Bank, the IMF and foreign capital. By the late 1970s the World Bank was placing increasing emphasis on economic liberalization, the curbing of state intervention and the benefits of export-oriented industrialization. By the second half of the 1980s, important liberalizing reforms were under way in Indonesia and changes at the cabinet and ministerial level saw the appearance of a number of officials more 'sympathetic' towards economic liberalization. At the same time, significant pockets of 'economic nationalism' persist, especially in the State Secretariat and the Ministry of Research and Technology.[37] The period from the mid-1980s has seen an increase in the influx of foreign capital, much of it from Japan (as well as South Korea and Taiwan), and the rapid emergence of an export-industry sector, producing things like textiles and footwear, strengthening Indonesia's connections to wider regional and global flows of capital and manufactured goods.[38]

These broad shifts in the Indonesian political economy (dictated in part by wider trends in the global political economy and by localized dynamics of subaltern accommodation and resistance) and the overall process of uneven capitalist development are occurring in the context of the continued public emphasis on loyalty to the New Order state. The importance of loyalty to the New Order is often articulated in the language of national development (*pembangunan*) under the leadership of the 'father of development', Bapak Pembangunan, Soeharto.[39] The Java-centred elite has also continued to reproduce itself with reference to the historic role of the administrative-aristocratic class that had risen to power in the Dutch period (the Javanese priyayi). More particularly, the Java-centred elite has sought to ground the legitimacy of the New Order by invoking and appropriating a perceived primordial past in which the Javanese aristocracy is seen to have played a key role. The trend towards the reinstatement and privileging of the aristocratic culture of the Javanese past in the wider Indonesian polity manifests itself in many ways. For example, one of the egalitarian legacies of the 1945 'revolution' (1945–1949) was the use of the term *bung* (brother) in political discourse. In recent years, in the context of the reassertion of hierarchical tendencies in Javanese culture, *bung* has given way to *bapak* (father) or at least *mas* and *mbak* (older brother or older sister) in political idiom – as in Bung Karno (Sukarno), Pak Harto (Soeharto) and Mbak 'Tutut' (Soeharto's eldest daughter).[40] This is part of a much wider trend by which the New Order has sought to generate national unity, encourage loyalty around national development, and also reconfigure the Javanese aristocratic past to fit the New Order present.[41] It is also worth noting that, in the same way that aristocratic marriages were regularly used in the pre-colonial and colonial era as a means not only of affirming the social hierarchy but also of cementing alliances, they have become a way by which promising young non-Javanese men from the Outer Islands are coopted into the Java-centred elite.[42] At the broadest level the Java-centred elite retains its position of dominance and reproduces itself by accommodating and coopting non-priyayi and non-Javanese. For example, while many military officers can point to priyayi ancestry, by becoming a military officer a young man effectively becomes a priyayi in terms of socio-political status regardless of his actual ancestry.

The power of the Java-centred elite and the New Order's conception of *pembangunan* have been transformed and mediated by the wider processes of the global political economy and uneven capitalist development and by the strategies of subaltern accommodation and resistance pursued at a multitude of regional and local sites. For example, the official ideology of Pancasila flows outwards and downwards in the context of a multitude of more particular ideas and practices at the local and regional level. Pancasila ideology (five principles of belief in one God, humanitarianism, nationalism, consensus, democracy and social justice) is regularly applied at the village level as a means of measuring state policy, and government rhetoric is regularly redirected by villagers towards local action, and not always unsuccessfully. Australian-based anthropologist Carol Warren has documented an incident in Bali where the people in a particular village objected to the way they had been excluded from a state-sponsored effort to improve the area's water supply; she highlights how they were able to base their successful demands for inclusion in the scheme on Pancasila ideology.[43] A quite different example of the various forms of resistance against the Java-centred elite that have emerged can be drawn from South Sulawesi where, as Thomas Gibson argues, repeated and violent efforts at resisting the central state in the colonial and post-colonial period have been driven by the complex dynamics of local social conflict and interaction, at the same time as they have been informed by the transnational idiom of militant Islam.[44]

As the case of South Sulawesi suggests, and as has been mentioned earlier, Indonesia's history has been driven by various, often Islamic, rebellions in the Outer Islands. For example, Aceh has a long history of rebellion, which has waxed and waned throughout the high period of Dutch colonialism and since 1949, not to mention the more recent expansion and revolt in Irian Jaya and East Timor.[45] These struggles have been driven by local ethnoreligious inflections, at the same time as they have been profoundly shaped by the power of the New Order and its efforts to facilitate resource extraction on the Indonesian periphery to the benefit of the centre and foreign capital. In the case of Irian Jaya, the central highlands at Grasberg are the site of the largest mine (copper, gold and silver) in Indonesia. Beginning in the late 1960s, the North American-based company Freeport-McMoran has extracted copper and gold from the Grasberg mine, which lies on the mountain range stretching eastward to the Ok Tedi mine in Papua New Guinea and the Bougainville copper mine beyond.[46] While armed resistance and an emergent nationalist movement have emerged in Irian Jaya, the struggle over East Timor provides a particularly acute example of the wider processes of integration and differentiation sweeping Indonesia. Indonesian occupation has provided the crucible for an East Timorese nationalism that was relatively non-existent twenty years ago but has become a potent political force. In official speeches Soeharto and other members of the Indonesian elite (not to mention the international media) always talk about the 'East Timorese', although the eastern half of the island of Timor is inhabited by around thirty relatively distinct ethnic groups. A common consciousness and a sense of shared identity have arisen as a direct result of the overwhelming power of the New Order state. In contrast to the Portuguese, the Indonesian state is far more intrusive, as manifested by the innumerable military posts which dot the landscape.[47] And if recent trends are any indication, the next generation of East Timorese, who have no direct experience of the pre-1975 period, are ready and willing to do battle with the Java-centred Indonesian state.[48] The East Timorese struggle also highlights the complicated character of globalization, insofar as while the movement to end Indonesian rule is centred on East Timor it is supported by a global network of sympathizers and East Timorese exiles stretching from Portugal to Australia.

## THE TWILIGHT OF THE NEW ORDER? GLOBALIZATION AND THE NEW LABOURERS, 1985–1995

While East Timor is a particularly acute example of social instability and national fragility, the Indonesia-wide process of uneven capitalist development and the increasing power of globalization also embody formidable challenges to the New Order and the Java-centred empire. While capitalist development is often still seen as the key to political and social stability, historically it has also been central to social diversification and the generation of conflict. Capitalism in Indonesia, as elsewhere, has given rise to both new or reconfigured elites and new or reconfigured subaltern classes, inserting them into a variety of hierarchies of production and accumulation, to which they accommodate themselves and against which they sometimes resist. A growing number of Indonesians, led by secular and Islamic intellectuals, journalists and students, are increasingly mobilizing in various parliamentary and extra-parliamentary ways against the Soeharto regime, under the banner of democratization.[49] Since the late 1980s student protests have been more frequent. Student activists have embraced rural disputes over land and the general questions of livelihood which are of central concern to the rural and urban poor. The response from the New Order authorities has varied, but there is some evidence to suggest that as in the mid-1960s the factions within the military have sought to establish links with students while publicly emphasizing the need for order and discipline. The still low-key student unrest continues to occur in the context of less vociferous dissension among sections of the elite.[50] While Soeharto's sixth term as President, which began in 1993, has done little to placate disgruntled members of the elite, the composition of his new cabinet was seen as a concession to a younger generation, at the same time as it also reached out to Muslims. However, because of its increased civilian character the military were marginalized relative to previous cabinets.[51] Recently, the possibility of an electoral alliance between the Nahdlatul Ulama (NU), which is the country's largest Muslim organization with 34 million members led by Abdurrahman Wahid, and the PDI (Indonesian Democratic Party) under Megawati Sukarnoputri, has begun to worry Golkar officials and point to the growing disaffection of various segments of the elite as well as the population at large.[52] (In the first half of 1996 the government successfully and flagrantly manipulated powerful factions of the PDI in a way which led to the ouster of Megawati Sukarnoputri as party leader. The government's actions, and a more specific military assault on Megawati's supporters holding out at PDI headquarters in Jakarta which occurred on the 27th of July, precipitated one of the most violent urban uprisings in the history of Indonesia's New Order.)

Against the backdrop of the wider Indonesian trajectory, the country's Java-centred elite has gone through many changes. For example, while many priyayi, in keeping with the historic bureaucratic and administrative role of the Javanese aristocracy, continue to take part in private business only indirectly through Indonesian-Chinese capitalists, under the New Order a growing number of priyayi, not least the President's children, have taken up a direct and dominant role in commerce. According to one observer the rise, by the 1980s, of priyayi merchants represented the 'last', and probably the 'most difficult', step in the Java-centred elite's 'consolidation of power'.[53] However, in the context of a mid-1980s shift towards increased foreign investment and export-oriented industrialization (between 1980 and 1991 the share of manufactured goods as a percentage of Indonesia's total exports rose from 3 per cent – a figure that had been more or less constant from the mid-1960s – to 40 per cent), it is very doubtful that the New Order is going to give birth to a cohesive priyayi capitalist elite, or even a broad Javanese commercial class, linked to the historic monopoly of state power exercised by the priyayi.[54] Indonesian social scientist Ariel Heryanto argues that, although there are now many important priyayi capitalists, the economically powerful Indonesian-Chinese business community has also been able to move beyond exclusive dependence on 'indigenous' (often priyayi) civilian and military officials of the state and establish links with the emerging tycoons and professionals of Javanese or other 'indigenous' background. From his perspective, a reconfigured and increasingly self-conscious 'multi-ethnic capitalist class' is emerging although it has not achieved anything like hegemony within the wider social formation.[55] This trend, which flows from the relative retreat of the New Order state from its historically dominant role in the economy, is still embryonic, but there is clearly an effort by some elements of the private sector to establish political networks and a collective organizational framework in a fashion which cuts across old divisions, and threatens established New Order patterns.[56] The New Order state had become far less able to support its often highly inefficient import-substitution industrialization sector, and the centre of economic gravity has shifted increasingly to foreign capital and domestic capital operating outside the

Java-centred state patronage framework. In this situation transnational capital (including some elements of Indonesian capital) is also strengthening its position in key sectors of the Indonesian economy and appears to be gaining socio-political strength.[57] The continued trend towards globalization was apparent in the second half of 1994 when, in the context of growing competition for foreign investment in the Asia-Pacific and the run-up to the APEC meeting in November 1994, Indonesia further opened up to foreign investment, eliminating a number of ownership restrictions and permitting joint ventures in areas of the economy that had previously been closed to foreign investment.[58]

The power of the Java-centred New Order elite is also threatened by the complex rhythms of local change and subaltern accommodation and resistance. As events in the industrial city of Medan in 1994, as well as elsewhere, suggest, a particularly serious challenge to the New Order may be coming from the workers' movements, born of the country's surging and globally integrated export-industrialization sector. The growing labour unrest has burst the boundaries of the framework of state–capital–labour relations laid down by the New Order in the 1960s and 1970s.[59] Some observers perceive a trend towards the emergence of a more cohesive working class, and culturally embedded discourses on class which flow in part from the activities of activists from urban middle-class backgrounds and the proliferation of labour theatre groups. At the same time, art exhibitions and public poetry readings have become important sites for the formation and articulation of consciousness about labour issues.[60] During the late 1950s and early 1960s Indonesian workers had been increasingly subordinated to the state capitalism of the late Sukarno era, while in the early New Order period urban workers were even more thoroughly domesticated, at the same time as the communist-led unions were wiped off the political map.[61] At the beginning of the New Order period state labour policy was aimed at eliminating the instability and worker unrest of the pre-1965 period and was premised on the view that the primary 'threat' to order and stability came from remnants of the pre-1965 'left-wing elements' which had dominated the trade union movement up to that time. The 'solution' was the setting up of a state-sanctioned and corporatist trade union body.[62]

Between 1965 and 1985 the New Order effectively contained independent labour activity and ensured labour peace apart from some outbursts at the end of the 1970s and in the first part of the 1980s. In 1973 the establishment of the All-Indonesia Workers Federation (FBSI – Federasi Buruh Seluruh Indonesia) as the only legal organization representing workers served to curtail the emergence of independent labour organizations. This was replaced by the highly centralized All-Indonesia Workers Union (SPSI – Serikat Pekerja Seluruh Indonesia) in the mid-1980s (and in 1995 it became the Federation of Indonesian Workers – FSPSI). Along with the denial of the right to independent organization, workers in Indonesia have generally been denied the right to strike. In 1974 Pancasila Industrial Relations (HIP – Hubungan Industrial Pancasila) was promulgated. This has served to legitimate widespread state involvement, at the same time as it has nullified the grounds for strike action because of its emphasis on familial and harmonious relations between labour, capital and the state. Soeharto has emphasized that in the context of Pancasila 'there is no place for confrontation'. Other proponents of HIP have contrasted Indonesian-style 'partnership' relations between employees and employers with the 'confrontational' type of labour relations which are said to prevail in 'liberal' North America, Western Europe and Australia.[63] The military (ABRI) has also played an ever increasing role in the trade unions and labour relations (not least being the practice of retired army officers taking up positions in the official trade union movement). As Indonesian intellectual Vedi Hadiz has noted, the fact that Admiral Sudomo, the former chief of security, could serve as the Manpower Minister (responsible for the management of labour relations) from 1983 to 1988 is a 'symbol' of the way in which military intervention in labour relations is central to the overall system of labour control under the New Order.[64]

By the 1980s the New Order was having to grapple with growing labour unrest, at the same time as labour leaders and activists sought to articulate 'new perspectives'. These sought to move beyond the moral and instrumental criticisms which were often levelled at the New Order in favour of a structural analysis of the exploitation of workers and peasants. Greater priority was given to conflicts between workers and capitalists. Activists and commentators also sought to analyse the role of the state in industrialization and while nobody was arguing that anything resembling a cohesive industrial proletariat had appeared, insofar as employers were often still able to 'divide and rule', both temporary and permanent workers were seen to be gaining an awareness that what interests they shared with management were far less than what they had in common with each other. The need for trade union independence emerged as a particular focus of concern in this period. While the highly centralized official trade union movement remained at the centre of labour relations in Indonesia, at the beginning of the 1980s a majority of the activists who sought some sort of progressive change felt that the potential existed for successful informal and grass-roots work within this framework. This resulted in a range of independent organizational initiatives which often operated formally as local branches within the approved union structure.[65]

These organizational efforts took on new significance from the mid-1980s when the export manufacturing sector began to grow dramatically. In 1971 the manufacturing sector employed an estimated 2.7 million workers (6.5 per cent of the total labour force), rising to around 4.5 million workers in 1980 (8.5 per cent of the workforce) and 8.2 million by 1990 (11.6 per cent of the workforce – 3.6 million women and 4.6 million men).[66] From 1965 until the 1980s the number of strikes was relatively low but rising.

Until the late 1970s it never rose above thirty-five annually and was often much lower. But in 1979 the figure rose to seventy-two, and then to over 100 a year in 1980 and 1981, and over 200 in 1982. By 1990 the number of strikes per year had reached pre-1965 levels and these strikes were centred on export-oriented manufacturing industries which produce garments, textiles and footwear.[67] In 1991 74 per cent of all strikes in West Java were in textile and garment factories. Although much of the unrest in the early 1990s has been centred on the new industrial areas in and around Jakarta it has now extended to other parts of Java and Sumatra. At the same time, many of the strikes reflect the inability or unwillingness of the government to ensure that employers abide by the government's own regulations – 90 per cent of reported strikes in West Java by the beginning of the 1990s centred on demands that companies pay their employees the official minimum wage (according to the independent union SBSI (Serikat Buruh Sejahtra Indonesia – Indonesian Prosperity Trade Union) wages comprise about 8 per cent of most company's operating costs, while an average of 30 per cent is spent on 'non-official expenditures' – that is bribes). By the early 1990s there had been some relatively tepid reforms, along with minimum wage rises. In September 1992 the average minimum wage in Jakarta was raised from Rp 2500 to Rp 3000 a day while in West Java it went from Rp 2100 to Rp 2600.[68] (As of early 1996 the official daily minimum wage for East Java was Rp 4000 per day, while in Jakarta and West Java it was 4600 rupiah – the equivalent of around US$2).

In early February 1994 there were widespread strikes in Java which again focused on demands that the new minimum wage actually be paid by employers. At the same time the government threatened to prosecute employers who failed to comply with the new minimum wage (the penalty was a maximum of three months in jail or 100,000 rupiah – equal to about US$50).[69] The wave of strikes in February proved to be the lead-up to the violent labour unrest which began with a peaceful demonstration on Friday, 14 April in which approximately 30,000 workers congregated in Medan. Driven by concern about military involvement in labour disputes, and the suspected involvement of military personnel in the assassination of union organisers the particular aim of the protest was also to increase the regional minimum wage which was 3100 rupiah (US$1.45–1.55) per day at the time. The independent SBSI, which helped to organize the protest was calling for an increase to 7000 rupiah (US$3.50) a day (but, at the time of the protest less than half of the factories in the Medan area paid their workers the legal minimum wage). The protesters were also seeking to overturn laws restricting the establishment of factory-level trade unions, to express their opposition to the recent 'arbitrary dismissal' of almost 400 workers from a local factory and to demand that the government look into the disappearance and death of a labour organizer named Rusli, whose body had been found floating in the Deli River only two days after he had played a prominent leadership role in a strike at the PT Industri Karet factory in Deli in West Sumatra. The initially peaceful demonstration escalated into a week-long series of violent confrontations with the military and the police, resulting in one death, at least twelve people injured, as well as 100 arrests and damage to 150 factories and shops, not to mention burnt and overturned automobiles. Between 14 April and 20 April the labour unrest and strike activity involved about 40,000 workers and over seventy factory sites in and around Medan.[70] In the wake of the unrest in Medan there appear to have been some minor improvements. As of August 1994 the minimum wage rose from 3100 rupiahs to 3750 rupiahs (US$1.72) a day, while over 90 per cent of the factories in the area are believed by some observers to be actually paying the minimum wage, in contrast to widespread avoidance prior to April. Forced overtime has also apparently been almost eliminated. At the same time, long-term industrial peace is thought to be unlikely. Apart from a few minor concessions, the government and employers have relied primarily on the heavy hand of the military, including sending soldiers in civilian clothes into factories. The government also sought to expand the SPSI to demonstrate to the 'international community', especially the USA, that workers in Indonesia enjoyed reasonable protection from exploitation. However, in Medan, between April and October 1994, only twenty extra SPSI units were set up. Employers, are wary of the state-sponsored SPSI even though it tends to take their side. Ironically, there is reported to be a concern among some business people that at some future date even the SPSI might begin to act in the interests of workers rather than employers.[71]

The unrest in Medan in April 1994 was possibly the largest outpouring of labour frustration and disaffection in the history of the New Order. It may mark a key juncture in modern Indonesian history. By the middle of the 1990s the country's 'new' labourers, many of whom had grown up in the burgeoning urban industrial areas in Indonesia, appear to be coming into their own.[72] At the same time, many workers now have more education than in an earlier era and this often makes them more aware of what rights they have. The reorganization of the official New Order union, giving more power to regional branches (which was accompanied by a change in name to the Federation of Indonesian Workers, or FSPSI), along with efforts to refurbish its international reputation, and the resulting relatively liberal industrial relations rhetoric, has also contributed to worker unrest. The new conception of labour rights which this rhetoric carries with it has not been lost on the workers; however, when they attempt to take this rhetoric seriously, the negative response from the FSPSI leadership simply leads to greater frustration and conflict. A likely medium-term reaction on the part of the New Order state will not be a sophisticated strategy of labour reform aimed at institutionalizing industrial conflict, but a continued approach to labour relations in which freedom of association remains non-existent while attempts are made to control the increase in working-class unrest using minor labour reform, such as moderate changes to minimum wage and exhortations for employers to comply with government regulations, in the context of the continued reliance on the repressive technologies of the FSPSI. At the same time, as cases such as South Korea and the Philippines suggest, an incremental and authoritarian reaction to growing working-class unrest can actually fuel militant activity. Minor changes in wages and conditions can often have a limited effect on workers' circumstances at the same time as a growing awareness develops that whatever has been gained has been because of working-class militancy rather than the generosity of the business or governing elites. In this situation the possibility of the emergence of a collective identity of resistance increases.[73] As the New Order increasingly becomes the *ancien régime*, there is every indication that labour unrest and the various modes of independent organization among workers will gain in significance.[74]

## CONCLUSION: POST-COLD WAR INDONESIA AND THE REVENGE OF HISTORY

It has been emphasized in this chapter that the dynamics of decades of dramatic capitalist development in Indonesia under the conservative leadership of Soeharto, Bapak Pembangunan, owes as much to the historical legacy of the Dutch colonial period as it does to the nationalist visions which emerged during the late colonial period and at the time of the struggle for independence in the 1940s. Indonesian nationalism, which was central to bringing the new nation of Indonesia into being, emerged out of a process of anti-colonial resistance, but was also profoundly rooted in the colonialism it sought to challenge. The rhetoric of national development and the need for loyalty to the nation, and efforts to generate an Indonesian identity, have been central to national political discourse. At the same time, Indonesia has increasingly become a Java-centred empire, a process which is now being challenged by the dramatic shifts in the global political economy and the rise of new social forces throughout the archipelago. As this chapter has suggested, one of the most important challenges to the post-Cold War New Order flows from the emergence of an export-oriented industrial sector with powerful linkages to the wider global economy and the related emergence of a growing urban working class. However, at this juncture, neither the new labourers, concentrated in the export-oriented industries, nor the independent union leadership is particularly unified. Some tendencies reflect relatively contemporary radical styles; at the same time, as there is a powerful moderate wing. There is also a vocal element of the independent union leadership which speaks in the language of the old PKI and looks to the 1920s and the 1950s (when the labour movement and the Communist Party played a powerful role in colonial and post-colonial politics) for inspiration. However, this very mechanical application of the idiom (and the categories and strategies) associated with 1950s-style Indonesian marxism, which is to a certain extent reincarnated in the recently formed Centre for Indonesian Working Class Struggle (PPBI), may well compound earlier failures rather than facilitate future victories. Although this particularly orthodox marxist discourse has its roots in Indonesian history it has transnational links to organizations in Australia and Western Europe and elsewhere.[75] At the same time, a revived marxist-derived radicalism could play an important role in any effort to build a progressive politics and an independent trade union movement in Indonesia. The character of the present working-class unrest, like the wider process of social transformation in Indonesia, has its roots in that country's particular historical trajectory, and that history, along with the marxism that played such an important role at various points in the twentieth century, needs to be subjected to a concerted process of re-examination and, where relevant, recuperation.[76]

## NOTES

*I would like to thank George Aditjondro, Arief Budiman, Gerard Greenfield, Vedi Hadiz, Paul Stange and Carol Warren who all read earlier drafts and made innumerable useful comments. However, I did not always heed their advice and it goes without saying that I am solely responsible for this chapter.

1 Ed Warner, 'Indonesia's Multi-Ethnic Pride' (Background Report) *Voice of America*, Washington, 15 November 1994, 11:54 am Eastern Standard Time. Robert Hefner is Professor of Anthropology at Boston University and Assistant Director of the Institute for the Study of Economic Culture, and Benedict Anderson is Professor of Government at Cornell University. According to the ILO (1988), 50% of the urban population of Indonesia live below the poverty line. See Michael Vatikiotis, *Indonesia Under Suharto* (London: Routledge, 1993), pp. 114–115. World Bank figures for poverty levels in Indonesia as a whole between 1970 and 1990 report a dramatic decline from 69% to 15% of population (from 70 million to 30 million people), By contrast, the trend in the Philippines was from 35% to 21% of the population; in Thailand it was 26% to 16%; in China it was 33% to 10%. Significantly the World Bank defines poverty 'as receiving less than 2,150 calories per day'. See *Far Eastern Economic Review* 24 March 1994, p. 15.

2 On classical modernization theory and modernization revisionism see Alvin Y. So, *Social Change and Development: Modernization, Dependency and World-System Theories* (Newbury Park, Calif.: Sage, 1990), One of the best-known approaches to emerge out of the revision of classical modernization theory in relation to Indonesia particularly has been the concept of patrimonialism, which gained considerable influence by the 1970s. For example, see Harold Crouch, 'Patrimonialism and Military Rule in Indonesia' *World Politics* vol. 31, no. 4, 1979, reprinted in Atul Kohli, ed., *The State and Development in the Third World* (Princeton, NJ: Princeton University Press, 1986), Patrimonialism is still the concept most regularly deployed by those seeking to explain Soeharto's New Order. See Jamie Mackie, 'Indonesia: Economic Growth and Depoliticization' in James W. Morley, ed., *Driven by Growth: Political Change in the Asia-Pacific Region* (London: M. E. Sharpe, 1993).

3 The parameters of the debate are clarified in Richard Robison, 'The Middle Class and the Bourgeoisie in Indonesia' in Richard Robison and David S. G. Goodman, eds, *The New Rich in Asia: Mobile Phones, McDonalds and Middle-Class Revolution* (London: Routledge, 1996).

4 Richard Robison, 'Indonesia: Tensions in State and Regime' in Kevin Hewison, Richard Robison and Garry Rodan, eds, *Southeast Asia in the 1990s: Authoritarianism, Democracy and Capitalism* (Sydney: Allen & Unwin, 1993), pp. 45, 49.

5 Partha Chatterjee, *Nationalist Thought and the Colonial World: A Derivative Discourse* (London: Zed Press, 1986), pp. 38–39, 161.

6 Nicholas B. Dirks, 'Introduction: Colonialism and Culture' in Nicholas B. Dirks, ed., *Colonialism and Culture* (Ann Arbor: University of Michigan Press, 1992), pp. 3–4, 7, 15, 23–24; Gyan Prakash, 'Introduction: After Colonialism' in Gyan Prakash, ed., *After Colonialism: Imperial Histories and Postcolonial Displacements* (Princeton, NJ: Princeton University Press, 1995), p. 16; Benedict Anderson, *Imagined Communities: Reflections on the Origins and Spread of Nationalism* (London: Verso, 2nd revised and extended edition 1992; first published 1983), pp. 3–7.

7 Greg Acciaioli, 'What's in a Name?: Appropriating Idioms in the South Sulawesi Rice Intensification Program' *Social Analysis: Journal of Cultural and Social Practice* no. 35, 1994, p. 39.

8 Ben Anderson, 'Old State New Society: Indonesia's New Order in Comparative Historical Perspective' *Journal of Asian Studies* vol. 42, no. 2, May 1983, reprinted in Benedict Anderson, *Language and Power: Exploring Political Cultures in Indonesia* (Ithaca, NY: Cornell University Press, 1990), pp. 96–99.

9 Ruth T. McVey, 'The Beamtenstaat in Indonesia' (1977) in Benedict Anderson and Audrey Kahin, eds, *Interpreting Indonesian Politics: Thirteen Contributions to the Debate* (Ithaca, NY: Cornell Modern Indonesia Project, Cornell University, 1982); Heather Sutherland, *The Making of a Bureaucratic Elite: The Colonial Transformation of the Javanese Priyayi* (Sydney: Allen & Unwin, 1979).

10 Anthony D. Smith, 'State-Making and Nation-Building' in John A. Hall, *States in History* (Oxford: Basil Blackwell, 1989; first published 1986), pp. 244–245.

11 Richard Robison, *Indonesia: The Rise of Capital* (Sydney: Allen & Unwin, 1986), pp. 10–15.

12 Burhan Magenda, 'Ethnicity and State-Building in Indonesia: The Cultural Base of the New Order' in Remo Guidieri, Francesco Pellizzi and Stanley J. Tambiah, eds, *Ethnicities and Nations: Processes of Interethnic Relations in Latin America, Southeast Asia and the Pacific* (Austin: University of Texas Press, 1988), pp. 348–349.

13 ibid.

14 Michael Adas, 'From Avoidance to Confrontation: Peasant Protest in Precolonial and Colonial Southeast Asia' in Nicholas B. Dirks, ed., *Colonialism and Culture* (Ann Arbor: University of Michigan Press, 1992).

15 Rudolf von Albertini, *Decolonization: The Administration and Future of the Colonies 1919–1960* (New York: Holmes & Meier, 1982), pp. 487–513.

16 Magenda, 'Ethnicity and State-Building in Indonesia', p. 350.

17 Anderson, 'Old State New Society' *Language and Power*, pp. 99–100.

18 Paul Stange, 'Inner Dimensions of the Indonesian Revolution' in Laurie Sears, ed., *Autonomous Histories, Particular Truths: Essays in Honor of John Smail* (Madison: Center for Southeast Asian Studies, University of Wisconsin, 1993), p. 219.

19 Anderson, 'Old State New Society' *Language and Power*, pp 100–103.

20 Robison, *Indonesia*, pp. 42–44, 57; Chris Dixon, *South East Asia in the World-Economy: A Regional Geography* (Cambridge: Cambridge University Press, 1991), pp. 190–191.
21 Richard Robison, 'Structures of Power and the Industrialization Process in Southeast Asia' *Journal of Contemporary Asia* vol. 19, no. 4, 1989, pp. 383–384.
22 Dixon, *South East Asia in the World-Economy*, pp. 191–192.
23 Karl D. Jackson, *Traditional Authority, Islam and Rebellion: A Study of Indonesian Political Behaviour* (Berkeley: University of California Press, 1980); Thomas Gibson, 'Ritual and Revolution: Contesting the State in Central Indonesia' *Social Analysis: Journal of Cultural and Social Practice* no. 35, 1994.
24 Rex Mortimer, *Indonesian Communism Under Sukarno: Ideology and Politics 1959–1965* (Ithaca, NY: Cornell University Press, 1974).
25 Dixon, *South East Asia in the World-Economy*, pp. 191–192.
26 Contrary to the official version, which lays the blame at the door of the PKI, it appears that an attempt by a general in the Palace Guard to seize power on 30 September 1965, ostensibly to pre-empt an expected coup against Sukarno, sparked off a series of events driven by the splits in the military which led to the marginalization of Sukarno and the effective elimination of the PKI. By mid-1966 the CIA and the State Department were estimating that anywhere between 250,000 and 500,000 alleged PKI members had been killed (in mid-1965 the PKI was reckoned to have 3 million members as well as 12 million people in associated organizations), Other estimates put the figure at over 1 million, and some estimates range as high as 1.5 million dead. The official Indonesian figures released in the mid-1970s were 450,000 to 500,000 dead. See Gabriel Kolko, *Confronting the Third World: United States Foreign Policy 1945–1980* (New York: Pantheon, 1988), pp. 173–185.
27 Magenda, 'Ethnicity and State-Building in Indonesia', pp. 350–353.
28 ibid., pp. 354–355.
29 Carol Warren, *Adat and Dinas: Balinese Communities in the Indonesian State* (Kuala Lumpur: Oxford University Press, 1993), pp. 271–272, 274–275; Max Lane, 'Voices of Dissent in Indonesia' *Arena* no. 61, 1982; Benedict Anderson, 'The Languages of Indonesian Politics', 1966, in *Language and Power*, pp. 136–139.
30 Anderson, 'Old State New Society' *Language and Power*, pp. 109–110, 116–117, 119–120.
31 Magenda, 'Ethnicity and State-Building in Indonesia', pp. 352–353.
32 Dixon, *Southeast Asia in the World-Economy*, pp. 193–194.
33 John Bresnan, *Managing Indonesia: The Modern Political Economy* (New York: Columbia University Press, 1993), p. 83.
34 Dixon, *Southeast Asia in the World-Economy*, pp. 194–195.
35 Robison, 'Structures of Power and the Industrialization Process in Southeast Asia', pp. 384–385.
36 Dixon, *Southeast Asia in the World-Economy*, pp. 195–200.
37 Robison, 'Structures of Power and the Industrialization Process in Southeast Asia', pp. 385–387.
38 Richard Stubbs, 'The Political Economy of the Asia-Pacific Region' in Richard Stubbs and Geoffrey R. D. Underhill, eds, *Political Economy and the Changing Global Order* (London: Macmillan, 1994), p. 372.
39 Acciaioli, 'What's in a Name?', p. 39.
40 Magenda, 'Ethnicity and State-Building in Indonesia', pp. 353–354.
41 John Pemberton, *On the Subject of 'Java'* (Ithaca, NY: Cornell University Press, 1994), pp. 148–235, 269–318.
42 Magenda, 'Ethnicity and State-Building in Indonesia', pp. 353–354.

43 Warren, *Adat and Dinas*, pp. 224–230, 278–279, 282–283.
44 Gibson, 'Ritual and Revolution: Contesting the State in Central Indonesia', pp. 62–63, 79–80.
45 For a recent analysis of elite accommodation and resistance in Aceh see David Brown, *The State and Ethnic Politics in Southeast Asia* (London: Routledge, 1994), pp. 112–157.
46 John McBeth, 'Indonesia's Last Frontier: Gold Rush in Tribal Hills' *Far Eastern Economic Review* 10 March 1994, pp. 48–53.
47 Benedict Anderson, 'Imagining East Timor' *Arena Magazine* no. 4. 1993.
48 John McBeth, 'Indonesia: Fresh Blood' *Far Eastern Economic Review* 1 September 1994, pp. 20–21.
49 Anders Uhlin, 'Transnational Democratic Diffusion and Indonesian Democracy Discourses' *Third World Quarterly: Journal of Emerging Areas* vol. 14, no. 3, 1993; Chua Beng Huat, 'Looking for Democratization in Post-Soeharto Indonesia' *Contemporary Southeast Asia* vol. 15, no. 2, 1993, pp. 144–145, 148–157.
50 Vatikiotis, *Indonesia Under Suharto*, pp 114–115.
51 Suhaini Azman, 'Indonesia: Civil Power' *Far Eastern Economic Review* 1 April 1993, p. 16. Liberal technocrats were also seen to have been downgraded relative to the economic nationalists led by Bachruddin Habibie, Soeharto's Minister for Research and Technology and a close adviser. See Henry Sender, 'New Boys' Challenge' *Far Eastern Economic Review* 1 April 1993, pp. 72–75. Also see Suhaini Azman, 'New Crew on Deck' *Far Eastern Economic Review* 22 April 1993, p. 41.
52 John McBeth, 'Indonesia: Power Couple' *Far Eastern Economic Review* 16 February 1995, pp. 26–27.
53 Magenda, 'Ethnicity and State-Building in Indonesia' pp. 356–359.
54 For details on the economic shift in the 1980s see Hal Hill, 'The Economy' in Hal Hill, ed., *Indonesia's New Order: The Dynamics of Socio-Economic Transformation* (Sydney: Allen & Unwin, 1994), pp. 103–104.
55 Ariel Heryanto, 'A Class Act' *Far Eastern Economic Review* 16 June 1994, p. 30.
56 Andrew MacIntyre, 'Power, Prosperity and Patrimonialism: Business and Government in Indonesia' in Andrew MacIntyre, ed., *Business and Government in Industrialising Asia* (Sydney: Allen & Unwin, 1994), p. 264.
57 Richard Robison, 'Industrialization and the Economic and Political Development of Capital: The Case of Indonesia' in Ruth McVey, ed., *Southeast Asian Capitalists* (Ithaca, NY: Southeast Asia Program, Cornell University, 1992), pp. 65, 88.
58 John McBeth, 'The Year of Doing Business' *Far Eastern Economic Review* 1 September 1994, pp. 70–72.
59 Vedi R. Hadiz, 'Workers and Working Class Politics in the 1990s' in Joan Hardjono and Chris Manning, eds, *Indonesia Assessment 1993* (Canberra: Department of Political and Social Change, Research School of Pacific Studies, ANU, 1993), pp. 186–187.
60 Heryanto, 'A Class Act', p. 30.
61 Olle Törnquist, *What's Wrong With Marxism?: On Peasants and Workers in India and Indonesia* (New Delhi: Manohar, 1991), pp. 176–177.
62 Vedi R. Hadiz, 'Challenging State Corporatism on the Labour Front: Working Class Politics in the 1990s' in David Bourchier and John Legge, eds, *Democracy in Indonesia 1950s and 1990s* (Clayton: Centre of Southeast Asian Studies Monash University, 1994), pp. 191–192.
63 Soeharto quoted in ibid., pp. 193–194.
64 ibid., p. 195.
65 Törnquist, *What's Wrong With Marxism?*, pp. 177–182, 215.

66 Hadiz, 'Workers and Working Class Politics in the 1990s', p. 190; Hadiz, 'Challenging State Corporatism on the Labour Front', p. 191.

67 Rob Lambert, *Authoritarian State Unionism in New Order Indonesia* (Perth: Asia Research Centre, Murdoch University, Working Paper no. 25, October 1993), pp. 4, 22.

68 Hadiz, 'Workers and Working Class Politics in the 1990s', pp. 187–188.

69 'Indonesia: Minimum Wage Sought' *Asian Labour Update* no. 14, January–March 1994, pp. 14–15.

70 'Indonesia: Medan Awakes' *Asian Labour Update* no. 15, April–June 1994, pp. 1, 3; 'Indonesia: Crackdown in Medan' *Asian Labour Update* no. 16, July–September 1994, pp. 20–21.

71 Margot Cohen, 'Indonesia: Still Hard Labour' *Far Eastern Economic Review* 27 October 1994, pp. 20–21.

72 Hadiz, 'Workers and Working Class Politics in the 1990s', pp. 191–193. Vedi R. Hadiz, 'The Political Significance of Recent Working Class Action in Indonesia' in David Bourchier, ed., *Indonesia's Emerging Proletariat: Workers and Their Struggles* (Clayton: Centre of Southeast Asian Studies Monash University, 1994), pp. 68–69.

73 Lambert, *Authoritarian State Unionism in New Order Indonesia*, pp. 22–25.

74 Hadiz, 'Challenging State Corporatism on the Labour Front', pp. 195–202.

75 This type of approach to marxism and socialist politics is apparent in James Petras and Steve Vieux, 'The Decline of Revolutionary Politics: Capitalist Detour and the Return of Socialism' *Journal of Contemporary Asia* vol. 24, no. 1, 1994.

76 Benedict Anderson, 'Radicalism after Communism in Thailand and Indonesia' *New Left Review* no. 202, 1993, p. 14. Also see Arif Dirlik, *After the Revolution: Waking to Global Capitalism* (London: Wesleyan University Press, 1994).

# 8 Anticipating the Pacific Century? Australian responses to realignments in the Asia-Pacific*

*Roger Bell*

## INTRODUCTION: AUSTRALIAN RESPONSES TO REALIGNMENTS IN THE ASIA-PACIFIC

The rapid economic transformation of much of Asia places Australia for the first time within, or at least closely adjacent to, the region of greatest global economic power. Australia's overriding desire to integrate closely into the region has, on one level at least, been substantially achieved: in 1995, almost three-quarters of its total exports flowed to the Asia-Pacific region, and APEC anticipated a multilateral regional economy grouping which eclipsed in importance either the European Union (EU) or NAFTA.[1] These developments intensify Australian government and business optimism that the so-called Pacific Century will be realized, integrating Australia further into the deepening prosperity of the region.[2] Equally, it is anticipated that the Pacific Century will be built on more balanced and reciprocal systems of multilateral political interactions which mitigate conflict and emphasize the shared interests of the diverse members of the region. And in Canberra, at least, this vision persists even as its global political equivalent – the so-called New World Order – is undermined by brutal conflicts, especially in Europe and Africa; a demoralized and impotent UN; bitter trade rivalries, especially in the Asia-Pacific; difficulties in limiting the proliferation of nuclear weapons; escalating expenditure on armaments, especially in the Middle East and Asia; the persistence of authoritarian governments on both the 'left' and 'right' of politics; and widespread abuses of human rights. This chapter traces Australia's often faltering efforts to adjust to the changing realities of the Asia-Pacific. It emphasizes the fundamental consequences for Australia of its uneven integration into the realignments – economic, political and cultural – which characterize the dynamic region on the eve of the much heralded Pacific Century. Australia's changing aspirations and policies are located throughout wider contours of regional and global changes – changes which are increasingly understood as essentially economic, but which are deeply embedded in political and cultural processes.

## COLONIALISM, THE COLD WAR AND AUSTRALIA'S 'ASIA'

The transformation of Asia did not begin with the overthrow of colonialism and the proliferation of independent nation-states in the post-war world. Japan's partial modernization and unexpected victory over Russia in 1902 were potent early symbols of emerging nationalism and embryonic state building in Asia. China also found a degree of unity and assumed some of the institutional trappings of a unified state at the turn of the century as it struggled to reduce foreign influence and modernize. Nationalist movements fuelled by opposition to colonialism surfaced throughout much of the region – from India to Indonesia. By the turn of the century, also, the USA had emerged as an economic giant, with a formal and informal empire in the Far East, the Pacific and the Caribbean. Developments in Asia and the Pacific intensified white Australia's exaggerated security fears. Anglo-Australian racism, already deeply embedded in its immigration policies and national culture, further fuelled Australian anxieties about Asia.

Though tied tightly to England and empire, newly federated Australia looked anxiously across the Pacific for US support against the uncertainties of Asia. During 1907–1908, Prime Minister Alfred Deakin proposed 'an extension of the Monroe Doctrine to all the countries around the Pacific ocean'. The magazine *Lone Hand* betrayed Australia's enduring racist anxieties when it proclaimed: 'Against the two white peoples with important establishments in the Pacific – the United States and Australia – are arrayed millions of brown men, ambitious and arrogant in Asia for more than 400 years.'[3] Just as commentators in the 1990s speak optimistically of the Pacific Century, so in the 1890s many anticipated and hoped their nation would share in the so-called American Century. And for race patriots, like the British writer W. T. Stead, the impending 'Americanization of the world' was to be welcomed as it 'would ensure the continued triumph of the Anglo-Saxon race'.[4] The rise of the USA as the major world economy and an expanding military and economic power in the Western hemisphere, the Pacific and East Asia prefigured in the 1890s its later global authority.

Throughout much of the twentieth century Australian society remained overwhelmingly Anglo-Irish in origin and defiantly 'white'. Yet traditional ties to Britain could not compensate for regional isolation and vulnerability. Attempts by Australian governments to forge new friendships in the Pacific through symbolic visits by the US navy, as well as calls for a regional security agreement with Washington, initiated a pattern that was to become a familiar ritual in its international behaviour throughout the twentieth century – even as it belatedly sought to accommodate its economic interests to those of its near neighbours.

War in the Pacific in the 1940s, followed by Cold War confrontations in Asia, especially Korea and Vietnam, drew Australia militarily into the region. Its involvement in Asia continued to be shaped by extreme, often exaggerated security concerns. Its understanding of Asia, as nations in the region strove to decolonize, remained shallow and anxious, linked increasingly to Washington's perceptions and policies. At the same time, however, the residual ties of empire and race nationalism continued to distort Australia's engagement with the emerging nations and peoples of the Asia-Pacific.

Despite the decisive role of the US in defeating Japan, and the escalating tensions of the Cold War, until it lost office late in 1949 Australia's Labor government refused to accept that Washington's international actions were in the interests of all former allies. Indeed, through its continuing imperial links, support for the infant UN, and through bilateral diplomacy, Australia encouraged other nations to join it in attempting to counter, resist or at least deflect US foreign policy initiatives. As a small state, it felt its particular economic interests and regional ambitions stifled by the predominance of US power and influence in the Asia-Pacific area. Only gradually, and against the background of an allegedly new Asian threat to its security in the form of communist China, did Australia accommodate itself to US authority in the Pacific. The war that erupted in Korea quickly became a brutal reminder that the divisions of the Cold War had been transferred to the Asia-Pacific region and would now be contested in virtually every sphere of international politics. Against this background, the conservative government of Robert Menzies (1949–1966) became increasingly receptive to US definitions of international threat, as it did to US interpretations of security issues and international politics more generally.

Yet if most Australians now welcomed the USA as their protector in a volatile region, they were much less enthusiastic about American culture and commerce, especially when these threatened to displace ties with Britain. As the *Sydney Morning Herald* protested during negotiations over the Security Treaty between Australia, New Zealand and the USA (ANZUS): 'Australia's relations with America are often imperfectly understood abroad. . . . They imply no weakening of the Commonwealth bond, nor any turning away from Britain.' Until the mid-1960s at least, Protestant Australians in particular continued to share what Russell Ward and others have described as a 'dual identity'. 'For most, but not all people, national and imperial patriotism were complementary, not contradictory', he observed.[5]

The fall of Singapore and bombing of Darwin in the early days of the war against Japan, and later the decolonization of Asia, dented but did not destroy the illusion of an imperial umbrella under which white Australia could shelter. 'We draw our main strength not from eight million of our own population,' Richard Casey, Foreign Minister in Menzies's government, claimed, 'but from the fact that we are a member of a great cooperative society: the British race, of which the senior partner is our mother country Great Britain'. Significantly, he added: 'We also have the very great potential asset of the friendship of the greatest single nation in the world, the United States of America.' Although Australian conservatives were anxious to negotiate a formal alliance with their potential new friend, royal visits, royal honours and celebrations of empire remained linchpins of public life in the Menzies years. Even in the late 1960s, while Australian troops fought alongside Americans in Vietnam, it was not uncommon for prominent Australians to announce, as did a former ambassador to Washington, Sir James Plimsoll, that 'we do not see our United States relationship as a threat to British relationships'.[6] Such assertions could not conceal the drift away from Great Britain. However, this realignment was much slower and more complex than historians have sometimes assumed.[7]

Anglophile Australia's relations with the USA were often uncertain and ambivalent as the small dominion reluctantly accepted that its future would be defined by developments in Asia rather than ties to Europe and empire. During negotiation of the ANZUS agreement in 1950–1951, for example, official Australian perceptions of China and Japan often contrasted with those of Washington. The USA agreed to the alliance because it paved the way for a 'soft' peace settlement with Japan, and provided another link in a broad anti-communist network in Asia. In contrast, Australia initially viewed ANZUS as a guarantee against a resurgent Japan. Four years later, during the Suez crisis, the two nations also acted from very different perceptions and pursued very different policies. Menzies's effort in support of British and French aggression against Egypt led to a sharp exchange with President Eisenhower, who condemned the attack as a debacle that merely accelerated the decline of Anglo-French prestige in the Middle East and paved the way for expanded Soviet influence. Under Menzies, Australia occasionally attempted to distance itself from Washington's Cold War policies, especially if these challenged British interests. Australian governments did not always follow the USA uncritically. Privately, Menzies portrayed ANZUS as a 'superstructure on a foundation of jelly'. However, the dominion's refusal to recognize the communist government of China, its willingness to fight in Korea under General MacArthur's leadership, and its anxious public promotion of ANZUS and SEATO were portents of the dominant direction in its foreign policy.[8]

As the Cold War intensified, the Asia-Pacific region joined Europe as a focus of superpower rivalries. Australia's foreign policies and strategic assumptions were radically recast by its association with the USA. Some on the left, in the trade union movement and the Labor Party (ALP), in Australia rejected the need for such a relationship and refused to view international events through what they saw as the distorting lens of the Cold War. Instead, they interpreted revolutions in Asia as legitimate manifestations of nationalism and evidence of long-overdue social change. They criticized the assumption that China or North Korea or, later, North Vietnam were merely willing satellites of the Soviet Union, or pawns in the global contest between 'marxism' and 'democracy'. But for members of the ruling Liberal–Country Party coalition, as well as the Democratic Labor Party which had recently splintered from the ALP, such interpretations were at best naive, at worst comfort to the 'enemy'. In the first months of war in Korea, for example, Liberal MP Paul Hasluck greeted his government's decision to send troops to serve under MacArthur with words that clearly echoed official US statements: 'This expansionist, imperialistic and aggressive policy of the Soviet Union must be resisted wherever it is exemplified.'[9] From stalemate in Korea to defeat in Vietnam, Australia joined the USA in a protracted struggle to contain communism, and nationalism, in Asia. To the Cold Warriors in Washington and Canberra, peasant nationalism had become merely a euphemism for communist subversion. In Australia, deep-rooted anxieties about Asian expansion and 'racial contamination' were now mixed with ideological alarm over the growth of communism in what came to be called the 'Near North'. The Menzies government, along with most Australians, understood communism as a monolithic movement that had spread from the USSR to Eastern Europe, China and the wider Asian region. Communities once obscure to Western interests, notably Laos, Cambodia and Vietnam, were interpreted as precarious strategic 'dominoes' by Australian officials now locked into the ideological imperatives of the Cold War. Justifying his government's decision to send troops to Vietnam, Menzies echoed this familiar argument. 'The takeover of South Vietnam would be a direct military threat to Australia and all the countries of South and South-East Asia', he said. 'It must be seen as part of a thrust by Communist China between the Indian and Pacific Oceans.'[10] Should one domino fall, all the others would topple in quick succession.

Yet even as it rushed to join the US in Vietnam, Australia's wider relationships with Asia were increasingly complex and distant from the divisive formulations of the Cold War. On the eve of the election of an unorthodox Labor government under Prime Minister Gough Whitlam, Australia's rapidly growing trade with Japan, loss of traditional markets in Europe, and re-evaluation of domestic policies on the sensitive issues of immigration and Aboriginal affairs foreshadowed a reorientation in Australian foreign policies. Under Labor (1972–1975) especially, the alliance with Washington was exposed to new tensions as Canberra searched for a more independent role in global affairs, anticipated US policy by recognizing the People's Republic of China, and immediately withdrew Australia's troops from Vietnam. Canberra's strident independence was short-lived, as the Whitlam administration was replaced by the conservative coalition government during the constitutional crisis of 1975. From Korea to the Gulf War examples of official Australian dissent from US actions and perceptions, like those fostered by the Whitlam administration, were fairly rare. Ironically, as recent disclosures about West Irian and Vietnam reveal, Canberra's most forceful initiatives in foreign affairs often sought not to offset US power, but to increase America's presence in Asia and bolster its military effort against 'communism' in the region. ANZUS remained the public cornerstone of Australia's strategic planning while enduring intelligence links and 'joint' security/communication facilities on Australian soil provided the backbone of an intimate relationship that survived undiminished despite the end of the Cold War. However, as superpower rivalries thawed, and economics challenged security as the central preoccupation in foreign policy, Australian governments, notably those led by Fraser, Hawke and Keating, did pursue more diverse and consistently independent initiatives abroad.

Indeed, after the defeat of the USA in Vietnam and promulgation of the Nixon Doctrine at the end of the 1960s, both sides in Australian politics grudgingly accepted that the nation must take greater responsibility for its own affairs – even in the military/defence field. It attempted to match more closely its security aims with commitments of money, equipment and personnel. As a key government paper on defence, the Dibb Report, acknowledged in 1987: 'The ANZUS Treaty provides for consultation in the first instance. There are no guarantees inherent in it. It is realistic to assume that the parties will continue to approach each situation in accordance with their respective national interests.' Official statements now emphasized that 'it is not this Government's policy to rely on combat assistance from the US in all circumstances'.[11] In the face of such official qualifications, the myth of the bilateral 'special relationship' evaporated. With the end of the so-called 'alliance era' of the Cold War, Australian officials accepted more restrained, and realistic, estimates of ANZUS. As Defence Minister Kim Beazley commented in 1989, Australia now wanted immediate, if practical, benefits from the US like 'day-to-day assistance in building up a self-reliant capability, intelligence, access to the best type of equipment, access to training opportunities'. Modest levels of defence cooperation had displaced 'ultimate guarantees' of protection as fundamentals of the bilateral relationship.[12] And increasing Australian–US bilateral disagreements over trade and regional arrangements hastened a long overdue re-evaluation of Australia's links with the many nations of the wider Asia-Pacific.

Constrained by its protracted identification with US policies and its Eurocentric political culture, Australia's positive reorientation towards Asia was realized slowly. In 1964 the Minister for External Affairs claimed, in words which echoed rhetorically in post-war Australia: 'Friendship with Asia, reciprocal trade, closer cultural relations and a clearer understanding of Asia and its people are in the forefront of Australian policy.'[13] By the early 1970s the white Australia policy was dismantled, Australian troops had been withdrawn abruptly from Vietnam, and Prime Minister Whitlam could speak with some justification of the 'withering away of xenophobia, isolationism, and racism'. No longer would insulated political leaders speak publicly of 'the riddles of the inscrutable East', as had the then

Treasurer, later Prime Minister, William McMahon in 1968.[14] Official Australian perceptions of Asia were more nuanced, its policies more pragmatic, its regional expectations more optimistic. As Richard Woolcott wrote, Australia's international policies and the assumption on which they rested had reached a fundamental turning point:

> What is happening is simply that the world around us has changed and we are responding to these changes. . . . [I]t was one thing for the Australian Government of the day to base a policy in Asia in the fifties on the containment of China and implacable anti-communism, when the United States was so doing, when the Korean War was being fought and when the French were still fighting in Indochina. But two decades later, by 1970, such a basis was completely outmoded. By 1972 we needed a new China policy, a different and more mature relationship with the United States, a new approach to our historic links with the United Kingdom. . . . The Government does not now look upon South-East Asia as divided between anti-communist 'goodies' and communist 'baddies'; it does not look upon the countries of South-East Asia as buffer states, as some sort of northern military line where some potential future enemy of Australia should be held. The approach is now less ideological and less militarily oriented.[15]

Australian government policies in the region were now more cooperative and reciprocal, constructed increasingly around a recognition that economic considerations obliged it to adapt flexibly to the new realities of its region.

## MULTILATERALISM AND THE ECONOMIC ROOTS OF AUSTRALIA'S 'TURN TO ASIA'

World War II, and the extension of US-sponsored economic multilateralism, punctured Australia's comfortable economic arrangements with the United Kingdom. By 1959 the imperial preference scheme was crumbling, and Great Britain had moved to secure its economic future in the European Economic Community (EEC, later EC). Significantly, two years earlier Australia signed its first major bilateral agreement with an Asian power – the Australia–Japan trade agreement. Recovery of the Japanese and European economies had been encouraged, in part at least, by the USA as it sought during the war years to reduce barriers to international trade and consolidate its pre-eminent position in a more open global economy. The GATT, the International Monetary Fund and the International Bank for Reconstruction and Development (the World Bank) embodied US plans for a more open world when established at Bretton Woods as the war ended. These were to be the principal instruments of a new international order which would ensure long-term stability and prosperity by undermining the power of competitive economic blocs. In particular, the

USA was anxious to dismantle 'closed' international arrangements which underpinned colonial systems, and separated socialist states along with many protectionist so-called mixed economies from integration into the global economy. Washington was determined to promote a liberal international economic order. This would be achieved, over time, by a series of multilateral arrangements based on the ideal of the 'open door' that would ensure non-discriminatory trade, currency convertibility and unrestricted access to materials and markets everywhere. As Emily Rosenberg has written: 'This brand of liberalism – emphasising equal trade opportunity, open access, free flow, and free enterprise – was advanced as a formula for global development, a formula that the Americans liked to think had succeeded in the US.'[16]

Multilateralism was portrayed as the way to undercut economic nationalism and replace closed spheres of influence with an open and efficient world economy, ostensibly benefiting all nations equally. In practice, however, multilateralism was often interpreted as a self-serving US initiative – especially by small and less efficient states anxious to establish their sovereign authority over post-war reconstruction and long-term domestic economic planning. These nations usually portrayed multilateralism as a vehicle to promote US domination of global trade and investment. While it remained the most efficient industrial nation, advantaged by economies of scale and boosted by the demands of war and reconstruction, the USA stood to benefit far more than any competing economy from a new, more open order.[17]

The US economy boomed in the two decades after World War II, but Washington was initially unable to win unqualified support for economic multilateralism (even in the so-called developed Western world). Nations like Australia which were heavily dependent on non-manufacturing sectors and commodity exports, remained particularly unhappy with GATT's emphasis on reducing barriers to industrial goods rather than agricultural products. Economic multilateralism, then, was an uneven and compromised process. And the formation of the EEC implied that the wealthier industrialized states would continue to put regional blocs and protection ahead of a genuine commitment to freer trade. Decades after the Bretton Woods agreements, commodities exports – largely unprocessed agricultural or mining products – remained subject to higher levels of protection and regulation than manufactured goods. Much of the so-called 'developing world', along with economies like that of Australia which depended heavily on commodities, were slowest to benefit from multilateralism. Furthermore, by the late 1970s as exports from Japan and the newly industrialized countries of Asia challenged the industrial dominance of the USA and Western Europe, support for general tariff reductions declined. Washington, for example, used a range of subsidies and later pursued so-called 'managed trade' to stall the very tariff changes and multilateral openness it had welcomed during the Bretton Woods negotiations. The US, the EC and Japan fought strenuously to protect local agriculture. Their embrace of economic multilateralism weakened as the benefits of open trade declined for the powerful industrialized nations. GATT's continuing reluctance to discuss a more open global trading system for agriculture was rejected angrily by Australia in 1982, for example, as an all-too-familiar fiasco. A year later Deputy Prime Minister Doug Anthony complained: 'The sorry state of agriculture is one that the founding fathers of GATT could never have foreseen in their most despairing moments.'[18] Anthony's pessimism grew out of his government's largely unsuccessful efforts to establish regional arrangements capable of overseeing freer trade in both industrial and primary products.

During the period of Liberal–National Party government under Prime Minister Malcolm Fraser (1975–1983), unprecedented emphasis was given to resource diplomacy and trade with ASEAN, while an embryonic Pacific Rim (or Pacific Basin) arrangement also won strong support. Officials claimed (in terms familiar a decade later) that the 'economic future of Australia points inevitably to our strong involvement with Asia'.[19] Foreign Minister Andrew Peacock foreshadowed a broad reorientation in Australian policies. 'Australia can't long delay important decisions as to how it as a nation is going to relate to the economic development of our near North', he stated in late 1979; 'if we want close political relations with our neighbours, we must appreciate that we cannot do so while remaining economically inward-looking and protectionist – economic and political relations are different sides of the same coin.'[20] Initially, however, the Fraser government made only minor concessions to the demands of its Asian neighbours for improved access to Australia's markets. Yet Canberra did support, in principle at least, the demands of developing countries for freer access to world markets. This position cannot be simply dismissed as hollow rhetoric, if only because as a major exporter of primary commodities Australia would undoubtedly have profited if these demands were met by the developed world. At the UN Conference on Trade and Development (UNCTAD) V meeting in Manila in 1979, for example, Fraser attempted to project Australia as a sympathetic broker between the protectionist industrialized blocs (EC, Japan and the USA) and the developing anti-protectionist states represented by the Group of 77. Like the developing states, Australia was disturbed that it would not be represented at a forthcoming Tokyo summit of OECD countries, and used the Manila meeting to attack protectionism. Understandably, most developing countries interpreted this as a criticism of EC barriers to Australian exports, rather than an unselfish general commitment to freer international trade. This suspicion was allayed slightly when, shortly after releasing its *Third World Report,* the government eliminated preferences for a wide range of imports from Britain (500 in all), and granted tariff preferences to a substantial number of products (sixty-six) from developing countries (most notably many clothing and footwear items). Australia also doubled its contribution to the ASEAN–Australian Economic Co-operation Program, bringing its commitment to almost $30 million. At the same time, Anthony foreshadowed other measures aimed at minimizing ASEAN's concerns with Australia's economic policies. 'We seek to give every product from ASEAN the maximum access and most favoured entry into our market that the economic and political realities in Australia will permit us to offer', he stated. In October 1979 officials from ASEAN and Australia met in Canberra and agreed in principle to a range of measures to improve trade – including bilateral trade and investment promotion programmes; an undertaking by Australia 'to take prompt action' if remaining British tariff preferences inhibited ASEAN access to Australia; and an undertaking to reassess duties on 'those items subject to the twelve and a half per cent import surcharge, on which ASEAN can provide specific evidence that its exports have been adversely affected by the surcharge'. Officials on both sides welcomed those decisions as marking 'a new beginning' in trade cooperation.[21] While these developments strengthened economic ties between Australia and ASEAN, East Asia remained far more important to Australia's economic prosperity than the ASEAN area. Moreover, there remained much greater economic 'complementarity' between Australia and the more heavily industrialized states of East Asia, than between Australia and ASEAN.

Regional negotiations to liberalize trade from the late 1970s complemented attempts by a succession of Australian governments to promote a formal regional economic arrangement. In a series of proposals which in some respects anticipated the formation of APEC a decade later, Australia embraced the so-called Pacific Rim idea. Significantly, Japan was also an enthusiastic supporter of this proposal. In broad terms, it envisaged closer formal economic interdependence between various states, or groups of states, in the Asia-Pacific region. The advanced industrial states, Japan and the USA, would provide capital, technology and planning; Australia, New Zealand and Canada would act essentially as sources of foodstuffs, raw materials and energy; and the developing, so-called cheap labour states of ASEAN and East Asia would provide manufactured goods. By the late 1970s the Asia-Pacific region accounted for almost half of total world GDP. It was argued that by exploiting the varied, allegedly complementary resources of countries throughout this region, the rate of development in the Pacific would quickly outstrip that of other regional groupings like the EEC. Various academic and business groups (especially those linked to mining industries) actively supported the idea, arguing that it capitalized on the existing interdependence of Pacific Rim countries. Anticipating the visit by the Prime Minister of China to Australia in January 1980, Foreign Minister Andrew Peacock announced that his department would recommend the government work towards developing a broad regional consensus on the idea. 'I personally think that in the eighties we will have a Pacific economic bloc', Peacock commented. 'The academic talk has ended. We have now moved on to inter-governmental discussions.'[22]

Expanded trading ties between Australia and ASEAN paved the way for closer and more cooperative regional relations. In the decade from 1980 the ASEAN states emerged as a more important export market for Australian products than either the EC or the USA (although as critics of Australia's trading performance pointed out, its overall share of this fast-growing market remained fairly static). ASEAN was also crucial to Australia's efforts to diversify its export base by becoming less reliant on commodities and winning recognition as a 'clever country'. From 1987 especially, ASEAN's purchases of value-added Australian manufactures rose more sharply than such exports to any other market. Member nations also became the principal focus of exports in the fast-growing educational services industry – an industry worth over $1 billion annually to Australia by 1993. Immigration trends complemented this new interdependence. By the early 1990s immigrants from Southeast Asia (largely ASEAN states) comprised 40 per cent of the annual migrant intake into Australia. Political cooperation also expanded. Most importantly, the Hawke government's APEC initiative built on careful negotiations with the ASEAN states, especially Indonesia. Like Australia, these states were keen to expand their voice and influence in multilateral commercial diplomacy, and were concerned by the prospect of large exclusive trading groupings or blocs focused on Europe and North America. Collectively, by the 1990s ASEAN and Australia made up about 2.5 per cent of the total global economy, and further growth demanded greater political unity and participation in multilateral trading initiatives. Canberra's relations with individual ASEAN states were sometimes brittle – as intermittent differences with Singapore, Malaysia and Indonesia demonstrated. All parties accepted, however, that continued economic growth should be complemented by regional initiatives as well as improved bilateral cooperation.

The Labor administrations of both Bob Hawke (1983–1992) and Paul Keating (1992–1996) agreed that fundamental structural changes and domestic reforms of the local economy were necessary if Australia was to benefit from a more open global or regional economy. Successive governments deregulated the exchange rate, reduced barriers to foreign investment, deregulated financial markets, further reduced levels of protection, initiated microeconomic reforms especially in transport, and took steps to free up the labour market. At the same time they introduced so-called structural adjustments which sought to make local industry – from textiles to motor cars – more efficient and less protected.

The continuing success of GATT in reducing protection of industry during multilateral negotiations from 1947 to 1979 did not translate into unqualified support for a liberal international economic order – even in the USA. Indeed, by the early 1980s as Australia attempted to restructure its domestic economy so that it was more open to competition from the outside world, strong symptoms of ongoing protectionism remained in the EC, Japan and the USA and in some of the Newly Industrializing Economies of Asia. Trading blocs remained, most importantly the EC, and new ones were in prospect, most notably NAFTA. During the Tokyo Round of GATT (1973–1979) and later during the Uruguay Round, many governments used qualitative controls, subsidies and export incentives as well as tariffs to protect local industries and agriculture. 'Managed trade' became a euphemism for such practices in states publicly tied to liberalized commerce but reluctant to commit themselves fully to more open regimes. The Common Agricultural Policy of the EC employed a complex of subsidies to privilege local producers; Japan maintained massive agricultural support; and from 1985 the US Farm Bill and Export Enhancement Program heavily subsidized that country's agricultural production and exports. Progress towards reduced protection for primary production at GATT was stalled by such practices. The effects on Australia's export earnings was dramatic. For example, during its first three years of operation the Export Enhancement Program increased the US share of the world's wheat trade from 29 to 43 per cent, while Australia's share declined from 20 to 12 per cent.[23] International trading regulations were easily sidestepped or compromised, creating distrust rather than genuine cooperation.

Confronted by a virtual impasse in GATT over continuing high levels of agricultural protection, in 1986 the Labor government convened in Cairns a meeting of fourteen countries,[24] anxious to bring the giant economies of the EC, USA and Japan into multilateral regimes which opened their agricultural producers to international competition. The Cairns Groups was a unique coalition of small and middle powers, from both the 'North' and the 'South'. Like many so-called developing countries of the South, Australia belonged to no trading bloc (other than a bilateral agreement with neighbouring New Zealand), and its commodity exports were stifled by barriers and subsidies erected in the major world economies. The fourteen states which joined Australia in the Cairns Group attempted to push multilateral trade negotiations, especially the Uruguay Round, towards genuine reform of agricultural trade. By the mid-1990s the Cairns coalition had won some major concessions under GATT, as barriers to mineral imports were virtually eliminated and a regime agreed for reducing agricultural protection.

However, changes in the global order did not consistently move towards increased openness. While protectionism generally declined, this change coincided in the 1980s and especially in the early 1990s with a somewhat contradictory growth in regional groupings and trading blocs. In addition, uneven responses by the seven major OECD economies to GATT processes, and the recurrent eruption of economic nationalism in such conflicts as the EC–US subsidy disputes of the mid-1980s or the ongoing trade dispute between Tokyo and Washington undermined progress. Fearing exclusion from new trading blocs, in 1989 the Labor government sponsored the forum for Asia Pacific Economic Cooperation (APEC). However, Canberra was careful to reassure its neighbours that this initiative did not foreshadow formation of a formal regional trading bloc. Rather, like the less conclusive Pacific Rim initiatives a decade earlier, APEC initially sought to provide both a focus for resolving regional trade difficulties, and a vehicle for promoting stronger regional and global commitments to the Uruguay Round of GATT. While bilateral trade liberalization outpaced multilateral change, by 1994 APEC had committed member states to a specific timetable of trade liberalization for the Asia-Pacific region. (See Table 8.1 for basic statistics on APEC member states.)

Despite the much publicized unity stated in the Leaders' Declaration issued at the Bogor meeting of APEC in April 1994, some differences between member states remained unresolved. The major partners, Japan

*Table 8.1* APEC (in brief), 1995

|  | Population (millions) | Per capita income ($) | % GNP growth* |
|---|---|---|---|
| Asia |  |  |  |
| Brunei | 0.3 | 15,640 | NA |
| China | 1,162.2 | 470 | 7.6 |
| Hong Kong | 5.8 | 15,360 | 5.5 |
| Indonesia | 184.3 | 670 | 4.0 |
| Japan | 124.5 | 28,190 | 3.6 |
| Malaysia | 18.6 | 2,790 | 3.2 |
| Philippines | 64.3 | 770 | −1.0 |
| Singapore | 2.8 | 15,730 | 5.3 |
| South Korea | 43.7 | 6,790 | 8.5 |
| Taiwan | 20.8 | 10,163 | 7.8 |
| Thailand | 58.0 | 1,840 | 6.0 |
| Oceania |  |  |  |
| Australia | 17.5 | 17,260 | 1.6 |
| New Zealand | 3.4 | 12,300 | 0.6 |
| Papua New Guinea | 4.1 | 950 | 2.3 |
| Americas |  |  |  |
| Canada | 27.4 | 20,710 | 1.8 |
| Mexico | 85.0 | 3,470 | −0.2 |
| USA | 255.4 | 23,240 | 1.7 |
| Chile | 13.6 | 2,730 | 3.7 |

*Source:* Adapted from *Newsweek*, 22 November 1994.
*Notes:*
*Average of annual growth 1980–1992.
   Total GDP of APEC countries by 1994 was more than $13 trillion, equal to half the world's total production.
   International trade within East and Southeast Asia by 1994 was more than the region's trade with the United States and Canada.

and the USA, disagreed over the fundamental question of whether participants should be permitted to deal on a most favoured nation (MFN)
basis with the rest of the world, or develop APEC into a preferential trading area with the characteristics of a trading bloc. Australia shared Japan's
support for giving negotiations MFN status. In contrast, Washington
favoured a 'preferential' grouping of trading states. APEC had become a
complex institutional symbol of trade liberalization and regional integration. Yet Japan and the USA were not fully committed to a specific timetable for removing barriers – despite decisions taken at the APEC leaders'
conference in 1994. These decisions anticipated the removal of obstacles
to trade and investment among industrialized members by 2010, and
among developing member states by 2020. However, as some critics
argued, bilateral agreements, along with progress under GATT, might
well have achieved equivalent results more rapidly. In addition, compliance
with multilateral APEC regimes and timetables was difficult to monitor
and even more difficult to enforce. To promote unanimous agreement, the
Bogor Declaration was necessarily vague. 'The pace of implementation', it
declared, 'will take into account the differing levels of economic development among APEC economies.' No attempt was made to define or specify
which states were 'developing' economies – although the deadline granted
this group of nations was considerably more generous than that for the
so-called 'developed' economies. Nor did the Declaration take account of
the prospect that some states, most notably China and perhaps Indonesia,
might grow rapidly and join neighbours like Singapore or South Korea in
the 'developed' category. Indeed, under the Bogor guidelines each state
was in effect free to identify the category which best described its level of
economic development.[25]

Despite these ambiguities, Australia welcomed APEC. Canberra was
pleased that the guidelines made no explicit distinction between industrial
goods and agricultural products, as this might pave the way for long-
overdue non-discriminatory tariff reductions which the GATT Rounds had
largely failed to achieve. Indeed, Canberra anticipated that by 2020
Australia's exports would have expanded by $7 billion annually. Prime
Minister Keating conceded after Bogor: 'We have a long way to go before
free trade is implemented in APEC.' But his government anticipated that
the next APEC summit, in Osaka in 1995, would formalize agreements
establishing a firm guarantee of genuine free trade and investment.
Publicly, Keating welcomed APEC in terms which reflected its extreme
significance for his nation's future. In his words, formation of APEC was
'an absolute triumph for the Asia Pacific, a triumph for the world trading
system, and . . . a triumph for Australia'.[26]

The Cairns Group and the APEC initiative were, in part at least,
exercises in domestic politics, as they reinforced Labor's argument that
Australia's economic difficulties resulted from its integration into a global
order of unequal states, over which it could exert very limited authority.

Australia's domestic difficulties were linked to the failure of the major states to give unqualified support to multilateralism. Unless these governments supported liberalized trade in agricultural commodities, Australia warned, it and other small economies would reject the GATT arrangements and be suspicious of its successor, the World Trade Organization, which was scheduled to begin in January 1995. Conveniently overlooking its own protection of manufacturing, Australia's leaders proclaimed that it was 'not prepared to be the only free trader in the world'. Bureaucrats and some business and union leaders publicly lamented the absence of a 'level playing field' in international economics. At the same time, Prime Minister Hawke conceded the limits of his own government's power in the more integrated world. The nation's economy has reached a point of 'absolute dependence in the international economy', he observed in 1986. A year later, as the Australian dollar fell to its lowest value against the major world currencies, Hawke protested lamely that Australia was 'part of a world wide situation and we can't affect the world'.[27] Yet as deregulation of the domestic economy and initiatives like APEC implied, both the Hawke and Keating administrations anxiously sought to influence the emerging economic configuration, especially in the Asia-Pacific. At the same time, the Labor government energetically pursued a range of foreign policy initiatives – notably efforts to reconstruct Cambodia – by which Australia sought to confirm that it was both an independent and a constructive partner in the region.

Under the leadership of Foreign Minister Gareth Evans, Australia encouraged UN peace-keeping operations; actively pursued international agreements on environmental matters; negotiated to protect the Antarctic; conceded that human rights issues could not be divorced from international politics; supported revised refugee agreements and protocols; and worked more independently through the UN to make issues like development equity, disarmament and restrictions on chemical weapons production more central to the international agenda. Such initiatives were complemented by a more realistic appreciation of the limits of alliance diplomacy and the ambiguous consequences of automatic Australian identification with US policies – especially in the Asia-Pacific.

As the contests over lend-lease, multilateralism and Article VII had demonstrated in the 1940s,[28] international economics were central concerns in Australian foreign policy as it adjusted to a world in which British 'protection' and imperial preferences would no longer dictate the dominion's economic plans. Genuine economic sovereignty in the post-war world could only be sustained at the expense of reciprocal involvement in multilateral developments fostered by the USA through the Bretton Woods agreement. By the late 1970s, Canberra belatedly accepted that the elaborate system of tariffs, quotas and incentives which protected local secondary industries would have to be modified if Australia was to participate more fully in the fruits of multilateralism. By the early 1980s about 70 per cent of Australia's imports faced 'non-protective rates of duty', while about 90 per cent of imports from the ASEAN nations entered under this duty or under a special low rate imposed on 'developing countries'. Canberra recognized that it must support concessions which expanded trade in industrial goods while seeking to induce GATT to implement genuine reforms in the agricultural area. Reform of the global economy was essential if Australia was to arrest its deteriorating terms of trade and declining role in an increasingly competitive international economy. Over four decades, from 1947, Australia's share of total international trade slumped from 2.5 per cent to 1.1 per cent; its ranking in terms of per capita income fell from third to thirteenth place; and its exports as a percentage of GDP remained static while exports by most other nations in the Asia-Pacific region grew rapidly. From the early 1980s, Australia's current account deficit, expressed as a proportion of total GDP, rose appreciably, hovering around 6 per cent from the late 1980s to the mid-1990s. Although located conveniently on the geographical edge of the fast-growing economies of much of East and Southeast Asia, Australian business and industry struggled to benefit from the transformation of the region. Finding it difficult to compete in the new regional environment, Australian governments were relatively quick to realign their state with the major industrial economy of the Asia-Pacific after World War II. Japan replaced the United Kingdom in 1969 as the major purchaser of Australian exports, and Japan became the most important destination for Australia's products – especially those from the mining and agricultural sectors (see Tables 8.2 and 8.3).

*Table 8.2* Trends in post-war trade (%)

|  | UK | Other EEC | Japan | South and Southeast Asia | USA |
|---|---|---|---|---|---|
| **Exports** | | | | | |
| 1949–1950 | 39.4 | 18.9 | 4.0 | 11.1 | 8.2 |
| 1959–1960 | 26.4 | 18.7 | 14.4 | 8.4 | 8.1 |
| 1969–1970 | 11.8 | 10.9 | 25.0 | 12.3 | 13.4 |
| 1979–1980 | 5.0 | 9.3 | 26.9 | 13.0 | 10.8 |
| 1989–1990 | 3.5 | 10.4 | 26.1 | 18.7 | 10.9 |
| **Imports** | | | | | |
| 1949–1950 | 53.1 | 6.3 | 1.3 | 13.5 | 9.9 |
| 1959–1960 | 35.7 | 11.7 | 4.5 | 11.3 | 16.2 |
| 1969–1970 | 21.8 | 12.8 | 12.4 | 6.5 | 24.9 |
| 1979–1980 | 10.2 | 13.4 | 15.6 | 12.4 | 22.1 |
| 1989–1990 | 6.5 | 15.5 | 19.2 | 12.1 | 24.1 |

*Source:* Adapted from R. A. Foster and S. E. Stewart, *Australian Economic Statistics, 1949 to 1989–90* (Sydney: Reserve Bank of Australia, Occasional Paper No. 89, February 1991), and B. Pinkstone, *Global Connections: A History of Exports and the Australian Economy* (Canberra: AGPS, 1992).

*Table 8.3* Australia's merchandise exports and imports by country, 1991–1992 ($ million)

|  | *Exports* | *Imports* |
|---|---|---|
| Associations of South-East Asian Nations (ASEAN) | | |
| Brunei | 19 | 82 |
| Indonesia | 1,635 | 995 |
| Malaysia | 1,106 | 867 |
| Philippines | 514 | 143 |
| Singapore | 3,189 | 1,301 |
| Thailand | 825 | 647 |
| Total ASEAN | 7,288 | 4,035 |
| European Community (EC) | | |
| Germany | 1,092 | 3,007 |
| Italy | 979 | 1,229 |
| Netherlands | 855 | 588 |
| United Kingdom | 1,930 | 3,102 |
| Total EC | 6,861 | 10,359 |
| China | 1,457 | 1,976 |
| Taiwan | 2,537 | 1,978 |
| Hong Kong | 2,104 | 792 |
| Japan | 14,589 | 9,290 |
| Korea, Republic of | 3,374 | 1,213 |
| New Zealand | 2,826 | 2,399 |
| USA | 5,221 | 11,743 |

*Source:* Adapted from ABS *Year Book* 1994, No. 76 (ABS Catalogue No. 1301.0), pp. 765–769; *Foreign Trade, Australia: Merchandise Exports and Imports, 1991–92* (5410.0).

Yet if Japan's rapid industrialization compensated Australia for the collapse of imperial preferences and Britain's withdrawal to the EC in 1961, it was the USA which exerted the most pronounced influence on Australia's economy after Bretton Woods. Australia was aligned far more rapidly with the economy of its powerful Pacific ally than with the proliferating growth centres of Asia. At the same time, Australia was a disproportionately important focus of US trade, investment, technology and popular culture as Washington, too, reoriented its economy increasingly from Europe and the Atlantic to Asia and the Pacific. Within a decade of VJ Day, the USA challenged the UK as the principal source of investment capital in Australia. By the early 1980s the Australian economy was affected by higher levels of foreign penetration than any industrialized nation other than Canada. Australia's balance of trade with the USA continued to deteriorate as the volume of bilateral trade grew. By the mid-1980s Australia was the second most important purchaser of US exports, and the value of its imports from the USA exceeded the value of imports from any other nation. As a stable, democratic, Anglophile and essentially risk-free nation, Australia, like Canada, was arguably a most attractive home for US investments. Australia's attractiveness was reflected in the fact that in the early 1990s it accepted higher levels of US investment than any single country in the Asia-Pacific area. Australia ranked fourth as a destination for US capital, and in 1994 outstripped the entire East Asia area as a target of US investment capital. Investments from the three major sources of overseas capital – the US, the UK and Japan – were by the early 1990s broadly equal in dollar terms, ranging between $58 billion and $51 billion. While Japan remained the principal destination of Australia's exports, the USA remained the major national source of overseas capital as well and the nation with which Australia had by far its most serious imbalance of trade. If, by the 1990s, the economic shift towards the Asia-Pacific was inexorable, it was uneven and far from complete. As late as 1992, for example, both direct and portfolio investments from the EC countries – mainly the UK – far exceeded those from either the USA or Japan. In the following three years, however, US investments grew rapidly outstripping those from the EU/UK or Japan (see Table 8.4).[29]

Increasingly, however, Australian trade was linked to Asia, especially to the most recently industrialized states of ASEAN, and to China and South Korea, as well as Japan. This region purchased over 70 per cent of total Australian exports by the mid-1990s, and commentators spoke

*Table 8.4a* Foreign investment in Australia by country (levels of investment at 30 June 1992) ($ million)

| Country | Investment |
| --- | --- |
| USA | 58,223 |
| Japan | 51,353 |
| UK | 52,117 |
| Total EC | 72,887 |
| ASEAN | 7,325 |

*Table 8.4b* Australian investment abroad by country

| Country | Investment |
| --- | --- |
| USA | 36,714 |
| New Zealand | 6,985 |
| UK | 19,730 |
| Total OECD | 77,871 |
| ASEAN | 3,041 |

*Source:* Adapted from ABS *Year Book*, Australia, No. 76, pp. 791–793.

optimistically of the 'ascendancy' of Northeast Asia as the region quickly emerged as the most powerful focus of industrialization and growth in the wider region.[30] Australia's trade surplus with the region now exceeded $8 billion annually, but at the same time its deficit with its major Pacific partner, the US, exceeded $10 billion annually.

Despite optimism about the generalized benefits of expanded global trade in a more open multilateral order, these benefits were distributed unevenly and were often slowly realized. At the same time, economic liberalism did not automatically foreshadow greater political liberalism, genuine human rights or democratic practices in the diverse states of the region. Indeed, Lee Kuan Yew and Dr Mahathir have led an assault on decadent Western values and asserted that Western-style democracy might not be compatible with Asia's varied social patterns, cultural traditions or economic ambitions. Moreover, market economies have been adopted by states as diverse as China, Vietnam and Indonesia, which remain rigidly authoritarian. The reluctance of the major economies to embrace trade liberalization fully did not, however, override bipartisan support within Australia for the view that the nation's long-term economic interests would be best served by adhering to the principles of liberal international trade and a 'rational' economic agenda. Yet the protracted GATT impasse over agriculture and divisions between the trade groups centred on the EC, North America and East Asia were symbols of international rivalry that some commentators likened to the divisions of the inter-war years. Multilateralism, as reflected in the operation of GATT, Strobe Talbott observed, remained '[t]he imperfect, spluttering engine of globalization'.[31] Economic regionalism persisted despite half a century of negotiations over multilateralism. President Bush's New World Order envisaged continued economic integration and broader political cooperation. But bilateral trade disputes, regional economic groupings, and partial liberalization of trade persisted into the 1990s – even as the rhetoric of global openness intensified.

## ADJUSTING TO ASIA

Well before the disintegration of communism in Eastern Europe, Australia, like many other capitalist nations, had embraced much of the rhetoric and practices of open-door liberalism. And, as in most Western democracies, 'economic rationalism' had been accepted as the new economic orthodoxy by government and opposition parties alike. Moves to deregulate finance, business and commerce, along with efforts to transfer government enterprises to private ownership, were indications of a fundamental shift towards a diminished role for state intervention and the public sector in the economic life of the nation. Both the Labor Party and the conservative parties also accepted that Australia must join regional as well as wider global economic arrangements, or risk isolation from the international processes that increasingly shaped the politics and prospects of national states.

Australia, like other small and medium-sized economies, was essentially powerless to resist integration into the more open economic order. Yet the benefits of this transformation remained, as Labor leaders had warned in the 1940s, at most very uncertain. In the half-century after World War II Australian living standards, had declined relative to those of other OECD nations; domestic inequalities had increased; the official unemployment rate hovered around 10 per cent; national debt levels and debt servicing levels exceeded those in all but one of the OECD nations; and Australia's terms of trade continued to decline as it failed to arrest its mounting annual trade deficits. Despite substantial integration into the dynamic Asia-Pacific region, Australia's overall economic performance had not kept pace with those of its major partners, notably Japan, the ASEAN states and South Korea. As Richard Higgott observed in 1994: 'As the Asia-Pacific region has become a major force in the global system of production and exchange, Australia's economic significance and influence in that region has declined.'[32]

Adjustment to these altered international circumstances demanded more than new trading agreements or domestic economic restructuring and reform. Cultural and constitutional change were also essential, it was argued by those anxious to secure Australia's future with Asia. Formal links to a European colonial past, symbolized by ties to the British monarchy, would retard Australia's quest to secure its future in the Asia-Pacific. A generation earlier, decisions liberalizing immigration policies and endorsing multiculturalism as a fundamental prescription for society were overdue responses to regional pressures for a more open and tolerant Australia. By the mid-1990s Keating spoke for a majority of Australians in claiming the need to redefine further his nation's political and cultural reorientation, when he stated: 'We can't succeed without the world knowing who we are, and much as we like and acknowledge the British and the institutions we have inherited, we are not British now.' Efforts to join the Pacific Century pushed Australia more rapidly towards political maturity. The quest for a republic came to symbolize national independence and sovereignty, not merely the end of formal ties to the UK. Even as he courted European investment and technical expertise on a visit to Germany, Keating emphasized that it was Australia's integration into the Asia-Pacific region and the global economy which obliged his nation to reshape its political culture and identity. Realignments in the region, he asserted, had created 'a tide of national renewal' and intensified the 'necessity for a Republic'.[33] Yet republicanism had not yet won formal acceptance, even if during the Keating administration it had the support of a growing majority of Australians.

Not surprisingly, as the occasional observations of Lee Kuan Yew and Dr Mahathir revealed, some Asian elites remained determined to identify Australia as Eurocentric, misinformed about the region, and culturally separate from its neighbours.[34] And its close ties with the USA, like links to a foreign monarch, intensified such criticism. US Under-Secretary of State Joseph Nye's claim of early 1995 that his government's relationship with Canberra is 'probably the most intimate we have with any Asia-Pacific country'[35] underlined Australia's difficult position in the region. Its independence could be asserted, but it remained closely identified with US policies, especially in military/strategic affairs. The sharp shifts in regional power, especially the rapid rise in Chinese economic power and military spending, reinforced Washington's determination to maintain a substantial 'forward presence' at least in East Asia. Australia's subtle distinction between greater self-reliance and continuing acceptance of the USA as a key element in defence policy was sometimes understood by its neighbours as a continuation of its close Cold War ties with Washington. Nor did bilateral acceptance of the limited, purely consultative nature of ANZUS quickly win recognition that Australian governments were genuinely independent actors on the international stage. In the post-Cold War world, the strategic architecture of the Asia-Pacific was being rebuilt by the emerging major powers of the region – China, Japan, India and Indonesia, as well as residual Russian and US influence. Conscious of its relative powerlessness in the face of escalating military spending by some Asian states, and the changing strategic alignments in the region, Australian independence was always qualified by reference – if not deference – to Washington. Australia remained intimately linked to US strategic and intelligence arrangements, and deeply penetrated by US popular culture, even as its contacts with Asian states and Asian peoples proliferated and matured.

Just as commentators exaggerated the vulnerability of Australian culture, both political and popular, to 'Americanization' during the period of US hegemony in the 1960s and 1970s, so too do they exaggerate its openness to 'Asianization' in the post-Cold War era. Typical of such routine claims is that in the *Far Eastern Economic Review* in 1994:

> The awakening of Australians towards Asia can be partly explained by the rise in Asian immigration, which has already rendered sweeping changes to the culture of the country. The 'Asianization' of Australia talked about in cautious tones in the early 1980s is becoming a reality as more than 40 per cent of the country's annual migrant intake now comes from Asia. By contrast, Australia's traditional migrant source, Europe, provides less than one third of new arrivals, and even that proportion is declining.[36]

But this claim, like those made by opponents of a more open society, obviously exaggerated the social consequences of Australia's new liberal immigration policies. It is estimated that by 2025 the proportion of its population of Asian descent will have grown to about 7 per cent. And these peoples, from a variety of ethnic and language groups, would remain heavily concentrated in the largest cities, especially Sydney. Based on the experiences of previous immigrants to Australia, assimilation into a plural society, not 'Asianization' of the host culture, is the most likely outcome of the more open policy.[37] Economic realignment does not necessarily foreshadow fundamental social disruption, or rapid cultural and political change, in contemporary Australia.

After World War II, Australia simultaneously welcomed US protection, clung to the symbols of the empire and monarchy, consumed imported popular culture with growing enthusiasm, and opened its doors to a widening stream of migrants from a range of linguistic and ethnic communities. Its cultural fabric was not torn by such influences. Rather it gradually absorbed and adapted these international currents of ideas, people and commodities into a more distinct and independent national culture. By the late 1970s, the celebratory label of multiculturalism symbolized the adaptation of Australian cultural and political life to international processes which eroded its insularity without rendering it merely imitative or dependent.

## CONCLUSION: ANTICIPATING THE PACIFIC CENTURY?

Modern Australia is neither a new Britannia in the South Pacific, nor a politico-cultural satellite of its powerful ally and influence, the USA. Nor is it a part of Asia, except arguably in a broad geographic or economic sense. It is increasingly linked to Asia, but remains culturally and socially very separate from the diverse nations and cultures of the region – even those with which it has shared a long history of British rule. Australia's population, cultural forms, external ties and educational priorities are increasingly informed by ties with Asian states and peoples. These influences have helped to shape a more plural Australian culture. Yet Anglophone Australia's particular history, traditions and identity as well as the complex legacies of British and US power remain the fundamental forces in contemporary Australian life. Recently, Asian peoples and influences have made Australia's multicultural complexion more diverse, further complicating traditional distinctions of class, religion, region and ethnicity. Developments in the Asia-Pacific have reoriented Australian diplomacy and economics unambiguously towards the region. While contemporary Australia is increasingly touched by these changes, domestic culture and society will not be quickly transformed by them.

The fields of material and cultural interaction between Australia and the diverse nations of Asia have expanded dramatically. Domestic society and culture, like the dominant Anglo-US sources which influenced them from abroad, are now challenged by new sources of material and cultural interaction – by new peoples, technology, commerce and ideas. Australians now negotiate their identity and culture from within an increasingly plural society on the periphery of the newly emerging Asia-Pacific. The nation's economic future is routinely understood as one dependent on further incorporation into the web of developments which continue to promote regional integration and growth. Yet Australia is arguably more culturally assertive and politically independent than at any time since Federation. Local differences have been sharpened as Australian society has responded to regional changes in a post-colonial world. The end of the Cold War hastened Australia's formal separation from dependence on the USA, although the small power remains deeply implicated in North American popular culture, political discourse and security networks. Like much of the modernized world, central fields of Australian life are touched by what Joseph Nye calls the 'soft power' of the USA, by its 'cultural and ideological appeal'.[38] The legacies of its involvement as an ally in the American Century persist, even as Australia prepares for the Pacific Century and a more fluid multipolar world. Australian governments, especially Labor under Keating, have responded flexibly to this more open international environment, finding their nation's status as a small or middle power less limiting than during the bipolar certainties of the Cold War. As it has attempted to accommodate to the transformation of the Asia-Pacific, Australia has sought to define itself in more distinctive national terms, and to promote more independently its separate national interests both within the region and on the wider world stage. Dr Mahathir's less than subtle assertion that economic considerations inspired Australia's belated efforts to become part of Asia is well-founded.[39] In many respects, Australian society remains largely distinct from the diverse nations of the region, despite efforts to engage more broadly with them.

## NOTES

* For research assistance I wish to thank Ellen Perdikogiannis and Damien McCoy.

1 While it is conceptually necessary to speak of 'Asia' and the Asia-Pacific, this should not imply that nations in the region share broadly similar features. The many nations of Asia do not comprise a coherent region, although most are obviously undergoing rapid industrialization and economic change, and participate as equals in various regional forums and institutions. In addition, all nations in the region, with the possible exception of Singapore, are extremely diverse, exhibiting profound domestic differences grounded in ethnic and religious distinctions, rural and urban contrasts, varied gender roles and family patterns, unequal levels of education, and sharply uneven rates of political participation by their citizens. Most obviously, political ideologies and governing structures in Asia range across a very wide spectrum – from rigidly authoritarian to essentially democratic. This plurality and these social divisions are emphasized in recent literature, especially that which seeks to puncture the simplistic optimism about the economic transformation of the Asia-Pacific and the coming of the Pacific Century. See, especially, G. Segal, *Rethinking the Pacific* (Oxford: Clarendon Press, 1990), For examples of Pacific Century optimism, see W. McCord, *The Dawn of the Pacific Century: Implications for the Three Worlds of Development* (New Brunswick: Transaction Publishers, 1991) and

the World Bank, *The East Asian Miracle: Economic Growth and Public Policy*, World Bank Policy Research Report (New York: Oxford University Press, 1993).

2 With regard to post-Cold War Asia, Senator Gareth Evans, Australian Foreign Minister, asked in 1991 if Australia was 'forever seen as a European outpost, a kind of cultural misfit trapped by geography in an alien environment? Or are we to recognise that Australia's future lies inevitably in the Asia-Pacific region – that this is where we live and must survive strategically and economically, and where we must find a place and role if we are to develop our full potential as a nation?'

3 See N. Meaney, *The Search for Security in the Pacific, 1901–1914* (Sydney: Sydney University Press, 1976); R. Megaw, 'Australia and the Great White Fleet, 1980' *Journal of the Royal Australian Historical Society* no. 56, 1970, pp. 121–131.

4 W. J. Stead, *The Americanisation of the World* (New York: 1901), pp. 53–55.

5 *Sydney Morning Herald* 26 November 1951; R. Ward, *A History of Australia* (Melbourne 1982), pp.51-52.

6 N. Meaney, 'Australia and the World' in N. Meaney, ed., *Under New Heavens: Cultural Transmission and the Making of Australia* (Port Melbourne, Vic.: Heinemann Educational, 1989) especially pp. 420–428; *Sydney Morning Herald* 26 November 1949; *The Australian* 2 January 1988 (cites Cabinet Papers from 1950).

7 For claims that post-war Australia was uniquely open to Americanization, see especially G. Serle, 'Godzone: Austerica Unlimited?' *Meanjin Quarterly* vol. 26, no. 3, 1967, pp. 239–242, and more recently P. Adams, 'Dolls on the American Knee' *The Australian* 12–13 September 1993. Compare P. Bell and R. Bell, *Implicated: The U.S. in Australia* (Melbourne: Oxford University Press, 1993) generally.

8 See Meaney, 'Australia and the World', pp. 428–429.

9 Hasluck, 27 August 1950, in *Commonwealth Parliamentary Debates* 209, 1950, p. 30.

10 Menzies, *Sydney Morning Herald* 6 June 1989, 2 January 1995, 1 January 1995; all cite confidential Cabinet Papers, 1960s.

11 P. Dibb, *Review of Australia's Defence Capabilities: Report for the Minister of Defence* (Canberra: Australian Government Publishing Service, 1986); also Australian Department of Defence White Paper, *The Defence of Australia 1987*, presented to Parliament by the Minister for Defence, the Hon. Kim C. Beazley, MP, March 1987 (Canberra: Australian Government Publishing Service, 1987).

12 For details of Australia's more independent posture in defence and foreign affairs, see especially Dibb, *Review of Australia's Defence Capabilities*, and G. Evans and B. Grant, *Australia's Foreign Relations in the World of the 1990's* (Carlton, Vic.: Melbourne University Press, 1991), For comments on Australia's new defence ambitions, see *Sydney Morning Herald* 1 May 1989, 16 July 1990, 12 June 1992, 9 March 1995; *Bulletin* 6 August 1986; *Time* (Australia) 6 April 1992. In 1994, the Commander-in-Chief of US forces in the Pacific, Admiral Richard Macke, confirmed America's downgrading of ANZUS in terms which intensified Australia's drive for greater independence: 'With regard to ANZUS, I don't believe that treaty organizations are what is required in the Asia-Pacific region', he said.

13 J. Angel, 'Australia and Southeast Asia' in P. Boyce and J. Angel, eds, *Diplomacy in the Market Place, vol. 7 1981–1992, Australia in World Affairs*, ed. G. Greenwood and N. Harper (Melbourne: Cheshire for the Institute of International Affairs, 1957–1992), p. 160.

14 William McMahon, in *Current Notes on International Affairs* vol. 39, no. 10, 1968.
15 R. A. Woolcott, 'Australia and Asia in the Seventies' in *Australian Foreign Affairs Record* vol. 45, no. 5, 1974, p. 315.
16 Emily Rosenberg, *Spreading the American Dream: American Economic and Cultural Expansion, 1890–1945* (New York, 1982), p. 232.
17 See, generally, R. Bell, 'Testing the Open Door Thesis in Australia 1941–1946' *Pacific Historical Review* vol. 51, August 1982, pp. 283–311; and M. Beresford and P. Kerr, 'A Turning Point for Australian Capitalism: 1942–1952' in E. Wheelwright and K. Buckley, eds, *Essays in the Political Economy of Australian Capitalism* vol. 4 (Sydney: Australia and New Zealand Book Company, 1980), pp. 148–171.
18 Doug Anthony, 'GATT Ministerial Meeting, Statement delivered on November 24, 1982' *Australian Foreign Affairs Record* vol. 53, no. 11, 1982, pp. 744–745.
19 Anthony, in *Sydney Morning Herald* 6 October 1983.
20 Andrew Peacock in *Backgrounder* 214, 28 November 1979; *Sydney Morning Herald* 18 September 1979.
21 In *Far Eastern Economic Review* 8 June 1979, pp. 44–45; *Backgrounder* no. 191, 20 June 1979, pp. 7–10; no. 208, 17 October 1979, pp. 5–6, and no. 209, 24 October 1979, pp. 8–9; *Sydney Morning Herald* 14 August 1979, 6 October 1979.
22 *Backgrounder* no. 190, 13 June 1979, pp. 5–6; *The Australian* 1–2 December 1979; *Sydney Morning Herald* 31 December 1979; *National Times* 24 November 1979, 6 October 1979, p. 72.
23 *Sydney Morning Herald* 24 May 1989.
24 Argentina, Brazil, Chile, Colombia, Uruguay, Indonesia, Malaysia, Thailand, the Philippines, Fiji, Australia, New Zealand, Canada and Hungary.
25 See generally, for reports on APEC and the Bogor meeting, *Sydney Morning Herald* 14 October 1994 and 16 November 1994; *The Australian* 12–13 November 1994; *Far Eastern Economic Review* 6 September 1994, pp. 14–16.
26 For a broader discussion of the origins and nature of APEC, see especially, 'APEC: Which Way Forward' Symposium, various essays in *Australian Journal of International Affairs* vol. 46, no. 2, 1992, pp. 161–202, and essays by Ippei Yamazawa, Andrew Elek and C. Fred Bergsten, in Ross Garnaut and Peter Drysdale, eds, *Asia Pacific Regionalism: Readings in International Economic Relations* (Sydney: Harper Collins, 1994), pp. 199–224.
27 *Sydney Morning Herald* 29 January 1986, and 8 October 1987; *Times on Sunday* 1 November 1987.
28 See R. Bell, 'Testing the Open Door Thesis' Article VII of the Lend–Lease agreements signed by the US with its wartime allies provided generous emergency assistance in return for commitments from recipient states to seek 'the elimination of all forms of discriminatory treatment in international commerce [and] . . . the reduction of tariffs and other trade barriers'. In the post-war years many states were reluctant to comply with these 'open-door' initiatives.
29 For excellent surveys of Australia's changing economic relationships with the UK and USA as well as Asia, see R. Higgott, 'Closing a Branch of Empire . . .' *International Affairs* vol. 70, no. 1, 1994, pp. 41–66; R. Higgott, *The Whole Economic Order: The Trade Crisis and its Implications for Australia* (Canberra, 1987); and R. Higgott, 'The Politics of Australia's International Economic Relations: Adjustment and Two Level Games' *Australian Journal of Political Science* vol. 26, no. 1, 1991, pp. 2–28. Also helpful are J. Ravenhill, 'Economic Objectives' in F. A. Mediansky, ed., *Australia in a Changing World: New Foreign Policy Directions* (Sydney: Maxwell Macmillan, 1992), pp. 102–123;

and H. Hughes 'Australia's Imaginary Export Boom' *The Independent Monthly* March 1995, pp. 74–77.

30 See especially R. Garnaut, *Australia and the Northeast Asian Ascendancy: Report to the Prime Minister and the Minister for Foreign Affairs and Trade* (Canberra: Australian Government Publishing Service, 1989), For figures on Australian trade with Asia and the Asia-Pacific region, see *Financial Review* 16 June 1995, p. 4, and OFFAT, *Asialine* 3, 5, May 1995, p. 6.

31 Talbott in *Time* (Australia) 15 June 1992, p. 39.

32 Higgott, 'Closing a Branch', p. 48.

33 Keating, in *Sydney Morning Herald* 10 March 1995.

34 The attitudes of Asian elites to Australia's efforts to forge closer links with the region are discussed in R. Trood, ed., *The Future Pacific Economic Order: Australia's Role* (Brisbane: Centre for Study of Australia–Asia Relations, Griffith University in association with the Australian Institute of International Affairs, 1993), See in particular the contributions by N. Viviani and J. Reid, and by J. Macleod and R. Trood. See also Australia OFAT, *Australia Through the Eyes of Asia: Adding Innovation* (Canberra: Australian Government Publishing Service, 1995) (summarized in the *Sydney Morning Herald* 10 April 1995), There is now a substantial literature on Australian (mis)perceptions of Asia and the debate over so-called Asianization (often referred to as the 'Blainey debate'), See, for example, M. Ricklefs, M. and A. Marcus, eds, *Surrender Australia? Geoffrey Blainey and Asian Immigration. Essays on the Study and Uses of History* (Sydney: George Allen & Unwin, 1983); 'The Blainey debate – 10 years on' Special Review, *The Australian* 15 March 1994; T. Faulk, 'Images of Asia' *Far Eastern Economic Review* 26 December 1992, pp. 44–45; D. Walker and J. Ingleson, 'The impact of Asia' in Meaney, ed., *Under New Heavens. Cultural Transmission and the Making of Australia*, pp. 288–324.

35 J. Nye, address by satellite to ACAS Seminar, 'Shaping the Future of the Australian–American Alliance', Canberra, 23 February 1995.

36 *Far Eastern Economic Review* 14 April 1994, p. 46. See also Greg Sheridan, 'Australia's Asian Odyssey' in Greg Sheridan, ed., *Living with Dragons: Australia Confronts its Asian Destiny* (Sydney: Allen & Unwin, 1995), p. 5. Sheridan speaks of 'the Asianisation of almost every sphere of Australian life'.

37 By 1991, almost 600,000 people born in the regions of East and Southeast Asia had migrated to Australia, with the largest numbers coming from Vietnam and China. Speakers of the Chinese languages comprised the fourth largest linguistic group, after speakers of English, Italian and Greek. See C. Inglis *et al.*, eds, *Asians in Australia: The Dynamics of Migration and Settlement* (Singapore: Institute of South East Asian Studies, 1992); Committee to Advise on Australia's Immigration Policies, 'Immigration: A Commitment to Australia' ('The Fitzgerald Report') (Canberra: Australian Government Publishing Service, 1988).

38 J. Nye, 'Popular Culture: Images and Issues' *Dialogue* no. 99, January 1993, p. 52.

39 In 1993 Mahathir observed that 'When Europeans were rich, you Australians were Europeans. Then you became Americans when America was rich. When Asia gets rich, you become Asians.

# Part II
# Asia-Pacific patterns

# 9 The romance of Asian capitalism: Geography, desire and Chinese business*

*Yao Souchou*

## INTRODUCTION: GEOGRAPHY, DESIRE AND CHINESE BUSINESS

In their elegiac reproach of the discursive fantasy of the 'Asian Pacific region', Rob Wilson and Arif Dirlik write, '[i]f such a region did not exist, it would have to be invented by policy planners and social scientists along the East–West axis to figure forth an integrated source of boundless markets, wondrous raw materials, and ever-expanding investments'. Talking about the vast Asia-Pacific as a single fixed geographical entity, they warn, not only belittles the region's 'staggering complexity, discrepant hybridity, and nomadic flux', but also sidesteps the questions: 'Whose "Asia-Pacific" are we talking about, whose interests are being served?'[1] Answers to these questions punctuate the complex entanglement of both the 'East' and 'West' in the making of the 'Asia-Pacific' discourse. The 'Asia-Pacific' is anything to anyone. For if the region – especially fast-growing East Asia – is the West's new-found land of expanding markets and disciplined but still relatively cheap labour, and if the discourse about the region fuels Asia's imagining of its rise in the globalized world, then 'Asia-Pacific' is no longer a purely geographical entity. It is a global space in which nations and political leaders have invested their dreams and wishes. In these imaginings, 'Asia-Pacific' becomes an object which would rescue the West from its current economic woes, on the one hand; and affirm (East) Asian states' emerging political and cultural confidence in the world, on the other. The agendas unite for a moment 'East' and 'West' in a common discursive enterprise. And the enterprise takes place even in the midst of heated contestations over the issues of human rights, information flow, environmental priorities and the impending 'clash of civilizations' predicted by the apocalyptic vision of Samuel Huntington.[2] What emerges is a reinventing of 'Asia', through an anxious rewriting of the texts about the place and its people. We see this in the remarkable East Asian discourse sponsored by Singapore and China which singles out the common Confucian heritage in the East Asian countries – China, Hong Kong, Taiwan, Japan, South Korea and Singapore – as the reason

for their spectacular economic performance.[3] In the West, a seductively figured text like Joel Kotkin's *Tribes: How Race, Religion and Identity Determine Success in the New Global Economy* serves to assuage nostalgic regret
for the loss of Calvinistic ideals which authorial fantasy miraculously redis-
covers in the work ethics and commercial instincts of Asian – and other –
'global tribes'.[4]

For those of us working in and writing about Asia, the reimagining of
'Asian culture' in the conjunction of desire and economic practicalities is
a crucial polemical issue. In this chapter, I would like to engage with one
articulation of this cultural invention: the inscription of Chinese cultural
virtues. What is involved is a dramatic celebration of the essential(ized)
cultural traits of the Chinese: hard work, commercial talent and family-
centredness. These are put forward as the unmistakable grounding of
their economic success. There is something spellbinding about this idea,
an idea born out of fantastical imagining and social 'facts' which many
find irresistible. Thus Thomas Sowell, in his *Race and Culture*, comments
on the Chinese and Japanese indentured labourers who came to Peru in
the nineteenth century:

> Seldom were those immigrants simply prosperous foreigners who
> brought their wealth with them. On the contrary, most of those who
> became middle class . . . were working class in origin. . . . What all
> those groups brought was not wealth but the ability to create wealth –
> . . . whether through specific skills or just hard work. They did not
> share the Spanish and Portuguese settlers' disdain for manual labour,
> or for commerce and industry, or for thrift.[5]

Sowell's admiration for Chinese and Japanese immigrants repeats his mis-
giving about the European aversion to the very pursuits for which the
Asian settlers are, to his mind, justly renowned. Other writings unify the
tropes of the Chinese penchant for hard work, love of the family and economic success into a single proposition. Among anthropological literature,
not untypical is Steven Harrell's suggestively titled 'Why do the Chinese
Work so Hard? – Reflections on an Entrepreneurial Ethic'.[6] The people in
the Taiwanese village where he studied, he tells us, are imbued with 'an
acceptance of work as a necessity, a willingness to do much, and an
assumption that whatever is necessary for economic betterment of oneself,
or more accurately, one's family, must be done and ordinarily will be
done without complaint'.[7] And to the question he poses so provocatively,
he answers:

> There is no doubt that Chinese culture does have a work ethic. Chinese
> have been, and generally still are, willing to exert enormous amounts of
> effort in search of familial improvements and security. . . . The Chinese
> have been socialized, after all, not just to work hard, but to work hard
> for the long-term benefits of the family. When they see this goal as

attainable, they will work hard toward it in an economically rational way.[8]

So they work hard because they have been socialized to do so. But the appeal to 'socialization' cannot so simply do away with the problem of essentialism. For if the term – with its assumption of unilinear social deterministic effects – means anything, it has to evoke the institutions and power relations framing the 'social entrenchment of values'. The making of subjectivity and cultural propensities is always complex and often unpredictable in outcome. What follows in my discussion emphasizes a major analytical point. This is that cultural traits do not exist 'out there' without history, without the self-conscious making and remaking by the people concerned in a particular circumstance. Nor are they homogeneously distributed. When the Chinese do display such qualities – and they do so just as frequently as they do not – what takes place is not a simple articulation of some deep-seated 'cultural instinct'. For, as I shall show among the Chinese traders in Belaga, Sarawak pioneering forbearance may be an observable 'fact' in the daily life of the outpost town; it still has to be discursively (re)produced in order to make it real. Self-inscription is a strategy which calls forth, and is moved by, ambiguous and contradictory wishes and longing. The narrative of toil told and retold has risen out of the need to recast the doubt about their life's work, and to convince themselves that all their endurance and sacrifice has been worthwhile. The making of virtue, I suggest, is an act of self-inscription which addresses a central irony of the position of the Chinese traders in the jungle. For if remarkable achievements testify to their unmistakable qualities of hard work and endurance, being in Belaga also reminds them of the social neglect and limited circumstances of their lives which brought them there to carve out a living in such a god-forsaken place. The self-inscription of virtue, if I may take a certain psychological turn, has to be seen as a ruling of desire which must anxiously (over)compensate a 'lack' in their lives and work. The writing of virtue is thus prompted by a need for affirmation. By writing and rewriting a cultural narrative, Chinese forbearance is reinscribed, not as some cultural instinct lodged in 'blood', but as something uncertain and malleable in which the inner prompting of these men can find its insidious articulations.

## SPACE, HISTORY AND THE MAKING OF A MARGINAL GEOGRAPHY

Travelling to Belaga is an arduous two-day journey by boat. From Kuching, the capital of Sarawak, you catch a hydrofoil to Sibu, a busy town of some 60,000 people, mostly descendants of Foo Chow people who came to Sarawak from southern China in the early 1900s during the Brooke regime. After spending a night in Sibu, you catch the early ferry to Kapit where a connecting motorized *tukang* waits to take you to Belaga. If the earlier journey from Kuching to Sibu leaves an impression of speed, brilliant surf and ear-splitting engine noise, the remaining journey from Kapit to Belaga is by comparison a quiet and contemplative affair. You are travelling up-river against the current. The waterway narrows, and for a few hours the boat moves among the thick mangroves with lush aerial roots twisting and curling in the shallow sand banks. Around noon, and still four hours from Belaga, the scenery before you suddenly changes. The water is now clearer and faster, and the thick vegetation covering the banks reaches high above the valley. The launch is moving through the rapids – the Pelagus, Bikiei and the Bungun – and huge boulders divide the river, forming deep waters and treacherous whirlpools. The launch reaches Belaga around four in the afternoon, nearly six hours after leaving Kapit. From the jetty the township is a five-minute walk up a flight of steps. On the high ground facing the river front is a row of some fifteen shops stocked with clothes, plastic wares, stationery, canned foods, beer and soft drinks. Practically all the shops, and the petrol pumps and marine engine workshops by the waterfront, are owned by the Chinese. These shops are, in all senses of the term, the social and economic centre of Belaga.

For this and other journeys I have made to the outpost town, I set myself the question: What has made the Chinese traders come to do business in such a place? This is first a question about business opportunity and its exploitation; they are here because there is money to be made. What prompts the Chinese traders to do business in the remote outpost town, I argue, also goes beyond the simple ruling of economic feasibility and profit. To have a stake in the town, to stay on even after they have made their modest fortunes, is also a matter of making something personally meaningful out of being in such a place. The geography of Belaga, which so dazzles the anthropologist-traveller, distils the sense of place that touches everyone who comes to know the town. If Belaga is an inaccessible jungle town, and if the physical hardship of living and working there is a reality, it is precisely these 'facts' which the traders turn into a text in order to say something about themselves. It is a text that makes much of the marginality of the place,[9] and the danger and deprivation that test true pioneers. The self-construction draws on the mythology of Belaga, and in the process (re)produces it into a phantasmic drama of 'a sense of place'. The discursive enterprise, then, is no mere solitary fantasy of the Chinese. More than that, it is an imagining made real not only by Belaga's location on the Rejang but also by the history of colonial enterprise.

The founding of Belaga and other trading towns along the Rejang – Sibu, Kanowit, Kapit – was part of the complex and bloody history of the colonial expansion in the interior.[10] After he took power in 1841 through a series of concessions agreed with the Brunei Sultanate and the British, James Brooke, the first Rajah, undertook several expeditions up-river. With the support of the British Royal Navy, Brooke's army of Malay and native mercenaries brutally suppressed local rebellion[11] and inter-tribal warfare, culminating in the massacre in 1849 of Sea Dayaks at Beting Marau off the mouth of the Kalaka. On 25 June 1859, two British officers were murdered in Kanowit by local Kayans. Reprisal came four years later – in 1863 – in the form of the so-called Kayan Expeditionary Force led by Charles Brooke, the Tuan Muda of Sarawak, with a force of 12,000 Iban warriors. The reprisal brought havoc to the Kayan, Kenyah and Kajang people of the Upper Rejang, effectively crushing the remnants of local resistance. Charles Brooke succeeded his uncle in 1868, and conso-lidated control of the vast territory he inherited. He carried out punitive campaigns throughout the 1870s and 1880s against the Ibans in the Upper Katibas and Lupar Rivers.

These pacification ventures provided the conditions for ensuring the suc-cess of the colonial enterprise: the exploitation of land and collection of tax revenue. To achieve these objectives, more stable communities than the tribal villages had to be established, communities which would devote themselves to the production of surpluses. Realizing the economic potential of the then untouched Rejang Valley, Charles Brooke began in 1880 to negotiate with Chinese clan leaders to bring their kinsmen to settle there. These immigrants, unlike earlier arrivals – numbering 40,000 in 1810 – who mainly went to the mines in the Simanggang areas in the northwest, built their homes on small farms in the Rejang Valley, growing vegetables and notably rice, an item of which there was a critical shortage in Sarawak at the time.[12] Some 600 Foo Chow Methodists from southern China arrived in Sibu in 1901, followed by a group of 550 the following year. With the success of the farming settlements, the Chinese gradually moved up-river to the interior through the beginning of the twentieth century. The movement was in pursuit of land or, where this was impossible under the land policy which protected native ownership, opportunities in trade.

The pacification of the Upper Rejang, and the subsequent movements of Chinese immigrants, were the dramatic background to the founding of Belaga. Following the Kayan Expedition in 1863, it was logical that an administrative foothold should be established in the Upper Rejang and in the Balui Basin. In 1884 the Brooke administration erected a bazaar build-ing and a military fort at the mouth of the Belaga River. Chinese traders were soon attracted to the Belaga station. Traditionally trade in central Sarawak was dominated by Malay traders under the protection of the Sultan of Brunei. In order to make tax collection easier, one of the first Brooke commands after establishing the Belaga station was to restrict the right of settlement in Belaga to traders and their families. Malay traders living in longhouses in the nearby communities were ordered to move to the Belaga bazaar 'where the administration could keep an eye on them'.[13] This restriction saw the beginning of the decline of the Malay traders' position in a system of trade extending from Brunei via the Kemena River to the upper reaches of the Rejang. In short, the changing fortune of the Malay traders transformed the whole opportunity structure in the Rejang, something which the Chinese were eager to exploit. By 1893 the *Sarawak Gazette* was to report: 'There are 14 shops in the bazaar and fifteen more will shortly be erected, 10 by the Chinese, 5 by Malays, before the present fort was built there was only one or two Chinese here.' Over the following decades, Chinese capital and entrepreneurs moved from Kuching to Sibu and Kapit; and some travelled further still, to Belaga where isolation from the other towns down-river was to become the very reason for doing business there.

## BELAGA: AN OUTPOST TOWN IN THE HIERARCHY OF PLACES

The history of the opening up of Rejang is an important narrative that helps to define Belaga's sense of place. The town simply marks the culminating point of the colonial penetration of the interior. In this narrative, Belaga is that disconnected place let loose by the physical terrain of Rejang River, the logical and discrete point at the far end from Kuching, the capital of Sarawak, centre of both past and present administration. Yet the 'natural isolation' of Belaga is a fact that still has to gel with other realities. Gupta and Ferguson write:

> The presumption that spaces are autonomous has enabled the power of topography to conceal successfully the topography of power. . . . [I]f one begins with the premise that spaces have *always* been hierarchically interconnected, instead of naturally disconnected, then cultural and social change become not a matter of cultural contact and articulation but one of rethinking differences *through* connection.[14]

The 'differences' of Belaga in relation to other places along the Rejang can be similarly rediscovered. The pacification of the Rejang by the Brooke administration had in a sense founded the place. But Belaga is also endowed with another connectivity, one at once more enduring and socially real: that of the riverine trade which links the towns of Kuching, Sibu, Kapit and Belaga in a system of social and economic relationships. In the context of these relationships the towns along the Rejang become 'hierarchically interconnected', in terms of their relative social, administrative and economic importance. The position of Belaga town in this hierarchy of places is shaped by the flow of capital and retail goods up-river from Kuching,[15] Sibu and Kapit to Belaga, and the moving of jungle produce back down the Rejang. Government initiatives – including moneys for development assistance and wages for school teachers and other civil servants – on the one hand, and revenue from the various licensing fees on the other, similarly move in opposite directions along the river. In all these ways, the connectivity of Belaga works powerfully in the social imagining of the town and what lies in other richer places on the Rejang. For the Chinese traders, towns down-river become the referencing points for the validation of their lives and achievements. If circumstances have forced them to come to Belaga, they still long for these more prosperous places where doing business is more profitable and enjoys greater prestige or 'face', places to which very few can return. As we shall see, it is this 'returning' to the 'home' down-river that traces the Othering for the making of Self by the Chinese traders in Belaga.

Belaga is now a town of some 1500 people. The Education Department runs a boarding school there for the children from the nearby native communities; about 600 students and some twenty-five teachers add to the total population during the school terms. The township is a trading centre for local produce. Rubber, pepper, coffee, cocoa, fish and game, jungle goods like ilipe nuts and rattan, as well as woven mats and basket wares, are sold and traded. The place is also a meeting point where the 'praise and blame' of government administration – school, medical care, agricultural assistance on the one hand, and political control, government licences and tax collection on the other – are made possible. Since 1973 a full district office with twenty-two administrative staff and development officers have been located in the town. The District Office is the centre of the government presence; it oversees the administration of land tenure, agricultural development, public health, education, and law and order (the District Officer – DO – also acts as the local magistrate). In addition, the DO handles the development fund and the salaries of government servants including some 25 school teachers working in the nearby longhouse; money from these sources are spent in Belaga on food, clothes, fuel and other daily necessities.

Apart from the District Office, Belaga's distinguishing feature is undoubtedly the Chinese shophouses. When one travels up the Rejang from Kapit to Belaga, after the long journey between brown muddy banks across swamp land, the row of well-constructed shop buildings, freshly painted and adorned with bright colourful signs in Chinese, English and Malay, are a welcoming sight. The shops are well stocked with clothes, plastic wares, stationery, canned foods, beer and soft drinks. Other than the shophouses, Chinese traders also operate the marine engine shops and petrol pumps at the waterfront as well as the twice-daily express boat services between Belaga and Kapit.

The fifteen-odd shops in Belaga stand in a straight row facing south towards the boat landing. These are the newer shops. Previously traders lived and worked in ramshackle wooden sheds at the present site, before the government completed the new lots in December 1978. Running adjacent to the new shops are the so-called temporary lots,[16] rows of twenty-eight wooden shacks which the government plans to pull down in the future. Here are found the smaller shops. Most of these are coffee shops offering simple food like boiled noodles and cakes, others sell soap powder, matches, dry batteries, mosquito coils, cooking oil and other sundry goods.

## STARTING BUSINESS IN BELAGA: THE NARRATIVE OF ENTREPRENEURSHIP

The shop Lee Ken Ong[17] in Belaga Bazaar is the largest trading store in Belaga with a turnover of just under $20,000 a month. It is a bright and cheerful place, with freshly painted walls and an old lacquered shop sign with calligraphy of gold to lend it luck and dignity. Plastic buckets, farming tools, umbrellas, nylon ropes and other useful wares dangle from above the counter and spread on to the verandah outside. Inside the shop are rows of steel shelves filled with rubber sandals, clothes, stationery, canned food and cosmetics. These goods, mostly of obscure brands from Thailand, Malaysia and China, may be a cluttered mess to the unfamiliar eye. But to the many government servants and school teachers who shop there, they are the latest and brightest available in Belaga, no less attractive than the more elegant offerings of a modern shopping mall. If the shop displays all the signs of commercial success, local people also talk in a somewhat envious tone of the owner Lee Ken Ong's other venture. The shop is also the largest dealer in fish, wild boar and deer in the Belaga area. This business involves both capital and an elaborate arrangement worked out over the years. A store with a refrigerator powered by diesel has been established in Long Jawi, a Kenyah longhouse village an hour's journey away by motorized *tukang*. There the appointed agent – a Chinese man married to a Kenyah woman – collects from the local hunters and fishermen, and keeps the purchases in cold storage. Once a fortnight or sometimes less, depending on the amount collected, the shop in Belaga sends its motorized *tukang* to Long Jawi. The goods are packed in ice blocks and covered in layers of gunny sacks and canvas sheets, before being transported down to Kapit and then to Sibu where they are sold to restaurants and wholesalers who come from as far as Kuching for the highly prized wild meat and fish.

The shop, which still carries the name of the original owner, is now run by his nephew Lee Sin Kin. The uncle Lee Ken Ong is something of a legendary figure in Belaga, as one informant describes him:

> Old Lee was an ambitious man, but a bit reckless. He always tried to start one business scheme after another when he should really stick to one and consolidate it (before beginning another). He really did not have much capital himself, and had to depend on his brother. . . . Well, you know, we Chinese say, brothers are close like hands and feet. But sometimes things don't work out so well between brothers. In a

place like Belaga, you don't need much capital. But even then, you should be able to stand on your own feet, and have some kind of independence after a while.

Lee first came to Belaga in the early 1960s to fish in the Rejang. It was a time when the river was still abundant with fish which fetched good prices in Kapit and Kuching, and he was the first to recognize the commercial opportunity. The venture was both profitable and promising, but it was hard work moving up and down the river from early in the morning till dusk. And one suspects that, as informants explain it, the business simply did not constitute the solid and grounded symbol of prosperity that a shop on land does. With savings from the business, and help from his brother, he started in 1971 the provision shop which still carries his name and, three years later, the first regular *tukang* ferry service between Belaga and Kapit.

Lee's elder brother is a merchant from Sibu who has made his modest fortune from dealing in pepper, rubber and timber. When Lee started the ferry service, the M\$25,000 capital was supplemented with a substantial loan from his brother. The elder brother also acted as a personal guarantor for Lee who depended on credit for the supply of petrol – an expensive item in Belaga at \$8 a gallon in October 1995 – and other goods for the store. So sibling support was crucial for Lee in realizing his business ambitions through a relationship based on both kin sentiment and economic pragmatism. Some of the loans were returned with interest. At the same time, as security against the outstanding loans Lee offered his elder brother a 40 per cent share of his cash-tight but otherwise booming business. Liquidity problems continued to plague him and, heavily in debt, Lee went into insolvency in 1969. In the end the elder brother took over the provision shop, installing his youngest son, Sin Kin, as the manager. Most of the orders for supplies now go through the main business in Sibu; the valuable wild boar and deer carcasses are sent there from Kapit before being transported to wholesalers in Kuching. Taking over the shop in Belaga has enabled Lee's brother to have a major stake in the profitable trade up-river through supplying retail goods and the sourcing of jungle produce. Even if the older Lee had not planned this, the arrangement could not have worked out better for him.

The story about Lee, as the local people tell it, exudes the bitter-sweet quality that often marks such narratives. If Lee's endeavour is a celebration of the forbearance and business instinct of all the Chinese traders in Belaga, it is also one charged with ambiguity. On one level, the narrative tells brilliantly of a man's remarkable achievement in taking a stake in Belaga. The marginal position of the outpost town, constituted by the geography of the Rejang and the opening up of the interior, has been crucial in defining the opportunity that awaits the more astute in business. In the words of one informant:

> Thirty or forty years ago, people (in Sibu) did not know very much about Belaga. We heard a lot about how difficult it was to pass through the rapids and people had died when their boats collapsed. Belaga was in the wilderness; and the older people always said 'there is a lot of business to do there with the Kayans, but no one is doing it'. So we knew life would be tough but opportunity was there. . . . For small-timers like us, we could not make it in Sibu (for lack of capital). Belaga was the only way of making something for ourselves.

It is a central feature of such narratives to transform Belaga's position of remoteness and marginality into one of economic advantage. Doing business here, as the case of Lee clearly illustrates, requires less start-up capital, and both rent and the wages of native labour are substantially cheaper than in other towns on the Rejang. At the same time, prices of retail goods and jungle produce can be charged – and profit appropriated – at a level commensurate with Belaga's long distance from town centres down-river. These are business decisions and calculations of loss and gain, of obvious importance in explaining why Chinese traders have set up shops there.

Yet the narrative of business foresight and the eager seizing of opportunity also betrays other facts that deeply touch the lives of the Belaga Chinese. While the tales of hardship and sacrifice may signal their legendary business undertakings, they also give an indelible sense of life's disadvantages for these men. So in the cool of the evening on the verandah over bottles of Anchor beer, the stories are told and retold as if to convince the narrators as much as the anthropologist that they are indeed endowed with special virtues. And the repetition harbours a secret of the heart's desire about which they become quite candid when the long evening's drinking begins to put them in a more open mood. As one man violently interjects, impatient with his companions' blowing their own trumpet and tales of face-saving bravado, 'We are in Belaga because we have to be; we have no choice.' Being in Belaga simply means that they cannot establish themselves in other places, socially and economically more desirable places like Sibu or Kuching. The interjection turns the narrative around and shows its other side. What is revealed here is not the glorious achievement of personal endeavours and individual talent, but things the story of Lee Ken Ong hints at: poverty, lack of capital, dependence on kinsmen for financial support, and conditions created by the power relations of the family. A certain melancholy or regret tinges the tales of entrepreneurship: these men, mired in their personal circumstances, find themselves in Belaga because it is the only place where they can make something of their lives.

## PUBLIC MYTH AND PRIVATE WISHES

The notion that the Chinese traders are 'forced to be in Belaga' decries the romance of their achievements. To understand this is to understand something of the psychic exchanges that move the narrative of toil. Before we come to that, it is necessary to point out that what I call 'the inscription of virtue' is a comprehensive process of construction of the Belaga Chinese traders in Sarawak. It is a construction operating at the level of common sense. From the State Planning Authority where you obtain your research permit, to the ferry jetty where you make enquiries about the travelling schedule, people you meet talk almost in awe about Belaga as the place in the jungle where life is hard and full of sacrifices. Then it emerges that you are travelling up-river to study the Chinese *towkays* (shopkeepers) there. Those who know Belaga, especially civil servants previously posted there, talk about the Chinese *towkays* in a tone that suggests curiosity and awe. The vague disbelief that there are men wanting to work and settle in such a god-forsaken place – even to make money – is quickly dispelled by the ready answer provided by the social mythology about the penchant for hard work and business foresight of the Chinese in Belaga and elsewhere. Another powerful source of inscription also adds to the myth making. Academic writings about Sarawak have also praised the Chinese for opening up the country for commercial profit and social benefit. John Chin writes in his *The Sarawak Chinese*: 'The Chinese immigrants came to West Borneo as peaceful people whose sole reason for settling in a strange land was to seek a better life for themselves and their families and kindred in China.'[18] At times, the discourse engages both the researcher and his subjects in a way which robustly reaffirms the common narrative:

> A recurring theme which ran through the interviews was that of pioneering hardship, which most of the interviewees tried to impress upon me. Sarawak is a physically harsh country and my observations of the ethnographic present, together with the conditions under which I conducted my interviews, gave me an inkling of previous circumstances and enabled me to empathize with my interviewees. Sometimes, interviews had to be carried out with my feet stuck ankle-deep in mud along a river bank . . . or by the dim light of a kerosene lamp at night . . . (giving me) a feel of what the past could have been like for Sarawak's Chinese pioneers.[19]

For these speakers – from the boatmen to the historian – there is a sense of 'ownership' in the way they talk about Belaga, as if the stories about these men are the story of their lives in Sarawak. Indeed, the sense of place of the outpost town carries traces of the territorial myth of the East Malaysian state itself: a land rich in natural resources, carved out of the jungle by tough and stout-hearted men under a wise government keen on development. Nature – and its ideological offspring, naturalization – form a crucial text moving between Sarawak's dramatic geography and its construction. What happens is a 'fragmentation' of landscape into metaphors widely dispersed in common social perceptions, a process which Bakhtin has so eloquently described:

> [W]hen collective labour and the struggle with nature had ceased to be the only arena for man's encounter with nature and the world – then nature itself ceased to be a living participant in the events of life. Then nature became, by and large, a 'setting for action', its backdrop; it was turned into landscape, it was fragmented into metaphors and comparisons serving to sublimate individual and private affairs and adventures not connected in any real or intrinsic way with nature itself.[20]

In a similar vein, the self-inscription by the Belaga traders retells the social myth in which nature becomes 'a setting for action', a mere 'backdrop' for the labour of these men. It is a retelling which marries political ideology and private desires, and in the process transforms the discursive economy of Belaga's geography into something personally meaningful for the traders.

Ng Ah Keng, aged 65, came to Belaga in 1961. His family were peasant farmers in Sarikei near Sibu, and his father brought up three sons and two daughters by growing vegetables and keeping pigs. Life was hard on the farm, and as time went by the smallholding could no longer support the expanding family. In 1959 Ng and his two elder brothers started a small bakery in the village market, making bread, cakes and biscuits. Though the business was quite successful by local standards, it was evidently too small to hold together three ambitious men. Ng decided to branch out on his own after a series of disagreements with his brothers 'over some financial matters'. He heard of Belaga from a supplier of confectionery who travelled regularly to the town from Sibu: it seemed the only suitable place to invest the small amount of money he had from his share of the bakery business. He took his wife and two children, rented a house for $30 a month in which to settle his family and start his own bakery business. He and his wife ran the business for ten years, getting up every day at dawn; from the wood fire oven at the back of the shop, they turned out bread, sweet buns with bean paste filling, and the ever popular *kaya* tarts of coconut jam. Business went down, however, when with the improvement of the ferry services shopkeepers began to bring in cheaper supplies from Kapit and Sibu. With his experience in the food business, Ng Ah Keng opened a small coffee shop in 1971 next to the main bazaar. He spent almost $3000 on the shop fittings and supplies, though the shop itself is rent free except for $90 a year land tax. Besides tea, coffee, beer and soft drinks, the shop also offers boiled noodles tossed in sesame oil and spring onions. The business has a turnover of just about $25,000 a year, providing him and his family of four children with a comfortable living by local standards.

Ng Ah Keng's experiences echo the personal histories of many local shopkeepers. The features of peasant family background, early deprivation, first venture into business with close kinsmen – entailing not infrequently financial and personal conflict – and coming to Belaga as a last resort are familiar recurring themes. If the story Lee tells of himself forms part of the general narrative about these remarkable men in Belaga, it achieves this only by deploying what is a notably central feature of all narratives. Narratives, Hayden White writes, take on 'an illusionary coherence and [the narrativization] charges them with the kinds of meanings more characteristic of oneiric than of waking thought'.[21] In the stories of the Chinese traders, coherence comes from making what they do and what they wish for economically consistent and ethically self-evident. At the same time, the narrative of business pioneering in the jungle creates vivid equivalents between private desire and public myth, personal ambition and the geography of the Upper Rejang. It also inaugurates, on another level, the making of the subjectivities of these Chinese men by reflecting on an idealized Other constructed from among the traders down-river, as I shall explain. The textuality of the geography reinhabits, while extrapolating from it, the anxious retelling of the narrative of toil. Ng's further adventure, told almost as an afterthought, takes the narrative to another height:

> When I came [to Belaga] there were only about ten shops, so business was quite easy. To make money you have to go to the jungle, to meet the *tu jen* [aboriginals] in their villages. There were in those days a lot of garu wood, rhinoceros horn and monkey gall stones, and the medicine shop in Singapore paid a lot of money for them. Though I was in the baking business, sometimes I went with friends to the longhouses and bought up what we could. But to go up to the river was dangerous. The long boat sometimes capsized and all the goods would be lost. People got drowned too. . . . In those days the Kayans would sometimes ambush you when they knew that you were passing through [with valuable goods]. I usually took some of the young fellows [nephews] with me but they had no guts. We slept by the river bank with parangs and long knives next to us. . . . One night we were attacked just before midnight. I told the young fellows not to be afraid and I stood in front of them with my long knife. I swung the knife around and around, so they [the Kayans] could see I was really fierce and not afraid. They ran away in the dark and never got near us.

## THE COMPLICITY OF SELF AND OTHER: NARRATIVE REPETITIONS AND THE INSCRIPTION OF VIRTUE

With an effective police force established in Belaga, such attacks and robberies by native people no longer take place. The significance of Ng Ah Keng's story lies not so much in its 'truth' or 'narrative embellishment'. Rather, what is worthy of note is the story's (re)turning to previous stories of hardship and danger told by other Chinese traders in Belaga and other parts of the Sarawak interior. The sense of *déjà vu* – that the story has been told and will be told again – impresses the listener, and turns each story into a cycle of repetition of a common theme. Repetition, J. Hillis Miller suggests, is an internally disposed character of a story.[22] Retelling is not straightforward going back or duplication, but riding 'on a narrative line . . . [which] trace[s] itself by some return or repetition, looping over its own length, crisscrossing, knotting up'.[23] Repetition moves, as if in a passionate tango, to and fro, lingering on the story line one moment and attempting to let loose from the narrative structure the next. What charts these movements, at once free and choreographed, is the inner wishes of the Belaga traders. The narrative of toil, I argue, told and retold by the Chinese, is charted by the need to return to the 'site of anxiety', while seeking assurance of the worth of one's endeavours. Narrative repetitions are attempts to resolve the feeling of ambiguity about their life and work. And on a more certain terrain constructed by the narrative, repetition gives birth to parallel thematic strands and the doubling of Self in its reflection in the narrativized geography of the Rejang.

It is an imagined geography evoking, as we have seen, a grand scenario of inaccessible jungle, dangerous rapids and, in the past, hostile natives. The reinvention of nature traverses the physical landscape to the communities of people along the river whose life and work have made them a part of this geography. If the exchanges of feelings and wishes of these men are so deeply implicated here, where do the Chinese traders find their Other who will mirror their real and imaginary perfections of virtue and hard work, and who will help to affirm what they believe they definitively are? They find it, I suggest, in different and opposite ways, in the native communities and the Chinese down-river.

Sitting in the Belaga Hotel coffee shop, Tiong, the owner, and I are having a couple of drinks well past dinner time. A man of about 50 comes over to the table. Tiong introduces us, and tells me the man is a pepper farmer from the Kayan community in Batu Kaloh about 5 kilometres down-river. They are clearly pleased to see each other, and Tiong offers him Guinness stout – a favourite beverage for the villagers when they come to town – while greeting him in Kayan, of which he is a fluent speaker. The man takes a long sip, and pointing at Tiong says to me with a shy smile, 'Towkay, dia kawan saya' ('The boss, he is my friend'). He has come to town to renew his shotgun licence and to buy some cartridges from Tiong. In the morning he withdrew some $200 from the post office which is the local agent for Bank Simpanan Nasional, the government national savings bank. For the villagers, coming to Belaga is an occasion for shopping, paying government tax and licence fees, and for having a good time with friends. After the drink, the two men go to the counter and the Kayan man gives Tiong the money for the cartridges, and hands over all the valuables from his pockets: the cash, licence, identity card and some bottles of pills for his wife. He is going drinking with a few friends, Tiong explains later. It is to be a long evening, and as on many occasions before, he gives his valuable things to Tiong for safekeeping and collects them the following morning before going home.

That native people and Chinese traders are in various ways locked in often unequal relationships is without doubt. But it is a relationship typified not so much by naked exploitation as by a mixture of friendship, patronage and commercial interest. More than any other event, it is the type of casual encounter I have described which sketches the subtle engagement between the Chinese shopkeeper and his client. On the one hand, as I have explained elsewhere[24], appropriation is tied in with the structure of indebtedness created by, for example, the extension of credit to the native customers who repay with interest or in jungle goods at a rate determined by Chinese traders. Other practices developed over the years further bind the native clients to their *towkays*, such as that of providing accommodation for the native clients when they are in town. In spite of elements of inequality, the general moral climate between the partners is one of trust and mutual respect.

There is a third element in the equation, one which cuts across the combination of economic relationship and personal ties: the prevailing ethnic perceptions. Among native informants, Chinese traders are talked about in a tone suggestive of admiration (for their ability to assemble wealth), trustworthiness (when a relationship benefits the client as well), commercial cunning and deception (when dealings clearly benefit only the *towkay*). What concerns me more, however, is the perception of the native people which mirrors and circulates the way the Chinese see themselves. In the context of the social and economic relationship, what emerges is an equally uneven understanding of the native people. They are seen as culturally simplistic, economically naive, yet fundamentally good and hard working, and jungle-wise in a way Chinese can never be. Tiong, notably, even as he chides his friend for being unable to hold his drink – which he sees as rather typical of the average *tu jen* (literally, people of the soil) – never lapses into ethnic contempt.

It is in this context that we may begin to understand something of the subtle figuring of the native people in the Chinese mind. If they are marked by a lack of sophistication and economic wit, Othering by the Chinese does not turn them into another version of the 'lazy native', the opposite of the Chinese cultural perfection of work and virtue. It is as if being in a place of wilderness and social neglect have bounded the Chinese and their native customers in a common destiny in place. Besides, the native people do have a skill which the Chinese admire: the ability to make a living from the jungle, the difficulties of which many Chinese know from experience. The result of all this is to undercut, even if not to cast doubt on, the Chinese self-perception of racial and economic superiority. What emerges is a significant hesitancy and even silence in the Othering of a people who do not appear unambiguously 'lazy' or 'virtuous'. Unable to settle in a fixed terrain of projection, the Native Other swings, in the imagining by the Chinese, between 'cultural and economic naivety' and 'fundamental goodness'.

Instead the Chinese traders look elsewhere, seeking an Other more satisfying of the cultural yearning which always falls short of fulfilment. And they find a more satisfactory image of themselves in the Chinese traders down-river in Kapit, Sibu and Kuching. Indeed for the Chinese in Belaga, these 'countrymen' not only share similar experiences of pioneering entrepreneurship but are also endowed with an impressive aura of social and financial success. Projection, in the Lacanian scheme of things, charts the transactions of desire which must imagine a perfection in order to transpose itself to a new register of release. The restless movement of desire in the futile search for fulfilment is motivated by a 'lack' or 'deficiency' which must seek compensation. But for the Chinese traders in Belaga, what is the nature of this 'lack'? And can we inject a social reading of this 'lack'?

My analysis here is not concerned so much with discovering the psychological unconscious of these men. Rather it hopes to reveal the inner prompting which calls forth the narrative repetitions and the discursive making of Belaga's geography in the first place. And this prompting, it can be suggested, is choreographed by the Chinese traders' experiences and understanding of their eventful lives. The sense of 'lack', I suggest, has a kind of 'actuality' which goes beyond the unconscious. For with all the talk of business talent and pioneering endeavours, there is a candid admission as they take account of their lives that if things could be otherwise, they would rather be somewhere else, in other places where having a business is clearer evidence of social and economic success. This admission of 'missed opportunity' and 'forced circumstances' is the other side of the discourse of entrepreneurship full of heroism and personal triumph. With the feeling of 'being done in by life', they begin to see their shops and businesses as both standing symbols of personal achievement and awkward evidence of their life's own disadvantages.

It is this sense of a 'lack' – at once social and lodged in desire – that has prompted the anxious repetitions of the tales of toil as a way of self-inscribing virtue. The marginal geography of the Rejang is crucial in this enterprise. The inscription of virtue transverses the (hard-working) body, to the formidable landscape of wilderness and danger, and back, in order to rewrite lives less glorious than their textual endorsement. Belaga's geography is transformed into a 'battleground' that tests the stout-hearted while it banishes the weak and those without talent. Thus what circulate in this geography are profound and melancholic imaginings which must create something more than the landscape and the people who have settled there.

At the same time, for these traders in Belaga, as the native communities cannot gratify the longing for an Other who can endorse one's worth in the world, construction of selfhood must turn to the Chinese merchants down-river. In these men of real and imaginary riches, Belaga traders invest their fantasies of their own cultural virtues of hard work, endurance and business talent. Othering is always a process of mutual entanglement. If the Chinese down-river look at those in Belaga somewhat curtly as men who have 'made it but not quite', the latter would view those in Sibu and Kuching as a measure of their 'missed opportunities' – what life could have been and crystallization of what the virtues of hard work and forbearance could have achieved 'if only . . .'. For those in Belaga, the Other down-river stands for the best flowering of Chinese cultural ideals in the fertile soil of Fate and kinship support which has been denied to them. The feeling is one of envy, circumspection and adoration. Othering is located in an ambiguous space of projection, and in one critical moment rescues from it the cultural perfection which they share by the virtue of their common heritage of 'being Chinese'.

## CONCLUSION: THE ROMANCE OF ASIAN CAPITALISM

The 'Asia-Pacific' is a site of cultural production, an invention by the West to deflect its uncertainty in a globalized world. It is above all a site that calls forth another round of Orientalism which serves to coalesce the historical hegemony of the West. The casting of Western complicity in the making of the 'Asia-Pacific' is undoubtedly an important intellectual project. But this (re)making of the 'East' into an object of imagination is no solitary undertaking of the West. Living in Southeast Asia – Singapore – this writer is all too keenly aware that the states and, increasingly, civil societies in this part of the world are deeply involved in the reinvention of their societies and people. The process of what might be called 'Self-Orientalism' creates an equally elegiac picture of the 'East' that duplicates the perfections that the new Orientalists have imagined at the end of the twentieth century.[25] This of course is not to suggest that the corresponding endeavours in Asia's remaking are similar, or come from the same configuration of power and global political economy. On the contrary, Asian discursive texts, such as that scripted by the Malaysian Prime Minister Dr Mahathir Mohamad, or by Senior Minister Lee Kuan Yew of Singapore, have come out of the significant 'differences' between the West and the Southeast Asian states. These 'differences', as prescribed by these texts, are located on two levels. First, the West still holds the cards in international politics, as the major source of capital and technology. Second, since the East cannot supplant the West from this leadership position, the strategy of Asian states like Malaysia and Singapore is to contest the West on cultural grounds. It is important to note that the increasingly political and economic confidence of the Asian NIEs never undercuts their realistic sense that their continuing growth depends largely on technology and foreign investment from the West. Perhaps it is this feeling of vulnerability, as I have argued elsewhere,[26] that has prompted the need to recast 'Asia' as a moral opposite of the West. Thus, in the famous 'Ten Asian Values that Help East Asia Prosper'[27]offered by Tommy Koh, Singapore's ambassador-at-large, the Asian penchant for hard work, frugality and love of the family are unproblematically figured as things the West lacks or has lost.

These are the dramatic global and national conditions in which I have cast my analysis of the inscription of virtue by a group of Chinese men in the jungle of Sarawak. The discussion obviously risks a forced and artificial linking of what takes place in the outpost town with happenings in the wider world. Yet it is equally fetishistic, methodologically speaking, to specify strictly when such a complex Orientalist enterprise begins and ends. Edward Said has located his particular example of Orientalism in the nineteenth century, in the Middle East and in the context of French imperial ambitions. It is the brilliant insight of Homi Bhabha who takes up Said's Lacanian nuances and reworks them into a general theory of colonial desire.[28] Lacan, particularly his notion of desire's seeking of a mirror of perfection in the constitution of Self, has offered me a way to examine the entanglement of a group of men caught within their own wishes and longing. The inscription of virtue by the Chinese traders in Belaga touches on culture and tradition, at once timeless and contingent. There are powerful echoes of Confucian prescriptions here: hard work and frugality as distinctive moral virtues because they ensure the continuity of the family. For the Chinese in Belaga, this has been an important rationale in explaining their dreams and achievements. But this text is more than what it says. Its 'surpluses of meaning' take us far beyond such pragmatic needs. The marginal geography from which they have to carve a living, the life circumstances that put them there, all deprive the tales of toil of their textual innocence. If the inscription of virtue is charted by the speculative principles of inner prompting, and if such an enterprise draws on supposedly timeless cultural values, what is involved cannot but help to reinforce a major discursive project undertaken outside the modest place/space where the men have made their life and work. What takes place in the outpost town in the jungle adds to the totality of texts written, in different ways, about a state like Singapore. The stories of Chinese pioneers have always been part of a myth about this remarkable people. It is a myth which installs legendary Chinese ancestors at home and abroad, a myth which a country like Singapore is quick to use as a foundation for its nationalist project. Virtuous hard-working Chinese fill the landscape not only in Belaga, but wherever Chinese have settled, and in the words of Joel Kotkin, in the virtual cross-border world of 'global tribes'. In this way the Chinese, at once endowed with cultural qualities self-inscribed and inscribed by others, are set free from the strictures of spatial and temporal definitions. The Chinese, always bracketed, become an object that belongs to no one, and yet an unmistakably free signifier that awaits the taking by all.

# NOTES

*This study is based on stretches of fieldwork in Belaga, Sarawak, between February 1992, and October 1995. A preliminary survey of Belaga was carried out in August 1987 on a grant from the Institute of Southeast Asian Studies, Singapore, as a part of the Community Network Programme. I am indebted to Jayal Langub, Dr Peter Kedit and L. K. Lee for their support and friendship. Thanks to Helmut Buhholt, Thomas Menkhof and Heiko Schrader for inviting me to the conference on 'Overseas Chinese and the Modernization of the Asia-Pacific' held in Bielefeld University, Germany, December 1995, where this paper was presented. The revision of this paper has greatly benefited from the valuable comments of Mary Somers Heidhues, Hubertus Pleister and other participants at the conference.

All values are in Malaysian dollars or Ringgit. In November 1996 the exchange rate of Ringgit to US dollars was M\$2.505 to US\$1.

1 Rob Wilson and Arif Dirlik, 'Introduction: Asia/Pacific as Space of Cultural Production' *Boundary 2* vol. 21, no. 1, 1994, pp. 1–2, reprinted in Rob Wilson and Arif Dirlik, eds, *Asia/Pacific as Space of Cultural Production* (Durham, NC: Duke University Press, 1995).

2 Samuel Huntington, 'The Clash of Civilizations?' *Foreign Affairs* vol. 72, no. 3, 1993.

3 A succinct summary of the discourse is given by Tommy Koh, Singapore's ambassador-at-large, in Tommy Koh, '10 Values That Help East Asia's Economic Progress, Prosperity', *The Straits Times* 14 December 1993, p. 29.

4 Joel Kotkin, *Tribes: How Race, Religion and Identity Determine Success in the New Global Economy* (New York: Random House, 1992).

5 Thomas Sowell, *Race and Culture: A World View* (New York: Basic Books, 1994), p. 35.

6 Steven Harrell, 'Why Do the Chinese Work So Hard? Reflection on an Entrepreneurial Ethics' *Modern China* vol. 11, no. 2, 1985.

7 ibid., p. 207.

8 ibid., p. 224.

9 That marginal places have special meaning and textuality is best argued in Rob Shields, *Places on the Margin* (London: Routledge, 1991), See also his extensive bibliography of the major theoretical works on the subject.

10 Details of the history of colonial expansion in Sarawak can be found in Steven Runciman, *The White Rajah: A History of Sarawak From 1841 to 1946* (Cambridge: Cambridge University Press, 1966), and Daniel Chew, *Chinese Pioneers on the Sarawak Frontier, 1841–1941* (Singapore: Oxford University Press, 1990).

11 The history of Sarawak has been written mainly from the perspective of the colonial government. Runciman, *The White Rajah*, is a good example of work which treats the suppression of local rebellion entirely in terms of the official attempt at suppressing piracy. It is interesting to notice that at the permanent exhibition at the Sarawak Museum the native 'rebel leaders' have been resurrected as national heroes.

12 See Chew, *Chinese Pioneers on the Sarawak Border, 1841–1941*; also Vinson H. Sutlive, Jr., *The Iban of Sarawak* (Arlington Heights: AHM Publishing Corps, 1978).

13 Ida Nicolaisen, 'Change Without Development: The Transformation of Punan Bah Economy' *Sarawak Museum Journal* vol. 32, 1983, p. 194.

14 A. Gupta and J. Ferguson, 'The Narrative of Nations and Places' *Cultural Anthropology* vol. 24, no. 2, 1992, p. 8.

15 Kuching is not physically situated on the Rejang, but they are none the less connected economically.

16 The shops in the temporary lots were burnt down during a fire in August 1995, and were being rebuilt during the time of my fieldwork in October that year.

17 Names of the shops and informants have been changed at the request of the interviewees.

18 John M. Chin, *The Sarawak Chinese* (Kuala Lumpur: Oxford University Press, 1981), p. 16.

19 Chew, *Chinese Pioneers on the Sarawak Border, 1841–1941*, p. 3.

20 M. Bakhtin, *The Dialogical Imagination* (Austin: University of Texas Press, 1986), p. 217.

21 Hayden White, *The Content of the Form: Narrative Discourse and Historical Representation* (Baltimore, Md.: Johns Hopkins University Press, 1987), p. 124.

22 J. Hillis Miller, 'Ariadne's Thread: Repetition and the Narrative Line' *Critical Inquiry* no. 3, Autumn 1976, pp. 57–77.

23 Garet Steward, 'Coppola's Conrad: The Repetitions of Complicity' *Critical Inquiry* no. 1, Spring 1981, p. 457.

24 Yao Souchou, *Chinese Traders in Belaga Town: Sarawak, East Malaysia: Geography, Indebtedness and Appropriation* (Report presented to the Institute of Southeast Asian Studies and the Sarawak Museum, 1987).

25 See Mahmut Mutman, 'Under the Sign of Orientalism: The West vs. Islam' *Cultural Critique* no. 23, Winter 1992–1993.

26 Yao Souchou, *Mahathir's Rage: Mass Media and the West as Transcendental Evil* (Perth: Murdoch University, Asia Research Centre Working Paper no. 45, 1994).

27 Koh, '10 values That Help East Asia's Economic Progress, Prosperity'.

28 Homi Bhabha, *The Location of Culture* (London: Routledge 1994).

# 10 Localized spaces, globalized places: virtual community and geo-economics in the Asia-Pacific*

*Timothy W. Luke*

## INTRODUCTION: VIRTUAL COMMUNITY AND GEO-ECONOMICS IN THE ASIA-PACIFIC

The new world order of sovereign nation-states, which was to have led to a progressive new system of international collaboration within the United Nations, did not last much longer than the victory parades after the global 1991 Gulf War. Something else has filled the void opened by the collapse of communism. Yet it does not look like the peaceful cosmopolitan harmonization of liberal democratic nation-states which former President Bush extolled after the UN coalition's victory over Iraq. Many nation-states are becoming increasingly fragmented and unstable; ethnic and class conflicts are spreading rapidly in both the developed and underdeveloped countries; and new supranational 'economic cooperation' communities or 'free trade' associations, like APEC in the Pacific Basin, are restructuring hitherto more insular or autarkic national economies. At the same time, the computerized capillaries of the Internet are diffusing at various rates of saturation in almost all corners of the globe, knitting together now more than 30 million users in a still mostly post-national/post-statal domain of rapid communication that blurs many traditional distinctions between 'them' and 'us'. This chapter, then, examines how new types of global order are gradually emerging above, below and within the modern nation-state, in part from the new technologies constituting the informational mode of production.

Transnational businesses, common markets and informational infrastructures are working together to remake existing national political economies and sovereign states. The European Community after Maastricht, the North American Free Trade Agreement or, perhaps most importantly, many Pacific Rim nations after APEC's formation in 1989 can provide some perspective on these changes. And the Pacific Basin region, as the main geo-economic venue for both NAFTA and APEC, may provide the best look at this development. Clearly, the members of organizations like the EU, APEC or NAFTA all have different competing visions of the future, and one should not reduce the complexities of such regional alliances to one simple truth. Instead, as this volume indicates, many of the contradictory tendencies at work all around the Pacific Rim need to be considered more fully, including any unusual global dimensions of technological change that frequently are ignored in country-by-country reviews.

Global flows of information and entertainment are often unbounded by spatial borders. They pass through existing boundaries, ignoring frontiers in the constant flux of informational exchange. Plainly, a 'transnational' flow of commodified goods, capital, people and ideas has existed for centuries; it certainly antedates even the rise of modern nation-states. However, these historical flows, at least until the late 1950s or early 1960s, tended to move more slowly, move less and more narrowly than the rush of products, ideas, persons and money that develops with jet transportation, political decolonization, extensive computerization, and, most importantly, electronic telecommunication after 1960. It is these greater intensities, rates, densities, levels and velocities in the informational flows of global capitalist production and the televisual flow of electronic mass media which transmute cultural community quantitatively into something qualitatively new, complex and different.

One obvious register of these shifts is the notion of 'virtual reality' in which computer-generated spaces or services begin to emulate all-encompassing material environments as sites of human activity. Individuals in different 'real' physical locations around the planet at different 'real times' during day or night can simultaneously exchange information, discuss ideas, or interact socially by accessing any one of many virtually real cyberspaces. A very realistic simulation in front of a computer screen at home or in the office can become a simulational reality which, in turn, begins to virtualize many economic, political and social practices. In keeping with these transformations, one already hears references to 'virtual corporations', 'virtual schools', 'virtual markets', 'virtual engineering' and 'virtual communities'. As Bell observes in Chapter 8 of this collection, an important contemporary vision of the Pacific Rim may well be to re-imagine it as the geographical location of the most developed iterations of the virtual corporation, virtual communities and perhaps even virtual states.

As the eighteen APEC nations have come to produce over half of the world's gross domestic project in the mid-1990s, this region has become one of the major centres of such informationalizing transformations. On the 'supply side', a transnationally articulated mode of production tied to virtual corporations – stretching from design centres in Tokyo, Los Angeles or Osaka to production facilities in Malaysia, South Korea or China to merchandising enterprises in Brisbane, San Francisco or Taipei – increasingly knits together disparate national pools of technology, capital, design, management, labour and markets around the Pacific Basin into common economic entities. At the same time, as these virtual firms operate around the clock, mass media representations and corporate public relations are spinning tales on the 'demand side' about the virtual geo-economic or geo-political communities of 'the Pacific Century', 'the Pacific Rim' and 'the Pacific Basin', which construct new imaginaries where new visions of the region's states, societies and economies can be seen as developing radically new hybrid formations of local and global order.

Characterizing these changes is difficult, but this chapter provides an initial move towards interpreting some of them. Such new spaces of cyber-spatial/televisual/informational interactivity fuse and confuse the material realms of the local and the global as virtual domains of 'glocality' sited in particular cyberspatial and televisual 'glocales', in many people's everyday lifeworlds. In many ways, the struggle for access to and control over the hyperreal estate of these virtual glocalized spaces now preoccupies political organizations, industrial markets and cultural groups in many regions of the existing capitalist world-system. Rupert Murdoch's quest to monopo-lize media markets in the Pacific Basin, Bill Gates's control over the oper-ating systems in 80 per cent of the world's personal computers, and Ted Turner's bid to dominate global news reporting with the CNN family of news channels are only the most obvious signs of this struggle. The Pacific Rim perhaps best represents one of these newly emerging glocales where a virtual political community may follow the material advances made by transnational businesses' virtual firms. Partly anchored in trans-Pacific trade, partly centred in the struggle between Japan and America for regional supremacy, partly generated in zones of the transnational cultural creolization of Asia/Australasia/America, and partly rooted in newly industrialized countries integrated with newly informationalizing countries, the increasingly integrated workings of APEC and NAFTA countries' poli-tical economies around the Pacific provide many examples of glocaliz-ation's virtual politics and economics. To rationalize the virtual economies of the APEC or NAFTA communities, their members are work-ing jointly to resolve international economic conflicts among themselves, to allay protectionist policies with trade liberalization frameworks, and to weaken intraregional compacts elsewhere in the world.

## POSTMODERNISM: COMMUNITY AS SIMULATION

Beginning with the early debates in the 1950s and 1960s about the nature of 'technological society' or 'postindustrial society', many critical dis-courses of social analysis, which deal with rapid changes in modern indus-trial society, have noted how individual and collective perceptions, discourses and interpretations are transformed radically by the electronic mass media. These shifts are still not completely understood, but they are reconstituting our most basic understandings of transnational community. Such transformations often are discussed as aspects of 'post-modernism'.[1]

The most pervasive influence driving these shifts in the structure and substance of the global community, however, appears to be the informationalization of the social means of production, consumption, administration and destruction during and after the 1950s and 1960s as the transnational impact of mass telecommunications, electronic computerization, cybernetic automation and rapid transportation began to be felt all across the globe.[2]

As Jameson claims, this coming of 'late capitalism' is a change 'which is somehow decisive but incomparable with the older convulsions of modernization and industrialization, less perceptible and dramatic somehow, but more permanent precisely because more thorough-going and all-pervasive'.[3] The mass mediations of informationalization in the economy and society, then, change existing structures of community as social action and cultural process in many different ways. Because of these global flows, as the successes of Hong Kong or Singapore illustrate, new microstates and city-states along the Pacific Rim are finding new comparative advantages for their economies in their labour forces, geographic location, resource endowments or business climates that attract investment, visitors and growth. And, as the post-Cold War crises of the USA and Russia indicate, older, established nation-states arrayed around the Pacific Rim are providing more volatile settings for the globalizing forces, restructuring large segments of their populations and territories as new informational glocales.

Obviously, the meanings of modernity as such change along with the growth of this type of advanced capitalist society as it becomes more entwined with the informational modes of production. Fukuyama's 'end of history' is not so much the end of the realist state's national history as much as it may be the beginning of hyperreal or virtual transnational communities.[4] A new reality logic based upon virtualized simulation rather than concretized representation may constitute the dominant organizing principle of this new era. In Baudrillard's vision of today's New World Order, 'McLuhan's formula, *the medium is the message*', appropriately is 'the key formula of the era of simulation (the medium is the message – the sender is the receiver – the circularity of all polls – the end of panoptic and perspectival space – such is the alpha and omega of *our* modernity), this very formula must be envisaged at its limit'.[5] Baudrillard suggests that the means of information in today's global transnational economy unhinge traditional symbolic relations. If the masses no longer act as conventional historical subjects in their traditional national communities, then what happens to that traditional context, namely the modern nation-state? It perhaps becomes increasingly meaningless in the Moebian logic of simulation that simultaneously creates new grounds for doubting the political sense of nation-state structures.

Theoretical abstractions, like the nation-state or national economy, can no longer be seen as 'the maps', 'the doubles', 'the mirrors' or 'the concepts' of any terrain metaphorically regarded as 'the real'. On the contrary, all abstract frames of the real begin to function only as simulations. For Baudrillard,

> simulation is no longer that of a territory, a referential being or a substance. It is the generation by models of a real without origin or a reality: a hyperreal. The territory no longer precedes the map, nor survives it. Henceforth, it is the map that precedes the territory – PRECESSION OF SIMULACRA – it is the map that engenders the territory.[6]

These postmodern shifts in the sign are a critical juncture in maintaining the 'hyperreal' collective order that transnational mass media and capitalism are fabricating today. Baudrillard now claims:

> When the real is no longer what it used to be, nostalgia assumes its full meaning. There is a proliferation of myths of origin and signs of reality; of second-hand truth, objectivity and authenticity. There is an escalation of the true, of the lived experience; a resurrection of the figurative when the object and substance have disappeared and there is a panic-stricken production of the real and the referential, above and parallel to the panic of material production: this is how simulation appears in the phase that concerns us – a strategy of the real, neo-real and hyperreal whose universal double is a strategy of deterrence.[7]

The practical mediations of generating hyperreality, as Baudrillard appraises it, are the electronic media and computerization. These networks carry the communal currents of informational identity and non-identity, community and otherness, unity and division. The social and the state, or the realms of labour, government and capital as co-producers of rational distribution, are becoming absorbed into communicative simulacra. In new zones of interaction, like the Pacific Rim,

> the radical sociality of the contract, dialectical sociality (that of the State and of civil society, of public and private, of the social and individual) gives way to the sociality of contact, of the circuit and transistorized network of millions of molecules and particles maintained in a random gravitational field, magnetized by the constant circulation and the thousands of tactical combinations which electrify them.[8]

The global restructuring of capital in APEC or NAFTA is reflected in both the corporate systemization and managerial particularization of virtual exchange throughout the Pacific Rim. Seeking greater profits, General Motors collaborates with Toyota at the NUMMI autoworks in California to transfer 'Japanese' efficiency and quality to GM's American product line, while Mazda cooperates with Ford to get the 'American' ruggedness and dependability of American-made 4WD sport utilities into its

Japanese-made product line. What the material corporation will not or cannot produce, the virtual firm provides quickly and reliably.

Moreover, traditional notions of causality, perspective and reasoning are undercut completely by electronic means of information like the World Wide Web on the Internet, which can efface many differences between cause and effect, ends and means, subject and object, active and passive. Baudrillard observes,

> we must think of the media as if they were, in outer orbit, a sort of genetic code which controls the mutation of the real into the hyperreal, just as the other, micro-molecular code controls the passage of the signal from a representative sphere of meaning to the genetic sphere of the programmed signal.[9]

Simulation goes beyond the distinctions of space and time, sender and received, medium and message, expression and content as the world's complex webs of electronic media generate unbound(ed)aries of new hyper-spaces with 'no sense of place'. In other words, the emulation of face-to-face exchanges of ideas and values in the mass media are forming post-national/astatal terrains for constructing new transnational communities as relations of 'contact' and not 'contract'. If Baudrillard is right about simulation, then the geo-political setting of the realist state is increasingly disappearing into transnational virtual imaginaries, like the Pacific Rim, where states are merely disparate local jurisdictions in which and from which capital, labour and power circulate within virtualized transnational geo-economies.

## COMMUNITY AND STATE POWER IN CONTEXT

As the primary container for modern systems of community, the modern state presumed a sociality of contract in discourses of instrumental action, rational reflection and linear causality to ground its political treatment of worldly space as perspectival and social time as neutral. The power of nations expresses itself in ways not unlike rhetorics of interpretation. Once granted, its power becomes motion-enforced, or energies moved from point to point or place to place, within space measured from some political centre. The power of this centre – a metropole, a capitol or royal court – might be seen as being specially appointed by some coercive in-statement, like the illustrative eye gazing/imposing a three-dimensional geometric grid in perspective-based painting. Such centred perspectival visions of time and space are the register of modern political power and its effects in action. Basic qualities, like sovereignty, authority, security and autonomy, are linked in a past, present and future that can be dis-closed, delineated and described in terms of the same uniform fungible units of time.[10] At some discernible point in the past, the state apparatus was in-stated, and it survives through the passage of invariant measures of homogeneous time that accumulate like territory or population.

Not only can the state realize 'space travel' for its power through territory as communal context, it also can attain 'time travel' for its power through temporality as a communally defined chrono-text. The future completes the present just as the present fulfilled the past, but, in each instance, a discourse of panoptic omniscience underpins the entire sweep of constructing this state power. In space, the state acts as an *omniscient illustrator*, drawing out lines of its domains from its ap-pointed instate-ments. Like a modern rationalist artist working in single-point perspective, instated omniscient illustration equals omnipotent construction as history 'illustrates' or the state 'draws a line in the sand'. In such re-presentational space where both sovereign and subject 'could grasp an invariant logic of relationships (a "world") that remained the same regardless of his or her position and that extended to infinity, thus having the value of universal truth'.[11] In time, the state speaks as an *omniscient narrator*, speaking of distant beginnings and far-off endings in equally absolute terms about its historical unfolding. Here, France, Japan, Mexico, Australia and the United States are invented in nationalizing parables of the state's origins, maturation and current powers. Again, like a modernist single-point perspective artist, in-stated omniscient narration equals omnipotent fabrication as 'history speaks' or 'the state commands'. In such representational time, both sovereign and subject experience

> the inscription of a single, homogeneous time stretching to infinity and carrying along in its powerful current absolutely everything . . . it leaves nothing aside or behind. The powers thus available to 'human' consciousness are enormous. In a convention that extends to infinity the rationalized powers of human attention, no atrocity need remain unexplained, no mystery unsolved, no mistake unrectified.[12]

National communities follow state sovereignty as governments preoccupy themselves writing and/or drawing lines of communal identity and antagonism on the Earth. Since 1648, nation-states have been regarded as those legitimate monopolies of violence charged with inscribing, discursively and coercively, writs of communal difference – in money, religion, markets, ideology and militaries – upon persons and places, delimiting them from what transpires within (and without) the geopolitical spaces framed by international borders. By endogenizing various disciplines of monopolistic order inside, and exogenizing diverse practices of free-for-all anarchist conflict outside, those borders defining each nation-state's instated place are inscribed on the planet's terrain.[13] Defending borders, controlling airspace and patrolling offshore waters all are regarded legitimately as essential practices for drawing, defining and then disciplining the various places of national territory to constitute the community of interests differentiating the geographical context and historical chrono-text of this nation-state from that nation-state. These logics, however, break down today as clearly illustrated by Germany's efforts to exert its legal jurisdiction over cyberporn available on American Internet access providers. Cyberspace cannot be bounded in the same ways as real space; and, when it is, access to or enjoyment of its benefits, as protests by many non-German users of America's on-line services show, may be seriously abridged.

## UNBOUNDED FLOWS

As this discussion suggests, the state always has been an essentially fictive construct of linear space in real time. The jurisdiction of states over nations, territories or possessions can be seen as discursive fields of state authority where rulers as authors have inscribed upon individuals and groups those attributes and behaviours they choose with the coercive gaze or normalizing hand of jurisdictive state power (or, literally, 'law speech' speaking). Informationalization, however, can alter the power dynamics of such heavily in-stated jurisdictions by generating new discursive fields with their own organizing cultural discourses, or perhaps alternate encoding dictions, nested in rapid and intense transnational *flows* of ideas, commodities, symbols, people and images on a global scale, which are disjunctive and fragmenting, anarchical and disordered.[14] These flows construct and carry the acts and artefacts embodying conventional understandings shared by individuals and groups in many different ethnonational communities around the Pacific Rim; they anchor the manifest and latent meanings valued by the transnational virtual communities being created within cybernetic, televisual and consumerist networks of information and exchange. In other words, 'Japan', 'America' and 'Australia' as flows of signs become open, fluid, multivalent forces on a transnational scale, allowing others to desire Japanese, American or Australian artefacts and to repeat Japanese, American or Australian acts at home or abroad in global culture spaces.

Castells, for example, argues

> what is facilitated by information technologies is the interconnection of activities, providing the basis for the increasing complexity of service industries, which exchange information relentlessly and ubiquitously. . . . Whatever becomes organizationally and legally possible can be technologically implemented because of the versatility of the technological medium.[15]

In appraising today's global economic changes, Reich asserts that collective forms of material prosperity are no longer national; instead, they all depend upon 'the same transnational trend. Barriers to cross-border flows of knowledge, money, and tangible products are crumbling; groups of people in every nation are joining global webs'.[16] As the networks of informational exchange unfold in the cybernetic spaces of information-alized processes, new communal codes and arrangements can arise. As Castells asserts,

> there is a shift, in fact, away from the centrality of the organizational unit to the network of information and decision. In other words, *flows, rather than organizations*, become the units of work, decision, and output accounting. Is the same trend developing in relation to the spatial dimension of organizations? Are flows substituting for localities in the information economy? Under the impact of information systems, are organizations not timeless but also placeless?[17]

These forces of flow can be seen most clearly shaping the venues of new glocales, or the new transnational sites and communities formed by elec-tronic mass media and global trade.

Actually, in the post-modern culture of global flow, 'culture' itself 'has become a product in its own right; the market has become a substitute for itself. . . . Postmodernism is the consumption of sheer commodification as a process'.[18] Rather than acceding to a privileged geo-political reading of global power, the geo-economics of virtual commerce and communication generate many new different grammars across a wide band of still less well-understood 'writings' and 'readings' of existing political communities. These other virtual forces, or collectively 'polydictions', today flow more placelessly beneath, behind, between, beyond in-stated boundaries set into space as these new artifices of encoding structure and process become quite fluid, defined by shifting networks of images and information mediat-ing these flows over existing state boundaries.

The unravelling of in-stated political communities today, or the loosen-ing of their jurisdiction(s), echoes the cacophony of new polydictive codes being made articulate in the mass media and cyberspace by informational transformations. New social discourses beyond the state, which are grounded in the market, science, the intelligentsia, technology, the mass consuming/producing public, medicine or even the global ecology, find individual and collective agencies allowing them alternative communities to write over/against/for and speak to/against/for the state. Exclusively political poles and polarities are slipping out of phase. In the informational discourse of virtual communities, different voices can and do speak outside (and within) the rationalized instrumental speech situations of statist jurisdiction.

Consequently, everything is not entirely pacific in the Pacific Basin. Who controls access to, and thereby many of the material benefits from, the transnational economy is a source of conflict in many Pacific Basin states. In some areas, like China and Vietnam, state socialist regimes are strug-gling to maintain the political supremacy of the Communist Party, while actively promoting an economic transition to capitalist relations of production by becoming industrial semi-peripheries to the informational core in North America or Japan. In other areas, like Taiwan or South Korea, more fragile democracies based upon the historic bedrock of authoritarian military regimes, which developed during the Cold War as bulwarks against communist expansion, are struggling with their own programmes for attaining greater democratization and civilian rule. In other areas, former socialist systems, like Cambodia or Russia, are attempting at the same time to stimulate the development of capitalism and democracy, but failing for the most part to see success on either front as intra-regime factions and black market entrepreneurialism are giving both capitalism and democracy a very bad name. And, finally, in Japan, Canada or the United States, mature industrial economies are grappling with informationalization's propensities for aggravating intranational structural contradictions and international market competitions, which are severely straining domestic political institutions as well as foreign diplomatic ties.

In each instance, astatist forces operating in multiple channels of the global marketplace or electronic mass media are making their own plural, parallel communities. With such new 'worlds', there are non-statist forces from the domains of commerce, finance, technology, ideas, health, etc. In these zones of operation, they, first, might rule off some space of exclusive control, and, second, rule as the most legitimate expert forces, and then, third, set the rules for definitive codes of new jurisdictions rooted in codes of financial, environmental, technological or scientific authority. These virtual power centres/speech communities exist, but their concrete existence as vital communities still floats inarticulately in realist readings of how the workings of global business circles, international technical exchanges, transnational environmental debates or multinational popular culture crazes affect the existing system of traditional nation-states.

Moving from place to flow, terrains to streams with virtualization introduces non-perspectival, anti-hierarchical and disorganizational elements into traditional spatial/industrial/national notions of sovereign community. Without conceptually making this turn, many events can escape analysis without any key distinctions being made. Having open and unconstrained access to global flows, not closed domination of local places, becomes a crucial attribute of power in informationalized societies. So many of China's southern coastal regions resist Beijing in order to exploit their own local capabilities in global trade by fostering 'special economic zones' where global flows can begin transforming their local economy and society into component parts. A chaotic cultural community spins from within the complex codes of the flow by providing individuals and groups with much more dynamic levels of access in the flows to make linkages, expand connections, broaden exchange, or enhance services in the flow. The diverse agendas of the various encoders and decoders build communal interactions, while a sense of communal security slips into concerns over the assuring integrity of codes, openness of access, extent of service, scope of linkage, and increase of turnover within virtual boundaries.

Caught in the currents of commercial, informational and televisual forces moving across the mediascapes of informationalization, the nation-state – with its more traditional geo-political concerns for policing its territories, populations and markets – often comes up quite short with nothing near complete closure over many political events within its boundaries. Even the United States no longer is that united as a state when millions of Asians, Latin Americans and Europeans illegally emigrate into its territories, as narcocapitalist enterprises mock its tax, police and administrative authorities, and as many businesses prey upon its consumers from around the world with less and less effective state regulation. When moving in these dimensions, as Der Derian observes, one might supplement existing categories exclusively tied to geo-politics and the control of space by teasing through alternative outlooks linked to chronopolitics and the setting of pace.[19]

Given these larger structural trends, the older concrete reality of place, expressed in terms of a peculiar sociocultural context defined in spatial location, gradually is being displaced by the tangible hyperreality of flow, understood in terms of the localized access to or enactment of new globalized practices through networks of informational circulation. The latter is not entirely displacing or destroying the former, but rather they are co-existing together. From these growing contradictions between organizational centralization and informational decentralization, or 'between places and flows', one might uncover in the workings of global change, 'the gradual transformation of the flows of power into the power of flows'.[20] Indeed, the televisual flows are the basis of defining new types of commercial/technological core, semiperipheral, peripheral and external areas as they restructure the market niches of cities, regions and countries.

## ECONOMIC AND MASS MEDIA COMMUNITIES

Most importantly, the postnational virtualized glocales emerging from informationalization conform to significantly different spatial, political and organizational rules. Global flows are partly post-national, partly post-sovereign, and partly post-statal structures, which are, in turn, the primary networking of a new kind of international community. The world-system of transnational capitalism gains its new figurations in the televisual/computational/cyberspatial conduits of the flow. For example, Reich contrasts the 'nominal nationality' professed by many modern major corporations with their 'actual transnationality' as global parts sourcing, foreign markets, expatriate management, multinational labour recruiting and world-wide financial operations increasingly typify their operations in places like 'the Pacific Rim'.[21] These distinctions are reshaping what is meant by economic community. Likewise, the 'nominal ethno-nationality' of mass culture, once defined by statesmen and parliaments, is becoming an actually transnational multiculturalism as computer codes, television images or pop music scramble what actually means what to whom. Hence, one sees Taiwanese Elvises, South Korean Sue Ellen Ewings, American Kung Fu sages, Australian Universal City funparks and Japanese Disneylands. Each of these traces marks a key site in the virtual communities in the Pacific Basin.

Believing that their security and prosperity are the products of national policies, national interests, or national decision makers, contemporary consumers and producers often mistake thoroughly transnational or largely local forces as the exclusive property of their nation-state. Xenophobic political appeals, stressing exclusively nationalistic benefits or costs, occlude how closely coupled most present-day core economies and societies have become. Borders today are highly porous, and flows of goods and services are continuously eroding them ever more. To take only one example, consumers and producers all around the Pacific Rim depend upon a global array of products in their localities: oil lifted in Alaska or Indonesia to be sold in Japan or New Zealand, fast food from Canadian-owned franchise operations, credit cards from Hong Kong-controlled banks, automobiles built in Mexico by Japanese firms transplanting their output as American cars, groceries produced in Central America, South Africa or Southeast Asia sold in British-owned store chains, newspapers held by Australian multinationals but published in New York, medicines developed in Germany and manufactured in California for sale in the Philippines, televisions fabricated in Taiwan by American companies to show programmes made in Canada by Japanese-owned studios head-quartered in Los Angeles, clothes designed in New York sewn together in American Samoa for sale in Hawaii, and information gathered by British wire services in Eastern Europe for broadcast on twenty-four-hour cable news networks centred in Atlanta.

The modelling of personal behaviour in both production and consumption is more glocal than national. Similar accounts of glocal interdependence can be adduced for virtually any 'nation-state' in the world today, but it arguably is most advanced in the regions around the Pacific Rim. Beyond Huntington's essentialist visions of civilizational cultures competing for hegemony in the Pacific, one must acknowledge the definite outlines of a globalizing transnational civilization that often is mislabelled in North America and abroad as 'American' when its material ecologies and metabolic energies are entirely transnational.[22] Pacific Rim cultures are displacing and reordering both Western and Eastern cultures in new transnational corporate ecologies of production, consumption and accumulation. The notion of 'national interest' has ever less meaning in these glocal webs of interdependence. Forcing these loosely coupled but vital connections of everyday life into the categories of realist state thinking results in xenophobic reactions: if something is not produced and/or consumed at home, then it allegedly must represent necessarily a weakening of 'national' power, productivity or prestige.

This archaic reading of transnational flows in national statist terms misses how embedded and efficient these glocal webs of exchange actually have become. Already, the virtual life is materially quite real. Outside the state, and inside shared technological goals, common ecological challenges, similar symbolic systems, parallel coding orders, or comparable product meanings, the global flows create new glocal communities that are blurring the old geographics of 'them' and 'us', 'other' and 'I', or 'friend' and 'foe' in new informational modes of organization. The origins and outlets of its many component currents can still be traced back to particular ethnonational settings, or the sovereign spaces of some state's nominal nationality; however, their effects, taken together in the streams of the global flow, are also being felt glocally, or locally and globally, as actual transnationality. These distinctions also can be extended to interpret the workings of many cultural networks, woven into the intermeshed telecommunication links of global media markets. Nominal nationality increasingly competes with actual transnationality in the processes of many international events and trends. Cultural products coming from Milan, Liverpool, New York, Kingston, Nashville, Hollywood or Dallas become global cultural forces eroding at the local level many larger political structures once made almost solely in Moscow, Washington or Tokyo.

These geo-economic transformations, then, carry along with them the acts and artefacts shared within a globalized transnational community. While new right-wing ideologies may prey upon the racial prejudices and economic anxieties of ordinary Americans by bashing Japan, South Korea or Taiwan, it is still obvious that millions of these same hard-working citizens troop off daily to Walmart, K-Mart or Target stores to buy high-quality, low-cost products from these Pacific nations. By the same token, American businesses are selling high-technology electronics, jet aircraft, defence goods, agricultural produce, and raw materials worth billions to these Asian economies. Despite all the rhetoric about 'a Japan that can say no' or 'a Fortress America', the geo-economics of virtual corporations, transnational markets and global consumerism are locking ordinary workers and everyday buying habits into the same industrial ecologies whose economic metabolism presumes transnationally shared values and goals. No other market can absorb the billions of dollars in business between the Pacific Rim economies. Without America, East Asia's economy cannot operate as efficiently; without East Asia, American markets cannot be served as effectively. Together in APEC, they produce nearly 60 per cent of the gross planetary product.[23]

Flows are decentring, despatializing and dematerializing forces as they work alongside and against the geo-political codes of spatial sovereignty. Their cultural force is redrawing new forms of community within and across the old national geographics written by states since 1648 by providing new psychosocial framing alternatives for reimagining moral values, political ends or economic needs. The values of Sky Channel advertising clips or the images on CNN news reports, for example, can establish common desires, shared fears, or collective needs in Japan or Mexico, New Zealand or South Korea, the Philippines or the United States, while forming a transnational discursive space to address them through the English language in corporate/technical/consumerist terms. 'Outside' the state, but 'inside' shared technological goals, common ecological challenges, or similar symbolic systems, the flow creates new transnational communities that are blurring the old geographics of 'them' and 'us', 'other' and 'I', or 'friend' and 'foe' in new informational modes of community. Again, like CNN sending signals from Atlanta by cable and satellite, the origins and outlets of its many component currents can still be traced back to in-stated ethnogeographic settings, or the spaces staked out by some nominal nationality. Yet their effects, like CNN 'Headline News' or the rush of global advertising in the televisual streams of global flows, are also being felt post-nationally – or locally and globally – as actual transnationality in new glocales like the Pacific Rim.

Beyond the realities of territorial national statics, fixed to state-structured processes inside of tightly inscribed borders, there are the new hyperrealities of global flows, fluctuating within televisually coded links along loosely coupled local/global networks. In the mass media sphere, every television receiver is a portal, opening into/looking out onto images of these teleterrains. Cultural meanings of these images develop out of codes set into the global flow of substantive and symbolic information. The Cable News Network is a globalized artificial space available in scores of nations around the world twenty-four hours a day. Much of the coverage is transnational, focusing on world politics, world economics, world sports and world mass culture, even though it is often framed by 'American' producers using American techniques for 'Americanized' consumers in Americanized markets. These hypermodernizing transformations in the flow, however, are not mediations of national realist modernizations. Instead, they act as the carriers of transnational postmodernity, because even Americans are being subjected to further 'Americanization' at this stage of postmodernity. As Jameson observes, 'postmodernism is what you have after the modernization process is complete and nature is gone for good'.[26] 'Being American' or 'becoming Americanized' in these infor-mational formations can take place almost anywhere and anytime as the discourses about Japanese Elvises, New Zealand political correctness, Australian new right-wing militias or Hong Kong gangster films all suggest.

Cyberspaces accelerate these transformations, as virtualized communities in the World Wide Web continue redefining traditional oppositions of us/them, same/other, friend/foe, in cultural codes; in a second sense, they alter categories of more/less, growth/stagnation, and elite/common in defining economic divisions; in a third sense, they delineate boundaries of inside/outside, foreign/domestic, ours/theirs in global community; and, in a final sense, they shift barriers of access/exclusion, power/powerlessness, order/disorder in the political frictions of transnational community. Thus, being plugged into 'the Pacific Rim' as an economic player in the 1990s is far more important to many people than being merely a solid American citizen in rural Ohio. Most workers would rather toil in the virtual enterprise of Japanese/American/Canadian/South Korean/Mexican/Taiwanese workplaces, like the Honda Corporation, for example, in Marysville, Ohio, to build cars that are exported to Japan instead of joining economic protectionist movements. Indeed, nativist resistance to the emergent Pacific Rim from rural America constitutes a serious threat to the virtual geo-economies rooted in this glocale as exclusively national, anti-transnational agendas from some small town in the American Midwest resist the transnational Pacific economic community with policies favouring trade barriers, immigrant bashing or mindless xenophobia.

Outside their efforts to guarantee national security or monetary discipline, nation-states in global flows often are little more than virtual realities imagineered on a geographic basis at a national level to regulate delivery of varied social services as their defining feature. Today, the attributes of 'nationality' often boil down to fleeting, floating coefficients of personal entitlement to a basic material standard of living that now marks the collective identity of different 'national' entities as states. Varying levels of individual and collective access to goods and services from the capitalist world-system, which are measured along a flexible continuum of statistical indicators, establish the essential socio-economic profiles of 'what is' a so-called First, Second, Third or Fourth World nation-state. Americans are 'Americans' or Thais are 'Thais' because they have this or that statistically defined higher or lower covariant chance to own a car, have a TV, eat red meat, see a dentist, use a VCR, possess a dwelling, or die after age 80. Such 'standards of living' also are little more than tactical hallucinations deployed to induct the silent majorities to 'live out standards' that are set in an endless precession of new corporate-generated goods and services in glocales mutating from simulation to simulation. Looking at these nation-states, *simulated differences*, driven again by copying models of meaning for which there are no originals, and *neutralized identities*, dynamicized by parallel processes of material production and consumption in each state's everyday lifeworld, are no more than parodies of national diversity or global community.

Despite the pretexts of 'national' cultural autonomy, the transnational commodity flow of McDonald's food products in Montreal, Moscow, Manila, Melbourne and Minneapolis is the same deterrent force arrayed against real local/national specificity. A simulation of cuisine in 'fast food' creates its own models of culture, behaviour, and desire within the confines of 'fast capitalism'.[25] Now, the territorial in-statements of nations simply provide territorialized historical imaginaries to shake and sort out such transnational economic and social welfare benefits in accord with their closeness to or distance from the central post-historical currents in the global flow of capital, energy, goods and power. What may be far more important are the glocales that these currents are cutting above and shaping below the realm of nation-states.

## CONCLUSION: LOCALIZED SPACES, GLOBALIZED PLACES

The economic, political and social forces behind these trends towards glocalization, therefore, are working on several different levels to realize divergent and diverse agendas in many different types of virtual community. On one level, corporate providers of telecommunication and computing services are constructing elaborate informational infrastructures, which essentially efface many of the existing borders of the prevailing Westphalian state system with the networks of global corporate exchange. On another level, corporate and individual users of these virtualizing networks are fabricating new semio-communicative communities, developing innovative techno-economic ensembles, and organizing unusual sociopolitical institutions within these cyberspaces. On yet another level, the glocal grids of exchange, manufacture and identity made possible by these networks are disembedding many cultures, economies and societies from their traditional nation-state milieux.

The nature of glocality, when viewed in conventional nation-state terms, appears as fluid and unbounded as ideological imaginaries like 'the Pacific Rim'. Several different virtualizing channels of glocalization exist, and they operate simultaneously in the current world-system. Nation-states continually attempt to contain and even resist their workings, but glocalities continue to evince decentred/differentiated/disorganized dynamics against the centralizing/standardizing/organizing logic of nation-states. In one pre-national web, ethnic/religious/linguistic/racial identities and interests spill over arbitrary national-statal (b)orders, bridging local frictions with central state authorities to transnational communities that seek a common dictive code. Inside a second non-national web, transnational trade networks buy and sell thousands of different commodities – necessary and sumptuary, legal and illicit, essential and frivolous, high-volume and high-value – in markets that thrive beyond, behind, and beneath any one nation-state's control. In an extra-national web, nature's various biotic, geologic, and atmospheric zones continue to evolve in thousands of different bioregions that surpass all national-statal efforts to manage them, while incurring all of the damage that human societies continue to inflict. Inside a post-national web, the informatic/telematic/robotic flow of cyberspaces are knit together in an emergent planetary infostructure, shredding the barriers once thrown up by modern industrial states to create national autonomy, national security and national identity. And, in a transnational web, the combined effects of all these webs are generating new cultural codes and practices that stress difference/resistance/multiplicity beneath and beyond national statal confines in a cybercreole of placelessness, eccentricity and simultaneity. All of these webs criss-cross the substance and form of new glocales, including those in the Pacific Rim.

These virtual communities, in turn, are designed to serve some very specific virtues that bolster the interests of their members. First, they support the agendas of transnational neo-liberalism inasmuch as they celebrate the virtues of markets over states. In pursuit of the most unfettered opportunities to produce goods, sell products, employ labour, invest money, and boost trade, government interference is downplayed against corporate freedom. Second, they embody one contemporary version of a post-Cold War New World Order in which tightly coupled regional alliances compete on global geo-economic playing fields rather than remaining tied into loosely coupled ideological alliances between nation-states struggling with each other geo-politically. To remake the world anew, transnational communities, like the new free trade communities of APEC, NAFTA or the EU, constitute new types of imagined communities for state elites and corporate managers to re-envision their nations' collective social activity beyond the project of anti-communism or anti-totalitarianism. Third, they create quite large, but very vaguely defined postnational spaces in which the operational goals of large corporations, scientific disciplines and global finance, as well as local entrepreneurs, ethnic minorities and localistic resistances, can be juxtaposed against the authority of particular national governments and the structure of individual national markets. In territory under APEC's or NAFTA's jurisdiction, jobs will be relocated in the name of global efficiency; environmental objectives will be loosened to enhance everyone's income; peasant uprisings will be undercut to support incumbent authorities tottering from internal crises and contradictions. All of these local moves simply enhance the global stability of the region's virtual economy and community.

Glocalities, therefore, are virtual social practices infiltrating the post-statal structures and postnational processes of transnational business with new routines defined by virtual modes of informational production. Transnational topographies and transcultural territories emerge in the flow from the daily traffic of international communication, travel, commerce and transportation. No longer grounded to one planetary place, one ethno-national location or one environmental site, these semi-imaginary/semi-concrete glocalities form their own diverse re-engineered cultural space in places like 'the Pacific Rim'. Increasingly, virtual domains also may become the most meaningful sites for contemporary individuals and groups. To be associated with 'the Pacific Rim' is seen, for better or worse, as being part of the sunrise sectors of the planet; to be elsewhere, like Rustbelt Ohio, West Africa or Greater Serbia, is regarded as being caught in the sunset regions of the world. Glocales matter, because they are made and unmade by the virtual flows of transnational informational utilities and corporate enterprises. They provide simulations of territory, models for behaviour, circuits of operationalization that reframe thought and action glocally. Glocalities remain in place, but become difficult to place as they integrate artificial spaces, built environments, and coded milieux into meaningful locations that fuse many nation-states into transnational economies and societies.[26] They provide new practical sites for economic, cultural and social interactions within glocal networks of subnational, national and supranational exchange. From these sites, individuals and communities can fabricate shared strategies for occupying these postmodernist spaces, imagining them in virtualized cultural conventions as 'the Pacific Rim' rather than as the traditional modernist regimes of Australia, the United States or Taiwan.

# NOTES

*An earlier version of this chapter was presented at the Third Conference of the International Society for the Study of European Ideas, 24–29 August 1992, and pieces of it appear in *Alternatives* no. 18, 1993, pp. 229–258, and *Journal of Pacific Studies* vol. 17, nos. 1–2, 1993, pp. 38–56.

1 See Jean-François Lyotard, *The Postmodern Condition: A Report on Knowledge* (Minneapolis: University of Minnesota Press, 1984), and Fredric Jameson, *Postmodernism, or the Cultural Logic of Late Capitalism* (Durham, NC: Duke University Press, 1991).

2 Timothy W. Luke, *Screens of Power: Ideology, Domination, and Resistance in Informational Society* (Urbana: University of Illinois Press, 1989), pp. 3–14.

3 Jameson, *Postmodernism*, p. xxi.

4 See Francis Fukuyama, *The End of History and the Last Man* (New York: Free Press, 1992).

5 Jean Baudrillard, *In the Shadow of the Silent Majorities* (New York: Semiotext(e), 1983), pp. 101–102.

6 Jean Baudrillard, *Simulations* (New York: Semiotext(e), 1983), p. 2.

7 ibid., pp. 12–13.

8 Baudrillard, *Shadow*, p. 83.

9 Baudrillard, *Simulations*, p. 55.

10 See, for example, John Breuilly, *Nationalism and the State* (Manchester: Manchester University Press, 1982), and Ernest Gellner, *Nations and Nationalism* (Oxford: Basil Blackwell, 1983).

11 Elizabeth Deeds Ermath, *Sequel to History: Postmodernism and the Crisis of Representational Time* (Cambridge: Cambridge University Press, 1992), p. 26.

12 ibid., p. 28.

13 See Charles Tilly, ed., *The Formation of National States in Western Europe* (Princeton, NJ: Princeton University Press, 1975), and E. J. Hobsbawm, *Nations and Nationalism Since 1780* (Cambridge: Cambridge University Press, 1990).

14 See Stephen Toulmin, *Cosmopolis: The Hidden Agenda of Modernity* (New York: Free Press, 1990).

15 Manuel Castells, *The Informational City* (Oxford: Blackwell, 1989), p. 142.

16 Robert Reich, *The Work of Nations: Preparing Ourselves for 21st Century Capitalism* (New York: Knopf, 1991), p. 172.
17 Castells, *Informational City*, p. 142.
18 Jameson, *Postmodernism*, p. x.
19 James Der Derian, 'The (S)pace of International Relations: Simulation, Surveillance, and Speed' *International Studies Quarterly* vol. 34, September 1990, pp. 295–310.
20 Castells, *Informational City*, p. 171.
21 Reich, *Work of Nations*, p. 131.
22 Samuel Huntington, 'The Clash of Civilizations?' *Foreign Affairs* 72, 2, Summer 1993, pp. 22–49.
23 Fred Bergsten, 'The Case for APEC' *The Economist* 6–12 January 1996, pp. 62–63.
24 Jameson, *Postmodernism*, p. ix.
25 See Ben Agger, *Fast Capitalism* (Urbana: University of Illinois Press, 1989).
26 Timothy W. Luke, 'Placing Power/Siting Space: The Politics of Global and Local in the New World Order' *Environment and Planning D: Society and Space* no. 12, 1994, pp. 613–628.

# 11 The triumph of the East? The East Asian Miracle and post-Cold War capitalism*

*Mark T. Berger*

## INTRODUCTION: THE EAST ASIAN MIRACLE AND POST-COLD WAR CAPITALISM

The end of the Cold War has drawn renewed attention to the emergence of East Asia as a dynamic and increasingly integrated economic zone. This regional dynamism and integration derive in part from the Cold War itself (particularly the period from the late 1940s to the early 1970s), during which the US-led push to contain communism and secure a capitalist economic order in Asia combined with the resurgence of Japanese corporate activity in the region to provide the overall framework for the so-called East Asian Miracle.[1] The East-Asian Miracle has emerged as a major and flexible concept, embedded in wider discourses on capitalist development and industrialization which homogenize and seek to manage a changing 'national', regional and international political and economic order. Some of the most influential explanations for the origin and character of East Asian dynamism continue to flow from liberal Anglo-American discourses which represent the dramatic industrialization of the region as a vindication of a free-trade model of capitalist development. A less influential, but still significant, set of Anglo-American approaches views the East Asian Miracle as a sort of lesson in neo-Keynesian economics. At the same time, a growing number of North American, West European and Australian observers now attribute the rise of East Asia primarily to Confucianism or other perceived cultural/racial characteristics. Linked to these approaches are more explicitly racial discourses, which regard the rise of the 'East', especially Japan (and now China), as a threat to the 'West'.

Since the end of the Cold War, North American- and Australian-centred discourses on the East Asian Miracle have been increasingly challenged by a variety of East Asian-based narratives, which are the main focus of this chapter. The best-known strands of these East Asian discourses represent the capitalist success of East Asia as grounded in Asian values (the Asian way). These triumphant East Asian cultural/racial visions are directly connected to the efforts of Northeast Asian and Southeast Asian elites to maintain hegemony within, or gain hegemony beyond, existing territorial boundaries and regional demarcations. East Asian discourses on the West are now producing what has been termed Occidentalism, and as the power of particular Asian states, whether individually or grouped, increases, the potency of Occidentalist discourses which hold up Asian values and virtues as both a key to the region's own success and as a panacea for an inferior and homogeneous West will become more marked (the shift in power relations is more pronounced in Australia than in North America). While there are numerous differences between and within East Asian and Anglo-American discourses on the East Asian Miracle, East Asian triumphalism is clearly complemented by some 'Western' narratives. Both the dominant Anglo-American discourses and the East Asian-based narratives continue to rest on a sharp distinction between East and West and on a generally fixed conceptualization of culture/race, which overlooks the hybrid character of the history of the region. Furthermore, it should be emphasized that the continued power of fixed conceptions of culture/race, and of the East–West dichotomy, is even apparent in those approaches to the rise of East Asia and the coming Pacific Century which speak of the need for an East–West synthesis. For example, regional elite integration in the Asia-Pacific is being facilitated by a process in which Anglo-American liberalism is effectively domesticated to East Asian cultural/racial triumphalism even as the relative fixity of the East and the West continues to be emphasized. At the same time, the elite Anglo-American and East Asian visions, and the emerging synthesis, not to mention the elite-oriented economic policy debate, have all worked to obscure the profound social costs of the capitalist miracles in Northeast and Southeast Asia, and of Cold War and post-Cold War capitalism more generally.

This chapter begins by charting the Anglo-American discourses on the East Asian Miracle and then turns its focus to key strands of the new East Asian triumphalism. This is done with an emphasis on the wider context of the continued but changing importance of racialized politics and fixed conceptions of culture/race in the Asia-Pacific and beyond. This will be followed by a discussion of the transnational processes of integration and fragmentation associated with globalization. A critical perspective on globalization directly challenges the utopian Anglo-American vision of an ever more integrated regional and international system of prosperous sovereign nation-states trading freely, which is anticipated by some supporters of organizations such as the Asia Pacific Economic Cooperation forum (APEC). A critical analysis of globalization also undermines the celebratory visions articulated by East Asian elites (and questions the fears of many in the West) that the end of the Cold War is producing, or will produce, a new global hegemonic configuration centred on East Asia. It is argued that the Asia-Pacific and the world have entered an era characterized by increasingly racialized politics and the continued potency of fixed conceptions of culture/race. At the same time, the centre of gravity of the global political economy is shifting away from an ostensibly US-centred Cold War hegemony towards a web of international power relations centred on transnational corporations (TNCs) and/or regionally integrated elites in the context of important changes to the position of territorial states. The overall trend is towards an increasingly decentred post-Cold War capitalism.

## UNDER WESTERN EYES

Against the background of the end of the Cold War (and the apparent victory for the USA and its allies) the most influential variants of Anglo-American liberalism, as already noted, still view the rise of the East as a free-trade miracle. Anglo-American liberalism also regularly discovers values and virtues in East Asia which are strikingly similar to those (Protestant) qualities which are perceived to have underpinned the rise of the West in an earlier era. At the end of the twentieth century the histories of a variety of social formations in Asia often continue to be read as belated versions of the rise of the West (or more particularly the rise of England and the United States of America).[2] This is connected to the reliance of North Americans and West Europeans, beginning with the colonial period, on an idealized version of North American and/or West European history as a model by which progress in Asia and elsewhere was interpreted. Prior to World War II, despite the appearance of secular ideas about historical development, the dominant Western discourses on 'Asia' continued to be shaped by fixed conceptions of culture/race and by nationalistic/racist assumptions about a Western civilizing mission. This trend continued into the Cold War era as the civilizing mission became an anti-communist modernizing mission. During the Cold War and beyond, Anglo-American theories of modernization and economic development have continued to reflect their linkages to the colonial era during which a cultural/racial pride in the perceived superiority of an Anglo-American (and/or a wider Western) historical model had been predominant. The continued power of Anglo-American visions after World War II clearly flows from the historic dominance of the British empire in the nineteenth and early twentieth centuries and from US global hegemony in the twentieth century. Under these circumstances, a commitment to gradual political and social change, representative government, individualism and free trade as universal values continues to have a profound impact on the lessons which are gleaned from the East Asian Miracle. For example, leaders of the British Conservative Party continue to invoke the East Asian Miracle, which they see as flowing from minimal state regulation and taxation, to legitimate their ongoing efforts at trade liberalization and financial deregulation in Britain.[3]

The centrality of free trade to Anglo-American narratives on the rise of the West and of the East is clear; however, the emphasis which has been placed on free trade at any given time has fluctuated both before and after the onset of the Cold War. In the early Cold War era, in the context of the Marshall Plan and the post-1945 reconstruction of Western Europe and Northeast Asia, greater emphasis was placed on economic planning, if not state intervention. This approach was part of what became known as classical modernization theory and worked to underpin the so-called 'golden age of capitalism' in North America, Western Europe and Japan (while it was very much a product of the Cold War, as already noted, post-World War II theories of modernization also built on the concepts deployed by the colonial powers in their civilizing missions of the pre-1945 era). The post-war boom ended by the 1970s, and by the early 1980s neo-liberal governments in North America and Western Europe (particularly the Reagan administration in the USA and the Thatcher administration in Britain), which explained national and international economic decline in terms of too much state intervention in economic and social life, were in the ascendant. Washington and London exercised predominant influence over the World Bank and the IMF, and decisively shifted the emphasis of international and domestic economic policy making to neo-liberal economics. Under these circumstances the East Asian Miracle was even more stridently invoked as evidence that free trade worked and this continued to be a dominant interpretation throughout the 1980s. At the beginning of the 1990s, the reading of the collapse of the Soviet empire as a victory for the type of capitalism that predominated in Britain and North America in the 1980s strengthened those approaches to the East Asian Miracle which asserted that it demonstrated the global applicability of the economic policies favoured by the IMF and the World Bank.[4]

The continuing influence of liberal economic ideas is reflected in the way that a recent World Bank report on East Asia – which was funded by the Japanese Ministry of Finance and carried out in the context of Japanese pressure on the World Bank to revise its commitment to an overwhelmingly neo-liberal development model – still only reluctantly acknowledged some role for the state.[5] The report, entitled *The East Asian Miracle* (which as of August 1995 had sold 110,000 copies – a record for a World Bank publication), extracted a range of liberal economic lessons and emphasized that government intervention aimed at promoting exports was the form of intervention most 'compatible with a wide diversity of economic circumstances'.[6] The report also continued to treat economic development as a technical policy question, and the role of the state (or government institutions), or wider historical considerations, were not seen as particularly relevant to an overall understanding of successful capitalist development.

Nevertheless, as the politics surrounding the 1993 World Bank report make clear, economic liberalism may be losing some ground as a result of the end of the Cold War and the growing power of the industrial states of East Asia, particularly Japan. There are an increasing number of revisionist Anglo-American (and of course East Asian-based) policy-oriented works which foreground the role of the state in capitalist development. Overall, a growing interest in identifying, and/or building, strong states (usually defined as states which have a high degree of coercive capability and relative independence or autonomy from certain classes or sectors of society, and are capable of intervening to restructure society or direct the market) has underpinned wider debates about economic and political change for a number of years now. The discovery of the important role of the state in capitalist development in East Asia and beyond is clearly reflected by James Fallows's recent book, *Looking at the Sun: The Rise of the New East Asian Economic and Political System*. Fallows, a US journalist, argues that: 'in Anglo-American theory the state gets *in the way* of the economy's growth and the people's happiness', but '[i]n the Asian model it is an indispensable tool toward those ends'.[7] His book has been roundly criticized for its cultural/racial reductionism and his analysis does rest on fixed conceptions of culture/race; however, it appears to have been his attack on economic liberalism which has attracted the most attention. At least one acknowledged revisionist has defended Fallows's heresy. In a recent review, Chalmers Johnson argues that it is now 'overwhelmingly' obvious that the state and the private sector have worked closely together to produce 'safe, sane societies with astonishingly high levels of evenly distributed income'. He also emphasizes that Japan and China are 'the only two foreign countries today that could threaten the national security of the United States' if the current relationships broke down.[8] In the early 1980s Chalmers Johnson wrote a pioneering state-centred analysis of Japanese economic development which is now seen as central to the revisionist or institutionalist approach to Japanese industrialization.[9] By the end of the 1980s the statist and wider institutionalist approaches to capitalist development in East Asia, which had emerged as much in response to the appearance of neo-liberal economics in the West, as they did to the rise of the East, had gained some influence.[10] Revisionist authors not only criticize free-market interpretations of the rise of the East, but they often emphasize that state intervention and protectionist policies have historically played far more of a role in the industrialization of Britain and the USA than the idealized image of the rise of the West would suggest.

What is of particular relevance here is the way in which the revisionist (state-centred or institutionalist) approaches clearly remain part of the dominant international economic policy discourses and perpetuate an elite-oriented ahistorical approach to capitalist development, articulating an analysis which either reifies culture/race (as a fixed and dynamizing or obstructing force) or treats it as irrelevant. For example, North American-based political scientist Jung-En Woo (Meredith Woo-Cumings) has argued that the rise of South Korea is 'neither a miracle nor a cultural mystery, but the outcome of a misunderstood political economy'. In her recent book she sought to 'merge Korea with the stream of world history by discovering universal aspects of its development'.[11] Although her book itself offers a detailed and historically particular analysis of the rise of South Korea, this kind of wholesale rejection of 'culture' results in the conclusion that South Korea's trajectory is a variation on a universally applicable state-centred late-industrialization model.[12] Jung-En Woo's book also reflects the ongoing process of synthesis between liberal political science and marxist political economy. This process has taken place in the context of the basically liberal academic and political structures and discourses of North America and was clearly reflected in the widespread exclusion of marxism from post-1945 social science and then its gradual appropriation on liberal terms from the 1960s onwards. Although her synthesis of liberal institutionalist and marxist-derived political economy is historically grounded, it continues to rest on the assumption that the rise of the East is effectively similar to the rise of the West. And to the extent that many of the marxist-derived political economy approaches which emerged in the 1980s continue to subscribe to a relatively unilinear conception of history, they work in complicity with Anglo-American liberalism. Although marxists challenge the privileging of free trade and the evolutionary conception of historical change, they remain part of an approach which stretches back to Marx's own work and presumes that the bourgeoisie is battering down the 'Chinese walls', compelling 'all nations' to embrace the 'bourgeois mode of production', and creating 'a world after its own image'.[13] Most marxist discourses, like liberalism, remain based on a 'universalizing narrative' about the rational progression of world history.[14] Of course, an increasing number of observers writing about Asia allow for a limited number of alternative paths to capitalist modernity, but a great deal of avowedly marxist and liberal work continues to evaluate capitalist development in East and Southeast Asia (and beyond) in terms of its apparent success or failure to follow idealized North American or West European paths to modernity.[15]

While the dominant Anglo-American discourses on modernization continue to assume that capitalism follows, or ought to follow, a relatively unilinear path to modernity, and relegate culture and cultural difference to the dustbin of history, there are also a growing number of North American, West European and Australian approaches which rest on deterministic cultural/racial explanations. At the turn of the century, Max Weber himself, along with many others, represented Confucianism as the key to China's historic decline and economic 'backwardness'.[16] By the 1950s the success of communist revolution in China, and the incipient communist revolt in Vietnam, ensured that Confucianism was deployed in some cases to explain the region's susceptibility to communism. By the late 1970s, however, some of the communist regimes of the region had already begun to orchestrate a return to capitalism, while the capitalist dynamism of South Korea, Taiwan, Singapore and Hong Kong was beginning to attract attention. Writing in the early 1980s Roy Hofheinz and Kent Calder attached considerable importance to the Confucian legacy in relation to East Asian industrialization. They pointed to Lee Kuan Yew as a 'quint-essential Confucian leader', they linked high saving rates and hard work, as well as the docility of the workforce, to Confucianism, arguing that the people of East Asia 'tend to prefer compromise rather than confrontation, and the work-place is an arena for cooperation in the process of growth not for conflict over the spoils'.[17] The importance of Confucianism now pervades the dominant North American, West European and Australian discourses on the rise of the East.[18]

The deterministic Anglo-American celebrations of Confucianism, and fixed cultural/racial explanations for the rise of the East more generally, have been characterized as the 'new Orientalism'.[19] The new Orientalism, as the term is used here, includes the continued stereotyping and caricatur-ing of East Asians in movies and on television, and is centred on, but cannot be reduced to, North American-based discourses which have his-torically imagined Northeast and Southeast Asia as the US frontier. The new Orientalism is, in effect, the flip-side of the Orientalism of the West European and US colonial period. In an earlier era, the perceived back-wardness and general failure of much of Asia to progress was attributed to inherent cultural and racial shortcomings. While the new Orientalism also falls back on essentialist cultural/racial categories, they are now deployed to explain the dynamic (and threatening) character of the rise of the East. While the new Orientalism bears the traces of the old Orientalism it now seeks to explain strength and power (success), while the latter sought to explain weakness (failure). Furthermore the new Orientalism draws on the increasingly important process of self-Orientalizing which is characteristic of East Asian triumphalism insofar as the explanations for Asian success offered by Asian leaders are readily domesticated to both the admiring and the fearful Western narratives. The new Orientalism is clearly linked to the powerful images of Japan as a threat to the West which had gained influence by the 1980s, and meshes with long-standing but fluctuating North American, West European and Australian discourses on the Yellow Peril which centre on China and/or Japan. The continuing influence of this trend was reflected in the cinematic and publishing success of Michael Crichton's *Rising Sun* and the high-profile debate about Samuel Huntington's 'Clash of Civilizations?'.[20] It is also apparent in a recent best-selling novel by the celebrated North American novelist Tom Clancy, which describes how a US–Japanese trade war escalates into a 'real' war in which a nuclear-armed Japan (with the support of China and India) sets out to cripple the USA financially and militarily, at the same time as it prepares to embark on the conquest of resource-rich Siberia.[21] The image of Japan (allied with India and China) as an undifferentiated Oriental threat to the USA and the West – which in Clancy's narrative (re)incorporates Russia – is made somewhat problematic by the way his book portrays the Japanese government as having been hijacked by a handful of powerful *zaibatsu* and military men who had not forgotten their crushing defeat at US hands in 1945. However, in an interview in 1994, Clancy registered a more straightforward Yellow Peril perspective, arguing that 'the Japanese think we are fools' and they 'still believe the master-race thing'. In his view, the USA 'pounded that out of the Germans, but not out of the Japanese' and '[t]hey still think they are the elected of God or Buddha or whatever. They just think they are better than everyone else'.[22]

## UNDER EASTERN EYES

In the context of the dramatic transformation of the global political economy, the new Orientalism and the Yellow Peril perspective, articulated by writers such as Tom Clancy, complement more than they conflict with an increasingly powerful series of discourses, which rest on the assumption that the roots of Eastern success lie not in the emulation of North America and Western Europe, but in the historic institutions and values of East Asia. Most strands of these triumphalist East Asian narratives assign a dubious homogeneity to the East and increasingly offer up an East Asian model to be emulated by the declining West and the rest of the world. East Asian discourses on the rise of the East, which emanate from a growing number of sources, often represent Japan as the historic leader in the region. And the emergence of a new 'Greater East Asia Co-Prosperity Sphere' centred on Japan continues to be either a goal or a concern for regional elites. Both the enthusiasm, as articulated most markedly by the Malaysian elite, and the concern, voiced by power-holders in countries such as China and South Korea, are reinforced by those Japanese commentators, such as Ishihara Shintaro, who view the rise of the Japanese state and Japan-based companies as a process which will 'liberate' the people of Asia from Anglo-American dominance.[23] For many people in Northeast and Southeast Asia the resonance between such pronouncements and the powerful culturally and racially based discourses which (like their European and US counterparts) buttressed Japan's formal and informal conquest of its neighbours and culminated in the Pacific War (1937–1945) remains a matter of some concern.

While Japan's dramatic economic rebirth after 1945 was not based on Japanese colonial and military power, the post-war economic miracle has clearly contributed to the resurgence of a variety of culturally and racially based explanations which are grounded in the pre-1945 period and have worked to legitimate the Japanese Miracle and Japan's historic role in the region. By the 1980s, with the rise of South Korea, Taiwan, Hong Kong and Singapore, the Confucian origins of Japan's success began to enjoy greater emphasis in Japan and the region (as we have seen above, this was also taken up in North America and beyond), although narrower cultural/ racial explanations for Japan's success have continued to flourish.[24] Michio Morishima's well-known book is a good example of an approach which emphasizes Japan's success as part of the wider Confucian heritage of East Asia.[25] More generally, writers such as Hung-chao Tai have argued that the 'cultural setting' of Japan and the East Asian NICs has given rise to what he describes as an 'Oriental' economic development model, which rests on 'human emotional bonds, group orientation, and harmony'. He contrasted this with the 'Western model of development' based on rationality, 'efficiency, individualism and dynamism'. At the same time, Hung-chao Tai emphasized that his 'Oriental model' was not culturally deterministic insofar as he viewed 'cultural factors' as 'necessary, but not sufficient, conditions for the shaping of a nation's economic future'. Hung-chao Tai also held the 'Oriental model' out to the rest of the world as the first 'meaningful alternative' to the Western model. He argued that although a number of 'developing countries' are plagued by 'cultural cleavages and social schisms', and did not have as 'long' and 'coherent' a 'cultural tradition' as East Asia, the 'Oriental alternative' was relevant because it sought to bring about 'economic growth' by 'emphasizing the union of these divisions rather than an intensification of them, which a competitive, individualistic, rational model of development may bring about'.[26] Such a model, despite the author's qualifications, is deterministic and homogenizing. And it is clearly linked to wider cultural/ racial discourses on the rise of the East which work to naturalize the authoritarian institutional and social relations of the East Asian Miracle.

The deployment of Confucianism and the 'Oriental Alternative' as the key to Japanese and East Asian industrial success has now become widespread, in the context of a trend in which Japanese and East Asian leaders continue to offer cultural or racial explanations for the rise of the East. But, despite Japan's special position in the dynamic changes that have swept East Asia, Washington's continued role as the guarantor of Japanese security has meant that most Japanese political leaders and intellectuals have remained relatively circumspect in the international arena regarding the cause and significance of the resurgence of Japan and the rise of East Asia more generally. It was possible for Meredith Woo-Cumings to write in 1991 that '[n]o one stands for (North) East Asia today and voices a distinctive regional perspective; rather its leaders tend to prefer a weak posture'. In her view, Mao Tse-tung (who died in 1976) was the most recent political theorist who had an international reputation as a spokesperson for the region. She argued that the 'East Asian response is reactive' and apart from infrequent conservative pronouncements from members of the Japanese elite (Ishihara Shintaro being one of the better known), East Asian leaders had a tendency towards restraint because the governments, and political and economic elites, of Japan, South Korea, Taiwan and China were still 'rule-takers' rather than 'rule-makers' in the international arena. In her view, Anglo-American liberalism was '*the* hegemonic discourse with nothing else challenging it in the international realm'.[27]

Since the beginning of the 1990s, however, increasingly influential Japanese voices have emerged seeking to speak for East Asia and/or to counter the dominant economic and political liberalism of North America, Western Europe and Australia (the West). For example, Sakakibara Eisuke, a senior official in the Japanese Finance Ministry, has emerged as a relatively outspoken advocate of the Japanese model. Fluent in English, Sakakibara rejects the more traditional forms of Japanese nationalism as vague and mystical at the same time as he expresses a determination to protect what he thinks is distinctively Japanese from the West. Furthermore, in his recent book *Beyond Capitalism*, he sees the 'Japanese Model' as being 'of great educational value for future economic development in areas such as Latin America, South-East Asia and Africa'. He argues that Japan is a 'non-capitalist market economy' insofar as companies compete in the market; however, they do not privilege profit over everything else and shareholders have virtually no power. From his perspective Japanese companies put people before profits, keeping loyal employees on the payroll even if there is an economic downturn, while the government works to protect industry even at the expense of wider questions of economic efficiency. Sakakibara, who is also involved with a new study group of Japanese politicians, academics and business leaders, holds the Japanese model up in sharp contrast to the US model and warns that if Japan went down the North American road the result would be 'a wider gap in income distribution, rampant money worship and the vulgarization of culture'.[28] The work of the Japanese development economist, Yoshihara Kunio, provides another example of this kind of approach. In the latest edition of his now standard work on the economic development of Japan he stresses the role of Confucianism, particularly its emphasis on loyalty and filial piety. Yoshihara argues that Confucianism was important in the Japanese case in the same way that Protestantism dynamized the rise of the West. He also argues that the best way to hasten economic development is through the intervention of the government or a developmental state which educates the people and initiates a dynamic private sector.[29] This interpretation reflects the wider Japan-centred discourses on the superiority of a Japanese and/or an East Asian model based on a developmental state which commands obedience and loyalty from the population over which it presides.

Interestingly, the loudest voices emphasizing both the superiority of the East, and the possible relevance of an East Asian model as a solution to the economic and social ills of the rest of the world appear to be coming from Southeast Asia, especially Singapore and Malaysia. Ironically, this may be a partial result of the fact that English remains an important language in these former British colonies which means that the views of politicians and intellectuals are more easily projected to the international media which are still dominated by English. Furthermore, the multiethnic character of these former colonies has meant that ruling elites have been attracted to political strategies based on appeals to Asian unity *vis-à-vis* the West. The new strength of these elite voices was apparent in the lead up to the Vienna Human Rights Conference held on 14–25 June 1993.[30] Prior to the conference a growing number of Asian leaders were already expressing dissatisfaction with prevailing Western conceptions of human rights, arguing in favour of particularly Asian notions of human rights. A central criticism has been that ideas of human rights based on the individual are Western and therefore irrelevant to Asia where individual rights are secondary to the community and the wider society. This distinction is often drawn by Singaporean leaders such as Lee Kuan Yew and Goh Chok Tong.[31] While the explanation for, and the lessons of, the rise of the East articulated by Lee Kuan Yew and the Singaporean elite are often expansive and vague in both spatial and temporal terms, they flow out of Singapore's particular historical circumstances. The colonial division of labour and the highly racialized social formation which grew up under British rule laid the foundations for race and ethnicity to serve as key social markers in the post-colonial period. Since the late 1950s the People's Action Party (PAP), under Lee Kuan Yew, has built a strong state aimed at a high level of political and social control, at the same time as it has provided rising living standards and dramatic economic growth. As the Singaporean state, under the PAP, embarked on an economic development programme, based after 1965 around export-oriented industrialization (EOI), it developed and extended its institutional power and emerged as a key element in the shaping of national identity and ethnic consciousness. In this context, the notion of Asian values has increasingly been deployed by Lee Kuan Yew and the Singaporean elite to legitimate and maintain the power of the PAP state and generate unity among a multiethnic population.

By the 1970s the PAP was pointing to the West with ever more frequency as the source of political unrest and social decay in the city-state. In his speech on National Day in 1978, Lee Kuan Yew argued that Singapore had, in effect, 'already been infected' by the West and the 'antidote' was the 'strong assertion of the Asian values common to all Singapore's ethnic groups, stressing the virtues of individual subordination to the community so as to counteract the disruptive individualism of western liberalism'. In the 1980s the elite increasingly represented Singapore as the embodiment of the communitarian, organic and corporatist social order which was believed to have underpinned the political stability and economic development of the other Asian NICs and Japan. Clearly demonstrating the complementary relationship between cultural/racial explanations for the rise of the East derived from Anglo-American discourses and East Asian-centred narratives, Lee Kuan Yew and Goh Chok Tong have both referred directly to a book edited by George Lodge and Ezra Vogel entitled *Ideology and National Competitiveness* in which a neo-Confucian developmental state is held up as the key to the rise of the East. This was complemented by the concerted promotion of Confucian values and the Mandarin language via the school curriculum and advertising campaigns. Chineseness was represented as a way of life which rested on Confucianism and Mandarin, and which emphasized the values of obedience to authority, discipline and community. From this perspective Confucianism was not linked particularly with China, but with the dynamic social formations of Japan, Taiwan and Korea. At the same time, this made it possible to represent Confucianism as the key element of a wider Asian culture. In late 1988 Goh Chok Tong proposed that the 'Asian values common to' all the ethnic groups of Singapore should be 'specified in a National Ideology' which would 'help Singaporeans keep their Asian bearings as they approach the 21st century'.[32]

With the end of the Cold War the Singaporean elite has gained a higher regional and international profile for its continued emphasis on Confucianism and Asian values. In the post-Cold War era, Asian values and related formulations are repeatedly deployed to generate unity among disparate ethnic groupings and loyalty to the state in Singapore and elsewhere. In particular, ideas about the necessity of putting the community before the individual, and fixed cultural/racial conceptions of Asia *vis-à-vis* the West, continue to be key aspects of the dominant narrative. For example, Lee Kuan Yew has emphasized on more than one occasion that the key to Singapore's success lies in the way its people 'used the family to push economic growth'. From his perspective, Singapore was 'fortunate' because it 'had this cultural backdrop, the belief in thrift, hard work, filial piety and loyalty in the extended family, and most of all, the respect for scholarship and learning'. At the same time his explanation for Singapore's continuing success is very quickly extrapolated to East Asia as a whole and he emphasizes that 'Eastern societies believe that the individual exists in the context of his family'.[33] The Singaporean leader also links this to Confucianism and has argued that a 'Confucianist view of order between subject and ruler' actually facilitates 'the rapid transformation of society' because 'you fit yourself into society – the exact opposite of the American rights of the individual'.[34] Interestingly, in late 1994, Lee Kuan Yew became honorary chairman of the International Confucius Association set up by the Chinese government. In their pursuit of market socialism, and the need to legitimate the Chinese state's dominant role in Chinese life, the CCP has also recently discovered Confucius. In October 1994, at the time of the 2545th anniversary of the sage's birth, the Chinese government held the inaugural meeting of the International Confucius Association (ICA), attended by scholars from the USA, Western Europe, and East and Southeast Asia. In an opening speech, Gu Mu, a one-time high-ranking party and government official, and now head of the ICA, argued that while China had benefited from Confucianism, it was also possible for the West to benefit. An article in *The People's Daily* emphasized that Confucianism had played an important role in the modernization of East Asia, and that it represented a solution to Western problems 'because it is a non-religious humanism that can provide a basis for morals and the value of life'. The article concluded that a culture based on Confucianism and science 'better suits the future era' and 'it will thrive particularly well in the next century and will replace modern and contemporary Western culture'.[35] In China, as in Singapore, the West is more than ever represented as decadent and caught up in a process of 'massive social decay'.[36] Of course not all China-centred triumphalism flows from China itself. The renewed use of the concept of 'Greater China' is more common in Taiwan, and throughout the Chinese diaspora, as well as in North America, than in China proper.[37]

East Asian triumphalism is clearly not monolithic and the causes of the rise of the East, and what constitutes Asian values, are contested from below, and within and between elite groupings. For example, the Malaysian Prime Minister Mahathir Mohamad's reading of the rise of the East and his vision of the future is often at odds with the more Chinese-Confucian orientation centred on Singapore and China. Of course, his vision is even more at odds with the Anglo-American visions being conjured with by the Australian and US governments.[38] At the end of 1990 he sought explicitly to counter the APEC initiative with a proposal that Japan and other East Asian countries form an East Asian Economic Group (EAEG) which would exclude the USA, Canada, Australia and New Zealand, as well as countries such as Mexico and Chile which are all members of APEC. (The EAEG has not come into being, but Mahathir has succeeded in having an East Asian Economic Caucus – EAEC – established within APEC.) Mahathir's vision of an exclusive Asia is linked to both domestic political contingencies and current regional trends, and rests on fixed racial categories which flow from the highly racialized politics of both the colonial and post-colonial era. The importance of fixed cultural/racial categories, which reflect the highly racialized politics of both the colonial and post-colonial era, was foreshadowed in his early political testament. *The Malay Dilemma*, which Mahathir authored in the late 1960s – while he was cooling his heels in the political background following his expulsion from the United Malays National Organization (UMNO) for publicly criticizing the leadership of Tunku Abdul Rahman – is replete with theories of genetic inbreeding and the use of reductionist cultural/ racial explanations for the subordinate educational and employment position of Malays in the country at that time.[39] From the moment he became Prime Minister, if not before, Mahathir has articulated a highly racialized anti-Western position which is grounded in an explicitly racial conception of national and international power relations. In this context Mahathir has increasingly positioned himself as the voice, not just of Malaysia, but of Asia. Mahathir's approach comes at a time when the memories of the colonial era are still relatively fresh, while the role of

Britain and the USA during the Cold War is littered with arrogant and racist incidents. Against this backdrop the leader of a political party which has held power in Malaysia without interruption for almost forty years (and who has personally been Prime Minister for a decade and a half) has been able to represent himself successfully as a revolutionary nationalist fighting against Western imperialism and racism. At the same time, his growing pan-Asianism, centred on Japan, rests on explicitly racialized conceptions of Asia and Asians which reinforce and mesh with wider cultural/racial explanations for the rise of the East.

Mahathir's effort to encourage a regional economic bloc, the EAEC centred on Japan, flows out of this racialized agenda, at the same time as it is grounded in the exigencies of Malaysian industrialization since about 1980 in which the Japanese state and Japanese capital have played a key role. At the end of 1980, while still Malaysia's Minister of Trade and Industry, Mahathir laid down what became known as Malaysia's 'Look East' policy which dramatically reoriented Malaysia's political economy towards using state-run enterprises to spearhead the diversification of the country's domestic industrial base by embarking on a range of import-substitution and capital-intensive industries which would complement private sector consumer and capital goods industries. Mahathir's shift made explicit reference to Japan and South Korea as models for Malaysia. Since the second half of the 1980s there have been significant increases in Japanese and East Asian investment flows into Malaysia, as well as Indonesia and Thailand, driven by the improved investment climate in Southeast Asia and a range of push factors linked to the rising cost of production in Northeast Asia, and the wider trend towards globalization. It was probably the decline of the value of the dollar in relation to the yen in particular, as a result of the Plaza Accord of 1985, which resulted in the dramatic increase in Japanese corporate investment southward. Before 1985 Japanese foreign direct investment (FDI) to the member countries of ASEAN totalled around US$900 million a year. By 1989 the figure was US$6.4 billion and a total of US$15 billion between 1988 and 1991.[40]

Against this background Mahathir declined to attend the APEC summit in Seattle in late 1993.[41] While Mahathir did attend the annual APEC conference in Bogor, Indonesia, in mid-November 1994, he spent some time prior to the conference in Japan seeking to convert the Japanese to his EAEC as an alternative to APEC. (He also attended the November 1995 APEC meeting in Osaka, Japan, but, like many other leaders, after the now ritual commitment to free trade within the region by 2010 for developed countries and 2020 for developing countries had been made, he was quick to qualify his government's support for this goal.) In 1994, prior to his visit to Japan he told the visiting Japanese Prime Minister that Japan ought to stop apologizing for its role in World War II and get on with business. This gesture was not sufficient to endear Mahathir's plan to the Japanese government, although, undeterred, Mahathir has been attempting to sell his message on Japanese television and in the print media. His biography appeared in Japanese in 1994 and he has also reached out to conservative forces in Japan by co-authoring a book in Japanese with Ishihara Shintaro, which also first appeared in 1994. The Japanese title is generally translated as 'The Asia That Can Say No: A Policy to Combat Europe and America'; however, the English-language version, which was published in 1995, is more diplomatically entitled *The Voice of Asia: Two Leaders Discuss the Coming Century*, although the actual content appears to be as unrestrained as the earlier Japanese edition.[42] Of course Ishihara is well known for an earlier book, *The Japan That Can Say No*, which came out in 1991. Ishihara's understanding of US–Japan relations, and international political economy more generally, rests on racial categories which see the US as a 'Caucasian' power and the friction between the USA and Japan as flowing primarily from the way in which 'racist attitudes are deeply entrenched in the Caucasian psyche' and 'no matter how much non-whites object, Westerners will not soon shed their prejudices'. At the same time he simplistically attributed South Korea and Taiwan's post-1945 success, and the economic failure of the Philippines, to their respective colonizers, implying Japanese cultural/racial superiority. Apart from sharing Mahathir's view of history as a struggle between races, Ishihara's earlier book also foreshadowed the Malaysian Prime Minister's concern to establish an EAEC insofar as he noted that Japan 'must be part of Asia's future' because 'as the Age of the Pacific dawns, the region will be even more vital to Japan's maturity than the United States' and Japan 'must, when matters of crucial national interest warrant, articulate our position and say no to the United States'.[43]

In his new book with Mahathir, Ishihara Shintaro emphasizes that 'Asia has a diverse and old civilization and culture in contrast to a much shorter one in the United States' and that 'it may be necessary' for Asian states to form 'an anti-American Asian front on the issue of values'.[44] Ishihara argues that the Japanese government should identify itself more with Asia and speak up more for the region even if that involves conflict with the USA and Western Europe. He rests this on the argument that 'Japan is an Asian country of Asian people with Asian blood' and '[i]t ought to realize that it exists for Asia rather than for America'.[45] In his section of the book Mahathir emphasizes that the region and the world are at a turning point. He is dismissive of Western decadence and argues that 'it is possible for Asia to create a cultural region of unmatched historical greatness. What is important is that we consciously strive to maintain our value systems. If we do so, we will never come under European domination again.'[46] Mahathir argues that '[t]he West would do well to learn from the success of East Asia and to some extent Easternize. It should accept our values, not the other way around.' From his perspective, 'Asians' permitted themselves 'to be overtaken by the West', failing 'to maintain and develop the achievements' of their 'forebears'. He concludes that '[n]ow,

Asia is awakening to a new era, and there is no reason we cannot regain our former glory. If we preserve our distinctive values and cultures as we master modern technology, I am convinced Asia will again be great.'[47] Mahathir and Ishihara's views have been represented as enjoying wide, although not necessarily deep, appeal among the general population in Japan. At the same time the 'Asia-first' approach emphasized by Mahathir continues to mesh with the views of other, more influential, members of the Japanese elite than Ishihara (who recently resigned from his seat in Parliament). Japan's Ministry of International Trade and Industry (MITI) has plans to establish a new position of director-general for Asian affairs, while the Tokyo-based Asia Pacific Club, which includes former Prime Minister Takeshita Noboru, has entertained the idea of an Asia-centred policy as articulated by Mahathir. This emphasis is also popular at the Asia Bureau of the Foreign Ministry. But other sections of the Japanese bureaucracy are more ambivalent and members of the Japanese elite are well aware that the USA still provides the military basis for Japan's economic power, while Japanese-based industry and finance have important interests in North America and Western Europe, well outside the boundaries of Mahathir's proposed EAEC.[48] Furthermore, Mahathir's enthusiasm for an East Asian Economic Group led by Japan has little appeal in South Korea or China (as well as a number of other countries in the region) where attitudes towards Japan are far more ambivalent.

## HYBRID HISTORIES

Nevertheless, as Mahathir and Ishihara demonstrate, the dominant discourses on Asia continue to rest on a powerful and very sharp distinction between East and West, which easily shades into fixed cultural/racial categories, overlooking the hybridity of the history of the region. Significantly, the term 'hybrid' first gained currency in late nineteenth-century Europe as a biological or physiological term for the offspring of parents of different 'races'. While the deployment of the concept of hybridity serves to criticize fixed conceptions of culture and ethnicity, given its own history, its very use also draws attention to the continued power of racist categories and racialized political discourses in ordering knowledge about the rise of the East and political and social change more generally.[49] While East Asian triumphalism rests on fixed cultural or racial conceptions of the East, as distinct from the West, Anglo-American discourses on Asia also continue to rely on a sharp distinction between East and West, which meshes with the culturally and racially determined understandings of historical change which flow from East Asia. Ironically, the continued power of the East–West binary, which assumes an incommensurability between East and West, means that Asian and Western observers actually agree on at least one fundamental point. Both the East Asian and Western discourses reinforce and reproduce Orientalist and Occidentalist conceptions of the world.[50]

In a wider sense, as already noted above, contemporary East Asian discourses are also linked in important ways to Orientalist discourses which took shape in the colonial period and complemented Western hegemony in much of the region prior to at least World War II. Orientalist discourses have usually involved a greater or lesser degree of complicity and involvement on the part of local and regional elites. Orientalist modes of conceptualization were effectively transferred and domesticated in the context of the wider process of colonial rule, anti-colonialism and the rise of nationalism in Asia. It can be argued that even in what became modern Thailand and Japan, which did not experience formal colonial rule by Europe or the USA, avoidance of colonial rule flowed in part from the successful appropriation and domestication of the technological, bureaucratic and intellectual frameworks and practices which flowed out of the earlier industrialization and colonial expansion of Western Europe and the United States. The Orientalist discourses which emerged as a complement to colonial rule in many parts of Asia have now been thoroughly indigenized, and as the global balance of power shifts eastward, the region's elites increasingly turn to the East–West dichotomy as a way of mobilizing domestic and regional support. The historical power of the East–West dichotomy, and the fixed conceptions of culture/race to which it is linked, have increasingly allowed the national elites of the region to speak not only for their 'nations', but even for Asia and Asians.

Furthermore, East Asian elites have also been anointed by North American, West European and Australian politicians and intellectuals as the authentic voices of Asia. Self-styled 'Westerners' have often uncritically privileged elite voices in an effort to display cultural sensitivity. Assertions about the inappropriateness of so-called Western concepts by powerful voices in Asia have met with support from North American, West European and Australian politicians, diplomats, business people and academics. There are numerous instances of Western scholars, intent on challenging North American and/or West European hegemony in both material and discursive terms, ending up uncritically privileging the elite narratives of power-holders in Asia as authentic representatives of a particular non-Western nation or social formation (and also contributing to the continued use of the East–West dichotomy). This problem is apparent in an article by Arif Dirlik, in which he argues that the 'Confucian revival' can be seen 'as an anti-hegemonic cultural movement that seeks to stamp upon the Pacific region the ideology of its East Asian protagonists'. Dirlik notes that the proponents of the Confucian revival 'seek to articulate it to a managerial capitalism at which East Asian societies have been remarkably successful'. Although the Confucian revival does not question the region's capitalist structure it is 'anti-hegemonic', from Dirlik's perspective, because it seeks to 'assert an East Asian identity' in the Asia-Pacific.

According to Dirlik, this may be why 'it has had more appeal among managers of capitalism in North America than among the peripheral societies of the Pacific region (whether of Latin America, the Pacific Islands or Southeast Asia) whose cultural characteristics it marginalizes'.[51] This qualification is important, and suggests that what Dirlik has identified as a counter-hegemonic discourse has already become a hegemonic discourse. The counter-hegemonic aspect of East Asian triumphalism is only apparent at the broadest international level (it is an elite narrative or series of narratives that counters the visions of the national elites of North America, Western Europe and Australia) and such an attribution clearly privileges elite discourses on the rise of the East. At this juncture East Asian triumphalist discourses, drawing on and reproducing Orientalist and racialized conceptions of Asia, still have more to do with the maintenance of hegemony within the region than they do with the projection of power beyond the region. And, as long as the USA remains a key military power in the Asia-Pacific and beyond, and North America continues to provide the institutional and cultural basis for the preponderance of Anglo-American concepts and ideas in regional and international relations, this will continue to be the case.

Nevertheless the discursive power of the East continues to grow and the world is in the midst of the altering of a long-standing international socio-cultural hierarchy, linked to a historical political economy, which conferred particular privileges on and assigned particular agency to Occidentals. A good example of this shift, and of the continued power of fixed conceptions of culture/race, was provided by the disturbingly influential *The Bell Curve: Intelligence and Class Structure in American Life*, which was published in 1994 in the USA.[52] While active white supremacists are in a minority in most parts of North America, Europe and Australia, the perspective on race articulated by Richard Herrnstein and Charles Murray's book is not as far removed from wider popular discourses on race and culture as liberal elites sometimes presume. Beneath a liberal veneer, explicitly fixed conceptions of cultural/racial hierarchy retain much of their potency, in North America, Australia and elsewhere. Although *The Bell Curve* was widely criticized, the fact that it was at the centre of a national (and international) debate and that its scientific claims were defended and/or had to be taken seriously makes clear that fixed and biological conceptions of race continue to have considerable power. What is particularly relevant to the discussion here is that, while the debate about Herrnstein and Murray's work focused on the authors' contention that African-Americans' lower IQ scores are fundamentally genetic, a less debated theme of the book clearly reflected a biological understanding of the East Asian Miracle and pointed to the historic re-ordering of the international socio-cultural hierarchy which has been a concomitant of the rise of East Asia. The authors argued that East Asians, on average, have higher IQs than whites. Interestingly, however, their idea that East Asians are more intelligent than other races rests almost entirely on the work of Richard Lynn.[53] The thrust of Lynn's analysis is drawn out nicely in a letter by him to *The New York Review of Books*, which had earlier published a particularly good critique of *The Bell Curve*. Lynn argued that his 'work on the intelligence of the Oriental peoples has shown that their average IQ is about 5 IQ points higher than that of whites in the United States and Europe'. He emphasized that he had 'published and summarised 25 studies which all point to this con-clusion'.[54] While this may be an extreme position, it highlights the con-tinued importance of fixed conceptions of culture/race in relation to the resurgence of racialized politics in the Asia-Pacific and many other parts of the world.

Despite both the resurgence of racialized politics and the emergence of triumphalist East Asian discourses which also rapidly shade into fixed racial conceptions of Asian superiority, the vision of a prosperous Pacific Century informed by, though no longer centred on, Anglo-American-style economic and political liberalism, continues to exercise considerable influ-ence on both sides of the Asia-Pacific. For example, George Yeo, a senior minister in the Singaporean government, has argued that 'the new Greater East Asia Co-Prosperity Sphere requires a common East Asian conscious-ness as its cultural foundation'. However, he also emphasized that the role of the United States was 'critical because an East Asian consciousness without the softening effect of Western liberal ideas will not gel'. He concluded that '[s]uch an inclusive East Asian consciousness will naturally welcome the participation of the West'. From his perspective, 'for world peace, East and West must each have the other at its core'.[55] Yeo's article and the work of a number of other writers, such as the latest book by John Naisbitt, much of which appears to have been written during an eighteen-month fellowship at the Institute of Strategic and International Studies in Kuala Lumpur, reflect the domestication of a historically power-ful Anglo-American liberalism to the cultural/racial triumphalism of East Asia, in the context of elite efforts to manage the process of capitalist industrialization in the Asia-Pacific. According to Naisbitt, '[a] new network of nations based on economic symbiosis is emerging: the Asian network'. It is founded, he says, on a 'spirit of working together for mutual economic gain' and a new Asian consciousness, the 'catalyst' for which 'is the free market'. He goes on to argue that '[t]he modernization of Asia must not be thought of as the Westernization of Asia, but the modernization of Asia in the "Asian Way"'. He warns that the 'West needs the East a lot more than the East needs the West'.[56] As the com-ments by Yeo and Naisbitt suggest, the triumphalist East Asian narratives of capitalist success, which are constructed and deployed as Asian, are produced within a wider framework which ensures that efforts to generate what Arif Dirlik calls 'alternative values to those of EuroAmerican origin' are already contaminated by the historic power of Anglo-American liberalism. From this perspective, the rise of the East does not represent the triumph of Eastern values, but the successful 'articulation' of East Asian cultures 'into a capitalist narrative'. What is taking place in East Asia is the 'successful globalization of capital' or 'the "deterritorialization" of capital from its EuroAmerican roots'.[57]


## THE NEW DYSTOPIA

A common element of these elite visions of a regional or universal capitalist modernity, regardless of their cultural/racial inclusiveness or exclusiveness, is their tendency to overlook the historically disruptive effects of uneven capitalist development. This is an obvious point (which is also widely overlooked) and it can be argued that, despite the proliferation of elite visions of a prosperous Pacific Century, the current post-Cold War trend towards globalization points to dystopia rather than utopia, to fragmentation rather than unity. For example, Arjun Appadurai has argued that the 'new' global political economy and socio-cultural order have 'to be seen as a complex, overlapping disjunctive order' of 'disorganized capitalism'. He notes that the end of the Cold War has highlighted that the USA was never an omnipotent master of the capitalist universe leading the capitalist world to prosperity and peace. He draws attention to the way in which a variety of 'forces' which flow from particular centres of power are rapidly 'indigenized' and the influence of the US and of Anglo-American forms of capitalist modernization was, and is, of less concern to many people than the power of more localized elites.[58] Nevertheless, during the Cold War the burgeoning US national security state and US-based corporations played a major role in the overall dynamics of post-1945 international political economy and socio-cultural change. And the post-Cold War era continues to be shaped, but not determined, in important ways, by a transitional type of Anglo-American capitalism which remains grounded in the politico-military power of the United States of America. However, it must be emphasized that even at its height US power was not a homogenizing force and, in the context of the rise of the East and the end of the Cold War, the new era of global capitalism represents an even less stable situation than the configuration of regional and international power associated with the heyday of Pax Americana.[59] However, if the contemporary Asia-Pacific has a key nexus of power, it is not so much the USA as the US–Japan relationship – a complicated web of economic rivalry and interdependence overlaid by Japan's military dependence on the USA – which is crucial to the wider network of regional economic linkages and political alliances. (Of increasing importance to this equation is, of course, the politico-military power of the Chinese state which flows from the dramatic industrialization since 1980 or 1985.)

The US–Japan relationship is linked to a central trend of the wider globalization process: the rise of TNCs. They have been the main beneficiaries, and in one sense the very product, of the post-World War II global politico-economic order. By the 1970s the trend towards privatization, capital market liberalization and the growing openness of the global economy precipitated a dramatic growth in both trade and foreign investment and in increasingly complicated structures of corporate ownership, cooperation and competition. By 1980 US-based companies and financial institutions still dominated FDI flows, but as FDI increased dramatically in the 1980s, EU FDI flows equalled those from US-based sources by 1989, and Japan-based FDI flows are expected to equal EU and US flows soon.[60] Apart from Japan, large companies based in Taiwan, South Korea, Mexico, India, the Middle East, along with numerous smaller corporations, have increasingly shifted towards the transnationalization of their activities. This has meant that efforts to identify a particular corporation with a specific nation are becoming increasingly problematic. The complex and interlocking array of multinational investments, ownership patterns, distribution networks and information flows which characterizes the global economy of the late twentieth century has ensured that what were once multi*national* corporations are increasingly *trans*national corporations in every sense of the word. Although the two terms are often used as synonyms, a distinction between them serves to highlight an important characteristic of globalization. The difference between MNCs and TNCs lies in the way that an MNC is primarily based in the territory of one nation at the same time as it operates within the territory of many others. The senior personnel of multinational corporations are generally passport holders of the country from which the company originates and while corporate loyalty is becoming more autonomous, an MNC is still seen to be identified with a particular nation. A transnational corporation, however, is one which is not linked to, and has no originating base in, any particular nation. It is even more mobile. At the same time, it is impossible to make a definite distinction between MNCs and TNCs insofar as the nationality or lack of nationality of a particular corporation is notoriously slippery to determine. Certainly companies such as Asea Brown Bovari (ABB), which originated in Sweden, appear no longer to have a national identity or a national centre of gravity. Yaohan, which originated as a Japanese grocery chain, shifted its centre of operations to Brazil and then Hong Kong, driven in part by a desire to avoid Japanese corporate tax. From its Hong Kong base Yaohan has its eye on the fabled China market. At the same time, the company continues to be organized around the teachings of the Seicho-no-ie Temple, which it claims is the source of its commercial prowess and which its management forcefully recommends to its employees despite some stiff resistance.[61]

In the context of the rise of TNCs and the wider trend towards globalization, states in the Asia-Pacific and elsewhere are emerging as major facilitators of regionalization and/or globalization. They have been drawn into service by interlocking national and transnational elite configurations. In Asia, Africa, Latin America and the Middle East certain sectors of the elite, with privileged access to state power, are turning their backs on the nation and are increasingly oriented offshore, where they open bank accounts, set up companies, invest in real estate, maintain business links, and send their children to school and university. A growing number of states and national elites are participating in a dramatic process of reconfiguration 'from above' as the myriad forces of globalization spread and deepen. At the same time, although political disillusionment is widespread there is renewed potential for conflict and resistance 'from below' in many parts of the world. In East Asia, China is often pointed to as a potential site of growing internal conflict as the Chinese state is buffeted by the growing power of its coastal regions and the dissatisfaction of people who have been left behind by uneven capitalist development. Connected to this trend is the potential for conflict between the Chinese state and its neighbours, while globalization has also resulted in the potential reconfiguration of territorial states into regional economic and even political blocs centred on East Asia, North America and Western Europe. The solidification of exclusive and competing regional blocs and their marked difference in terms of internal coherence and power could result in greater international and/or inter-regional conflict. While the basis for regional politico-economic and socio-cultural blocs in Europe and the Americas may be in place, the emergence of an exclusive East Asian-centred politico-economic and socio-cultural bloc is mitigated, in the short to medium term, by the continued importance of the North American market to the East Asian economies. Furthermore, apart from Mahathir's EAEG, which as yet Japan appears neither to support nor discourage, there is nothing to rival APEC which is ostensibly aimed at avoiding regional politico-economic blocs. The emergence of APEC is indicative of the post-Cold War transition to a weakened form of Anglo-American-style economic liberalism, which is still grounded in US politico-military power, and represents an effort on the part of Asia-Pacific elites to manage the post-Cold War political economy in a direction commensurate with the interests of transnational capital.

While APEC provides a focus for elite visions of prosperity and stability based on economic liberalism, the liberalization of trade and investment in the 1980s and 1990s has been paralleled by greater concentration of income, high rates of underemployment and unemployment, widespread poverty and the marginalization of a growing number of rural and urban poor around the globe. Even for a significant percentage of the population of the Asia-Pacific, the prosperous new post-Cold War era remains illusory. In this context a convincing vision of post-Cold War capitalism as it relates to East Asia and the Americas can be found in the science fiction novels of William Gibson. Gibson's work is part of a wider series of textual and cinematic techno-global dystopian narratives running at least from *Blade Runner* to the recent *Johnny Mnemonic* (the latter movie was loosely based on Gibson's most recent novel, but the terrible acting, low-budget special effects and poor stunt direction did Gibson's work and ideas a serious disservice).[62] Gibson's future is not a prosperous democratic paradise, nor does the nation-state or inter-state conflict loom large. Power appears to be centred on global conglomerates, with dynastic management structures and shifting alliances, that are locked in high-tech combat, while a vast series of ethnically diverse underclasses move across a post-modern landscape, finding solace in religious cults and post-industrial tribalism. In all Gibson's novels the central characters are the ordinary people of the future who find themselves enmeshed in the Byzantine machinations and tectonic struggles of interlocking but conflicting globalized elites. In Gibson's future the subaltern classes engage in an array of localized rebellions and everyday forms of resistance, but the overall prognosis is bleak. In his vision the 'people' are fragmented and national, communal and individual destinies have been completely subsumed by dynastic-corporate power structures. The majority of the population is engaged in the basic politics of survival refracted through shifting ethnic, religious and neo-tribal loyalties. Gibson's novels convey the way that globalization and the ever greater diffusion of capitalism generate an overarching unity, at the same time as they have resulted in fragmentation and differentiation exacerbating and reconfiguring social inequities. Even as the world becomes increasingly integrated, processes of integration contribute to the creation or reconfiguration of a diversity of underclasses, migrant proletarian communities and working classes grounded in a multitude of social and cultural contexts.

## CONCLUSION: THE TRIUMPH OF THE EAST?

Throughout the Cold War the most influential interpretations of what has come to be regarded as the East Asian Miracle flowed from the dominant Anglo-American discourses. These interpretations were grounded in theories of modernization which often assumed that their descriptions and prescriptions were scientific and universally applicable, but flowed from the fixed cultural/racial assumptions about progress which emerged during the colonial era and were subsumed into ethnocentric Cold War discourses on economic development. With the end of the Cold War, Anglo-American approaches – which have placed particular emphasis on the centrality of free trade to successful capitalist development – have continued to prevail; however, with the growing power of industrial states in East Asia, the universality of the *laissez-faire* approach to economic development has been increasingly challenged by liberal and marxist-derived state-centred perspectives on the rise of the East. Also linked to the Anglo-American state-market debate are a growing number of North American, West European and Australian perspectives which rest on fixed cultural/racial assumptions and often see the industrialization of East Asia as a menace to the West. At the same time, so-called Western discourses on the East Asian Miracle have been increasingly challenged and/or complemented by discourses which flow from East Asia and also rest on fixed conceptions of culture/ race. Significantly, the dominant Anglo-American and East Asian narratives on the East Asian Miracle all continue to rest on an East–West dichotomy which reinforces fixed cultural/racial conceptions of historical change and ignores the centuries of contamination which have characterized the hybrid history of the Asia-Pacific. The rise of East Asia and the end of the Cold War have been accompanied by the international resurgence of racialized politics and have meshed with the continued importance of fixed cultural/racial categories to the ordering of knowledge in and beyond the Asia-Pacific. While this chapter has questioned the East–West dichotomy and emphasized the historic hybridity of the Asia-Pacific, it has also pointed to the growing significance of global processes of integration and differentiation and the possible shift in the balance of global power from territorial states to transnational corporations and regionally and internationally integrated elites. In contrast to the celebratory visions offered by powerful Anglo-American and East Asian narratives, it has been argued that the Asia-Pacific and beyond has entered an era of post-Cold War capitalist dystopia characterized by profoundly racialized politics, uneven capitalist development and processes of cultural transformation and socio-economic differentiation refracted through global patterns of integration and fragmentation.

## NOTES

* An earlier version of much of this chapter was published as 'Yellow Mythologies: The East Asian Miracle and Post-Cold War Capitalism' *positions: east asia cultures critique* vol. 4, no. 1, 1996, pp. 90–126 (acknowledgements to Duke University Press), I would also like to thank Ien Ang and Catherine Waldby of the Centre for Research in Culture and Communication, School of Humanities, Murdoch University, and Lily Ling (Department of Political Science, Maxwell School of Citizenship and Public Affairs, Syracuse University) who read and commented on this chapter. Thanks also to Stephen Frost (Asian Studies, University of Western Australia) for intellectual input and also to Tani Barlow for her comments and criticisms.

1 Bruce Cumings, 'The Origins and Development of the Northeast Asian Political Economy: Industrial Sectors, Product Cycles and Political Consequences' *International Organization* vol. 38, no. 1, 1984; reprinted in *The Political Economy of the New Asian Industrialism*, ed. Frederic C. Deyo (Ithaca, NY: Cornell University Press, 1987).
2 Mario Rutten, *Asian Capitalists in the European Mirror* (Amsterdam: VU University Press, 1994).
3 Will Hutton, 'Tory Fantasy of Far Eastern Promise' *The Guardian Weekly* 5 November 1995, p. 13.

4 William Keegan, *The Spectre of Capitalism: The Future of the World Economy After the Fall of Communism* (London: Vintage, 1993; first published 1992), p. 4.

5 'East Meets West', *Far Eastern Economic Review* 20 February 1992, p. 8.

6 World Bank, *The East Asian Miracle: Economic Growth and Public Policy* (Oxford: Oxford University Press for the World Bank, 1993), pp. 347, 366–368.

7 James Fallows, *Looking at the Sun: The Rise of the New East Asian Economic and Political System* (New York: Pantheon, 1994), pp. 216–217 (Fallows's italics).

8 Chalmers Johnson, 'Intellectual Warfare' *The Atlantic Monthly* January 1995, pp. 99–104.

9 Chalmers Johnson, *MITI and the Japanese Miracle* (Stanford, Calif.: Stanford University Press, 1982).

10 A key institutionalist work is Robert Wade, *Governing the Market: Economic Theory and the Role of Government in East Asian Industrialisation* (Princeton, NJ: Princeton University Press, 1990).

11 Jung-En Woo, *Race to the Swift: State and Finance in Korean Industrialization* (New York: Columbia University Press, 1991), pp. ix, 2–4.

12 Alice Amsden has also argued that the processes by which industrialization in South Korea flowed from 'government initiatives and not the forces of the free market' can be seen as 'general propositions applicable to similar countries'. See Alice Amsden, *Asia's Next Giant: South Korea and Late Industrialization* (New York: Oxford University Press, 1989), p. 27.

13 Karl Marx and Friedrich Engels, *The Communist Manifesto* (New York: Viking Penguin, 1986; this translation first published 1888), p. 84. The classic contemporary work in this vein is Bill Warren, Imperialism: Pioneer of Capitalism (London: Verso, 1980).

14 Robert Young, *White Mythologies: Writing History and the West* (London: Routledge, 1990), pp. 2–3.

15 For example, see Kevin Hewison, Richard Robison and Garry Rodan, eds, *Southeast Asia in the 1990s: Authoritarianism, Democracy and Capitalism* (Sydney, Allen & Unwin, 1993).

16 Max Weber, *The Religion of China* (New York: Free Press, 1951; first published in German in 1916).

17 Roy Hofheinz, Jr., and Kent E. Calder, *The Eastasia Edge* (New York: Harper & Row, 1982), pp. 41–45, 58, 109–113, 121.

18 See, for example, Robert Elegant, *Pacific Destiny: Inside Asia Today* (London: Headline, 1991, first published 1990), pp. 35–36, 628–631.

19 Meredith Woo-Cumings (Jung-en Woo), 'East Asia's America Problem', in *Past As Prelude: History in the Making of a New World Order*, ed. Meredith Woo-Cumings and Michael Loriaux (Boulder, Colo.: Westview Press, 1993), p. 138.

20 Michael Crichton, *Rising Sun* (London: Arrow, 1992); Samuel P. Huntington, 'The Clash of Civilizations?' *Foreign Affairs* vol. 72, no. 3, 1993.

21 Tom Clancy, *Debt of Honour* (London: Harper Collins, 1994).

22 Rich Cohen, 'Master of War: Novelist Tom Clancy Keeps Making New Enemies', *Rolling Stone Yearbook*, 1994, p. 143; Martin Walker, 'Millionaire Minstrel of the Military', *The Guardian Weekly* 25 December 1994, p. 20.

23 Shintaro Ishihara, *The Japan That Can Say No: Why Japan Will Be First Among Equals* (New York: Simon & Schuster, 1991), See Arif Dirlik, 'The Asia-Pacific Idea: Reality and Representation in the Invention of a Regional Structure' *Journal of World History* vol. 3, no. 1, 1992, p. 71.

24 Gavan McCormack and Yoshio Sugimoto, 'Introduction: Modernization and Beyond', in Gavan McCormack and Yoshio Sugimoto, eds, *Modernization and*

*Beyond: The Japanese Trajectory* (New York: Cambridge University Press, 1988), pp. 2–7.

25 Michio Morishima, *Why Has Japan 'Succeeded'?: Western Technology and the Japanese Ethos* (Cambridge: Cambridge University Press, 1989; first published 1982).

26 Hung-chao Tai, 'The Oriental Alternative: An Hypothesis on Culture and Economy' in Hung-chao Tai, ed., *Confucianism and Economic Development: An Oriental Alternative?* (Washington, DC: Washington Institute Press, 1989), pp. 6–7.

27 Woo-Cumings, 'East Asia's America Problem', pp. 142–143.

28 Sakakibara Eisuke cited in 'Japan: The New Nationalists', *The Economist* 14 January 1995, p. 20; Eisuke Sakakibara, *Beyond Capitalism: The Japanese Model of Market Economics* (Washington, DC: University Press of America, 1993).

29 Yoshihara Kunio, *Japanese Economic Development* (Kuala Lumpur: Oxford University Press, third edition 1994; first published 1977); pp. 196–197, 202. Also see Yoshihara Kunio, *The Rise of Ersatz Capitalism in Southeast Asia* (Kuala Lumpur: Oxford University Press, 1988); Yoshihara Kunio, *The Nation and Economic Growth: The Philippines and Thailand* (Kuala Lumpur: Oxford University Press, 1994).

30 Susumu Awanohara, Michael Vatikiotis and Shada Islam, 'Vienna Showdown' *Far Eastern Economic Review* 17 June 1993, pp. 16–20.

31 Michael Vatikiotis and Robert Delfs, 'Cultural Divide' *Far Eastern Economic Review* 17 June 1993, pp. 20–22.

32 Lee Kuan Yew and Goh Chok Tong cited in David Brown, *The State and Ethnic Politics in Southeast Asia* (London: Routledge, 1994), pp. 77–81, 84–86, 89–99, 106, 284–285. See George Lodge and Ezra Vogel, eds, *Ideology and National Competitiveness: An Analysis of Nine Countries* (Boston, Mass.: Harvard Business School Press, 1987).

33 Lee Kuan Yew cited and discussed in Gabriel Lafitte, 'Reorientations' *Arena Magazine* no. 12, 1994, pp. 13–15.

34 Lee Kuan Yew cited in 'Confucianism: New Fashion for Old Wisdom' *The Economist* 27 January 1995, p. 33.

35 *People's Daily* cited and discussed in Frank Ching, 'Confucius, the New Saviour' *Far Eastern Economic Review* 10 November 1994, p. 37.

36 Kishore Mahbubani, 'The Dangers of Decadence: What the Rest Can Teach the West' *Foreign Affairs* vol. 72, no. 4, 1993, p. 14.

37 Stephen Uhalley, Jr., '"Greater China": The Contest of a Term', *positions: east asia cultures critique* vol. 2, no. 2, 1994, p. 286.

38 Michael Vatikiotis and Robert Delfs, 'Cultural Divide', *Far Eastern Economic Review* 17 June 1993, pp. 20–22.

39 Mahathir bin Mohamad, *The Malay Dilemma* (Kuala Lumpur: Federal Publishers, 1982; first published 1970).

40 Richard Stubbs, 'The Political Economy of the Asia-Pacific Region' in *Political Economy and the Changing Global Order*, ed. Richard Stubbs and Geoffrey R. D. Underhill (London: Macmillan, 1994), pp. 371–372.

41 Sandra Burton, 'The Stubborn Holdout' *Time: International* 22 November 1993, p. 27.

42 Mahathir Mohamad and Ishihara Shintaro, *The Voice of Asia: Two Leaders Discuss the Coming Century* (Tokyo: Kodansha International, 1995), See Mahathir Mohamad and Ishihara Shintaro, 'East Beats West' *Asiaweek* 8 September 1995.

43 Ishihara, *The Japan That Can Say No*, pp. 61–62, 82–83. The earlier version, which was co-authored with Morita Akio, the head of Sony, was published in Japanese in 1989 as *No To Ieru Nihon*. The unauthorized English-language edition which, significantly, was financed by the US Department of Defense, included Morita's contribution; however, he withdrew from the authorized North American edition. See Richard J. Barnet and John Cavanagh, *Global Dreams: Imperial Corporations and the New World Order* (New York: Simon & Schuster, 1994), p. 55.

44 The Japanese-language version of Mahathir Mohamed and Ishihara Shintaro, 'The Asia That Can Say No: A Policy to Combat Europe and America', is cited and discussed in Richard McGregor, 'Mahathir Fumes as Japan Plays Hard to Get' *The Weekend Australian* 12–13 November 1994, p. 16.

45 Edward W. Desmond, 'One Happy, Culturally Superior Family' *Time: Australia* 21 November 1994, p. 54.

46 ibid., p. 54.

47 Mahathir Mohamad, 'East Beats West' *Asiaweek* 8 September 1995, p. 41, excerpted from Mahathir Mohamad and Ishihara Shintaro, *The Voice of Asia*.

48 'Saying No', *The Economist* 25 November 1994, p. 31.

49 Robert Young, *Colonial Desire: Hybridity in Theory, Culture and Race* (London: Routledge, 1995), pp. 6, 10, 27–28.

50 Huntington, 'The Clash of Civilizations?', pp. 41, 45–49.

51 Dirlik, 'The Asia-Pacific Idea: Reality and Representation in the Invention of a Regional Structure', p. 74.

52 Richard J. Herrnstein and Charles Murray, *The Bell Curve: Intelligence and Class Structure in American Life* (New York: Free Press, 1994).

53 See Charles Lane, 'The Tainted Sources of "The Bell Curve" *The New York Review of Books* vol. 41, no. 20, 1994, pp. 14–19.

54 Richard Lynn, 'Letter to the Editors', *The New York Review of Books* vol. 42, no. 2, 1995, p. 45.

55 George Yeo, 'A New Greater East Asia Co-Prosperity Sphere', in Greg Sheridan, ed., *Living With Dragons: Australia Confronts Its Asian Destiny* (Sydney: Allen and Unwin, 1995), p. 179.

56 John Naisbitt, *Megatrends Asia: The Eight Asian Megatrends That Are Changing the World* (London: Nicholas Brealy, 1995), excerpted in John Naisbitt, 'Dawn of the Dragon Century' *Far Eastern Economic Review* 16 November 1995, pp. 80–82.

57 As Dirlik notes further, 'the very success of capital has given rise to a new set of contradictions' insofar as '[t]he emergence of non-EuroAmerican capitalisms has been accompanied by the emergence of new voices that challenge Euro-American models by calling for forms of organization that are derived from alternative cultural constructions'. See Arif Dirlik, *After the Revolution: Waking to Global Capitalism* (London: Wesleyan University Press, 1994), pp. 51–52, 73–74.

58 Arjun Appadurai, 'Disjuncture and Difference in the Global Cultural Economy' *Public Culture: Bulletin of the Project for Transnational Cultural Studies* vol. 2, no. 2, 1990, p. 4–6.

59 Stephen R. Gill, 'Neo-Liberalism and the Shift Towards a US-Centred Trans-national Hegemony' in Henk Overbeek, ed., *Restructuring Hegemony in the Global Political Economy: The Rise of Transnational Neo-Liberalism in the 1980s* (London: Routledge, 1993), p. 246–247, 280.

60 Mathew Horsman and Andrew Marshall, *After the Nation-State: Citizens, Tribalism and the New World Disorder* (London: Harper Collins, 1994), pp. xii, 35–37.

61 Masao Miyoshi, 'A Borderless World?: From Colonialism to Transnationalism and the Decline of the Nation-State' *Critical Inquiry* vol. 19, no. 4, 1993, pp. 735–737.
62 According to one observer, Gibson's work is 'as much an expression of transnational corporate realities as it is of global paranoia itself'. See Fredric Jameson, *Postmodernism, or, The Cultural Logic of Late Capitalism* (London: Verso, 1993, first published 1991), pp. 38, 419; William Gibson, *Neuromancer* (London: Grafton, 1995; first published 1985); William Gibson, *Count Zero* (London: Grafton, 1987; first published 1986); William Gibson, *Mona Lisa Overdrive* (London: Grafton, 1990; first published 1988); William Gibson, *Virtual Light* (London: Penguin, 1994; first published 1993).

# Conclusion: The coming of the Pacific Century: the Cold War and after in the Asia-Pacific

*Mark T. Berger*

## INTRODUCTION: THE COLD WAR AND AFTER IN THE ASIA-PACIFIC

The end of the Cold War has thrown into sharp relief a major trend in global affairs which has been the focus of increasing attention since the early 1970s: the rise of East Asia as an increasingly significant zone in the international economy.[1] As has been argued in this book, the basis for the East Asian Miracle flows in part from the political economy of the Cold War.[2] Furthermore, during the Cold War, and into the post-Cold War era, Anglo-American liberalism offered, and continues to offer, both the most influential explanations for the rise of East Asia and the most powerful visions of where the Asia-Pacific is going.[3] While influential East Asian-based narratives on the coming of the Pacific Century have increasingly challenged the hegemony of Anglo-American liberalism, elite East Asian visions continue to be domesticated by, or remain subordinate to, Anglo-American narratives on the Pacific Century.[4] While the contributors to this book come from a number of disciplinary backgrounds, hold differing politico-intellectual positions and focus on particular 'nations' and patterns, they are united by an attempt to engage critically with the dominant narratives on the causes and significance of the rise of East Asia and the end of the Cold War in the Asia-Pacific. This Conclusion will briefly outline the main arguments and concerns of the various chapters and locate them in relation to the overall critique of the celebratory visions of the Pacific Century. Finally an important alternative way of both viewing and challenging the complex processes of capitalist development and integration in the Asia-Pacific, which builds on the critical perspectives laid out in this book, will be outlined and discussed.

## MIRACLES AND MODELS: THE RISE OF EAST ASIA AND THE END OF THE COLD WAR

For many years now Japan has occupied a particularly prominent position in the debate over the causes and significance of the rise of East Asia.[5] As

Haruhiro Fukui and Shigeko N. Fukai argued in Chapter 1, the influential academic and popular image of Japan as a 'developmental state' and a 'new capitalist' model characterized by steady economic growth and political stability is out of step with important changes which have been brought on by, or have coincided with, the end of the Cold War.[6] They emphasized that since the mid-1970s the trend in Japanese politics towards greater 'convergence' among the most important interest groups and the main political parties has been paralleled by growing 'political instability'. The reasons for the growing political instability include the increasingly volatile voting behaviour of the Japanese electorate and are linked to the growing policy convergence of the major parties which has meant that politics, especially elections, are increasingly perceived as 'boring' and 'uninteresting' by the citizenry of Japan. When this is combined with 'an endless series of political scandals amidst a seemingly endless recession' the result has been 'growing ranks of disillusioned and increasingly cynical voters'. Fukui and Fukai make clear that while the image of a dynamic and stable Japan, acting as a major buttress of the wider US-centred Cold War framework, was always exaggerated, the end of the Cold War, a growing array of economic problems and the instability and uncertainty associated with Japanese politics in the 1990s have resulted in the 'end of the miracle'.

Another trend in the region that has problematized talk of an easily discernible East Asian model and clearly signalled the demise of the regional Cold War framework, and Japan's particular position in it, is the dramatic economic growth of mainland China, particularly its southern coastal provinces. At the same time in Chapter 2, Martin Farrell argued that the ability of a resurgent Chinese state to take on a regional and international 'leadership' role in the post-Cold War era is constrained by problems associated with maintaining the spectacular rates of economic growth which China has registered since the early 1980s. The transition to capitalism in China is uncharted territory and, as Farrell made clear, a whole range of problems associated with maintaining capitalist-style economic growth have yet to be confronted. At the same time, even if China remains on its present economic course for the next twenty years profound problems threaten the country's 'unity' and 'stability' and therefore its 'superpower potential'. To begin with, the succession question looms in the background and there is considerable uncertainty surrounding the future coherence of the Communist Party and its ongoing potential as a unifying force. Related to this is the question of the future role of the PLA, while the peasantry, which has been generally perceived as the 'backbone of the Chinese revolution', is becoming more and more 'alienated' from the Communist Party. Last, but certainly not least, 'corruption' is undermining the government's 'effectiveness' and its 'legitimacy'. As we have seen, many observers continue to articulate a celebratory vision of the Pacific Century which represents China as an emergent 'economic superpower' at the centre of a dynamic capitalist East Asia.[7] Farrell is much more doubtful. But, regardless of how unlikely it is that a stable, united and prosperous China, under the stewardship of the Communist Party, will emerge over the next few decades, events in that country will have a significant impact on regional and international affairs as the Pacific Century approaches.

South Korea is another key state which has often been pointed to as a model for other countries to follow and which has been at the centre of the Cold War in the region. Kwan Kim in Chapter 3 has argued that a crucial aspect of South Korea's modern history has been the 'preservation of state authority' in relation to 'particular class interests'. In a chapter stressing the importance of South Korea's very particular historical trajectory and pointing to the difficulties inherent in extracting lessons from the East Asian Miracle, Kim emphasized that the overwhelming primacy of the South Korean state is grounded in Korean culture and more particularly the peninsula's modern history beginning with the Japanese colonial period followed by the Cold War.[8] At the same time, as in the case of Japan, the policies and government–business alliances that brought about the rapid economic growth of the 1960s and 1970s also paved the way for the decline of the 'comprehensive developmental state' in South Korea and the increasing emphasis on economic and political liberalization by the 1980s. At the same time, the process of economic and political liberalization is resulting in new pressures on the state to play a greater role in mitigating the social costs of globalization. This is taking place against the background of a powerful historical and cultural legacy of authoritarianism, the privileging of the relative autonomy of state power and the unresolved Cold War division of the Korean peninsula between North and South.

While Kwan Kim sought to put South Korea's dramatic industrial success in historical context with a focus on the state, and emphasized that economic success and the waning of the Cold War have resulted in a range of challenges to the South Korean miracle, Gerard Greenfield in Chapter 5, shifted the focus southward and critically examined a country that is increasingly being characterized as Asia's 'next Tiger'. He argued that, in the context of the increasingly powerful perception of Vietnam as 'Asia's next Tiger', a process of 'convergence' is under way between Anglo-American visions of Vietnam's transition to capitalism as the triumph of liberalism and East Asian narratives which view Vietnam as following the 'Asian way'. This convergence is at the centre of the 'contemporary imaginings of Vietnam's elites as they reposition themselves at the helm of a capitalist developmental state'. Although the elite visions emanating from Vietnam are grounded in nationalist impulses they also stem from the process of privatization and the articulation of Vietnam's elite into the regional and transnational capitalist elite. At the same time, Greenfield argued that the capitalist transition has been accompanied by increasing 'social disorder' which threatens the likelihood of Vietnam becoming 'Asia's next Tiger' and also challenges the processes by which this elite narrative is generated and maintained. As Greenfield makes clear, with his focus on the mining areas of Quang Ninh, major challenges to Vietnam's dominant elite are coming from a large number of localized sites and they represent a serious threat to the image of Vietnam as 'Asia's next Tiger'.

Another country in Southeast Asia, which is seen by many commentators to have already joined the ranks of the Asian Tigers, is Malaysia. Steve Majstorovic, in Chapter 6, focused on the formation and trajectory of the post-colonial 'ethnic state' in Malaysia, setting his analysis in the context of the ongoing debate about the relationship between the material and the discursive. He argued that his analysis of the Malaysian trajectory makes clear that the material and the discursive are crucial to our understanding of social and political change. From his perspective modernity has not undermined or corroded ethnonational sentiments. He emphasized that 'ethnonational identity' has been transformed and politicized in response to the 'alienation and dissociation' of the modernization process. Meanwhile, Mark Berger in Chapter 7 also argued that post-1945 Indonesia should be seen as an 'ethnic' state rooted in the particular history of the Netherlands East Indies. Berger emphasized that the overall framework for the capitalist development of the archipelago which has been carried out under Soeharto is grounded as much in the complex historical legacy of the Dutch colonial era as in the nationalist initiatives which led to independence in 1945. The nationalist movement in Indonesia tapped an increasingly widespread anti-colonialism; however, it was also dramatically shaped by colonialism. The early promise of the nationalist period has given way to a (re)turn to colonialism as Indonesia has become a Java-centred empire. Within the wider political economy of Indonesia, it is the Javanese, especially the hereditary aristocracy of Java, the priyayi, who (having been initially incorporated into the Dutch colonial state) have survived and reproduced themselves within the New Order state. At the same time, Berger emphasized that a major post-Cold War challenge to the New Order is coming from the country's globally integrated export-oriented industrial sector and the new social forces which are linked to the growth of this sector. For example, it is this sector which has been the site of considerable working-class unrest. And this unrest, like the overall process of social change, is grounded in the particularity of Indonesia's historical trajectory and the country's dramatic but uneven incorporation into the wider process of post-Cold War capitalist development in the Asia-Pacific.

## REINVENTING THE REGION: THE ASIA-PACIFIC AND POST-COLD WAR CAPITALISM

With the rise of East Asia and the end of the Cold War, along with a growing emphasis on regional integration, new imaginings about the region have redrawn the boundaries of East Asia and what is increasingly termed the Asia-Pacific.[9] This book reflects these changes insofar as it includes chapters on Russia and Australia. Some commentators have sought to deploy Russia's Asian heritage as part of elite efforts to redefine the role of the Russian state in the post-Cold War era, while Australia is at the centre of a complex domestic and regional debate about whether it is part of 'Asia' or not. With regard to Russia, in Chapter 4 Douglas Borer anticipated that as the economic boom in East Asia continues the role of Russia in the Pacific Century, initially as a major supplier of weaponry and natural resources, and then as a field for investment and a market for consumer products, will grow. As a result of its geographical propinquity, and because of its continued neglect by Moscow, Russia's Far East has dramatically reoriented its economic and trading linkages in favour of South Korea, Taiwan and China. Borer argued further that these growing linkages between the Russian Far East and its dynamic neighbours may be laying the groundwork for the day when Russia might be 'rebuffed when looking West' and will find a better reception in the courts of 'a less critical, less liberal East'.[10]

In Chapter 8, Roger Bell put the growing turn to Asia by the Australian government and Australian-based companies in historical context and sought to address the issues it has raised about national identity in Australia. He argued that contemporary Australia 'is neither a new Britannia in the South Pacific, nor a politico-cultural satellite of its powerful ally and influence, the USA'. At the same time, he insisted that apart from the obvious geographical proximity and growing economic linkages, Australia is not 'part of Asia'. While Australia is increasingly integrated with Asia in various ways it continues to be socially and culturally distinct from the wide array of nations which have emerged in the region in the twentieth century. Although contemporary Australians 'negotiate' their cultural and national identity in the context of an 'increasingly plural society on the periphery of the newly emerging Asia-Pacific', Bell argued that Australians are also more inclined towards political independence and cultural assertion than they have been in the country's entire history as a nation. Australians have increasingly sought to define and identify themselves as citizens of a distinct and independent 'nation' ensuring that despite the turn to Asia, Australia 'remains largely distinct from the diverse nations of the region' even as Australian business and government leaders seek a greater role in the Asia-Pacific.

In Chapter 9 Yao Souchou, following Arif Dirlik and Rob Wilson, argued that the Asia-Pacific can be seen as an important 'site of cultural production'. He took the view that it was a particularly Western invention which serves to 'deflect' Western 'uncertainty' in a 'globalized' and changing world. He emphasized that the Asia-Pacific is a key site where 'another round of Orientalism' is being called forth 'which serves to coalesce the historical hegemony of the West'; however, the process of (re)imagining and '(re)making' the 'East' is not driven solely by the West. Using a particular case study which focuses on Chinese traders in Sarawak to discuss the wider construction and romanticization of Chinese business, Yao outlined the way in which the government and peoples of Asia are also deeply implicated in the process of what is increasingly called self-Orientalization. At the same time, he emphasized that the process of self-Orientalization is not a unitary one and there are numerous differences even among influential elite commentators such as Malaysian Prime Minister Dr Mahathir Mohamed and Senior Minister Lee Kuan Yew of Singapore. He also noted that the dramatic increase in self-assurance which was a concomitant of the industrialization process in East Asia was tempered by a continuing awareness that the region's economic dynamism depended very heavily on Western investment and technology. Yao Souchou concluded that this continued sense of 'vulnerability' may well be an important key to the reconfiguring of Asia as the 'moral opposite' to the West.

In an effort to come to grips with the dramatic post-Cold War shifts and the related exercises in regional redefinition in Chapter 10 Timothy Luke focused on the trend towards what he calls 'glocalization'. From his perspective the forces driving glocalization operate on a range of 'levels' and seek to achieve an array of objectives. He pointed to the corporate level where computing and telecommunications companies are setting up complex 'informational infrastructures' which work to obscure, if not completely 'efface', the boundaries of the global nation-state system and replace them with international corporate exchange networks. At the same time, the use of 'these virtualizing networks' by individuals and corporate or non-corporate collectivities is resulting in the fabrication of what he called 'new semio-communicative communities' which have set up 'innovative techno-economic ensembles' and 'unusual socio-political institutions'. Meanwhile, the 'glocal grids' which have been brought into being by these new networks are disrupting and dramatically reconfiguring 'cultures, economies and societies' which have been historically constructed and grounded by the nation-state. In this context, the nation-state seeks to obstruct or at least 'contain' these trends at the same time as the proliferation of glocalities contributes to an overall trend towards differentiation, decentring and disorganization, challenging the centralizing and standardizing imperatives of the nation-state. 'Semi-imaginary/semi-concrete glocalities' have no particular territorial, geographical or ethnonational anchor, while they contribute to the formation of, and map themselves onto, complex and reconfigured cultural spaces such as the 'Pacific Rim'. Furthermore, to be part of the Pacific Rim or the Asia-Pacific, in contrast to being a citizen of the USA, or Taiwan, or Australia, is seen as participating in a future-oriented endeavour and could increasingly emerge as a key element in wider processes of self-identification in the Pacific Century.

In the final chapter of the book, Mark Berger also focused – from a somewhat different perspective – on the regional and international post-Cold War processes of integration and fragmentation in an effort to contextualize the overall debate about the rise of East Asia. He argued that, during the Cold War, Anglo-American narratives on the cause and significance of the East Asian Miracle were particularly dominant. In the post-Cold War era, those Anglo-American narratives which understand the rise of East Asia as a 'free trade' miracle remain predominant, although by the 1980s an important Anglo-American challenge to *laissez-faire* conceptions of East Asian capitalism had emerged which adopted a liberal or marxist-derived state-centred perspective on capitalist development. Connected to the Anglo-American debate about the role of the state *vis-à-vis* the market has been a range of narratives flowing from North America, Western Europe and Australia which deploy fixed ideas about culture/race to explain East Asian industrialization and tend to view the rise of the East as a serious threat to the West. By the beginning of the 1990s, Anglo-American and West European approaches to the coming of the Pacific Century were being questioned by increasingly powerful narratives which were anchored in the socio-political forces of East Asia. Significantly, both the Anglo-American discourses on the rise of East Asia and their East Asian-based challengers ground their analyses on a dubious distinction between East and West which strengthens fixed notions of culture/race and deflects attention from the hybridity of Asia-Pacific history.

## POWER AND PROGRESS IN THE PACIFIC CENTURY: ELITE INTEGRATION AND CRITICAL LOCALISM

Against the background of the dramatic process of globalization and the continued influence of a diluted form of Anglo-American liberalism, Berger concluded that a key trend in the post-Cold War Asia-Pacific was the integration of self-serving elites into a complicated set of overlapping regional and transnational networks.[11] Repugnant and racist as his political agenda is, when perennial US Republican presidential hopeful Pat Buchanan talks in condemnatory language of a 'new' North American 'managerial class, which seems to lack roots or values or loyalties, which forgets that our people do not exist to serve the economy; the economy exists to serve Americans', he is lashing out at the process of elite integration.[12] The USA and Britain stand out for the unwillingness of their increasingly transnationalized elites to make any sustained effort to address the socio-economic imbalances and fragmentation which are a particular characteristic of globalization.[13] Significantly, annual wages in the USA for people without high school education have declined by almost 25 per cent since 1973, while there was a 17 per cent drop for high school graduates, but a 5.2 per cent rise for college graduates. Even more dramatic is the claim that 1 per cent of the wealthiest households in the USA now control 40 per cent of the 'national' wealth, while in Britain the top one per cent controls 18 per cent of the 'national' wealth.[14] According to conventional economic indicators, the US economy grew between 1992 and 1995 at a rate reminiscent of the boom years of the 1950s. However, the growth in investment, increases in productivity, continued low inflation and the appearance of new jobs numbering more than 8 million (a trend which is anticipated by most economists to continue throughout 1996) were not accompanied by an improvement in living standards. After taking inflation into account, the weekly earnings of the average 'rank-and-file worker' fell by almost 20 per cent between the mid-1970s and the mid-1990s, while the annual pay of corporation heads went up by almost 20 per cent during the 1980s and almost 70 per cent after taxes. Since the beginning of the 1990s, the 'real wages' of a majority of workers in the USA have not risen, despite the dramatic economic recovery after 1991. Technological change, among other things, is making it possible to replace large numbers of skilled white-collar and blue-collar workers with relatively unskilled and lower-paid workers.[15]

Since the early 1980s the Hawke and Keating governments in Australia have pursued economic liberalization, financial deregulation and industrial reform in an effort to emulate and integrate with the dynamic economies of East Asia.[16] Both the ALP and the Liberal–National coalition elected in March 1996 are publicly committed to eliminating tariffs by the year 2000 (with the exception of the textile and automobile industries which will continue to receive protection, although much less than in the past). The March 1996 election and the subsequent change in government in Australia have raised questions about whether the country's turn to Asia will continue with the same force and direction. However, there is every indication that although the Liberal–National coalition is intent on significant domestic reorientation, there appears to be little change in its overall approach to engagement with Asia. The current government appears more or less set to continue on the liberalizing path charted by the previous government. Australia's deeply rooted egalitarianism and an array of institutional arrangements aimed at protecting wages, working conditions and welfare rights continue to act as a brake on the unqualified pursuit of an Anglo-American economic and social policy agenda; however, the growing gulf between the rich and the poor in the Antipodes is clearly captured by statistics which indicate that between the mid-1970s and the early 1990s household incomes in the richest 5 per cent of the country's neighbourhoods grew by over 20 per cent while there was at least a 20 per cent drop in household incomes in those Australian neighbourhoods at the bottom of the scale.[17] The tax cuts of the past few years have flowed to high income earners with no clear indication that this has resulted in the kind of spending and investment which create jobs.[18]

At the same time as late twentieth-century Australia is being integrated with Asia in the interests of an outward-oriented elite rather than of the 'nation' as a whole, the social and economic conditions in the former Soviet Union also reflect the ongoing process of elite integration. Russia today is characterized by the more or less unrelieved misery of the majority of the population combined with the spectacular prosperity of a relatively small elite. In 1994 official Russian statistics estimated that less than 1 per cent of the population were earning over US$300,000 a year, while 27 per cent of the population were 'poor' (that is they could afford to feed themselves), while another 33 per cent lived on or below the basic subsistence level. This is against the backdrop of spectacular levels of capital flight and the growing power of increasingly transnationalized organized crime networks.[19] Meanwhile, in South Korea, Taiwan and even Japan, dramatic income rises have in many cases created new inequities and the relatively egalitarian character of the social order in South Korea and Taiwan in the 1950s and 1960s has been steadily eroded.[20] According to the World Bank, the total number of people living in poverty in Asia will only drop from the 805 million which it recorded for 1985 to 435 million by the beginning of the twenty-first century.[21]

The vision of a prosperous and stable Pacific Century is primarily something with which globalizing elites can conjure, while power relations in the Asia-Pacific and beyond preclude anything resembling equitable distribution of the benefits which flow from the new era of global capitalism. Although political disillusionment is widespread in the context of the deepening of globalization and elite integration, there is renewed potential for conflict and resistance 'from below' in many parts of the Asia-Pacific, as has been outlined in some of the chapters in this book. Some of the most interesting contemporary strategies of progressive action focus on the importance of local modes of empowerment and mesh with the cultural and socio-economic concerns of particular groups and organizations which face problems refracted through global, regional, national and local relations of power. On the margins of the Pacific Century a range of challenges to the dominant narratives, and efforts to articulate alternative trajectories to development in the Asia-Pacific, can be found.[22] In an effort to sketch out a way of moving beyond the dominant discourses on the Pacific Century I want to conclude with a discussion of the work of a well-known (albeit marginalized) radical North American-based commentator on the Pacific Century. Arif Dirlik, a China specialist and professor of history at Duke University, has produced a number of works which seek to articulate an alternative politico-intellectual position in the context of the triumph of global capitalism and the perceived dawning of the Pacific Century.[23]

Dirlik's most complete discussion of an alternative theory and practice can be found in an important and agenda-setting book entitled *After the Revolution: Waking to Global Capitalism*. In this extended essay Dirlik provides a wide-ranging history of capitalism, at the same time as he attempts to historicize marxism (he focuses on Chinese marxism which he argues is 'a localized or vernacular version of a global Marxism that claimed a subject position for itself within a universalized Marxist discourse') and evaluate the rise, demise and significance of the state-socialist model. From his perspective, all the main concepts of marxism, including class analysis, are inadequate to the task of 'liberation'. Nor do they represent a sufficient means by which to come to grips with 'the full complexity of contemporary capitalism' and 'the social formations and problems that it has generated'. He is opposed to efforts at totalization and attempts to inject new categories and formulations which are not 'implicit' in marxism. Ultimately, he argues that a new 'vision of liberation' has to come from outside because, despite what advocates have believed, 'it is not immanent in Marxism'. In particular he argues that the crucial shortcoming of 'actually existing socialism', in those countries – such as China and Vietnam – where marxism became a hegemonic discourse, was that it attempted to duplicate capitalist goals which both 'distorted socialism' and 'undermined the legitimacy of the system'. He argues that earlier forms of marxism are no more capable of addressing the processes of 'fragmentation' brought on by the global spread and reconfiguration of capitalism than are the dominant modernization perspectives.[24]

In a concise statement of the problem facing those in the Asia-Pacific and beyond who want to bring about progressive political and social change, Dirlik argues that the 'challenge' is to mesh 'a non-totalizing discourse of liberation with a theoretical discourse that of necessity must address the problem of totality (however fragmented) under capitalism'. From his perspective, if any particular project of liberation is going to be faithful to its goals, it can only concern itself with 'local propositions for general consideration' or 'general propositions for local consideration' and it must avoid either 'binding axioms formulated in accordance with teleological presuppositions' or 'the reification of local cultures'. At the same time, Dirlik emphasizes that 'capital' remains a '"foundational" principle of contemporary life' and '[a]ny discourse of liberation worthy of the name must address the problems of material and social existence that it presents'. In this context, marxism remains relevant, and rather than signalling the 'death of marxism', the demise of state socialism in East Asia and beyond ends marxism's 'servitude to bureaucratic modernizationism'. Ultimately Dirlik proposes what he calls a 'critical localism'. He argues that the local is a key site of resistance against global power, but it must also be the site where efforts to abolish oppression and inequality grounded in particular histories are carried out. This 'critical localism' must continue to evaluate the present from the perspective of the past, at the same time as it examines the past through the lens of modernity (including various forms of revisionist marxism). From this perspective Dirlik is highly critical of those decidedly uncritical localisms which include 'romantic nostalgias for communities past' as well as 'hegemonic nationalist yearnings of a new kind (as with the so-called Confucian revival in East Asia)' and 'historicisms that would imprison the present in the past' such as the wide variety of explicitly anti-modernist fundamentalist movements in many parts of the world.[25] Critical localism represents an important attempt to engage with the overwhelming material and discursive power of capitalist modernity and its destructive consequences in the Asia-Pacific and beyond.[26] It reflects the persistence, and possible renaissance, of a marginalized but still significant body of theory and practice which is committed in various ways to the idea that it is time for the people in the Asia-Pacific and beyond, whose voices have for too long been silenced, to find their own path to the Pacific Century.

## CONCLUSION: THE COMING OF THE PACIFIC CENTURY

The transition to the post-Cold War era in the Asia-Pacific has seen the emergence of Anglo-American discourses which represent the dramatic economic growth and industrial dynamism of East Asia as the harbinger of a prosperous, and even peaceful, Pacific Century. In the context of the wider reconfiguration of the international political economy, Anglo-American discourses on the Pacific Century have been increasingly challenged and/or complemented by cultural/racial discourses which flow from an institutional base in Northeast and Southeast Asia. At the same time, Anglo-American liberalism continues to have a basis in Northeast and Southeast Asia, and this meshes with wider regional and international elite discourses on economic development and globalization. These efforts at elite integration in the Asia-Pacific and elite visions of regional capitalist development, in the context of a wider international trend towards integration, continue to perceive the process of capitalist industrialization as a unifying and even a homogenizing force. However, the emphasis in this book has been on the growing significance of global processes of both integration and differentiation, which point to a very different vision of the Pacific Century than those offered by powerful regional elites. While the backdrop to this book is the changing character of the political economy of the Asia-Pacific, it is a somewhat different contribution to the literature on the coming of the Pacific Century. Many of the chapters have emphasized the uncertainty which hangs over the Asia-Pacific with the end of the Cold War and the continuing dramatic and uneven spread of industrialization. The contributors have all suggested or implied that the Pacific Century may well be an era of fragmentation as post-Cold War capitalism continues both to transform and be transformed by local, 'national' and regional processes of accommodation and resistance. All of the chapters have, in various ways, sought to challenge elite visions of the Asia-Pacific as a region of increasingly prosperous nations integrated into, and/or leading the way towards, a wider global capitalist modernity. Taken together, they represent a broad critique of the dominant narratives on the coming of the Pacific Century.

## NOTES

1 Alvin Y. So and Stephen W. K. Chiu, *East Asia and the World Economy* (Thousand Oaks, Calif.: Sage, 1995).

2 Bruce Cumings, 'The Origins and Development of the Northeast Asian Political Economy: Industrial Sectors, Product Cycles and Political Consequences' *International Organization* vol. 38, no. 1, 1984, reprinted in Frederic C. Deyo, *The Political Economy of the New Asian Industrialism* (Ithaca, NY: Cornell University Press, 1987); Richard Stubbs, 'The Political Economy of the Asia-Pacific Region' in Richard Stubbs and Geoffrey R. D. Underhill, eds, *Political Economy and the Changing Global Order* (London: Macmillan, 1994), pp. 366, 369–373; Peter A. Petri, 'The East Asian Trading Bloc: An Analytical History' in Ross Garnaut and Peter Drysdale, eds, *Asia Pacific Regionalism: Readings in International Economic Relations* (Sydney: Harper Collins, 1994).

3 Mark Borthwick (with contributions by selected scholars), *Pacific Century: The Emergence of Modern Pacific Asia* (Boulder, Colo.: Westview Press, 1992); Samuel P. Huntington, 'The Clash of Civilizations?' *Foreign Affairs* vol. 72, no. 3, 1993.

4 George Yeo, 'A New Greater East Asia Co-Prosperity Sphere', in Greg Sheridan, ed., *Living With Dragons: Australia Confronts Its Asian Destiny* (Sydney: Allen & Unwin, 1995); Mahathir Mohamad and Ishihara Shintaro, *The Voice of Asia: Two Leaders Discuss the Coming Century* (Tokyo: Kodansha International, 1995).

5 E. Wayne Nafziger, *Learning from the Japanese: Japan's Pre-War Development and the Third World* (New York: M. E. Sharpe, 1995).

6 A good recent example of the 'developmental state' approach can be found in Chalmers Johnson, *Japan: Who Governs? – The Rise of the Developmental State* (New York: W. W. Norton, 1995), pp. 8–9.

7 William H. Overholt, *The Rise of China: How Economic Reform is Creating a New Superpower* (New York: W. W. Norton, 1994); Murray Weidenbaum and Samuel Hughes, *The Bamboo Network: How Expatriate Chinese Entrepreneurs Are Creating a New Economic Superpower in Asia* (New York: Martin Kessler Books, 1996).

8 One of the best analyses of cultural change as it relates to the economic rise of East Asia generally, and South Korea particularly, can be found in Roger L. Janelli (and Dawnhee Yim), *Making Capitalism: The Social and Cultural Construction of a South Korean Conglomerate* (Stanford, Calif.: Stanford University Press, 1993). On the legacy of Japanese colonialism see Bruce Cumings, 'The Legacy of Japanese Colonialism in Korea' in Ramon H. Myers and Mark R. Peattie, eds, *The Japanese Colonial Empire 1895–1945* (Princeton, NJ: Princeton University Press, 1984); Carter J. Eckert, *Offspring of Empire: The Koch'ang Kims and the Colonial Origins of Korean Capitalism 1876–1945* (Seattle: University of Washington Press, 1990); Jung-En Woo, *Race to the Swift: State and Finance in Korean Industrialization* (New York: Columbia University Press, 1991).

9 The boundaries of the Asia-Pacific are unclear and flexible. The Asia-Pacific is sometimes defined as that part of the world stretching from Siberia in the north to New Zealand in the south and encompassing Northeast and Southeast

Asia, Australia and the Pacific Islands, or Oceania, but excluding South Asia. It is also conceived more broadly as including the west coast of North America and the Pacific Rim as a whole.

10 Evidence of this trend may be found in Boris Yeltsin's high profile visit to Beijing in April 1996 which resulted in the signing of a host of agreements on economic, technological and military cooperation. See Matt Forney and Nayan Chanda, 'Comrades in Arms: Russia's Rapprochement Could Boost China's Clout' *Far Eastern Economic Review* 2 May 1996, pp. 17–18.

11 Kees van der Pijl, 'The Second Glorious Revolution: Globalizing Elites and Historical Change' in Björn Hettne, ed., *International Political Economy: Understanding Global Disorder* (London: Zed Press, 1995).

12 Pat Buchanan cited in Martin Walker, 'Why the South Holds Politicians In Its Thrall' *The Guardian Weekly* 10 March 1996, p. 6.

13 John K. Galbraith, *The Culture of Contentment* (London: Sinclair-Stevenson, 1992); Christopher Lasch, T*he Revolt of the Elites and the Betrayal of Democracy* (New York: W. W. Norton, 1995); Michael Lind, *The Next American Nation: The New Nationalism and the Fourth American Revolution* (New York: Free Press, 1995); James Petras and Morris Morley, *Empire or Republic?: American Global Power and Domestic Decay* (New York: Routledge, 1995).

14 Richard Cohen, 'Capitalism Brings Rich Pickings' *The Guardian Weekly* 30 April 1995.

15 Simon Head, 'The New, Ruthless Economy' *The New York Review of Books* vol. 43, no. 4, 1996, pp. 47–52.

16 Ross Garnaut, *Australia and the Northeast Asian Ascendancy: Report to the Prime Minister and the Minister for Foreign Affairs* (Canberra: Australian Government Publishing Service, 1989).

17 Elisabeth Wynhausen, 'The Working Rich: Our New Elite' *The Weekend Australian* 23–24 September 1995.

18 Mike Steketee, 'Keating's 1000 Days' *The Weekend Australian* 7–18 September 1994.

19 Jack F. Matlock, 'Russia: The Power of the Mob' *The New York Review of Books* vol. 42, no. 12, 1995, p. 14.

20 Walden F. Bellow and Stephanie Rosenfeld, *Dragons in Distress: Asia's Miracle Economies in Crisis* (San Francisco, Calif.: Institute for Food and Development Policy, 1990); Matthew Horsman and Andrew Marshall, *After the Nation-State: Citizens, Tribalism and the New World Disorder* (London: Harper Collins, 1994), pp. 98–100.

21 For the Caribbean and Latin America the projected trend is from 75 million to 60 million people, while it is anticipated that the number of people living below the poverty line in sub-Saharan Africa will rise to 265 million by 2000 from a 1985 figure of 85 million. See James H. Mittelman, 'The Globalization Challenge: Surviving at the Margins' *Third World Quarterly: Journal of Emerging Areas* vol. 15, no. 3, 1994, pp. 439–441.

22 Walden Bello, *People and Power in the Pacific: The Struggle for the Post-Cold War Order* (London: Pluto Press, 1992); Ravi Arvind Palat, ed., *Pacific-Asia and the Future of the World-System* (Westport, Conn.: Greenwood Press, 1993); Ed Tadem and Lakshmi Daniel, *Challenging the Mainstream: APEC and the Asia-Pacific Development Debate* (Hong Kong: Asian Regional Exchange for New Alternatives, 1995); Vivian De Lima and Carmencita Karagdag, eds, P*eace, Disarmament and Symbiosis in the Asia-Pacific* (Quezon City: Conference on Peace, Disarmament and Symbiosis in the Asia-Pacific, 1995).

23 Arif Dirlik, 'The Asia-Pacific Idea: Reality and Representation in the Invention of a Regional Structure' *Journal of World History* vol. 3, no. 1, 1992; Arif

Dirlik, ed., *What Is in a Rim?: Critical Perspectives on the Pacific Region Idea* (Boulder, Colo.: Westview Press, 1993); Rob Wilson and Arif Dirlik, eds, *Asia/Pacific As Space of Cultural Production* (Durham, NC: Duke University Press, 1995).

24 Arif Dirlik, *After the Revolution: Waking to Global Capitalism* (London: Wesleyan University Press, 1994), pp 6, 31, 44, 81–82.

25 ibid., pp 82, 84, 105–106, 108–109.

26 Mark T. Berger, 'Post-Cold War Capitalism: Modernization and Modes of Resistance After the Fall' *Third World Quarterly: Journal of Emerging Areas* vol. 16, no. 4, 1995.

# Index

304    *Index*